Mark Twain and
the Brazen Serpent

Mark Twain and the Brazen Serpent

How Biblical Burlesque and Religious Satire Unify *Huckleberry Finn*

DOUG ALDRIDGE

McFarland & Company, Inc., Publishers
Jefferson, North Carolina

ISBN (print) 978-1-4766-6845-1
ISBN (ebook) 978-1-4766-2763-2

LIBRARY OF CONGRESS CATALOGUING DATA ARE AVAILABLE

British Library cataloguing data are available

© 2017 Doug Aldridge. All rights reserved

No part of this book may be reproduced or transmitted in any form or by any means, electronic or mechanical, including photocopying or recording, or by any information storage and retrieval system, without permission in writing from the publisher.

Front cover (left to right): Mark Twain, 1884; image of the brazen serpent (*Illustrated Bible Dictionary*, published by Thomas Nelson, 1897); drawing of Huck Finn by E. W. Kimble (*Adventures of Huckleberry Finn*, 1884 first edition)

Printed in the United States of America

McFarland & Company, Inc., Publishers
  Box 611, Jefferson, North Carolina 28640
    www.mcfarlandpub.com

To Bärbel, my wife,
the love of my life,
and
in memory of
Spc. Fred Greene,
a friend of our family,
killed at Fort Hood
attacking the shooter
with a pen.
He saved lives that day
and proved his pen
mightier than bullets.
"Greater love hath no man."

Table of Contents

Preface	1
Introduction	9
One. Perspectives on Point of View: A Tale with Three Tellers	33
Two. Precedents for Viewing *Huck Finn* as Biblical Burlesque and Religious Satire	56
Three. Catching the Brazen Serpent in Clemens' Net of Allusion: *Huckleberry Finn, Paradise Lost,* and the Bible	73
Four. To *Vilify* "the Ways of God to Men": *Huck Finn, Pilgrim's Progress, The Inferno* and *Paradise Lost*	117
Five. "Dark, Deep-Laid Plans": The Evasion as Religious Satire	171
Six. Author-Real Intention: *Huckleberry Finn* as Religious Satire	203
Seven. Dancing with the Devil	235
Afterword: "Sam Clemens Arrives at the Pearly Gates: A Dialog between the Author and the Doorman"	255
Appendix A: The First Person Huckleberry Finn *Chapter Titles*	259
Appendix B: Pap Confronts Huck in Chapter V and Genesis 3: 9–24	261
Appendix C: Samuel Clemens' Burlesque of Milton's Hell	263
Appendix D: Awakening in Paradise	265
Appendix E: The Duke and the King Introduce Themselves	266
Appendix F: Huck's "Great Debate" and Satan's	267
Chapter Notes	273
Bibliography	283
Index	287

Preface

"Let me make the superstitions of a nation and I care not who makes its laws or its songs either."[1]
—Mark Twain

I. Genesis

Long ago, as an undergraduate at a small college, I suffered an epiphany while studying *Huckleberry Finn*. I say "suffered" even though an epiphany is a joyful experience because the long-term effects of this particular one were transformative in ways that were a source not only of wonder to me, but also of the painful loss of beliefs I had grown up with, especially Bible based religion. What I saw back then that nobody had noticed before (or since) in the extensive commentary on Mark Twain and *Huckleberry Finn* was to prove an entrée for me into a lifelong fascination with Mark Twain's writings in general and *Adventures of Huckleberry Finn* in particular. There is a name for this condition; it's called *delirium Clemens*. Many years later, while pursuing an MA, I wrote a thesis exploring the extensive religious satire, both explicit and covert, contained in the novel. This book is an extensive revision and expansion of that work. While it is by no means an attack on anybody's faith, it should be considered a precautionary note on the dangers of taking scripture—any sacred text—literally and uncritically.

The world today offers far too many examples of the dangers of religious extremism, and the deepest intention of Mark Twain's best, most famous, and much misunderstood novel is to attack the notion that any "revealed" system of morality can work for the betterment of society. As Mark Twain later wrote, "Plainly God never knew anything about human beings, or he would not have trusted the idiots with so dangerous a thing as a Bible."[2] For all the ink that has washed over Huck's and Jim's raft, no one has ever published an explication that comes to grips with its deepest meaning as religious satire.

Yet another interpretation of *Huckleberry Finn* after so much commentary has already appeared might seem superfluous, even presumptuous. The foremost literary scholars of six or seven generations and every school of literary criticism have investigated the novel exhaustively (if inconclusively). Huck's closing comment, "There's nothing more to write" takes on a prophetic ring in this regard, as if his creator were looking ahead and seeing the confusing proliferation of theories about what he called "motive," "moral," and "plot" in Huck's narrative. Did he know that on some deep textual level he had said all—and precisely what—he meant? Is his verbally ironic "Notice" a hint that there's poisoned ground or buried treasure beyond this "Keep Out" sign?

That is what he may have been saying when he said of the book as it neared completion, "No one else may like it, but I shall *like* it."[3] When he said that, he was writing privately to his close friend William Dean Howells, as if, in *Huckleberry Finn* at least, he had found the means and freedom to express himself fully. That's the hypothesis this study is based on. Otherwise, about all that remains to say would fall into the realms of providing historical contexts for the novel or reader response commentaries in which the personal reflections of the writers are of greater moment than the artistry of the author on whose work they reflect.

II. Breaking New Ground

In view of the deep divisions among scholars about the meanings that Mark Twain may or may not have intended to convey—or failed to confront—through Huck's limited perspective, one of two things must be true: Either the author stands remote from his fictive world and it's up to the reader to make whatever one can or will of the story (as has been claimed by George Carrington); or readers—casual ones and literary scholars alike—have been overlooking aspects of the novel's construction that are essential to comprehending its meaning from the perspective of "THE AUTHOR," as Mark Twain signs his prefatory "Notice" and "Explanatory."

These features include Mark Twain's deceptively simple management of point of view, which has baffled every critic I can name from Arnold Bennett to Bernard DeVoto to Henry Nash Smith to Victor Doyno to Andrew Levy and a host of others, to create sub-textual levels of meaning on which both Mark Twain and the implied author, Samuel Clemens, get to add their own fully elaborated viewpoints to the background of Huck's realist narration. Mostly, these extraordinary twins, Mark Twain and Samuel Clemens, interact in the text much as do Huck and Mark Twain: with, as Henry Nash Smith observes of Huck and Mark Twain, "an almost unbroken irony that pervades the whole account of Huck's adventures."[4]

The following extract from Clemens' 1882 notebook (two years prior to the first publication of *Adventures of Huckleberry Finn*), a self-contained dialog between two Negro deckhands on a Mississippi steamboat, which was not published until 1975, puts his views on the status of the Bible—and, by extension, all texts purporting to present revealed truth—into bold relief. The notebook dialogue's expression of Clemens' notion that this theme was one that must be simultaneously spoken and suppressed anticipates his handling of biblical satire in the novel. It begins:

> Wanted to send a message to His Chillen, & didn't know no way but to sen' it in read'n & writ'n, w'en he know'd pow'ful well dey warn't no niggers could read it— & wouldn't be 'lowed to learn, by de Christian law of de Souf— & mor'n half er de white folks! [...]—if 'twas a man dat got up sich a po' notion, a body'd say he [...] can't invent worth shucks; but bein' its *Him*, you got to keep yo' mouf shet.

At the end of this dialogue, its first speaker drives home the point he has been making with a concluding statement that resonates with many of Mark Twain's writings on religion and the Bible, some of which have been published for the first time since the 1970s:

> [A] man is [...] mo' juster en what de Lawd is! Kase de Lawd take en buil' up a man so he jis *boun'* to kill people, en lie en steal en embellish, en den he take en jam him into everlast'n fire en brimstone for it! [...] De Lawd ain't no sich po' trash. I'll resk it, dat any book dat's got any sich stuff as dat in it warn't ever writ by de Lawd—en [...] de Lawd warn't even roun' in de neighborhood when she *wuz* writ, nuther.[5]

While the implied author's attack on the Bible in *Huckleberry Finn* is more subtle, its point is the same.

We are so used to regarding Mark Twain's somewhat unreliable narrator as the sole character in the novel from whose point of view we experience the action that making thematic sense of the first edition text of *Adventures of Huckleberry Finn* by itself is widely viewed as a hopeless task. Alas, concludes a swelling chorus of critics, *Huck Finn* is a great American narrative, but not a good novel. Admirers of the book, however, praise its language and its life-like portrayal of Huck and Jim and the Mississippi River and the sleepy little towns along its banks and the colorful characters who swarm through its pages; they love its language and its episodic structure and the humorous and satirical effects to which Huck is oblivious.

Much of *Huckleberry Finn* criticism reminds me of a fable I once heard about a group of blind men who visited a zoo and were introduced to a docile elephant that permitted them to feel its body and one even to climb on its back. One walked among its legs and declared it to be like a forest. One felt its trunk and declared it to be like a serpent. One grasped its tusks and declared it to be limbed like a tree, and one pulled its tail, declared it to be like a bell rope, and when it sat down he didn't say anything more. The one who climbed a ladder onto its back declared it to be like a mountain. Afterward, they could not agree on what it was, although each had his own vivid impressions, and all declared it to be something great, except for the one on whom it sat. He cursed it.

Huckleberry Finn is just such a literary monster. It was written by one of the great satirists of all time, and it is revolutionary in many ways. The problem for critics is that Mark Twain deliberately keeps his reader in the dark about its full meaning because the fallout he could have suffered from the bomb it plants in the reader's mind could have destroyed his reputation as a teller of moral tales who never crossed the line between irreverent satire and blasphemy. He didn't want his "kag of powder"—Huck's metaphor for telling the truth in a tight place—touched off, because he knew where it would land him. He didn't want his elephant to sit on *him*, so he also never pulled the bell rope to ring out his meaning. Nor did he need to; as Michael Patrick Hearn writes: "The book has been debated and reinterpreted according to every current critical trend, so much so that one would hardly think that anything new could possibly be said about it. Unfortunately, not all the sage critics have kept in mind Twain's sane advice, 'Don't explain your author, read him right and he explains himself.'"[6]

III. Reading Mark Twain Right

Reading him right is the challenge Mark Twain implies in his prefatory "Notice." I believe that I have learned to read *Huckleberry Finn* right. It has been a long process of study—over forty years—but this study's explanation of Mark Twain's meaning may convince those who are open to viewing him as something more than the Divine Amateur he pretended to be, and who are open to the idea that in this one work at least, he created a coherent masterwork of literary art the like of which was never seen before him and has not been seen since.

To Hearn's wise cautionary note I must add Janet Smith's comment: "All his life, Mark Twain complained that whenever he wanted to be especially devastating, his irony became so subtle that people missed the point.[7]

This has been the problem by which critics have been frustrated in their efforts to understand Mark Twain's narrative. No one set of critical tools is adequate to get at its meaning. We need a bigger box of tools—a longer "lead line"—for the task than critics have applied to the job before now, and plumbing the depths of *Huck Finn* is the purpose of this study. The religious satire of *Huckleberry Finn* lies buried deep in its structure and the author veils it with his meticulous management of point of view. It consists of archetypal material, allusions to the Bible and other works of literature that lend Huck's narration subtextual levels of meaning of which Huck is entirely unaware. Perhaps readers who have found this narrative subversive and irreverent have sensed these meanings, but no one has ever put his or her finger on just how subversive and irreverent it is.

Most discussion of the religious satire of *Huck Finn* treats this theme as being subordinate to the broader social satire of the mores of the antebellum South; Mark Twain's targets, we are told, include customs like slavery and institutions like churches that justify it and house hogs every day and hypocrites on Sunday, and ordinary people who perpetrate atrocities against each other in accordance with principles misnamed "honor" and "justice" and "religion"—but not religion itself; and not the Bible, which Mark Twain handles with kid gloves in his *overt* satire, and certainly not the Trinity, which he doesn't even mention in so many words. No, we have been told ever since Brander Matthews wrote the "Biographical Introduction" to his collected works, he was never irreverent to the point of blasphemy; he was only pointing out how well-meaning people fall short of their own ideals because human beings always try to make moral progress by looking backward, and it never works. But after many years of research that resulted along the way in a master's degree in English and an award-winning thesis on which this study is based, I have come to see that exactly the reverse is true of Huck's narrative: Its social satire is subordinate to its religious satire. That is the point on which this microcosm spins; and critics have been missing it for over 130 years.

I do not believe that Mark Twain thought his America was ready for what he had to say, but I know he had to have his say, anyway. Perhaps we're ready now. The world is festering with fundamentalism, and radical religionists of every creed are trying to tear down secular, democratic institutions around the world and throw civilization back into the dark ages of universal theocracy. Only the brands—crescent or cross or what-have-you—differ. Mark Twain would have decried this trend, wherever in the world it manifests, and my purpose in this book is to add his voice once again to the chorus of protest against the radicalism and violence of all these misguided modern fanatics. We have to learn to read him right. That is what this book is about.

IV. About Huck's Racist Conscience

There is one issue that I feel obliged to deal with at the outset of this study: the novel's portrayal of Huck Finn as a racist. This section of my preface is a condensation of more thorough discussion in Chapter Six that revisits this perennial bone of contention in the controversies that swirl around Mark Twain's masterpiece.

Many apologists for *Huckleberry Finn* have made much of Huck's transcendent recognition of Jim's humanity in his decision to "*go* to hell" for his friend. Nothing of the kind happens in the novel. Huck decides to go to hell for the cardinal sin of stealing back "his nigger." Yet while this is a story told from the point of view of a racist, it is not a racist book, but a book about racism, the ultimate evil of this fictive world. Mark Twain's scrupulous avoidance of using generically human words like "man" or "woman" in Huck's references to African Americans underscores Huck's belief in the racist dogma that black people are sub-human. That Mark Twain finds that offensive is evident from his later allusion to Acts 17, a biblical passage that emphasizes the spiritual equality of all people in the eyes of God.

Huck persistently refers to Jim as "nigger" because he is incapable of thinking of Jim as his friend or as a man. To deny Huck's racism is to distort his character and underestimate his monumental moral achievement—as Mark Twain summarized the meaning of the novel— in choosing the dictates of his "sound heart" over those of his "distorted conscience."

Huckleberry Finn's 215 iterations of the n-word encapsulate the racist dogma that African Americans are not fully human. All of the foregoing facts reveal and underscore the necessity in this realist satire of its author's pervasive use of this increasingly offensive term. It is neither a sign of Mark Twain's own racism nor a stale and nauseating joke, and verisimilitude is the least of his motives for his unrestrained use of this epithet. He could not have expunged it from the novel without undermining its thematic integrity. Huck's repetitious use of the n-word is necessary to an understanding of his character as a product of his socialization; it is necessary in the satirical scheme of the novel to point up the institutionalized inhumanity of which race-based slavery is Mark Twain's main case in point; and it is necessary for a measure of comprehension of Jim's situation as a fugitive enslaved man and his yearning for dignity and freedom.

This distillation has been condensed from a more extensive discussion exploring the veiled power of Jim's role in Huck's narrative. That section of this study addresses Mark Twain's presentation of Huck's racist perspective, showing how it turns the testimony of Twain's racist narrator into a powerful condemnation of racism itself—and not just of Huck's racism, but of the bias that can distort the reader's perception of Jim as well. For a thorough discussion of the novel's treatment of its racial themes, see Chapter Six, Section V: "About Jim."

I recommend this section especially to those who find Huck's unregenerate racist attitudes and comments an insurmountable barrier to appreciation of Mark Twain's treatment of this unavoidable and strongly relevant theme of Huck Finn's tale. As you will see, Huck's "narrative" and Mark Twain's novel are two very different stories.

V. Mark Twain on Slavery and the Art of Satire

I close this Preface with three quotations from Mark Twain's writings to which this study repeatedly refers; the first two concern slavery and his thoughts on growing up in a slaveholding community, and the last discusses the relationships among literary burlesque, travesty, and satire:

> In my schoolboy days I had no aversion to slavery. I was not aware that there was anything wrong about it. No one arraigned it in my hearing; the local papers said nothing against it; the local pulpit taught us that God approved it, that it was a holy thing, and that the doubter need only look in the Bible if he wished to settle his mind—and then the texts were read aloud to us to make the matter sure; if the slaves themselves had an aversion to slavery they were wise and said nothing.[8]

> It is commonly believed that an infallible effect of slavery was to make such as lived in its midst hard-hearted. I think it had no such effect—speaking in general terms. I think it stupefied everybody's humanity, as regarded the slave, but stopped there. There were no hard-hearted people in our town—I mean there were no more than would be found in any other country; and in my experience hard-hearted people are very rare everywhere. Yet I remember that once when a white man killed a negro man for a trifling little offence everybody seemed indifferent about it—as regarded the slave—though considerable sympathy was felt for the slave's owner, who had been bereft of valuable property by a worthless person who was not able to pay for it.[9]

> Shall I tell the real reason why I have unintentionally succeeded in fooling so many people? [...] One can deliver a satire with telling force through the insidious medium of a travesty, if he is careful not to overwhelm the satire with the extraneous interest of the travesty, and so bury it from the reader's sight and leave him a joked and defrauded victim, when the honest intent was to add to either his knowledge or his wisdom.[10]

Regarding the last of these quotations, the technique it inversely describes for *hiding* meaning is the very one that Sam Clemens used in *Adventures of Huckleberry Finn* to create a firewall of irony between himself and his audience. But there is a back door. And he hid the key in plain sight.

Introduction

I. The Controversial *Adventures of Huckleberry Finn*

Although deeply flawed, as generations of critics and commentators have argued, *Adventures of Huckleberry Finn* is Mark Twain's masterpiece and one of the greatest novels ever written in English. Not all readers have endorsed this valuation. Dissenters have occasionally prevailed in having the book banned from libraries and academic reading lists on a variety of grounds having to do with its "motive, moral, and plot"—its language aside—as the author terms these intentional, thematic, and structural considerations. His famous "Notice" ostensibly warning readers against taking Huck's story too seriously actually challenges them to match wits with Mark Twain. As he predicted to his friend W. D. Howells, "Nobody else might like it, but I shall *like* it."[1] What the author liked so emphatically about the book he didn't say, but the "Notice" hints that it has less to do with matters of style (for which Huck's narrative has been praised) than of meaning (for which it has been faulted). The purpose of the study that follows this introduction is to explore Huck's fictive world from the viewpoint of its author in "detective fashion," as Tom Sawyer would say, on the basis of clues scattered throughout the text, in order to reveal what he meant by it and why he liked this tale so well.

This exploration of the meaning of Huck's story from the viewpoint of "THE AUTHOR," as the book's introductory "Explanatory" and "Notice" are signed, makes sense of the many puzzling incongruities that have vexed readers since 1884 when the novel was first published. It reveals a consistent pattern of meaning that runs through the book's three sections and enables one to see that the best way to understand this book's meaning and to appreciate the artistry of the man who wrote it is to pay attention to its religious satire. From this perspective the book is consistent in its intention and coherent as a work of literary art. There is hardly a passage in the text that cannot be read in support of this idea. All of the major plot developments, from the "Notice" through "Chapter the Last," line up as support for the assertion that the author constructed this novel to be a covert parody of the major religious works that in his view had shaped the world in which he lived.

Of course, such a view of a literary work by Mark Twain contradicts what has been the prevailing opinion about his literary artistry since his own day—an estimation of his work as "magnificently episodic," as English novelist and critic Arnold Bennett described *Tom Sawyer* and *Huckleberry Finn* in 1910 (the year of Samuel Clemens' passing), adding:

> but as complete works of art they are of quite inferior quality. Mark Twain was always a divine amateur, and he never would or never could appreciate the fact [...] that the most important thing in any work of art is its construction. He had no notion of construction, and very little power of self-criticism. He was great in the subordinate business of decoration, as distinguished from construction; but he would mingle together the very best and the very worst decorations. The praise poured out on his novels seems to me exceedingly exaggerated.[2]

Critics have contested the appropriateness of the conclusion of *Adventures of Huckleberry Finn* so long and hotly that Harold Kolb in 1979 characterized Tom Sawyer's "evasion" as "the best roasted chestnut in American fiction."[3] While the debate has died down of late, the reason why it has subsided seems to be not so much consensus as exhaustion. Having explored the implications of the Phelps farm sequence to the fullest as it reflects on the various themes and structures they have found in the book, both the pro-evasion and anti-evasion camps appear to have run out of ammunition, and their great—albeit inconclusive—battle seems to have ended in an uneasy cease-fire.

Henry Nash Smith (1962) defines the grounds on which the majority of critics have based their negative estimations of the conclusion's appropriateness in an influential chapter titled "A Deformed Conscience and a Sound Heart." *Huckleberry Finn*, according to Smith, "contains three main elements": flight to freedom, social satire, and the developing characterization of Huck.[4] Since, as Bernard DeVoto, Leo Marx, Henry Nash Smith, Walter Blair, and Jane Smiley have all contended over the years, the evasion parodies the flight to freedom with an inharmonious burlesque of romantic escape fiction and reduces Huck to the level of Tom Sawyer's sidekick and Jim to the status of "a 'darkey' in a minstrel show,"[5] the novel winds up as an incoherent and self-contradictory work that demonstrates its author's inability to sustain and fulfill the thematic potential of the middle chapters.

Furthermore, many readers regard Twain's insensitive burlesque of his heroes' quest as utterly overwhelming the social satire implicit in the fugitives' adventures at the Phelps farm, so that they finish the book feeling "sold." As Leslie A. Fiedler (1960) puts it:

> Twain himself confuses the [tragic and comic aspects] hopelessly at the end, when Huck, calling himself Tom, *becomes* Tom; when Tom himself appears and reveals his whole role as fiction, a lie; and the tragic moral problem of Jim's freedom is frittered away in a conventional Happy Ending that we owe our idyllic vision of Childhood on the Mississippi.[6]

The defenders of Twain's ending have taken their stand on critical ground extraneous to the novel's central themes as defined by Smith and perceived by many readers. Lionel Trilling (1948) and T. S. Eliot (1950), for example, find the recessional quality of the closing chapters satisfying on formalist grounds, and numerous formalist apologies have followed theirs. Critics who see literature as the mirror of history have found in Tom Sawyer's evasion a satire on the implementation of the Thirteenth Amendment (Bassett, Gibson, Doyno, Levi, et al.).

This view comes nearer than most to fulfilling detractors' demands for a thematic justification of Twain's cavalier treatment of his protagonists, for it is at least true on the level of social realism, but as Leo Marx (1954) complains, "To take seriously what happens at the Phelps Farm is to take lightly the entire downstream journey."[7] It is not the slave's quest for freedom so much as Huck's quest for enduring values that seems trivialized at the end; as William R. Manierre (1968) laments, Huck's six thousand dollar treasure signifies his relation to society, and he mentions it on only three occasions. The first is in Chapter I, where it occasions his adoption by the Widow Douglas and attainment of respectable standing in St. Petersburg. Next, in Chapter IV when Huck "sells" it to Judge Thatcher, Manierre sees in this act Huck's "rejection" of this new status. Finally, in "Chapter the Last" Huck learns that his fortune is still intact, and that with pap's death there is no longer any obstacle to his reclaiming it and becoming once more a "respectable" member of the society that he has rebelled against: "Somehow," sighs Manierre, "it is all rather sad."[8]

Considered in this light, the development of Huck's character—the innocent picaro pursued by the society he abandons—ends in his selling out, and Huck's flight to freedom ends in a trap. On none of the thematic levels indicated by Smith may the conclusion be taken as an unequivocal affirmation of the values Huck appears to espouse at the climax. On the level of Huck's developing character, he relapses into acting as Tom Sawyer's lackey, and many readers wax indignant that their hero's hard-won moral victory over his conscience has no more lasting effect on his behavior than his camp-meeting conversion in Chapter XXII of *Tom Sawyer*.

On the level of social satire, his final resolve to "light out" would be a devastating indictment, if it were convincing, but Smith and others have argued that "there is *no evidence in the text*" (italics added) that compels us to take Huck's rejection of society seriously.[9] Huck's behavior for the past eleven chapters has undermined his moral stature, and the threat of pap and plight of Jim have been resolved—indeed, revealed for the illusions they were almost all along—so he has only the petty strictures of "sivilized" life left to flee. With wealth and security beckoning, he could get used to those discomforts "by and by." As Franklin Rogers (1960) opines:

> The entire final section represents an admission of defeat in the attempt to give the book a coherent form. The book is essentially a structural failure because the travelers reach no physical goal in their journey, and during the Evasion Huck fails to act in accordance with the instinctive humanity which characterizes his relations with Jim during the journey.[10]

Of course, not all readers who defend Twain's ending are indulging escapist fantasies. James Cox (1954), who can take Huck's final decision to "light out for the Territory ahead of the rest" more seriously, nevertheless finds Twain's conclusion stylistically flawed by "flatness" that indicates "Mark Twain could not keep a proper balance" between Tom Sawyer's values and Huck Finn's.[11] Cox's reading of the climax in *Mark Twain: The Fate of Humor*, according to Harold H. Kolb Jr. (1979), "unhinges the moral structure" that both defenders and detractors have assumed to be the moral heart of the novel: the idea that Huck's decision to "*go* to hell" for Jim is right.[12] Cox asserts that the climax is a subtle confidence game that leads the reader to "fatally approve the climactic commitment to a moral system" that forces Huck "to play the role of Tom Sawyer that he *has* to assume in the closing section of the book" because "he has forsaken the world of pleasure to make a moral choice. Precisely here," claims Cox, "is where Huck is about to negate himself ... with an act of positive virtue."[13]

David Burg (1974) and George Carrington (1976) have both proposed *diminuendo* readings of Huck's moment of moral transcendence. Burg finds an existentialist bias against *all* moral systems in the novel and sees the "disturbing prolixity" of the conclusion as a feature that "may be necessary to convince the reader he has misconceived the theme of the book."[14] For Carrington, Chapter XXXI provides a satisfactory climax if one views Huck's narrative as the story of his moral growth, but his decision to save Jim is just a moment in an endless succession of situations. Rather than view the novel as a comedy, Carrington suggests that transforming it to tragicomedy by admitting the ending, accepting that Huck's moment of "'life'" in Chapter XXXI is the prelude to his "'death'" in the next chapter and his "'rebirth'" as Tom Sawyer.

Carrington finds Huck's climactic mental struggle "unsatisfactory reverie" and "a noble melodrama of self-sacrifice" that shows Huck engaging in the same "sophistical use of gestures" that he and Jim used previously to justify their chicken thieving. In this new situation, Carrington finds this moral strategy neither satisfying nor funny.[15] This critic downplays the significance of the moral and emotional apex of Huck's flight, and he finds the deepest meaning in it to be that Chapter XXXI suggests the "unlimited gap" that separates pretense from behavior. He also finds it true to human nature, which demands that people dramatize the situations in which they find themselves entangled.[16]

Of course, in retrospect, the conclusion ceases to appear morally anticlimactic once we have thrown out the moral climax, but the power of that moment for most readers, combined with Mark Twain's 1895 statement that the book is about the conflict between Huck's "sound heart" and "deformed conscience" coming "into collision" and conscience suffering "defeat,"[17] strongly suggest that, as Harold Kolb has explained, Huck's moral victory is "not a subtle trap ... for naïve readers," even though Huck's "moral adventures ... are so satisfying, so wholesome, so perfect, that they invite suspicion."[18] In Kolb's view, reading strategies that attempt to justify the conclusion by sacrificing our view of Huck as a boy who transcends the corrupt value system of his culture—at least for a moment—are "perverse" because they distort Mark Twain's moral vision[19]—up to the point, anyway, where Huck is "reborn" as Tom Sawyer.

Bruce Michelson (1980) suggests that while "the last one-third of the novel is too anti-climactic and too long to please ... in allowing Huck to flee back into the world of children, Twain keeps faith with Huck."[20] This of course harks back to what Eliot (1950) and Trilling (1948) had to say about the formal perfection of the book. Their appraisals prompted Leo Marx's famous attack (1953) on Twain as an artist whose failure of nerve "shielded both Clemens and his audience" from "painful answers to complex questions of political morality."[21]

In other views of the novel, John Seelye (1981) explains the story as a literary practical joke, and characterizes Huck as "a ventriloquist's dummy, playing Mortimer Snerd to Tom Sawyer's Charlie McCarthy..., a juvenile version of Simon Wheeler, the perpetrator of "The Celebrated Jumping Frog" as narrative joke..., a prankster ... stretching the truth for three hundred and sixty-six pages, then letting it snap back with a bang."[22]

More recently (1984) Catherine Zuckert has argued that

> Twain's novel has thematic as much as literary unity, i.e., that Huck's return to society is a necessary, even logical conclusion of his attempt to find freedom in nature. This return constitutes as important a part of Twain's realism as his careful presentation

of the various dialects, because, as he shows, it is not possible to attain freedom through flight.[23]

Zuckert's view complements Burg's (above); the latter asserts that the "primary theme of the novel ... is simply flight" and that "the real moral of Mark Twain's masterpiece is that there is neither a valid moral code, nor the possibility that human beings could live by one if there were. The best that can be hoped for is a sound heart."[24] In another qualified defense of the conclusion from *Huck Finn*'s centennial year, John Bassett observes: "The characters we meet throughout the book are in part transformations of the meaning of 'Huck' and 'Tom' in an adult world. By the end neither has achieved a promising transformation."[25]

Yet another critical camp deserves mention here: The school of archetypal criticism has also had its day playing hooky with Huck. Archetypal critics have commented on various ways in which Huck's adventures resonate with myths and literary archetypes to enhance the universality, subliminal impact, and underlying meaning of various episodes and even, in Kenneth Lynn's (1960), Daniel Barnes' (1965), and Billy G. Collins' (1976) views, the structure and meaning of the novel as a whole, which Collins finds to be based on Huck's identification with Moses and Jim's with the Israelite people captive in "The American Egypt."

In Collins' eyes the novel becomes a re-enactment of the liberation drama of Exodus that relies on biblical authority to disprove that slavery was "the peculiar pet of the Deity" (Twain's phrase).[26] Although his case is based on parallels too extensive to be dismissed as coincidental, Collins' call for a general reassessment of the structure and meaning of the novel has, unfortunately, been widely ignored, at least in part because it is so well known—thanks to scholars like Allison Ensor and Stanley Brodwin—that Mark Twain's attitude toward biblical authority was more skeptical than reverent (to put it mildly), and the kind of appeal to Higher Authority that Collins reads into these parallels is too inconsistent with Clemens' beliefs and his characterization of Mark Twain to constitute more than a *leitmotif* in the novel's design. Nevertheless, his insights have great value when integrated into a reading of the novel that considers what Barnes characterizes as Clemens' ironic treatment of his biblical allusions,[27] many of which have gone undetected until this study.

II. After a Century of Controversy

Are we any nearer to consensus now, after more than one and a quarter centuries of wrangling, about the meaning of Huck's *Adventures* or its artistic merit? Leslie Fiedler's commentary in his centennial essay on "the book we love to hate" suggests that the very standards critics had been using to judge Twain's novel are inappropriate, that "*Huckleberry Finn* is a travesty of High Art quite as much as of conscience and duty and 'sivilization.'" That Mark Twain won "the masses he wooed" is evident from the book's popularity since "long before official critics and moralists had managed to come to terms with it." Fiedler adds that "the self-appointed guardians of culture and morality have continued to regard it with suspicion ..., [and] those who still insist that Twain's novel is dangerous and 'vulgar' speak the truth: What falsifies *Huckleberry Finn* is the begrudged and belated praise of elitist critics, who have done their best recently to persuade us that Twain's untidy masterpiece, more improvised than structured, is a "great novel" in terms of the "culture standards" by which they also find *Pride and Prejudice* or *The Wings of the Dove* great.[28] This of course harks back to Arnold Bennett's condescending 1910 dismissal of Mark Twain as a "divine amateur" (above, I)

Jane Smiley (1996) sees the book as overrated, asserting that the critical community has downplayed its formal and thematic flaws in order to further their agenda of easing the burden of guilt on whites who have been slow to relinquish the bias that gives rise to Huck's—and in her view Mark Twain's—point of view in the novel.[29] In suggesting that *Uncle Tom's Cabin*, a novel easier to defend—and teach—within the tradition of the English novel, be substituted for *Huck Finn* in the classroom, Smiley rejects the notion that there is anything sufficiently redeeming in Twain's work to justify its substitution for as passionate and coherent a fictional presentation of anti-racist sentiment as she portrays Stowe's novel being. *Uncle Tom's Cabin* may be a better choice for teaching the evils of slavery and by extension racism itself, especially at the junior level, but while this conventionally structured novel *is* more accessible, Smiley's comments reveal that *she needs* a less challenging read than *Huck Finn*, because she does not begin to understand either Huck or Jim, as she shows when she argues that "The entry of *Huck Finn* into classrooms sets the terms of the discussion of racism and American history, and sets them very low: all you have to do to be a hero is to acknowledge that your poor sidekick is human; you don't actually have to act in the interests of his humanity."[30]

Where in Mark Twain's text does Huck ever acknowledge Jim's humanity? The closest he comes is his statement toward the end of the book that "I knowed he was white inside"—in other words, an exception to the rule of white supremacy. If Huck deserves to be regarded as a hero, it is because he sacrifices his hope of salvation and acts on Jim's behalf despite his conviction that Jim is a sub-human. As Joseph Wood Krutch opined in 1954, "Huck's incredulity in face of the fact that ... Jim is as grief-stricken by a personal loss as a white man would have been when he remarks, ['I do believe he cared just as much for his people as white folks does for their'n. It don't seem natural, but I reckon it's so,'] is worth, artistically at least ... all of *Uncle Tom's Cabin*."[31]

Mark Twain's novel succeeds better than Stowe's in condemning racism, but one has to learn to "read him right" first. Twain succeeds neither by condemning his protagonists nor by falsifying them with phony transformations. And Huck does act on Jim's behalf. But this study has a long way to go before it shows just how wrong Smiley is. She is correct, however, in pointing out that the task of scholarly criticism should not be to impute greatness to inferior works in the pursuit of supposed or real socio-political agendas. Rather, it is to discover why certain books stand the test of time while others fade into obscurity. As Hearn affirms (2005), Smiley's political argument moves her to embrace Harriet Beecher Stowe's overt condemnation of slavery and racism, but "Mark Twain's verbal invention and philosophical depth"[32]—and, I must add, his insight and authenticity in laying bare the cultural evils that were "the several natural props" (Twain's phrase)[33] of American slavery and racism—surpass Stowe's. As Twain said, "Experience is an author's most valuable asset; experience is the thing that puts the muscle and the breath and the warm blood into the book he writes."[34]

Summing up critical response to the novel's conclusion, Ron Powers comments in his 2005 biography, "The meaning of Huck's response to his friend's [Tom Sawyer's] high-spirited depravity, and, indeed, of his complicity in it, has been endlessly debated and never resolved."[35] Powers joins "Mark Twain scholar Thomas Quirk" in a "replenishing call": "an invitation to read *Huckleberry Finn* less for what its various claimants would have it be, and more for what it is: an act of imagination, and one so propulsive that it pulled the author himself along into its created verities. [...] Imagination, not political courage or piety, is what finally ennobles the book."[36]

Whether Powers overlooked Victor Doyno's landmark genetic explication of the novel in *Writing Huck Finn* (1991) and Doyno's at least equally important edition of the novel that includes variant passages from Twain's working manuscript, *Adventures of Huckleberry Finn: The Only Comprehensive Edition* (1996), or if Powers has simply joined the legions of readers who have resolved to regard the closing travesty as inexplicable, it is understandable that the long debate has deafened many readers to *all* of the competing arguments that critics continue to put forward.

Doyno's genetic explication in his earlier book finds that "Once the reader knows the relevant historical background, the Phelps section offers an enjoyable, powerful, comedic, artful conclusion with timeless cultural importance"[37] and that its literary satire completes the novel both thematically and artistically. His analysis of the closing sequence focuses primarily on the conflict between Tom's authoritarian European romanticism and Huck's pragmatic approach to stealing Jim, and his focus on this dimension of the text—Mark Twain's literary satire—does enhance our understanding of Twain's motive, moral, and plot. With regard to the concluding Phelps sequence Doyno comments that the readers and critics who have been morally outraged at Twain's violations of realism and his "authorial deception and deceit," which in their view ruin the end of his otherwise "good adventure story," should redirect these "genuine, appropriate" emotional reactions with "additional knowledge." They could focus their anger not on Twain, but instead on a Southern society that derailed Reconstruction by imprisoning free African American men in the 1870s and '80s and effectively ushering in an even more vicious form of bonded servitude in violation of the spirit of emancipation.[38] According to Doyno, their indignation and outrage are "misplaced" when modern readers and critics blame the deception on Twain instead of appreciating his ingenuity in setting up a situation in which Tom Sawyer becomes an exemplar of de facto re-enslavement: "For the book, and perhaps for Twain and the nation, the recurrence of slavery has massive thematic and structural importance."[39]

In the later book, Doyno provides interpolated variant texts from the manuscript along with commentary on them and facsimile pages of the manuscript. I have found his *Comprehensive Edition*, which he represents as a resource to scholars until the full text of the manuscript becomes available after 2027, when the copyright expires, to be an invaluable resource in writing this study. As Doyno characterizes his publication of variant texts, along with commentary and facsimile pages of the manuscript in his "Textual Addendum," his *Comprehensive Edition* "will serve [scholars] as a primary means of understanding how Mark Twain invented his masterpiece."[40]

Furthermore, Doyno's analysis of the structure of the novel finds that it binds together several satiric themes: racism institutionalized in slavery before the war and in convict lease laws after Reconstruction—symbolized in the novel by Jim's imprisonment and re-enslavement—which effectively perpetuated slavery in an even more vicious form; religious satire lampooning the ways in which Christians used the scriptures to justify practices that promulgate societal evils—emblemized by the practice of slavery on the pious Phelpses' plantation; and literary satire that pillories the proponents of Europeanizing American culture through the degrading influence of the romanticism typified by Sir Walter Scott and all the other "authorities" with whose books Tom Sawyer is infatuated.

Doyno's structural paradigm asserts persuasively that Mark Twain's central focus is on the subversive power of literacy and literature to overwhelm the democratic impulse at the heart of the American experiment, personified by Huck and Jim, and that the deep motive of the novel is to free not just Huck, but the reader also, from pernicious effects of a literary culture that uses literacy to promote authoritarianism. While his focus on literature ultimately investigates Tom Sawyer's heartless use of it to hijack Huck's mission to steal Jim, delving into the texts Tom cites as his authorities and revealing a multitude of ironies that arise from seeing how they relate to the evasion, Doyno's discussion of religious abuses centers on the political connivance between Pulpit and Throne (or State) to perpetuate the power of this mutually dependent elite. In short, while the literary satire he observes as the essential meaning of Twain's satire is indeed literary, the ancillary religious satire as he reads it is essentially social—aimed not at religion itself but at abuses of the social authority and political power inherent in most religious institutions.

III. Literary Satire

This last is the point on which the analysis of this study diverges from Victor Doyno's. He gets Mark Twain, and his explication reveals many previously unrecognized dimensions of this quintessentially American novelist's literary artistry. I have learned a great deal that is indispensable from Doyno's work. For example, his discussion of Twain's uses of Shakespeare's plays sees in the entire Wilks episode "an inverse repetition of *King Lear*." Parallels that Doyno notices between the two works include a "king" attempting to deprive three daughters of their inheritance, "a false duke ... a true and false brother"—in Twain's work, "in fact, a pair of them"—"a trial scene [,] and a stormy heath scene in which a body is uncovered." At the end of this episode, "as if to punctuate the extended parallel," upon Huck's escape back to the raft, Jim greets him in his King Lear outfit. For those unfamiliar with Twain's burlesque techniques, these parallels might seem at most suggestive of the author's intention to import *Lear* into the novel, but as will be shown as this study goes forward, he uses this parodic technique over and over again, so that the sheer mass of such possible allusions to other texts with which he is known to have been familiar—and in the end, even his own plot—itself becomes evidence of these references being intentional. As Doyno writes:

> The inclusion of enough elements to create an observable resemblance also creates a progression from the burlesque of relevant Shakespeare plays in the earlier sections

to a subtle, perhaps accidental parody of the Wilks episode [in the Phelps farm sequence]. Huck, of course, never realizes that he may be wandering around in a parodic situation.

With regard to Twain's use of literary sources, Doyno finds that this reference to *King Lear* founds Jim's deep feeling as a grieving father on Lear's tragic story even though the fugitive slave is "a politically and racially contrasting human." Doyno finds in Twain's novel an "overwhelmingly negative attitude toward nobility," exemplified by the "rascal king on stage in the nude" and "the outlandish distortion of Jim in King Lear's outfit: The honored piece of literature is absorbed, transformed, made into a quite new and quite different thing as the king and the duke attempt to swindle three orphaned girls. This significant use of literature prepares for the blatant—and all encompassing—parody of literature in the Phelps farm sequence."[41]

This literary burlesque is not entirely dismissive of the concept of nobility, however. Twain has prepared for this inverse repetition of *Lear* by showing how Jim fills the role of Lear as grieving father in Jim's mourning over the likelihood of his never again seeing his children, little Johnny and 'Lizabeth, just before the Wilks episode begins, at the end of Chapter XXIII, where he confides to Huck his remorse and shame at having unwittingly abused his deaf daughter. Remarking on Twain's revision of this passage, Doyno points out that Twain wrote "never" into Jim's dialog in a "highly unusual modification of dialect form to standard language," possibly alluding to King Lear's famous line, "Never, never, never, never, never," and the critic opines that this allusion may imply that "tragic emotions can occur in the life of a low-status, traditionally voiceless person such as Jim just as they can in those of higher birth." Finding in "this richly allusive context, a dramatization of immense, irreparable human sadness, the inconsolable grief about a sick child that can torment any parent," Doyno concludes that this "suffering, limitless in depth, transcends cultural status and racial boundaries to serve as the best argument in favor of Jim's shared humanity."[42]

In an alternative view, Jim's inconsolable remorse raises him to tragic status in the eye of the reader and confers on him truly noble stature that is devoid of aristocratic pretense. Although he looks outlandish in his King Lear costume, it suits him thematically as the only really noble character—Huck eventually excepted—in this burlesque of Shakespeare. What Kenneth Lynn has called Huck's "parenthood problem" as he unconsciously seeks a worthy role model receives ironic treatment here, but the irony transforms the negative literary satire on aristocracy to a positive characterization of nobility by associating Lear with Jim, the only man in the book who consistently models heroic virtues.

Doyno's discovery of this and other Shakespearian parallels confirms something I have long suspected but could never quite put together from Huck's narration: the broad similarity of Huck's plight—having to choose between helping Jim (the commission of a crime) and social conformity (betraying Jim, his noble father figure)—to the parallel plight of Hamlet who must make a choice between avenging his father (and committing the crime of regicide) and social conformity in betraying his memory (filial disloyalty). I doubt that this parallel is accidental. In both the novel and *Hamlet*, the protagonist's moral dilemma creates the field through which the plot moves forward.

These socially inverse re-enactments of Shakespeare's plots and characters define for readers the characteristics of nobility and heroism as they manifest in a democratic society stripped—like the king's camelopard—of the trappings of hereditary aristocracy and politically enfranchised religion. Jim is as worthy as any king, and Huck is his prince and heir.

Doyno's revelation of the depth, breadth, and complexity of Mark Twain's literary satire has impressed me with the brilliance of Twain's use of allusions to a wide range of literature relevant to Huck's predicament and manifested prodigiously in the concluding travesty where Tom Sawyer does intentionally what Huck Finn has been doing unconsciously: re-dramatizing classic literature in a way that ironically enforces truths of human experience within the framework of Twain's democratic ideology. However, the appreciation of this ironic inversion of nobility, fealty to legitimate authority, devotion to the principles of kindness, mercy, love, and heroism takes years of study and voluminous reading to achieve, as Doyno's explication also demonstrates.

Was it Mark Twain's intention to force readers into a literary situation in which they had to go back and, in order to appreciate his art, do that from which, in Doyno's view, Twain was attempting to free them? Or is there another strategy in operation that renders all Mark Twain's and Tom Sawyer's literary hijinks merely the frosting on the cake of Samuel Clemens' profoundly anti-authoritarian and irreverent argument throughout the novel? This is a question that this study sets out to answer. The treatment of religious satire in the pages that follow focuses only secondarily on the political and social effects of religion run amok; its primary aim is to investigate the anatomy of Huck's conscience in order to discover exactly what the author meant when he described his tale as one of a boy's "sound heart and deformed conscience" coming "into collision," and "conscience" suffering "defeat."

Doyno's persuasive genetic studies reveal in part the extent to which the reader's recognition of covert allusions to classic literature contributes to fuller appreciation of the author's richly allusive style. Doyno's analysis—

rightly in my view—finds in *Mark Twain's* allusions a great deal of support for his theory that the motive, moral, and plot of the novel are to be found in its literary satire on the pernicious effects of anti-democratic and aristocratic European literary models for social organization and morality. This theme is of course exemplified and emphasized by Tom Sawyer's concluding evasion and the long section, in which Huck recounts his and Jim's adventure aboard the foundered steamboat *Walter Scott*, which Twain inserted into Chapter XII as the story neared completion. My own analysis follows Doyno's in many respects, but not his conclusion that the implicit meaning of the book is to be found at the level of Mark Twain's point of view.

Doyno, however, comes to the very border of the ground covered by this study in his treatment of the theme of religious/literary satire and his identification of many of the literary archetypes of the novel; and his publication of many of Twain's manuscript revisions along with his insightful discussion of them in his comparison of the manuscript and first edition texts gives readers a window into Mark Twain's creative process. Doyno's work lends support to the theory presented here that a subtext of biblical and Miltonic parody undergirds the various subtexts that he and other critics have discovered in *Huck Finn*. And it has helped to refine my thinking and intensify my conviction that at bottom, the most devastating literary satire in the novel is "THE AUTHOR's" burlesque of the Bible and *Paradise Lost*.

IV. Further Views

Another important recent contribution to our understanding of *Huck Finn* is *The Jim Dilemma: Reading Race in Huckleberry Finn* (1998), in which Jocelyn Chadwick-Joshua analyzes Mark Twain's portrayal of Jim to reveal his heroic character and the many ways in which he functions as a father figure to Huck. In the process, Chadwick-Joshua provides many insights into the coherence of Twain's vision, focusing on the many African American characters for whom Jim stands as representative; analyzing Twain's artistic techniques for showing how deeply embedded racism is in both ante- and post-bellum American society; and setting the record straight on the difference between a racist book and a book about racism, which is what Chadwick-Joshua finds *Huck Finn* to be.

Michael Patrick Hearn's expanded edition of *The Annotated Huckleberry Finn* (2005) is a valuable resource to anyone pursuing a deeper appreciation of Mark Twain's artistic achievement because it features an insightful book length introduction and many useful notes to the text of the first edition along with the original Kemble illustrations. I have found it to be a "go to" volume in composing this study.

Most recently, Andrew Levy's landmark "cultural biography of Twain in his era" in *Huck Finn's America* (2015) contributes mightily to our understanding of topical aspects of Clemens' novel—in our own day as in his—showing how "*Huck Finn* is *the* great book about American forgetfulness, and how our misjudgments of the book's messages about race and children reveal the architecture of our forgetting."[43] Levy's assertion that the history of *Huck Finn* criticism has been a history of misreading the novel and that it is "a complicated parable of the persistence of racism" that, read rightly, reveals the "unconscious parable of the persistence of racism we built, in turn, by celebrating the book according to the terms we have."[44] And he explores Twain's concerns with "literacy, popular culture, compulsory education, juvenile delinquency, at-risk children, and the different ways we raise boys from girls, and rich from poor." Twain, Levy contends, "was vastly more interested in how many Americans *play* with race than in how they rise above it."[45]

Levy observes also that Twain delivered *Huck Finn* in the early years of Jim Crow, the system of segregation and oppression of African Americans that limited voting rights and rigged elections, denied blacks economic and educational opportunities, and under which "a racially biased judicial system drove many African-Americans into convict leasing systems that rented out their bodies for pennies a day." In today's America, he adds, "large percentages of the African-American male population of major cities … are either imprisoned—where their labor can be sold for pennies a day—or released from prison, but with restricted voting rights, mobility, and access to economic benefits." "Likewise," continues Levy, Twain "offered *Huck Finn* to a country where parents, educators, and politicians worried that children … were too exposed to violent media … that made them anarchic and violent themselves. The twenty-first century reader lives in a country worried about the exact same things." Some of the facts have changed, but the dynamics shaping our reality have not changed since *Huck Finn's* debut. "In this light," Levy writes:

> it matters that we have been misreading Huck Finn, because that misreading is both wasted opportunity and metaphor for our larger failure to recognize our close relation to the past. […] We misread *Huck Finn* […] for the same reason we repeat the cultural and political schema of the Gilded Age—because the appealing idea that every generation is better off than the one before conceals our foreboding that we live in a land of echoes.[46]

Levy's emphasis on what Mark Twain saw as the cyclical pattern of history comprises an important dimension of this study's analysis as well, and his deep research, lucid discussion, and clear focus on Twain's topical concerns make *Huck Finn's America* an excellent companion to the analysis presented here; indeed, all five of these recent books are compatible with and complement this study's focus on an aspect of Twain's argument concerning a related issue: *Why* is it that we live in perennial re-enactment of the misguided policies and cultural manifestations of the past? As we shall see, *Huck Finn* provides Mark Twain's solution to this riddle as well, and his solution goes beyond Americans' faith in progress and the national state of denial to which Levy attributes our tendency to repeat the past.

These five important books by Victor A. Doyno, Jocelyn Chadwick-Joshua, Michael Patrick Hearn, and Andrew Levy contribute greatly to an understanding of the novel that is true to Mark Twain and his era, but they deal with aspects of his artistic achievement that are mostly peripheral to this study. What we are concerned with here is penetrating to a deeper subtext of the novel to explore the fullness of its religious satire, not its topical relevance to a host of societal evils that these able critics rightly perceive Mark Twain attacking, and which do contribute greatly in the various ways they point out to the unity and coherence of the novel. Doyno especially recognizes the importance of Twain's satiric portrayal of the form of Christianity with which Huck is acquainted, but in his discussion of this aspect of Twain's satire he overlooks a great deal of evidence that it was not just Southern, fundamentalist Christianity that the author was satirizing, but the entire edifice of biblically based morality that provided the archetypes for our national identity. And readers of Levy—one of whose primary observations has to do with history repeating itself rather than progressing—will find here an explanation—according to Mark Twain—of why this recycling of the past goes on and on.

V. Where Do We Go from Here?

The foregoing introduction to the problems with which critics have been wrestling in their efforts to explain *Huckleberry Finn* has, inevitably, oversimplified matters. But I think it is fundamentally accurate as a measure of the present stage of our ongoing response to a novel that has stirred up more controversy than perhaps any other in American literature—not just in the scholarly press—but in the mass media and the public schools of our nation as well. Clearly there is something wonderfully perverse about a book than can remain a bone of contention not only among the highly literate, but also across the spectrum of American culture for as long as *Adventures of*

Huckleberry Finn has been in print. That the voice of Huck has been powerfully influential is a fact of our cultural history, but why his fictional autobiography has occasioned such storms of controversy has yet to be fully explained.

My intention in the pages that follow is to show that all five of the critical camps we've been attending to—the approving formalists/condemning moralists, to apply Marx's reduction to the Huck Finn controversy once more[47]; along with the mavericks like James M. Cox, Leslie A. Fiedler, and John Seelye; the biographical/historical/genetic analysts who impose extraneous materials onto the text in order to gauge its meaning; stylistic critics who focus only on the language of the text at hand and use its evidence as the sole basis for their conclusions; and archetypal critics who too often conflate the meaning of a derivative text with that of its source—have overlooked matters of point of view and mythic displacement. Mark Twain's literary artistry does provide grounds to *refute* Henry Nash Smith's assertion that "there is no evidence in the text that compels us to take Huck's rejection of society seriously."[48]

Along the way, rather than merely providing yet another view of the novel to confuse its students further, I shall attempt to integrate the views of generations of literary scholars into the discussion to show how different perspectives on the novel—even ones written in reaction to one another—like Harold Kolb's response to James M. Cox (above, Section I)—can contribute to fuller understanding of Mark Twain's artistic achievement in *Huck Finn*. Of course, there isn't room for *everybody* on this bus, so the goal has been to select a representative sample of commentary from the various critical camps.

VI. Clemens vs. Twain

Another of Mark Twain's recent biographers, Andrew Hoffman, raises an issue that has received little attention over the years: To what extent are we to regard Mark Twain as a character in this text rather than its author? In Hoffman's view,

> Sam Clemens hides behind the scenes in *Huck Finn* pulling the narrative strings, and he does not mind weakening Mark Twain's authority in the process. Tom's incursion at the end of the book, which challenges the moral foundation carefully set by Mark Twain, represents Sam's disguised effort to secure recognition for himself as both the author of *Huck Finn* and the inventor of its titular author.[49]

Pursuing Hoffman's proposal that there is an underlying tension between Clemens and Mark Twain in the novel, the method of the ensuing study is to conduct rigorous examinations of both Clemens' handling of point of view and his use of literary sources in *Huck Finn*. The ironies to which both of these techniques give rise support the hypothesis that the implied author of this novel, Samuel L. Clemens, doubly disguised as Huck Finn and Mark Twain, transforms Huck's picaresque monologue and Mark Twain's social/religious/political/literary satire into a largely covert satire on the Judeo-Christian worldview. By modeling villainous characters on biblical heroes and basing key episodes of the novel on passages from the Bible, *Pilgrim's Progress*, Dante's *Inferno*, and *Paradise Lost*, Clemens frequently causes Huck's narrative to reflect satirically on these sources. Thus Clemens structures the novel in a very different pattern from that which has been observed until now.

The theme that emerges from this two-fold consideration of point of view and literary archetypes in the text is religious satire. This theme unifies the novel's much-maligned closing section with the chapters set in St. Petersburg, on Jackson's Island, on the river and shore, and in the closing Phelps farm sequence, where Tom Sawyer—and Mark Twain—do indeed make a mockery of all that has gone before. It is necessary to consider Clemens' management of point of view and his handling of literary archetypes as one pursues a just appreciation of the motive, moral, and plot of his greatest and most controversial novel.

Reference here to Samuel L. Clemens rather than Mark Twain is deliberate and necessary, as will be explained thoroughly in Chapter One. Lest anyone find me in contempt of the current scholarly fashion of referring to the writer as Mark Twain, and only the historical man as Clemens, I feel obliged to offer a word of explanation here. Only by acknowledging the love-hate relation Clemens had with his *nom de plume* and opening one's mind to the possibility that he used the invented character it named as a comic foil—a straight man, to put it another way—have I been able to unravel portions of the narrative that otherwise defy full explication. Much of this study's discussion relies on the distinction between Mark Twain as "implied narrator" and Samuel Clemens as "implied author": I define these terms as part of my analysis of point of view, so if you go browsing in the chapters that follow and come across them, consult Chapter One for clarification of their meaning. When we get to the end of the book, we can all get back to referring to "THE AUTHOR," as he signs his introductory "Notice" and "Explanatory," in the usual way.

VII. Samuel Clemens' Burlesque Technique

As Franklin R. Rogers has shown, to account for his "dependency upon ideas found in other works of fiction to which Mark Twain confessed on several occasions," he claimed to W. D. Howells that he was "the worst literary thief in the world, without knowing it."[50] Rogers makes the case, however, that:

> that borrowing which is rooted in his burlesques was, *of necessity, conscious*. To such deliberate borrowing Twain has also confessed [… in] a letter written in 1876. [...] Since the ideas only are borrowed, the result is nothing like the originals when Twain has completed the transplantation, for they become in his hands mere foundations upon which he rears a structure of episode, character-axis, and theme all his own [italics added].[51]

I intend to show that Huck's confrontation with his conscience occurs after his experiences have carried him through burlesque re-enactments of the great myths of Eden and the Fall of Man, Cain's slaying of Abel, Abraham's near-sacrifice of Isaac, the Deluge, key elements in the story of Moses, the fall of King Saul, David's grief at the death of his friend Jonathan, and the Crucifixion. These experiences have forced Huck into personal conflict with the God of the Old Testament and the Satan of *Paradise Lost*, and Clemens has conferred on him numerous archetypal identities which, through his ritual suicide/patricide/deicide in Chapter VII, Huck casts off.

The opening chapters set the stage for his rebirth as a new Adam on Jackson's Island, ritually prepared for his voyage through what, by the time of the novel's composition, had already become the heartland of the American Eden. As W. R. Moses has speculated, Chapters V through XXXI constitute a tour of Hell—Dante's *Inferno*—in which Huck descends ever-deeper into confrontation with first Incontinence and Wrath, then Violence, and finally Fraud and Treachery, in a progression of episodes that mirrors Dante's infernal structure.[52]

As the raft drifts, covert biblical satire is a consistent theme and unifying *motif* that substantiates Clemens' assertion that Huck's character is "no better than that of David and Solomon and the rest of the Sacred Brotherhood."[53] The climax confers the identity that Stanley Brodwin has described as Mark Twain's "Adamic Satan" on Huck,[54] and Tom Sawyer's "evasion," in which the struggle between Moses and Pharaoh plays a prominent role, as Billy G. Collins has pointed out, becomes, when viewed in this light, the novel's supreme expression of the conflict between Huck's compassionate pragmatism and Tom Sawyer's conscientious conformity.

In a series of parallels between Tom's evasion—an apt name for a liberation plan designed to re-enslave the one it is supposed to set free—and the story of the first fourteen chapters of Exodus, Clemens' patterning his plot on the Bible's plan for freeing the Israelites provides a closing blast of religious as well as social/literary satire. This previously undetected burlesque unifies the conclusion with the rest of the book as religious satire, and it attributes the evils of "sivilization," from which Huck resolves to "light out" at the end, to its reliance not only on Tom's "dime novel" models for conformity, as Doyno has revealed in copious detail, but also and more fundamentally to its biblically informed social order and morality.

Although Doyno finds few "explicit references to religion" in the Phelps episode,[55] Collins establishes that the parallels between Exodus and the evasion are too numerous, too exact, and too pervasive to be dismissed. Collins marshals strong evidence that Mark Twain identifies Huck as Moses, and Tom as Moses' brother Aaron; Jim and all the other slaves represent the Hebrew people captive in The American Egypt (Lincoln's epithet),[56] and the slaveholders stand for the Egyptian captors of the Hebrews in the Bible story. But the interpretation Collins imposes on Clemens' uses of the Bible—especially in the Phelps farm sequence—is out of alignment with the pattern of biblical parody we are about to explore.

To accept his view that the conclusion manifests the *implied author's* concern with disproving that the Bible condones slavery is to view the novel as being *less* unified thematically than its detractors have maintained it to be all along. In view of the author's attacks on biblical morality found everywhere else in the text, this reverent interpretation of the novel as a whole—and of the closing chapters especially—under*mines* rather than under*scores* the thematic unity of the novel. For it imputes to the implied author a pro-biblical posture that affirms what the text explicitly denies: the moral authority of a biblically based code of ethics and conduct.

What Collins fails to notice is that Tom Sawyer, in his motivation and methods, caricatures the Mastermind of Exodus in ways that appropriately conclude the novel's overt and covert religious satire attacking the moral authority of the Bible. Tom's words throughout this section frequently echo Exodus and burlesque biblical characterizations of the deity Mark Twain held in derision. Huck's subservient behavior and Jim's humiliation are simply the logical, inevitable consequences of their renewed participation in a society founded on Tom's biblically informed code and divinely inspired hunger for kingdom, power, glory, honor, and bloodshed. And racism. And slavery.

Archetypal critics who conclude that they have discovered the meaning of a passage once they have identified its source often miss Clemens' irony. Biblical allusions in *Huckleberry Finn*, many of which have gone unnoticed, *invite* one to read for irony. As Allison Ensor points out, Twain's "adult life, and even his early years were to a high degree informed by skepticism"[57]:

> The nonrespectable side of Twain wished to deride and ridicule the Bible for all it was worth. The impulse to do so appeared as early as 1870 and increased progressively [; …] he wished to reveal the book's foolishness and pernicious influence. […] The

respectable side of his nature realized that the public regarded the Bible and Christianity as sacred [; …] Twain was thus led to suppress in some manner the more outspoken and extravagant attacks which he made on religion and particularly on the Bible.[58]

In *Huckleberry Finn*, as we are about to see, Clemens displays both sides of his nature by borrowing his narrative structure from *Paradise Lost, The Inferno, Pilgrim's Progress*, and the Bible to create a covert satire on the very sources to which he alludes.

Thus, in view of the author's frequent, conscious borrowing of ideas from literary sources, and of his well-known familiarity with and attitude toward the Bible and *Paradise Lost*, extensive biblical and Miltonic burlesque cannot be dismissed as either a minor or an unintentional theme of the novel. Rather, such burlesque will be shown to constitute a central theme of this novel: *Huckleberry Finn* is a thoroughgoing satire on biblical religion and Judeo-Christian metaphysics and cosmology. The failure of readers to recognize religious satire based on Clemens' burlesque of the Bible and *Paradise Lost* has resulted in general incomprehension of this undergirding structure and overarching theme of the novel. *Adventures of Huckleberry Finn* can be seen in its many-layered unity—a masterpiece of kaleidoscopic satire—only when we view it as the powerful indictment of Huck's biblically informed conscience that Samuel Clemens intended his novel to be.

Most readers who have expressed disappointment in the novel's ending have misjudged the depth and breadth of its religious /literary/social satire. Readers' blindness, not Clemens' "failure of nerve,"[59] is what has prevented the conclusion from being seen for what it is: an appropriate finale to the novel's satirical attack on the biblical world-view in which American culture in the nineteenth century—to say nothing of the twenty-first—was still firmly rooted.

Tom Sawyer and Mark Twain do engineer a parody of Huck's and Jim's adventures that violates their democratic spirit and authentic morality by superimposing on many of the very same situations the overlay of European-style, romantic, chivalric "authority" that Doyno explores thoroughly in his discussion of the novel's literary satire. This glaring travesty is exactly the type of sensational red herring that Sam Clemens discovered he could use to succeed in "fooling" his audience. Once he had discovered the technique that enabled him to simultaneously express and suppress his opinion of the Bible (see Preface, Section II and Section V: final quotation), he was able to construct *Huck Finn* with a deeply concealed subtext in which he lays the blame for the immoralities performed in the name of religion—and the fascination with literary authority that perverts Tom's play—at the fountainhead from which all Western literary authority springs: the Bible.

VIII. Upcoming

This study focuses on the first edition text of *Huck Finn* and integrates a wide range of critical perspectives into discussion of the structure and meaning of the novel as a covert satire on the Judeo-Christian world-view. Its analysis of Huck's narrative finds that while the whole story is committed to Huck's voice, the perspectives of the book's implied narrator and author are accessible to readers alert to Mark Twain's allusions to literature beyond the ken of his naïve narrator. The burlesque of the Bible and *Paradise Lost* to which these allusions give rise spans the entire novel, constituting both the undergirding structure and overarching theme of the book.

The first chapter points out the extent to which Clemens' management of point of view creates a layered text of complex irony, and it discusses one of the critical controversies that arose in the late 1970s when Harold Kolb took exception to James Cox's radical reading of the climax and Phelps farm sequence. The point of this section is to demonstrate that the apparently contradictory assessments of these two critics are actually both valid when applied to different dimensions of the text—different levels of meaning. Chapter One concludes with a section that provides an overview of this reading of *Huckleberry Finn* as religious satire.

Chapter Two reviews some precedents for treating *Huck Finn* as a work that is deeply and consistently concerned with constructing a parody of the Bible, and the argument also attends to ways in which apparently contradictory readings can be reconciled with one another when the reader regards their arguments as complementary expressions of the differing points of view of the author (Clemens) and the implied narrator (Twain).

Chapter Three begins the introduction of new evidence that literary burlesque of the Bible and *Paradise Lost* is the foundation of Clemens' religious satire and goes on to explicate nineteen major episodes (more than one per chapter, on average) in the opening (1876–1880) portion of the novel that show the author's persistent concern with biblical and Miltonic burlesque; in fact, almost every chapter of the recently discovered first half of the manuscript, up to Chapter XIX of the finished novel, advances Clemens' religious satire.

In Chapter Four of this study, the main focus is on the portion of the novel begun in 1883—up to Chapter XXXII—in which Clemens makes extensive use of parallels to the Bible, *The Inferno, Pilgrim's Progress,* and *Paradise Lost* to ground Huck's experiences in a context of mythological and theological concerns that have profound moral implications. The section on Huck's climactic debate with his conscience traces its parallels to the once-famous soliloquy of Milton's Satan on Mount Nephates (prior to his intrusion in Eden), in which he acknowledges the justice of his damnation, resolves to think no more about his chances for pardon, dedicates himself to evil, and sets out to hold "divided empire" with God. The defeat of Huck's conscience that Mark Twain declared thus marks his achievement of moral autonomy and his advent as the original avatar of what Stanley Brodwin has termed "Mark Twain's Adamic Satan."

Chapter Five investigates the religious satire of the Phelps farm sequence and Tom Sawyer's evasion with emphasis on its long recognized but little understood burlesque re-enactment of the events of Exodus 1–14. The events of the evasion are broadly parodic: Clemens burlesques both his biblical source and the plot of the novel up to Chapter XXXII to reveal how "stealing" Jim in accord with Tom's and Mark Twain's "authorities" reduces Huck and Jim to props in Tom's play and temporarily dims their hard-won moral authority. When the dust Mark Twain tosses in the reader's eyes clears, however, it is Tom's role that Clemens reveals to be villainous. Jim and Huck emerge from this analysis as heroes.

Both chapters Four and Five also consider the significance of Clemens' revisions as he wrote and re-wrote until he felt that it was probably safe to publish the novel. His manuscript and revisions frequently testify that religious satire was a theme with which he was constantly wrestling in composing what became an amazingly complicated narrative with overtly realistic first-person narration erected on a framework of allusions to religious literature that conflate and thereby negate the moral polarity of his source archetypes. However, the primary focus of the discussion—even as the sidelights of the manuscript shine on the text—is the first edition, which for better or worse is the novel as Clemens published it and as we have it. In the great majority of instances this study finds that his extensive revisions do serve the purposes of improving both characterization and thematic development even as they tone down the overt religious and social satire.

The sixth chapter investigates the question of authorial intention, focusing on the role of the prefatory "Notice" as a rhetorical key designed to unlock the otherwise impenetrable irony of Clemens' text and to confirm that the themes traced from the novel in the pages that follow are indeed the meanings that the implied author meant to convey. This chapter also includes a section discussing the role of Jim in the archetypal structure of the novel, along with some observations on his heroic character and his function as a surrogate father to Huck. Chapter Six continues with consideration of the novel as an organic work of art that has much greater unity and coherence than most of its critics have deemed it to possess. A short, concluding section returns to a question raised in Chapter One: How can one be "prosecuted, banished, or shot" by a fiction?

Chapter Seven of this study is devoted to consideration of a wider range of relevant matters: This final chapter seeks to place *Huck Finn* in the continuum of Mark Twain's major fiction, advancing my own—no doubt debatable—belief that despite the heartbreak, bitterness, and cynicism that threatened to overwhelm him in later life, Clemens never lost his deep faith in the possibility of improving the human race, damned though it may be by its own persistent, pervasive, and pernicious superstitions. This chapter also includes excerpts of Mark Twain's 1870s essay, "God of the Bible vs. God of the Present Day" (first published in 1995), which stands as his religious manifesto during the period he was writing *Huck Finn*.

The Afterword is a relevant piece of short fiction, "Sam Clemens Arrives at the Pearly Gates: A Dialog between the Author and the Doorman," that came to me early one morning while waiting for my head to clear so that I could get back to work on this study.

Six appendices, four of which consist of parallel redactions of passages in *Huck Finn* and the biblical or Miltonic texts on which I propose that they are modeled; one more that displays the differing texts of the duke's and king's self-introductions as they appear in different combinations in the manuscript and in the first edition; and one that lists the intriguing first person chapter titles that Mark Twain, presumably, later substituted for the more prosaic, third person ones in the first edition, extending the author's portrayal of Huck—and diminishing the appearance of Mark Twain—as being "the maker of the book."

IX. A Note on Citation and Cross-Reference Methods

Generally, I have tried to conform to the Chicago style of documentation; however, because Mark Twain's chapters are fairly short and there are many editions of the novel in circulation, I have resorted to an unconventional method of citing passages in the text for the convenience of readers who wish to follow the discussion in their own copies of *Huck Finn*. Rather than giving the page number in a particular edition, I simply note parenthetically the chapter of *Huck Finn* in which any given passage is located. This is convenient for me, too, because I have found several editions useful in composing this study. For textual authority, I have used the first edition text in Michael Patrick Hearn's *The Annotated Huckleberry Finn*, a book that is also very helpful to anyone pursuing a just appreciation of the novel.

This study attempts to discuss *Huck Finn* as much as possible in its narrative order. No matter what approach one takes to explicating Huck's tangled web, the task is complicated by Mark Twain's characteristic style of composition that employs a great deal of repetition with variation, so that each time he repeats a motif the repetition creates an echo in the attentive reader's mind, a resonance that conditions the meaning of not only the present passage but also the previous and/or successive one(s).

For example, the closing burlesque of Huck's and Jim's flight to freedom contained in Tom Sawyer's evasion reminds readers of Huck's authentic experiences, making them more admirable for their authenticity and rendering Tom's attempts to outdo them more despicable for their arti- and superficiality (see Chapter Five, Section XI). Because this "echoic" character, as both Doyno and Levy describe it, pervades the text, it frustrates any attempt to deal with the text in a linear way. One has to continually jump back and forth between and among episodes in order to comprehend Clemens/Twain's meaning. The method that I have resorted to for dealing with these reverberations is to include occasional parenthetical cross-references like the one in the middle of this paragraph that look forward, sideways, and back in the discussion to support readers in following these motifs in the design of Mark Twain's text. The printed number refers to a chapter of this study; the Roman numeral cites the relevant section.

CHAPTER ONE

Perspectives on Point of View
A Tale with Three Tellers

I. A Tale Told (in Code) by an Idiot

The narrative structure of *Adventures of Huckleberry Finn* conforms to the formula for storytelling that Mark Twain elaborated in "How to Tell a Story." *Huck Finn* is unique among Clemens' works, John Lindberg reminds us, in that it is the only novel in which he committed the entire story to the voice of a boy. Attending to the way that Huck's limitations cause "foreshortening in the narrative," Lindberg points out that "the reader sees and hears only what Huck sees and hears, and the reader must supply his own sense of irony. ... Huck has the primitive awareness of a child awakening to the confusing world of adults."[1]

Because Huck's point of view is the only window Mark Twain gives us into his world, George Carrington speaks for a whole school of critics when he claims that Mark Twain "can give us none of the 'guidance' Wayne Booth prays for in difficult fictional situations."[2] Therefore, according to Carrington, we can never know what was on Mark Twain's mind as he composed the novel. The only point of view to which we have access is Huck's, and we must content ourselves with that. On this basis, we can observe what Huck reports, gather some understanding of Huck and his environment, and proceed with a reader response, but we walk away with nothing more than that; it appears useless to ask what the author thinks about any of the implications of the action because he appears to have absented himself from the text. All that a critic can say is essentially reader response, and one reader's coherent response need not agree with another's, nor with what biographical information suggests the author may have meant to imply by the words and deeds of his characters.

Yet his chapter divisions, with their third person subheadings, do convey the idea of an implied author contributing to what Wayne Booth calls "the reader's intuitive apprehension of the completed artistic whole,"[3] as do the prefatory "Notice" and "Explanatory," especially the latter, for it claims what Huck denies: that "THE AUTHOR" is the creator of Huck Finn's words. In later editions of the novel, Twain changed the first edition's third person chapter descriptions to first-person chapter titles, furthering the illusion that Huck *is* the maker of the book and further distancing himself from his text. Even Twain's use of the word "narrative" in the "Notice" strikes a modest note.[4] This is not art, it seems to say, but just a story, the autobiographical memoir of a child who, having found out the hard way "how much trouble it was to make a book … ain't a-going to no more" (Chapter the Last).

Evidently, this separation of the author from the text is what Mark Twain meant to accomplish by putting the whole story into Huck's own words. As Twain's manuscript shows, he considered putting "Reported by Mark Twain" on the title page, and he rejected the idea of claiming even that much authorial responsibility for Huck's words.[5] Nevertheless, he does inject a sense of ironic humor that relieves the grimness of the realities of Huck's narrative. And he could not deny his responsibility for immersing the reader in the horrors Huck reports: foraging for food from swill barrels, pap's drunken abuse, episodes of violence, brushes with death, random murders and bloodshed, disasters, fraud, treachery, hypocrisy, greed, lust, human degradation, slavery, and Huck's own racism, to itemize several of these horrors. His genteel readers were appalled and did hold Mark Twain responsible in no uncertain terms, but the public loved him.

Of course, no author can completely divorce himself from the implications of the story he writes. Nobody believes that Huck Finn is a real character who wrote a memoir. And, clearly there is a dimension of the text in which Mark Twain makes his presence known. Huck's claim to be the maker of the book is one example: How clever of the author, readers may respond, to claim that his persona is a real person—how charmingly absurd! In this dimension, Mark Twain becomes responsible for the humor of the story. The primitive Huck hardly possesses a sense of humor; whenever he says anything that is truly funny, he doesn't intend to make the reader laugh—he is just reporting what happened with no sense of irony or wit, yet irony pervades his tale, as Henry Nash Smith and a host of other critics have observed: Huck's tale is characterized by "an almost unbroken irony," Smith points out,[6] as the reader marvels at his innocence, ignorance, and naiveté.

Yet, as Lindberg's observation (above) makes clear, Twain leaves it up to the reader to supply the information Huck lacks in order to fill in the blanks in Huck's comprehension. The author supplies none of it. Once we enter Huck's world in Chapter I, the only glimpse we get of "THE AUTHOR" behind him, looking back at us over Huck's shoulder, comes in the first paragraph, and from Huck's point of view. *Tom Sawyer* "was made by Mr. Mark Twain," Huck informs us, and since he is in a position to judge the veracity of that work, being a creature of it, he identifies himself as both a fiction who owes his existence to the author and a character whose existence is independent of "Mr. Mark Twain." Filling in the blanks in Huck's comprehension appears to be the whole game that Mark Twain sets up with his reader: Can the reader fill in enough of these blanks to make sense of "a tale told by an idiot"?

Lindberg views the novel as an application of Clemens' advice about how to tell a humorous story; his analysis suggests that "the hero's earnestness" and other virtues swiftly charm readers into tolerating his ignorance and character flaws, and that Clemens' characterization of Huck predisposes the reader "to share Huck's concerns until the point of the story becomes our own. ... Huck maintains the unifying reality of the book—himself and his voice."[7]

Lindberg's insight into the method Clemens developed for telling a humorous story (as contrasted with a "comic" or "witty" story in "How to Tell a Story") suggests "a grouping of events" to which Huck's point of view gives shape, "a sense of timing by contrast and process ... that imparts a rhythm of climaxes to ... episodes arranged to illustrate Huck's increasing anxiety."[8] This insight brings an important aspect of Clemens' creative process into focus. By immersing his imagination in the personality of his child persona, and by committing the entire narrative to Huck's voice, Clemens liberated himself as AUTHOR from accountability for the novel's deepest satirical elements and freed himself to write without restraint as long as he kept his satire covert. Huck's beguiling voice assures us that all the novel contains is the truth of Huck's experience. It is one measure of Clemens' genius that on the level of pure story, Huck's character and voice always sustain the narrative, charming us into embracing the preposterous idea that "Huck Finn *is* the maker of the book," as George Carrington assures us.[9]

Moreover, the storytelling technique Lindberg observes in the novel is characteristic of Mark Twain's platform manner of storytelling adapted to a book-length tale. One distinctive feature of the telling of *humorous* stories is that the speaker remains unaware that he has said anything funny, and looks up in puzzled surprise when his audience is tickled by what he has said, just as Huck would wonder why anybody would laugh at his hunting for the mate to a wooden leg. Harold Kolb has commented on "the unceasing procession of moral idiots" that peoples the fiction of Mark Twain.[10] Huck, in this respect, is in good company, and Clemens lets us know that, when Huck comments on Jim's folklore: "Jim said bees wouldn't sting idiots; but I didn't believe that, because I had tried it lots of times myself, and they wouldn't sting me" (Chapter VIII).

II. Real and Make-Believe Narrators

This study is primarily a consideration of two aspects of Samuel Clemens' literary art in *Adventures of Huckleberry Finn:* his handling of point of view and his rendering of literary archetypes into Huck's vernacular. Obviously these aspects are interrelated, for Huck, as a barely literate narrator, has been isolated by his creator from literary influences that have helped to shape the consciousness—and consciences—of both the author and, at least indirectly, his audience. As the opening chapters reveal, Huck has had a smattering of Bible and romance by word of mouth, at first, from the Widow Douglas, Miss Watson, and Tom Sawyer, and then along with his schooling. In the "three or four months" that pass between Chapters III and IV he learns to read and write, and naturally would attend Sunday school and church; and, as required of him in Chapter I, he participates in customary daily household devotions with the widow and her sister Miss Watson. In Chapter XIV he reads a little farther along these same lines, but Jim's take on chivalric and biblical lore challenges Huck's conventional wisdom so that this exposure to literature hardly has the effect on Huck that similar reading has had on Tom Sawyer. Its effect is to undermine conventional interpretations of these texts—and to defamiliarize them to the reader.

In Chapter XVII Huck reads some Bunyan; his comment that *Pilgrim's Progress* is "about a man that left his family it didn't say why" reveals that he misses Bunyan's point completely even as it invites the reader to compare Huck and Christian with each other and all the other nominal Christians Huck encounters along his way, on a level of which this naïve narrator is unaware. This level *would* be that of the implied author, Wayne Booth's term for the characterization of an author implied by the total intellectual, emotional, and moral content of a literary work, *if* his theory were capable of accounting for the full complexity of Clemens' management of point of view in the novel.

Booth's insights do allow one to distinguish between Huck's point of view and the *implied narrator's;* thus Booth comments that Huck "claims to be naturally wicked while the author silently praises his virtues behind his back."[11] But simply to observe a dual perspective implicit in *Huckleberry Finn* is to overlook the extent to which Mark Twain is actually a narrator—and a none-too-reliable one, at that—rather than the author of the book. Since Booth disregards the phenomenon of pseudonymous authorship in his discussion of novelists' self-characterization in their work, his *Rhetoric of Fiction* provides only the basis for the present discussion of point of view in Clemens' novel. Because *Huckleberry Finn* is in essence the product of three tellers, the three levels of telling that Booth terms "real author," "implied author," and "narrator" or "persona" are fully elaborated elements of Clemens' narrative paradigm. In the course of defining his terms, Booth comments:

> Our sense of the implied author includes not only the extractable meanings but also the moral and emotional content of each bit of action and suffering of all of the characters. [...] It includes, in short, *the intuitive apprehension of a completed artistic whole*; the chief value to which *this* implied author is committed, regardless of what party his creator belongs to in real life, is what is expressed by the total form [italics added].[12]

In regard to Samuel Clemens, whose *nom de plume* emphasizes the irony that pervades his work, one must realize that his art reflects his awareness of the extent to which it is nearly all a characterization of his persona Mark Twain. During Clemens' life, he was perhaps even more popular as a speaker than he was as a writer, and he made a fair part of his living as a performer. The role he performed was the character Mark Twain, and even though the general public knew his real identity, it was not Sam Clemens they attended his lectures to hear, and whose books they bought, but Mark Twain, the fictitious character he brought to life on the platform and the printed page. Booth asserts, "The emotions and judgments of the implied author are ... the very stuff out of which great fiction is made."[13] This being so, Clemens' experiments with literary form gave rise to an art one of whose primary functions is to imply the mythical Mark Twain's personality and convictions. There were pseudonymous authors before Mark Twain and there have been others since, but Sam Clemens took his alter ego to a level that was unprecedented in literature or on the platform. And there has been no one like him since.

Mark Twain, therefore, is not a *maker*, but a *product* of fiction; his emotions and judgments are not the source but an important theme of the works of Samuel Clemens. Thus, while it is tempting to label Mark Twain the implied author of *Huckleberry Finn*, to do so without reservation would be a misleading misuse of Booth's term. The Samuel Clemens implied by the collaboration of Mark Twain and Huck Finn is, in Booth's strict sense, the true implied author of this work, just as the Mark Twain implied by Huck's narrative is, as the first paragraph of Chapter I makes clear, a character in the background of the novel, the source of its pervasive ambiguity and much of its humor. Thus Mark Twain is the *implied narrator*—not *author*—and the personality characterized by the "total form" is the novel's version of Samuel L. Clemens, the true implied author whose point of view it is the purpose of the present chapter to access. For the purposes of this discussion, then, the implied author of *Huckleberry Finn* is Samuel Clemens; the implied narrator is his alter ego Mark Twain; and the narrator—their persona—is Huck Finn.

Since these three levels of narration are explicit in the novel's form, one could say in fairness to Booth that the character of Samuel Clemens, the historical creator of the "completed artistic whole" (as Booth distinguishes the "real author" from the "implied author" above), is what the author implies by his self-characterization in the text, and that Clemens, as the implied author, has in effect given a self-portrait by writing a novel that consciously includes the three levels of viewpoint that Booth indicates. Regardless of what "party" Samuel Langhorne Clemens belonged to "in real life," the version of him that can be extracted from the narrative is the level of narration that gives Huck's story its most basic literary form and produces its deepest ironies.

Much of the critical disunity reviewed in the introduction to this study stems from readers' inadequate appreciation of Clemens' ironic handling of viewpoint in the novel. The commitment of almost the whole narrative to Huck's voice marks Clemens as a maverick in matters of literary form. The implied author does make his presence felt throughout, but only to the reader who is sensitive to verbal and structural allusions of which Huck and, to a great extent, the implied narrator appear to be unaware.

The pattern of allusion Clemens structures into Mark Twain's and Huck Finn's ostensibly realist narration enables one to see Huck's experience on the complementary levels of dream and myth. Huck's story, considered strictly as his personal experience, has the significance, immediacy, pathos, and apparent confusion of an individual's dreams. What aligns Huck's vision with larger social, historical, and religious realities is Clemens' patterning the book's incidents—Huck's experience, Mark Twain's realist fiction—on other texts, primarily the Bible, Dante's *Inferno*, Bunyan's *Pilgrim's Progress*, and Milton's *Paradise Lost*. These literary sources provide a backdrop of Christian theology and cosmology, a background that Clemens burlesques in the overtly picaresque, Realist adventures of his naïve narrators. To Henry Nash Smith's observation, "The contrast between the two levels of perception [Mark Twain's and Huck Finn's] creates an almost unbroken irony,"[14] must be added that the contrasts among the points of view of the highly literate implied author, the less sophisticated implied narrator, and the naive narrator give rise not only to the book's most subtle ironic effects but also to its fundamental "motive," "moral," and "plot."

Until fairly recently, the distinction between Mark Twain and Samuel

Clemens has been regarded as more of a problem for bibliographers than for critics. This fact has oversimplified criticism of the Mark Twain *oeuvre*; I hope that modern scholarship (including Justin Kaplan's biography, *Mr. Clemens and Mark Twain*; Alan Gribben's *Mark Twain's Library: A Reconstruction*; Baetzhold's study of Clemens' indebtedness to British writers in *Mark Twain and John Bull*; and numerous other works cited in Alan Gribben's "Removing Mark Twain's Mask," in addition to the three most recent biographies, Andrew Hoffman's *Inventing Mark Twain*, Fred Kaplan's *The Singular Mark Twain* and Ron Powers' *Mark Twain: A Life*, and most of all Victor Doyno's genetic studies of the literary satire of *Huck Finn*) has helped to prepare serious readers to consider Mark Twain as a main character in most of Samuel Clemens' writings. This character, especially in *Adventures of Huckleberry Finn*, masquerades as the implied author in the text and invites us, by his very presence in the text, to consider the discourse from a third point of view: that of "THE AUTHOR," as Clemens signs his introductory "Explanatory" and "Notice."

III. Distinguishing Huck from Mark Twain and Samuel Clemens

William R. Manierre's discussion of the opening chapters of the novel demands attention as one begins to examine Clemens' management of point of view and his religious satire in *Adventures of Huckleberry Finn*. In the course of justifying his labeling Huck an "empiricist member of society," Manierre points out that the book's "cavalier introduction of Christianity" in Chapter I establishes "a dichotomy of two kinds of experience": as Huck characterizes them "the deadly dull ... cramped up, ... dismal regular and decent" way of life in his new home versus the "free and satisfied" ways of his former life. At first he rejects the "sivilized" ways of the widow and her sister along with threats about "the bad place" and promises about "the good place," as Manierre points out, noting Huck's pragmatism: "He accepts the immediate gratification of his pipe and the reliability of his 'superstitions' ... because they produce desired results."

Among "the basic oppositions" of the first chapter Manierre lists the form of Christianity approved by the widow and Miss Watson versus the 'superstitions' by which "the uneducated" attempt to protect themselves from misfortune. According to this critic *"the book approves the latter and disapproves the former"* (italics added). Huck's ambivalent view of the versions of Providence he hears from the sisters adds another layer to these basic oppositions, and his rejection of the efficacy of Christian prayer, previously only implied, becomes explicit in Chapter III, observes Manierre, as he tests it and finds that it does not deliver the fish hooks to go with the line that he prayed for. As to what the Widow Douglas defines as "the proper object of prayer," adds Manierre, Huck can "see no advantage about it—except for the other people—so at last I reckoned I wouldn't worry about it any more, but just let it go."

Manierre reasons, "Thus the two opening paragraphs of chapter 3 test and reject two cardinal principles associated with the nominal religion of organized society," and he asserts that in Chapters III and IV, "Twain's juxtaposition of unworking prayer and of working river lore is as direct a commentary on one set of values by another as flat statement would have been—and far more effective." Pointing out another implied comment on the efficacy of prayer, this critic states, "Parallelism of action links the concept of Christian prayer, with which the [third] chapter begins, with that of the [unworking] magic formula with which it ends." Thus the third chapter, in Manierre's view, equates praying with rubbing "an old tin lamp and an iron ring" in an effort to call up a genie.[15]

But who makes this equation? Coming as it does in Huck's vernacular, we cannot simply conclude that the implied author stands literally behind every statement in the book. As H. N. Smith observes, the narrative is characterized by "an almost unbroken irony" exemplified in its extreme double vision by the wooden leg joke of Chapter IX. Even the dullest reader can laugh at a narrator ignorant enough to have "hunted all around" for the mate to the wooden leg Huck and Jim find in the floating house, but in the case of Huck's views on prayer, are we to agree with Miss Watson, who calls Huck "a fool," but "never told me why" (Chapter III)? Not all of the novel's readers have disagreed with her. Or are we to stand behind Huck, as Manierre suggests, in outright heresy?

The implied narrator, Mark Twain, does neither, notwithstanding Manierre's assertion that the book approves Huck's irreverent attitudes. In the long run it does, but in the immediate context Mark Twain as implied narrator sets up another set of possibilities: Huck is an ignorant boy, Miss Watson an unenlightened Calvinist, and the widow, who mediates between their extremes, represents the attractive form of Christianity that contrasts with Miss Watson's by offering a view of Providence "that could make a body's mouth water" (Chapter III). The fact that Huck decides "to belong to the widow's Providence if he wanted me" stands the implied narrator behind both the irreverent Huck and the kindly, pious Widow Douglas. Clemens' text does not commit Mark Twain to what a large segment of his public would have regarded as blasphemy.

Manierre points out some of the earliest irreverencies in the text. These set the stage for the satire to come by setting in motion the process of defamiliarization, which forces the alert reader to examine critically what he or she has been socialized to accept uncritically. Huck's reflections on prayer, however, do not require the reader to align with Huck's pragmatism, Miss Watson's religion, or the widow's kindly, pious vagaries. The real pleasure of reading Chapter III derives from seeing these three modes of belief played off against each other.

To assign any stance to the book or the author is to lose sight of the text's ambiguity. So it is not Samuel Clemens, Mark Twain, "the book," or even Chapter III that equates praying with trying to call up a genie; it is Huck Finn, who knows no better, and William Manierre who do that without regard for the tongue-in-cheek expression of Mark Twain and a poker-faced Samuel Clemens in the background. To lose sight of the implied tellers of Huck's tale is to make oneself the text's victim, the unwitting butt of Clemens' joke (see Preface, Section V, final quotation).[16]

Clemens' posture as implied author challenges the reader to discover this author's emotions and judgments behind the double wall of irony he erects by his management of points of view. He proposes stakes for this game in the form of his prefatory "Notice." Although the bait is unattractive, one can take its triple threat to emphasize ironically that motive, moral, and plot are indeed ascertainable in Huck's narrative, but only when the reader's wit is on a par with that of "THE AUTHOR." As Wayne Booth declares, "To collaborate with the author by providing ... mature moral judgment is a far more exhilarating sport" than to collaborate with him by providing "the source of an allusion or by deciphering a pun."[17]

The tradition of contentious debate this novel has generated reflects at least one certainty: The judgment Clemens challenges readers to provide is all that makes sense of the story. Because it is ironic, one can also take the forbidding tone of the "Notice" as a promise; Mark Twain observes in his *Autobiography* that "the experienced" know what he learned at a tender age: the supreme sweetness of watermelon "acquired by art" rather than "come by honestly."[18]

Irony is thus the keynote of the narrative, and Clemens quickly establishes three-dimensional point of view at the outset. "THE AUTHOR," an exacting literary artist as the "Explanatory" implies, slips into his double disguise as Mark Twain, implied narrator, and Huck Finn, narrative persona, in the first three paragraphs following the title page. From there on, readers must sort out the perspectives for themselves.

So it is that while "Huck approves superstition while dismissing Christian prayer as on a par with 'Tom Sawyer's lies,'"[19] the implied author and narrator remain noncommittal despite Manierre's inference that one should read Huck's impressions as Mark Twain's ideology. The reader who accepts the challenge of the opening three paragraphs regards every statement skeptically, notes that the implied author has remained noncommittal, and awaits further developments.

Ideology, at this stage of the discourse, is subordinate to viewpoint. Here, it is Huck's ignorance and the process by which he learns that the text emphasizes. Insofar as Huck's character is Manierre's topic, his analysis is correct. However, when he holds forth on the basis of Huck's associations that these chapters introduce and define "the moral standards" that invest the ensuing story with meaning and that "Twain's tying together here of methods and themes ... serves clearly to define his terms with emphasis and to establish *once and for all* a number of the book's central value judgments" (italics added),[20] Manierre attempts to bridge the ironic distance between Huck's views and Mark Twain's, despite the text's clear demand that we keep them separate:

> You don't know about me, without you have read a book by the name of *The Adventures of Tom Sawyer*, but that ain't no matter. That book was made by Mr. Mark Twain, and he told the truth, mainly. That is nothing. I never seen anybody but lied, one time or another, without it was Aunt Polly, or the widow, or maybe Mary. Aunt Polly—Tom's Aunt Polly, she is—and Mary, and the Widow Douglas, is all told about in that book—which is mostly a true book; with some stretchers, as I said before [Chapter I].

Huck's debut as Mark Twain's persona emphasizes the ironic relations among implied author Clemens, implied narrator Mark Twain, and narrator Huck Finn. For here, Huck, whom one soon discovers to be an inveterate and unabashed liar, introduces Mr. Mark Twain as yet another. If there is a reliable level of narration implied in the text, it is on neither the level of narrator nor that of implied narrator. Only on the level of "THE AUTHOR" have we been warned that this text is in some sense dangerous to the reader.

IV. Of "THE AUTHOR" and His Narrative Twins

Huck's self-introduction in Chapter I, often read as a clever plug for the book to which it was a sequel, as well as a recap of the outcome of the earlier book along with assurance to the reader that one need not have read *Tom Sawyer* in order to enjoy *Huck Finn*,[21] is also essential to an understanding of the novel's tripartite point of view. Here, Huck, whose status as a naïve narrator makes his ability to tell the whole truth less than reliable, introduces Mr. Mark

Twain as a co-narrator in the background. According to Clemens' characterization of Mark Twain, this implied narrator seems "to share ... contempt for 'book-larnen,'" as Michael Patrick Hearn notes, and quoting Twain he continues: "The most valuable capital or culture or education usable in the building of novels is personal experience. I surely have the equipment, a wide culture, and all of it real, none of it artificial, for I don't know anything about books."[22]

Thus, the twin narrators of this text are an ignorant boy backed by an "anti-intellectual backwoodsman," a narrative convention in Southern and Southwestern humorous storytelling.[23] And the boy, a stretcher of the truth himself, stands the veracity of the man into question, rendering the narrative that follows a quicksand of lies and half-truths. The only level of narration on which the reader can rely, "THE AUTHOR," seems to be absent from the text after the two prefatory paragraphs and the opening one.

Having thus established the firewall of irony that shields Clemens from reader responses that could have injured his reputation as a droll teller of inoffensive tall tales, as happened in England with *A Connecticut Yankee* (see Chapter Seven, Section VIII), the author proceeds in the first chapter to cast Huck as his ingenuously irreverent child Moses, which begins his satire on Judeo-Christianity.

V. A Mystery Wrapped in a Code

In what sense can one be "prosecuted," "banished," or "shot" by a fiction? This question is really the subject of this study, and although it will take a long time to answer it, the circuitous route leads back to this question with answers that shed new light on the dark places of the text where readers have often stumbled into damning or praising Mark Twain blindly. Huck's narrative is a multifaceted riddle, a mystery wrapped in a code. Its solution is a full understanding of the ironies of the text, the foundation for which is the three-fold perspective from which the alert reader views each episode.

While many of Mark Twain's readers have held views differing sharply from Huck Finn's on the subject of Christian prayer, some even of these readers have been able to endure the book's "cavalier introduction of Christianity"—even applaud it—because it shows nothing more, as Miss Watson concludes, than that Huck is a "fool" waving a banner in (to borrow Harold Kolb's phrase once more) the "unceasing procession of moral idiots" that peoples the fiction of Mark Twain.[24]

The literary art with which Clemens equates praying with rubbing a tin lamp implies no authorial agreement with his naïf. It only shows his skill and insight in portraying the mental processes of a nearly feral waif. Attributing the conclusions Huck reaches to Mark Twain or Samuel Clemens does violence to the ironic fabric of the text into which their views are separately woven. What Clemens does reveal about himself here is that he is capable of viewing religious matters irreverently—no news to Mark Twain's contemporary audience—and a necessary phase of the narration thematically as well as a delightfully humorous one, at least for those who have cut their literary teeth on tracts, Sunday school books, and the popular 19th century genre of the novel that presented "saintly children in conflict with a corrupt society."[25] Only retrospectively can one engage in speculation about where "THE AUTHOR" in fact stands.

However, Clemens does communicate his meaning through his treatment of literary sources; his allusions constitute a code that allows him to "comment" on significant actions of the characters as they engage in situations, and subtle repetitions of plot motifs, with variations in motivation, outcome, or both, provide important clues to his meaning. Huck's struggle with his conscience illustrates a situation where the plot motif of his inner conflict plays out differently in Chapters XVI, XXVI, and XXXI. In XVI he decides to ignore his ethical issue and to do right or wrong, "whichever come handiest at the time"; this fence straddling leads to the anarchic outcome of the rest of the raft voyage. In XXVI he breaks this resolve and risks his safety to do right and "steal the king's plunder" (the first-person chapter title of this episode; see Appendix A)—hardly the handiest way—to protect the orphaned sisters who have treated him kindly. In XXXI he relives the crisis of XVI and commits to "wickedness" and to Jim—again not the easiest way—and the outcome of his decision restores order to his experience in a number of surprising ways that comprise the author's commentary on his plot and characters, much of which this study will attend to in due time and order.

VI. A Wolf in Sheep's Clothing

VI-A: Distinguishing Samuel Clemens from Mark Twain

Unless one can establish textual grounds for differentiating among the three levels of narration that the text indicates in its opening three paragraphs, such speculation must remain highly suspect. The opposite view, that "THE AUTHOR" accepts uncritically all or most of Huck's ingenuous heresies, barefaced bigotry, and self-contradictory devotion to Jim, has led to the novel's banishment from public schools and libraries. Throughout the novel, we cannot attribute Huck's opinions arbitrarily to the author. No matter how closely one identifies with Huck or how intensely one agrees or disagrees with his ideas, they remain his own and/or his culture's.

To pin Huck's beliefs onto the implied author or the implied narrator, one must find other grounds than the realism with which he presents them. Huck Finn, alas, is an unreliable guide to the abstractions of his narrative, even on the rare occasions when he is aware of them. One of these, for example, is his unwavering conviction that slavery and racism are right. Conflating the viewpoints of the tellers of the tale leads inevitably to the conclusion that *Huck Finn* is a racist novel because its narrator is a racist and remains one throughout the book, despite the exception he makes for Jim.

Clemens' management of point of view softens the irony of the third chapter's irreverent commentary on prayer, making the narrator even more than the religious doctrine he tests empirically—and inappropriately—the butt of Mark Twain's humor. As Wayne Booth declares, "The price of ambiguity is a loss of satiric force."[26] And that is what is wrong with William Manierre's analysis (above). If there is so little agreement among the three points of view under consideration here (implied author Clemens, implied narrator Mark Twain, and narrative persona Huck Finn), how then can one make sense—*vis-à-vis* "THE AUTHOR"—of this text? Since the narrative is committed to Huck's voice, distinctions among the three angles of viewpoint established in the "Notice," the "Explanatory," and the first paragraph of Chapter I have in the past been based upon congruency of the text with biographical and historical information (including genetic criticism) about Clemens/Mark Twain; considerations of structure and style; and the incidence of literary archetypes.

Biographical and historical views such as Walter Blair's, Dixon Wecter's, Alan Gribben's, Andrew Hoffman's (along with other biographers), and to a certain extent Victor Doyno's and Andrew Levy's, while they shed much-needed light on the text, tend to impose standards from outside the work instead of discovering its internal coherence and unity. Knowing that Clemens' childhood took place in a village that provided him with the setting for *Tom Sawyer* and *Huck Finn* can be helpful to our appreciation of his realistic descriptions and the authenticity of his characters and their dialog, and knowing what he read can help us appreciate his work more fully, and there has been plenty of that sort of discussion of his work. When it comes to matters of coherence, unity, and meaning, however, these critics frequently view his work as deeply flawed. Thus *internal evidence* is the primary subject of this study. "The intuitive apprehension of total form" takes place within the confines of the interaction of the reader with the *published* text.

Stylistic evaluation of course reveals that Clemens took painstaking care to make his rendering of the various dialects in the novel, especially Huck's and Jim's voices, as authentic as he could make them without obstructing the flow of his narration. And it has turned up a few instances of authorial intrusion. One can view these as minor lapses in control of viewpoint or gentle prods from the author to remind readers that while this is Huck's autobiography, he remains a fictional character (as does Mark Twain). An outstanding example of such authorial intrusion is Colonel Sherburn's speech to the mob in Chapter XXII. Since Huck hears it only once, his ability to recall its relatively refined diction and syntax along with its content seems like one of Mark Twain's "stretchers." But this crack in the ceiling sheds no light on the relationship between the twin tellers of Huck's tale in the background; it only reminds us of their presence.

Similarly, Janet McKay's explication of Huck's climactic monologue again alerts readers to the author's presence. Finding Huck's climactic debate with his conscience to be "a beautifully constructed dramatic moment that captures the major forces at work in the novel," McKay nevertheless faults the author's characterization in this passage, pointing out that Huck's language is out of character as he makes his famous decision to "*go to hell*" for Jim (Chapter XXXI). Despite the terms in which Huck's conscience speaks being "external to Huck," Clemens causes Huck's narration to internalize them, as if they were consonant with the dynamics of his personality, and Clemens' intrusion "actually does some violence to Huck's character" by putting these words in his mouth. McKay supposes that the "best excuse for dropping these sentiments into Huck's narration is ... that *within the confines of this scene* they present a powerful impediment to Huck's following his sound heart and therefore display to the fullest his personal growth."[27]

Thus McKay's stylistic analysis supports the view that the reader can detect the author's presence in the text even as he pretends to stand remote from it, but he stands mute and forces McKay to invent a reason for his abuse of his child-narrator. The limitation of this method of explication is that, while it attends strictly to the text and allows us to appreciate the stylistic brilliance of Clemens' art and occasionally alerts the reader to the participation of the author in the text, it sees every intrusion as a flaw that weakens the illusion of Huck's reality, and yet it does not enable one to draw firm conclusions about the author's reasons for intruding into Huck's narrative (see Chapter Four, Section XVIII).[28]

To their discredit, the many schools of structural analysis have largely ignored the textual boundaries that separate implied author, implied narrator, and narrative persona. In so doing, critics from Bernard DeVoto to Leo Marx,

Henry Nash Smith, William Van O'Connor, and George Carrington to Victor Doyno, regard the text as a dramatization of Mark Twain's *Weltanschauung*, regard Huck as the author's droll mouthpiece, either disregard Clemens completely or conflate his point of view with Mark Twain's, and consistently overlook the ironic interaction of points of view, beyond that between Huck and Mark Twain. This approach leads to a view of the novel that is fairly true to the implied narrator at the expense of deeper understanding (as Clemens expected).

Since Clemens characterized Mark Twain as a "jack-leg" novelist[29] who did not "know anything about books,"[30] it might not seem too farfetched to view Mark Twain, the implied narrator of *Huck Finn*, as losing control of his story to another of its characters, Tom Sawyer, at the end, as many of these critics do. Hardly ever do structural critics question whether Mark Twain's lapse is also Samuel Clemens' because they have conflated the viewpoints of the implied author and the implied narrator *a priori*.

While it remains to be shown to what extent the text bears out this distinction, an inquiry into Clemens' place in his own fiction is worth conducting at this stage of Mark Twain studies, for scholars have increasingly come to recognize that Mark Twain was to a greater extent than is commonly recognized a disguise, a work of conscious art, an intermediary between Clemens and his audience.

In his Foreword to Alan Gribben's *Mark Twain's Library: A Reconstruction*, Henry Nash Smith sums up a stumbling block that has impeded Mark Twain criticism (his own included): "Samuel Clemens ... repays our attention not only from the standpoint of history but even more abundantly from the standpoint of art." Smith writes that knowing what he read is "essential" to understanding what he wrote. The fact that writers develop by imitating or reacting against the work of other writers, Smith submits, is what makes Gribben's catalog important. As Mark Twain, Clemens' pretended to be "a man of no education and no acquaintance with books," Smith writes. "This pose was ... a collaboration between the writer and his readers." Mark Twain embodied for his audience "a version of [the] ... myth of the American Adam": "According to this powerful cultural image, the Europeans who crossed the Atlantic to settle [North America ...] abandoned the complex culture of the Old World [...] in order to make a completely fresh beginning in the New World."[31]

VI-B: Sam Clemens Disguised as Mark Twain

None of the above treatments—biographical/historical, stylistic, or structural—of point of view in the novel takes one beyond the perspective of Mark Twain, the implied narrator. The remaining method of analysis, discussion of what Northrop Frye terms literary archetypes, has proven more fruitful. Such commentary can respect the bounds of viewpoint in the text, for a reader who recognizes that Huck's story structurally mirrors texts of which Huck is ignorant or in which he "takes no stock" has gotten at least as far as the purely structural or stylistic critics, Manierre, Carrington, and McKay, for example, who bump their heads on the ceiling of the implied narrator's viewpoint and mistake it for the ultimate vantage point of the implied author. The rare commentator who sees in the implied narrator's text structures that mirror texts of which the implied narrator was also ignorant, or that imply views inconsistent with the conventional morals Mark Twain stood for—according to Clemens' characterization of him—can legitimately claim to have penetrated into the depths of Clemens' ironical manipulation of viewpoints.

Clemens identifies the archetypal villain of this book, conscience, by gradually building up a composite portrait that draws its features from many "eye-witness accounts." Biblical parallels are foremost among these, and allusions, both explicit and covert, to Bunyan, Dante, and Milton—with all of whose works to which this study refers he was well acquainted by the 1870s—emphasize the author's concern with not only conscience but also its derivation and anatomy. This villain, the dramatic presence that lurks in the shadows "laying" for Huck, is not the abstraction "conscience" but the anthropomorphic Author of the Moral Sense, Milton's "Author of this Universe."

With respect to Clemens' familiarity with the Bible, Alan Gribben's catalog of Mark Twain's personal library is instructive:

Bible.
Clemens and members of his family owned or referred to more than twenty-five copies of the Bible. In the course of reading Clemens' literary works, letters, and notebooks, I have identified more than 400 instances in which he alludes to specific biblical passages—excluding his references to Adam, Eve, Noah, or other familiar figures. He mentions or alludes to thirty-seven of the sixty-six books in the Bible: twenty-three of the thirty-nine Old Testament books and fourteen of the twenty-six New Testament books figure in his writings. The majority of his allusions (sixty-eight) refer to the Book of Genesis; he alluded to passages in other books in the following descending order: Matthew (fifty-eight); Luke (forty-four); John, especially the raising of Lazarus (twenty-six); Exodus (twenty-five); Judges (sixteen); Isaiah (thirteen); Numbers (twelve); I Samuel (twelve); I Kings (twelve); Mark (eleven); the others ten or fewer.
Such computations reveal little about the manner in which Mark Twain approached the Bible as a literary source, but they do indicate the breadth of his familiarity with scripture as well as his interest in the narratives of Genesis and those attending to the life of Christ.[32]

This study pursues Clemens' art into his characterization of the deity within, the "Moral Sense" as it is personified by pap Finn and Tom Sawyer. Clemens' art is deeply involved in exploring and defining the nature and sources of not only Huck's but also the reader's acquired moral consciousness, even though, from Huck's culturally determined point of view, his decision to help Jim is as clearly wrong as it is right from the implied narrator's (and in the judgment of most readers).

VII. Reconciling Antithetical Critiques 1.0: Kolb *and* Cox

VII-A: Of Huck the Realist

Huck's sojourn with pap in Chapter VI exposes him to pap's drunken, abusive behavior, further recounts the progress of the custody fight (which will later resonate with the one over the infant in the Bible story of Solomon's judgment, in Chapter XIV; see Chapter Three, Section XIV), and then attends to the positive aspects of living at the remote cabin: "I didn't see how I'd ever got to like it so well at the widow's." After "two months or more" of this "lazy, jolly" life with pap, remembering the deadly dull routine at the widow's, he concludes, "I didn't want to go back no more." This decision leads to his plan to flee both pap and civilization when the opportunity arises—that and pap's getting "too handy with his hickory, and I couldn't stand it. I was all over welts." "Once he locked me in and was gone three days." Huck reports feeling "lonesome," and "scared" that pap might lock him up and never return, and so he tries with increasing desperation to find a way to escape, "but I couldn't find no way."

The text testifies to Huck's interest in process, and the great detail with which he narrates that process is one of the hallmarks of his personality and character. Deeply involved in his environment and what is going on in it, Huck fully regards events and the process by which they occur as all that is real. Very rarely does he look around him and interpret reality as being emblematic of any inner emotional or psychological state, and when he does, as in Chapter XV, he does it to "fool" Jim into interpreting the symbolism of what has actually just happened. He does it as a practical joke that turns in part on the assumption that reality has no meaning—even though Jim's reading of it turns out, ironically, to be prescient. Huck's commitment to the actual adds another layer of insulation to the firewall of irony that Clemens imposes between himself and the reader.

VII-B. Of Huck Living His Rituals

Matters of symbolic meaning and abstraction lie far below the level of Huck's awareness, which means that he works them out not intellectually but dramatically. As James Cox points out, Huck doesn't intellectualize his rituals, he lives them.[33] The consequences of Huck's decision to go to hell are inevitable, dramatically, once one infers what Huck's language can never articulate and Clemens' art can only imply: the equivalence of the God and Satan of the Judeo-Christian tradition and the moral inferiority of its fiendish God to Clemens' "Adamic Satan," Stanley Brodwin's term for Clemens' concept of the person who has transcended culturally imprinted motives of religion and morality to achieve moral autonomy.

One of the most interesting developments in the interminable controversy over *Huckleberry Finn* has been Harold Kolb's attack on James Cox's reading of the novel as a literary confidence game that lulls the reader into a false sense of moral superiority while upending the principle—conscience—on which this false comfort rests. If Cox is right, then the radical view the novel sets forth is that conscience itself is villainous. If Kolb is right, Mark Twain stands squarely behind the moral system Huck appears to reject. Actually, Cox's and Kolb's views complement each other in a reading of the novel that takes all three tellers' points of view into consideration. Having once seen how such apparently contradictory explications as these actually highlight the discreteness of persona (Huck), implied narrator (Mark Twain), and implied author (Clemens), one can begin to comprehend the utility of this paradigm of threefold point of view in the analysis of the subtlety with which Clemens develops his covert religious satire in *Huckleberry Finn*.

The disagreement between Cox and Kolb arises from Cox's characterization of the climax as a moment in which the reader "fatally approves" Huck's taking a moral stand when it has been his ingenuous inability to strike such a pose that has distinguished him from all the hypocrites he has encountered along his way. In Cox's view, Huck's fundamentally moral choice marks the end of his amoral innocence and makes inevitable his subsequent "rebirth" as Tom Sawyer. Kolb, on the other hand, sees the climax as the fulfillment of Huck's moral growth—as, he observes, have most of the novel's critics, both detractors and defenders.[34] In the reading Kolb defends, Huck's moment of decision becomes not the fall from innocence Cox reads it to be, but his transcendent discovery of a truly moral basis for action.

Each of these critics explains the ending in terms of his reading of the climax. For James Cox, Huck's fall from amoral grace necessitates his return to society—to hell, as Cox regards the scene of the evasion[35]—and to his full participation in all the games society approves of boys' playing. Kolb, on the other hand, sees Huck's playing Tom Sawyer's games as Mark Twain's closing affirmation of the moral pattern of Huck's flight: "Jim's debasement and Huck's suppression are precisely what the whole novel is about."[36] Mark Twain, according to Kolb, attacks "not the moral but the providential universe—at least that nineteenth-century version which demanded proof in this world. Virtue, Mark Twain insists, is not always rewarded; evil is not always punished."[37]

Each of these critics makes a strong case for his reading. Focusing on the author's attack on conscience leads Cox to explore the ethical implications of the text on the level of the implied author; Kolb's interest in the moral consistency of Mark Twain's vision leads to his discussion of another dimension: the ethics of the implied narrator. The method by which one can confirm both readings and reconcile them is to show how each contributes to the full articulation of the conflict between Huck's sound heart and his deformed conscience.

Clemens dramatizes the moral polarity of the novel in two ways. First, there is the celebrated conflict between Huck's heart and conscience; second, the relationship between the implied narrator and the implied author dramatizes this conflict in contradictory attitudes toward the conflicting values that Huck embodies. Few today would argue that there is much good in Huck's social conscience. "Deformed" is a charitable description of a moral code that approves of slavery. Most critics, like both Kolb and Cox, have found in Huck's climactic rejection of his conscience's dictates an affirmation of higher morality; thus, as Cox observes, Huck loses one conscience only to adopt another more compatible with the ideals of the reader: "His acceptance of a moral system—albeit one based on rebellion—is explicit in his conclusion that 'if I could think of anything worse, I would do that too,' [which] follows his resolution to set Jim free" (Chapter XXXI).[38] Huck, as Cox has shown, falls into collaboration with Tom Sawyer "on principle." So it is not merely the defeat of his old conscience, but the apparent victory of his new one that one needs to come to terms with in order to understand what Clemens meant when he wrote unequivocally, "his conscience suffers defeat." Harold Kolb finds that Huck's story succeeds "because we, like Mark Twain, wish to believe in the ethical ideal Huck represents. ... Mark Twain's book has at its center an angel in homespun. The most realistic of our realists has created a hero who is a gilt-edged, tree calf, hand tooled, seven-dollar Friendship's Offering moral idealist."[39]

Was the author wrong about Huck's conscience suffering defeat? Did he just mean Huck's Southern, pre-war conscience? Is the "sound heart" he referred to really Huck's same old conscience with a new ethical ideal, or not even that? For according to Kolb, "in spite of his protests, his much-proclaimed rebellion, Huck's code is precisely that of the Widow": to do good for others, and not think of the cost to himself.[40]

Is James Cox setting out on the wrong track when he asserts that without a radical vernacular vision the style of the novel would be mere décor? Huck's "counter-conversion" sets up the conclusion as the working out of its consequences,[41] and these are surely not the unqualified triumph or tragedy that many readers have wished for. As Kolb has shown, the implied narrator's theme, the "suppression and humiliation" of his "angel in homespun," is precisely what Mark Twain's book is about. As Cox has shown, the implied author's vilification of *all* conscience is the radical vision that effects this suppression and humiliation. To the extent that Huck gets into Tom Sawyer's "evasion" on principle, his participation destroys his newfound faith in principle itself, and he exits to the Territory on the characteristically expedient but comprehensive grounds that "I can't stand it. I been there before" (Chapter the Last).

VII-C: *Of Clemens' Attack on Conscience*

Clemens' ultimate blow to conscience is his attempt to debase *the reader's moral absolutes*, not just Huck's. With his revelation that Huck's moment of moral transcendence—his acquisition of "higher" conscience—leads to the fall from grace of the novel's final section, Clemens provides the novel's final object lesson in socio-ethical despair. Huck's moral quantum leap lands him in hell, as Cox observes. However, the extent to which social Christianity has also imprinted his "higher" conscience undermines Cox's argument that the novel stops short of portraying *all* conscience as finally social.[42] The consistency of moral vision that Kolb perceives is Mark Twain's; the debasement of it for which Cox makes a strong case is Samuel Clemens'.

The author's proliferation of points of view in the text accommodates both of these critics' readings. Mark Twain, the implied narrator, is the author of the book as Kolb reads it, a generic nineteenth-century novel conforming to a best-selling formula of which its author was no doubt aware. According to Kolb, "Huck Finn is firmly in the camp of Jacob Blivens, a cousin to what Anne T. Trensky has called 'The Saintly Child in Nineteenth-Century American Fiction.'"[43] Attending to the implied author's perspective, on the other hand, reveals the "radical vernacular vision" that James Cox perceives through his analysis of the moral logic of Huck's battles with his conscience, penultimate decision to go to hell, and final resolve to "light out for the Territory" alone. Despite Cox's reluctance to refer to the author as Clemens because it seems "excessively formal,"[44] it is only on the level of the implied author that his analysis is compatible with the many explications of the novel that Kolb claims it unhinges.

The threefold point of view that makes both of these readings indispensable is the central structural principle that enables one to perceive underlying order in this moral chaos where conscience appears by turns villainous and heroic. The Mark Twain implicit in this novel is a popular author whose métier is humor, melodrama, and conventional morality, as Brander Matthews characterized Mark Twain in 1897.[45] Seen through Mark Twain's eyes, Huck Finn *is* an "angel in homespun" who appeals to his public's appetite for saintly children in conflict with a corrupt society.

Samuel Clemens, however, undermines the set of moral assumptions implicit in Mark Twain's narration through his handling of the novel's literary archetypes. Thus the novel polarizes moral vision along pro- and anticonscience lines through the contrasting religious visions of Mark Twain and Samuel Clemens, and Mark Twain becomes Samuel Clemens' straight man in this book; or, to put it another way, every time Mark Twain plays one of his moral aces, Clemens trumps it. So it happens that the Mosaic theme of the novel explored by Kenneth Lynn, et al., leads to the liberation of Jim only after delays, humiliation, and further enslavement that comprise many of the biblical parallels by which Clemens and Mark Twain point out Huck's main biblical prototype, Moses.

Those readers who see Huck as a "Mississippi Moses" are not wrong, but they are only partly right. For on the level of the implied narrator, the reverent comparison of Huck with Moses is as clear as the similarity between Huck and Bunyan's Christian explored by Alfred Bendixen. Mark Twain casts Huck as Moses, and Clemens points out that the bigotry, cruelty, hypocrisy, and stupidity implicit in his literary archetypes provide the principal elements in Mark Twain's reverent analogy. Mark Twain, then, like Tom Sawyer, *represents* conscience; Samuel Clemens, through Huck Finn, dramatizes the rebellious heart and all his own religious skepticism.

VIII. The Argument of "THE AUTHOR"

By keeping the novel's threefold point of view in mind, the reader who fully considers the literary burlesque of *Huckleberry Finn* can reconcile a number of apparent textual inconsistencies that have given rise to so many contradictory interpretations. This reading strategy reveals a pattern of allusion in the background of the text that shows Clemens' concern with themes and sources beyond the ken of his narrative personae, Huck Finn and Mark Twain.

The text gains richness, depth, and coherence as one focuses on Clemens' sources. In Chapter I, where Huck's unconsciousness of parallels between his situation and that of his biblical counterpart Moses renders his chapter title, "I Discover Moses and the Bulrushers" (see Appendix A), "ironically false,"[46] Clemens establishes a threefold perspective on the action. This tripartite point of view enables the reader to look through Huck's perceptions, and through the structure imposed on his narration by implied narrator Mark Twain, into the mind of the artist Samuel Clemens, the implied author.

Pursuing this approach through the next two chapters shows that his handling of controversial material like Huck's empiricist rejection of the doctrine of Christian prayer blunts its satiric edge. Mark Twain renders heresy good fun by making it the measure of the narrator's ignorance rather than making prayer the object of the author's immediate scorn. Thus Clemens tempers Huck's overt irreverence toward Moses and prayer and transforms it to Mark Twain's humor, furthering his characterization of his twin narrators. But one cannot yet conclude from the text where "THE AUTHOR" stands in this ambivalent context.

Chief among the textual matters on which I shall focus are pap Finn's role, Clemens' ironic presentation of archetypal material throughout the story, the climax, the evasion, and the prefatory "Notice." By discussing a perspective on structure that reconciles readings as contrary as those of James Cox and Harold Kolb, this study offers a unified reading of the novel as religious satire. Pap's role as a burlesque characterization of the Old Testament God and Milton's Arch-Fiend—combined in one despicable individual—anchors Clemens' religious satire. Huck's journey is a tour of Dante's Hell that exposes a society damned by its own perverse mythology. Huck's "counter-conversion" at the climax, in which he "converts" into Milton's Satan, reveals what Clemens believed to be absurdities in Judeo-Christian cosmology. The evasion also burlesques its biblical prototype and assaults the Most High. It is of a piece with the rest of the book, the most subtle but devastating of Clemens' anti-religious satires. The most important function of the "Notice" is to encode the structural paradigm that makes this reading necessary.

Without a firm grasp of Clemens' management of viewpoint critics have advanced a bewildering array of hypotheses regarding the structure and meaning of this novel (see Introduction, Sections I–III). Yet the inherent tension between the implied author and the implied narrator in the text has been largely overlooked, although this omission has not stopped numerous critics from dropping the name "Clemens" into their discussion of the novel to signal to their readers that they have penetrated the deepest meanings of Huck's narrative. This tension, manifested in Clemens' inversion of the moral polarity of Mark Twain's biblical archetypes, is the source of the novel's most profound ironies. And it is the primary means by which Clemens transforms Mark Twain's picaresque morality play into a cosmic satire on the mythology in which nineteenth-century Western culture (not just the ante-bellum South) was, in Clemens' view, mired.

The next step toward seeing this satire as a unifying factor in the text is to review the existing criticism in search of instances where either explicit or covert allusions to various religious texts are implicit in Huck's narrative. By the end of the fourth chapter, this study will have reviewed enough of the evidence that religious satire is a central theme of the novel to justify the evasion and the conclusion artistically, thematically, and dramatically with the rest of the story.

While Billy G. Collins' reading distorts Clemens' view of the Bible, his conclusion is in harmony with Harold Kolb's perception of the novel as an example of the "saintly child" formula in nineteenth-century American fiction. Thus Collins is right in contending that *Mark Twain's* purpose in modeling the evasion on the Book of Exodus is to prove that the Bible did *not* approve slavery, and that teaching that it did caused "moral blindness, hypocrisy, and violence."[47] But the implied author, true to form, trumps Mark Twain's moral ace with his own attack on the moral blindness, hypocrisy, and violence of the biblical texts on which the implied narrator relies for moral authority.

Having shown, in the process of reviewing existing criticism and examining new textual evidence of Clemens' satiric intent, that most theories regarding Clemens' use of Judeo-Christian literary sources in *Huck Finn* can be integrated, with some corrections, into this reading, the reader will be ready to consider other sources reflected in the text: both previously overlooked biblical parallels and a new dimension of literary burlesque that helps structure the novel's frame: an intricate and vitriolic assault on Christian mythology, cosmology, and theology as they are expressed in *Paradise Lost.* Chapters Three through Six of this study pursue this line of analysis to the conclusion that the purpose of Clemens' religious satire in *Huckleberry Finn* is not just to upend the Bible as an unchallengeable source of moral authority; by burlesquing Milton, Clemens broadens the scope of his argument in order to *vilify* "the ways of God"[48] to "the damned human race."

CHAPTER TWO

Precedents for Viewing *Huck Finn* as Biblical Burlesque and Religious Satire

I. Reconciling Antithetical Critiques 2.0: Lynn *and* Barnes

Was Clemens so concerned with disproving that the Bible condones slavery, as Collins asserts that he was, that he played down his satire on the Bible's pro-slavery texts in the novel? As Tom Quirk has pointed out, the Jackson's Island sequence features a re-enactment of an incident in the legend of Noah that churches of the pre-war South held to be one of the principal biblical props supporting slavery. A more probable explanation for the presence of the Mosaic parallels observed by Lynn, Barnes, Collins, and Briden, especially between the frame of the novel and the first fourteen chapters of Exodus, is that Clemens' allusions to the story of Moses are intended ironically to heighten the novel's religious satire by revealing how freeing Jim in Mosaic fashion actually protracts Jim's bondage, dehumanizes Jim, and demeans Huck.

Daniel Barnes, among the first to discuss the impact on the reader of parallels between the legend of Moses and *Huckleberry Finn*, commented in 1965, "Critics of *Huckleberry Finn* have ... generally overlooked the significant role that the Bible ... plays in Twain's conception of the characterization and ... the structure of the novel":

> they fail to perceive the extent to which the lives and actions of [...] Huck, Jim, Tom—and even the Duke and the King—are paralleled in biblical prototypes. [...] The effect on the reader's awareness of these parallels is generally to heighten the ironic impact of the novel [... and] offer valuable new insights into Twain's technique as a literary craftsman.[1]

Barnes focuses on the irony of the title of Chapter I:

> The important point here ... is not the *fact* that Huck's situation parallels that of Moses; it is, rather [...] the further ironic implications; in making his protagonist reject Moses, Twain renders the statement of the title of Chapter I ["I Discover Moses and the Bulrushers"; see Appendix A] ironically false: Huck has not, in any sense, "discovered" Moses; his rejection [...] provides a fundamental sort of irony which pervades the whole account of his adventures.[2]

Barnes thus highlights what Kenneth Lynn, the first critic to comment on the significance of parallels between the Mosaic legend and the novel, largely overlooks in his preoccupation with "the novel's grand theme, the Mosaic drama of liberation," which, in Lynn's view, "depends ultimately on the outcome of Huck's search for a father."[3] According to Barnes, Huck's blindness to all he has in common with Moses is the starting point for a consideration of the "ironic impact" of Mark Twain's use of the opening chapters of Exodus as one literary archetype for Huck's adventures. In Lynn's view (and the implied narrator's), the *fact* of the parallel is of paramount importance:

> The liberation theme is announced in the title of the novel's very first chapter. [...] Huck soon loses all interest in the Moses story, "because I don't take no stock in dead people," [but] the humorous introduction of the Biblical saga [...] ushers in the majestic theme of slavery and freedom [and] inextricably associates Huck [...] with the biblical liberator.[4]

In Barnes' analysis, though, Clemens' rendering the first chapter's title "ironically false" becomes a central feature of the discourse, the announcement of the implied narrator's presence as a consciousness that comprehends irony of which the narrative persona is unaware. Samuel Clemens' major objection was not, as Billy Collins attempts to demonstrate that it was, to any particular misuse of the Bible—whether to support slavery or war or persecution or imperialism; his fundamental objection was to regarding the Bible as a divinely inspired source of moral instruction. Harnesberger explains, quoting Mark Twain:

> When he dissented from the "unjust, pitiless God" pictured in the Old Testament, or when he complained:
> "What God lacks is convictions—stability of character. He ought to be a Presbyterian or a Catholic or *something*—not try to be everything," he was referring to the biblical God and objecting to the depiction because he considered the Book to be entirely the work of man, not inspired by God.[5]

As Clemens told his best friend, the Rev. Joseph Twitchell, in a confession during their walking tour in the Alps in 1878:

> Joe, [...] I'm going to make a confession. I don't believe in your religion at all. I've been living a lie right straight along whenever I pretended to. For a moment, sometimes, I

have been almost a believer, but it immediately drifts away from me again. I don't believe one word of your Bible was inspired by God any more than any other book. I believe it is entirely the work of man from beginning to end—atonement and all. The problem of life and death and eternity and the true conception of God is a bigger thing than is contained in that book.[6]

As pointed out in the previous discussion of the dispute between Kolb and Cox, the way to reconcile these contrary readings is to affirm both critics' opposing points of view; by attributing these contrasting attitudes toward specific biblical texts—to which *both* Mark Twain and Clemens allude—to the opposing points of view of the implied narrator and implied author toward these biblical texts, the reader can hold both perspectives in mind without invalidating either one, and await further developments.

II. Of Moses, Prayer, Sunday-School, Slavery, Hogs and "Tom Sawyer's Lies"

Critics have recognized at least since the 1950s that Mark Twain's ironic treatment of religion as a dimension of Huck's moral growth culminates at the climax in Chapter XXXI in what Norris W. Yates has described as a "counter-conversion"[7]: Huck's "*go* to hell" moral victory over his conscience. Although there has been no single, comprehensive discussion of the novel's implications as religious satire before this one, numerous critics have commented on aspects of Mark Twain's ironic presentation of Huck's experience of religion. Most perceive his "cavalier treatment of Christianity" as one feature of the general disenchantment with "sivilization" that leads to Huck's decision "to light out for the Territory ahead of the rest"; thus Henry Nash Smith observes:

> Pretended or misguided piety and other perversions of Christianity obviously head the list of counts in Mark Twain's indictment of the prewar South. And properly: for it is of course religion that stands at the center of the system of values in the society of this fictive world and by implication in all societies.[8]

Most critics who have touched on the theme of religious satire in the novel, whether they focus on Moses, prayer, Sunday school, slavery, hogs, or "Tom Sawyer's lies," follow Smith in viewing it as a feature of the larger social satire that Smith indicates as one of the novel's three main elements. Thus, Victor Doyno points out the overt religious satire of the text at many points, but always in subordination to the larger social criticism of credulity, sanctified hypocrisy/greed/racism, and cruelty as they manifest in Huck's conscience and environment.

In contrast, this study suggests that readers have consistently misapprehended this satirical element and that *religious satire is the point of Clemens' social satire*. Through his satirical treatment of Milton's Puritan attempt to "justify the ways of God" to humankind, Clemens imputes the evils of a depraved society to its tawdry mythology. "Let me make the superstitions of a nation and I care not who makes its laws or its songs either," he wrote in the 1890s.[9] He thus elevates his satire out of the implied narrator's concern with Southern culture before the war—and after Reconstruction—into the implied author's critique of the Judeo-Christian heritage and its impact on American culture.

III. Of Puritanical Religion

While it is true that Huck's world manifests a particularly perverted form of provincial Christianity, the cosmology in the background of his experience derives from seventeenth-century Puritan theology—and the branch of Clemens' family that he claimed was instrumental in beheading Charles I. The rootstock of American Puritanism is not native, so it is appropriate that Clemens should allude to classics like *Paradise Lost* and *Pilgrim's Progress* in formulating his attack on the Judeo-Christian world-view—especially so in view of the novel's extensive *literary* satire, which Victor Doyno has explored. Apart from the Moses motif, Mark Twain shows no great respect for public forms of religion or institutionalized Christianity anywhere in the novel. As William Manierre comments, religious institutions and practice contribute little positive value to society while serving as sources of emotional excesses and hypocrisy even as they fail to make Huck's world a better place.[10]

Huck's early views on Moses, prayer, Sunday school, Providence, and "Tom Sawyer's lies" suggest Clemens' concern with religion even through the firewall of irony that he imposes between himself and the reader, as Manierre's comments quoted above point out (see Chapter One, Section III). Jim's critique of the legend of "Sollermun" in Chapter XIV—with its emphasis on Solomon's inhumanity as a function of his upbringing in a polygamous society—can be taken more seriously because it introduces Clemens' own views on the influence of "training and association"—what today we call "socialization"—on individual development and links a biblical text that illustrates such influence with the effects on Huck of socialization in a slave-holding, racist society. As Hearn notes, this incident "reflects the earlier custody battle between pap Finn and the Widow Douglas."[11] Huck's dismissal of Jim's argument in turn reflects the orthodox bigotry that his own upbringing has produced. "Jane Lampton Clemens," a memorial essay the author wrote about his mother, contains the following comment on her attitude toward slavery:

> As I have said, we lived in a slaveholding community; indeed, when slavery perished my mother had been in daily touch with it for sixty years. Yet, kind-hearted and compassionate as she was, I think she was not conscious that slavery was a bald, grotesque, and unwarrantable usurpation. She had never heard it assailed in any pulpit, but had heard it defended and sanctified in a thousand; her ears were familiar with Bible texts that approved it, but if there were any that disapproved it they had not been quoted by her pastors; as far as her experience went, the wise and the good and the holy were unanimous in the conviction that slavery was right, righteous, sacred, the peculiar pet of the Deity, and a condition which the slave himself ought to be daily and nightly thankful for. Manifestly, training and association can accomplish strange miracles.[12]

Huck dismisses Jim's interpretation of the story of Solomon with the culturally imprinted slur, "you can't learn a nigger to argue" (Chapter XIV). His attitude provides a second illustration of the "miraculous power" of "training and association." Huck never questions the moral assumptions that he has acquired from his culture, and he remains a racist throughout the novel (which makes it increasingly painful to read as the years roll by, especially for African Americans); however, his subsequent experiences with Jim undermine the power of this negative socialization to control his actions.

As Huck grows acquainted with the widow's ways, in Chapter I, his comments reveal how ignorant he is of the customs of polite society and religious practice: "You couldn't go right to eating, but you had to wait for the widow to duck her head and grumble a little over the victuals; though there warn't really anything the matter with them."

Huck's comment here is not comic but humorous, which means that he doesn't see any irony about it: He is so ignorant that he doesn't even understand that the widow is blessing the meal, not complaining about it. Huck's religious education is just beginning. Here also one can see Mark Twain's management of Huck's point of view, for by the time Huck supposedly writes his narrative, he knows very well that the widow's "grumbling" is a prayer.

In Chapter I Huck goes on recounting his time with the widow and Miss Watson, her spinster sister, who tortures him with a spelling lesson. Huck wants none of the stuffiness and "deadly" dullness of living with these sisters, who exemplify the morals and mores of the village culture. He comments that the widow found "a power of fault with me for doing a thing [smoking] that had some good in it. And she took snuff too; of course that was all right, because she done it herself." Here, of course, Mark Twain is poking fun at the small hypocrisies of an upper class woman who means to do right by Huck, but the boy is becoming sensitive to the ways in which adults do not always do as they say.

IV. Of Tom, the Widow, Pap and Huck

Chapter III of the novel is very closely concerned with developing Huck's character. Mid-way through this episode he declares that the boys "quit the robber band because ... we only just pretended." Unlike Tom Sawyer, Huck is at that developmental crossroads where "pretend games" cease to be fun and the real world of natural processes absorbs his interest and attention; Huck rarely even speaks of his dreams. At the same time, Clemens gently advances the religious/social satire with Huck's unconsciously humorous comments on prayer, with which the third chapter begins, and "Tom Sawyer's lies," with which it ends, as William Manierre has observed.[13]

Chapter IV, which Clemens interpolated at some time after his initial spate of composition,[14] begins with a recap of what has happened to Huck in the intervening "three or four months" since the story's beginning. He has learned to read, spell, and misrepresent the multiplication table, and in a general way he has settled in at the widow's and adjusted to going to school. The time span of Huck's stay with the widow and Miss Watson indicates, as Huck reports, that he has had time to absorb some of the mores of the class of people the "patrician" Widow Douglas and Miss Watson represent. This helps to explain his dismissal of Moses as being "no good to anybody, being dead, you see," in Chapter I at the beginning of his stay with them, as Barnes has noted, while some six months later he takes a lively interest in Solomon in his argument with Jim (Chapter XIV). His report of the first day of his stay is his report of *every* day, except Sunday, when he no doubt would be required to attend Sunday school and church. As Daniel Barnes was the first to notice, the widow plays the Pharaoh's daughter to Huck's Moses in Chapter I (see Chapter Two, Section II and Chapter Three, Section XIX),[15] and as his surrogate mother, she takes her responsibility for his spiritual welfare very seriously.

When Huck reports in Chapter XVIII that his church attendance with the Grangerfords "was one of the roughest Sundays I had run across yet," he is speaking from experience of his life at the widow's, the only time of his young life when he is likely to have attended church regularly, and during which he absorbed far more cultural imprinting than he knows, as one can observe in Chapters XIV, "Was Solomon Wise?" and XXXI, "You Can't Pray a Lie" (see Appendix A). In short, he is on his way to becoming a young gentleman, by the local standard, when pap returns to St. Petersburg. By this time he is sleeping in a bed every night, it having gotten too cold to "slide out" and "sleep on the ground any more."

Chapter IV foreshadows pap's involvement in the plot as he arrives at the widow's grounds, leaving tracks in the snow that tip off Huck to his presence. His distinctive boot-prints reiterate the sign of the Cross that Tom and the boys earlier used as the sign of their gang, only this time its presence is truly ominous (see Chapter Three, Section I). Huck's quick-witted reaction of running to Judge Thatcher to keep his fortune out of pap's grasp is all that frustrates pap's claim on it. This action begins and necessitates pap's active involvement in the plot. Without the custody fight between the widow and pap, he would presumably have taken the money and gone. Jim's "hair-ball oracle" serves to foreshadow pap's mythic role in the archetypal development of Clemens' religious theme (see Chapter Three, Section IV-A).

Frustrated at being unable to lay his hands on Huck's money, pap tries to con "the new judge" in order to convince him that he should have custody of Huck in the first of the novel's series of feigned—and real—conversions. Conversion scams are one of the king's specialties, as we learn in Chapter XIX, and he and pap are closely related morally as perpetrators of religious fraud. It is clear from the start that pap will stop at nothing to get Huck's money, but his depraved character cannot sustain this ruse, and his scam misfires to both humorous and mythic effects.

It is worth noting at this point that, as F. Kaplan has written, from July to September of 1876, Clemens "had written 146 of his manuscript pages, chapters 1 to 2½, and 5 to 8½."[16] The import of these initial episodes of the novel testifies to his conception of it as religious and biblical satire, as will be shown in Chapter Three of this study. Chapters V and VI report the progress of the custody-fight between "the old man" and the widow. Pap's temporary victory in V needs celebration, so he threatens Huck with a beating "if I didn't raise some money for him." Huck borrows "a few dollars from Judge Thatcher and pap took it and got drunk and went a-blowing around and cussing." Here we see the intemperate, violent, wrathful pap of W. R. Moses' analysis of the parallels between Huck's narrative and Dante's infernal vision.[17] This parallel burlesque of Dante's work does not feature the parodic character that is one of the hallmarks of nineteenth-century literary burlesque, but it is firmly rooted in that school of comic literature, as Chapter Four of this study reveals.

V. In the First Circle of Hell

Chapter VI (also part of the author's original conception of the story), Clemens' literary version of hell (see Chapter Three, Section V) advances all three perspectives on the plot, revealing the powerful mythological undercurrents that flow in Huck's psyche without overt analysis or even comment from the author or implied narrator. Social satire is of course implicit in pap's diatribe against the "govment," but religious satire underlies Chapter VI as the deepest of these levels of point of view.

For Huck the literalist, pap's being "all over mud" from having spent the previous night in town lying drunk in the gutter, calls to mind the creation story in Genesis 1, about which he probably learned in Sunday-school while living with the widow or in daily household devotions there: "A body would a thought he was Adam, he was just all mud," but otherwise, Huck reports just what happened. Remember, here, that Huck is not trying to be funny; his seeing pap as Adam is based on his literal understanding of the Bible story as depicting a man made of mud.

Farther along in Chapter VI is the passage in which pap, having failed in his attempt to kill "the Death Angel," dozes off, and Huck takes down pap's gun and prepares to kill his father if he has to. While Hearn notes Edgar M. Branch's discovery of a possible source for Huck's account of pap's fit of *delirium tremens* in an 1861 article in *The Missouri Democrat* and also the resonance, pointed out by Paul Baender, of "Tramp ... tramp ... tramp" with the refrain of the temperance movement anthem "The Dead March," none of these commentators finds much more religious significance in pap's fits.[18] Hearn does comment, however, "The belief that [the Angel of Death] comes to people who are about to die comes from the Bible. ... The old drunk follows his own superstitious beliefs in Heaven and Hell."[19] As Victor Doyno comments: "Although the Christian story gives honor to an almighty father who permits his son's death as a requirement for others' salvation, the reality of a murderous father frightens Huck."[20] Once one recognizes Huck's pap *as* the archetypal murderous Father in Clemens' scheme, and Huck as His Son, this satirical blow to Christianity becomes especially telling. It also sets up Huck's "burlesque Resurrection" in Chapter XXXII (see Chapter Five, Section III).

VI. Further Precedents: Of Cain and Abel, Solomon, and Moses

In Chapter XIV of the novel, Hearn points out Clemens' implicit theme undermining the idea that moral authority derives from relying on the letter of Scripture; as he asserts:

> Huck exploits the widow's religious instruction ... when it serves his purpose in trying to win the argument with Jim. Like Miss Watson, he uses his knowledge of the Bible to put an "inferior" in his place. [...] An important theme of the novel [is] that one's

morality must come naturally from within oneself [...] and not from some abstract set of values or [...] some "authority."[21]

But this is not just "some" authority; it is *biblical* authority that Clemens uses to illustrate this point, and, as will be shown in the next chapter, his treatment of this passage from I Kings 3: 16–28 is much more complex and satirical than critics have previously seen it to be.

Again in Chapter XVI, when Jim tells Huck of his plans to buy or steal his children free once he and his wife win their freedom, Hearn points out the biblical resonance of the passage, noting that the law assigning ownership of a slave's children to the owner of the mother derived from Mosaic law: Exodus 21: 3 rules that "If a master have given him a wife, and she have borne him sons or daughters; the wife and her children shall be her master's, and he shall go out [of servitude] by himself." Clemens thus forges a link between the legal structure of slavery and Bible based religious beliefs that supported the "peculiar institution."

In regard to the feud episode in Chapters XVII and XVIII, Hearn comments that the names of the warring clans—*Shepherd*son and *Granger*ford—resonate with the story of the *first* herder, Abel, and the *first* farmer, Cain, and the first murder in the Bible.[22] However, Hearn does not point out that these clans, neighbors who, by their professed religion, should love one another, and whose duty it is, by the same token, to treat each other as "brothers," instead prosecute a deadly feud from which Huck is lucky to escape with his life. Hearn also comments on the passage in the same sequence where Huck narrates his experience of the church service he attends with the Grangerfords and Shepherdsons: "One would think that the blood feud would have damned their eternal souls, but being of 'the first aristocracy,' both [families] believe they remain among God's elect. The 'ornery' preaching only reinforces their immorality and hypocrisy."[23]

As Norris Yates points out, by the time of his "counter-conversion" in Chapter XXXI, Huck has heard the "ornery" preaching about brotherly love delivered to a congregation of murderers who sit "with their guns handy," and he reports that afterwards, "from some of these same gun-toters" he hears "conversation about 'faith, and good works, and free grace, and preforeordestination,' and he feels that this was 'one of the roughest Sundays I had run across yet.'"[24]

Randy Cross notes that "the hypocrisy of church-goers" comes under fire in Chapter XVIII, when, "Upon entering the church building while on an errand for Sophia Grangerford, Huck expresses his feeling on the reason for church attendance"[25]: "There warn't any lock on the door, and hogs like a puncheon floor in summertime because it's cool. If you notice, most folks don't go to church only when they've got to; but a hog is different" (Chapter XVIII).

Notice, though, that his comment is neither sarcastic nor witty: Huck is just observing a difference between human beings and hogs. This passage *is*, however, ironic, and the irony compounds itself with the divergent perspectives of the implied author and implied narrator. From the viewpoint of Mark Twain, this comment injects humor into the text as the reader once again marvels at the truths that may come blurted "from the mouths of babes and innocents." Clemens has bigger game in view, however, than Mark Twain comprehends, for at this point in the story all hell is about to break loose, and the presence of hogs in the church symbolizes Clemens' conflation of "God's house" with a hog-house—a moral sty—and it reiterates his emblemizing the biblical God as a hog, as will be shown in the next chapter (see Chapter Three, Sections III and IV-C).

Collins points out a number of parallels between the legend of Moses and the feud episode, some overt, as in Buck Grangerford's riddle about where Moses was "when the lights went out" in Chapter XVII, some less obvious, such as the Grangerfords, as slaveholders, being cast in the role of "Egyptians" in the Bible story, making them appropriate targets for a modern-day Passover plague of death,[26] despite their status as Christians and rank among "the quality."

Moreover, Vaneta Nielson has disclosed intriguing parallels to the biblical book of I Samuel in her discussion of the feud episode; Neilson finds that the author's treatment of "King Saul's tragic reign" and "the savage prophet" Samuel puts Clemens among the ranks of "religious writers."[27] However, she fails to see that a close reading of this Bible story of ritual genocide and the punishment of the guilty by the slaughter of the innocent—a biblical theme Clemens was fond of pointing out—might have had different implications for a man of Clemens' religious skepticism than for less critical Bible readers (see Chapter Three, Section XVI).

Having put the feud behind them, Huck and Jim return to their idyllic freedom from the "sivilization" that Hearn characterizes as lurking "around every bend in the river." As long, he comments, as Clemens' fugitives abide on the raft and avoid contact with the society of the shore, "they need not leave Eden."[28] But of course they do have to co-exist with this society, especially after the duke and king come aboard later in Chapter XIX.

In this and the following chapter the king especially reveals himself to be a vicious fraud who exploits his marks' ignorance and credulity, using their religious faith to bilk them out of cash. His histrionics at the orgy of religious frenzy in Chapter XX, the camp-meeting episode, demonstrate his expertise in this line of fraud, and his vastly greater take than the duke's on this, their first outing as partners in crime, makes clear that his is a more lucrative racket than his younger colleague's.

This overt religious satire becomes even clearer when one compares the texts of the first edition version and the version in Clemens' working manuscript, which Doyno has published in its entirety and Hearn quotes in large measure.[29] The much more intensely sarcastic manuscript version had to be thoroughly revised to make it "fit" for publication in Mark Twain's time. However, as will later be made clear in Chapter Four of this study, the revisions Clemens made to downplay the social satire have positive effects of preserving Huck's sympathetic character and sharpening Clemens' covert religious satire.

In the closing section of the novel, Collins finds a wealth of allusions to the first fourteen chapters of Exodus, and he views them, whether Clemens frames them as parallels or parodies, as fundamentally serious efforts on Mark Twain's part to create a biblical frame for the closing sequence that completes the novel's religiously based indictment of the South for crimes against humanity. Did Clemens really call on the Perpetrator of what he regarded as the *original* crime against humanity for support in condemning the institution that both Noah and Moses were instrumental in founding?

VII. The Brazen Serpent in the Wilderness

As overt religious satire intensifies, the Bible becomes an ever-present influence on the lives of the people Huck meets on shore. As Joseph McCullough remarks, although he misattributes the words of a preacher there to Huck's "royal" companion, "the phony king invades the camp meeting ... holds up the Bible and shouts, 'It's the brazen serpent in the wilderness! Look upon it and live!'" (Chapter XX). McCullough writes that the brazen serpent of Moses, originally a symbol of healing, came to be regarded as an object of worship in itself, and he suggests that Mark Twain is pointing out "the dangers of worshiping a symbol."[30] In this case, however, as in the Bricksville episode in the next chapter, the symbol seen as an idol is the Bible itself, whose authority shaped "the social order, morality, and even the most intangible aspects of civilization in the nineteenth century," as Stanley Brodwin has written.[31]

In the Bricksville incident the mortally wounded Boggs gasps and expires beneath the crushing weight of a large Bible:

> They laid him on the floor, and put one large Bible under his head, and opened another one and spread it on his breast—but they tore open his shirt first, and I seen where one of the bullets went in. He made about a dozen long gasps, his breast lifting the

Bible up when he drawed in his breath and letting it down again when he breathed it out—and after that laid still; he was dead [Chapter XXI].

At both the camp meeting and in Bricksville, the reverence with which credulous people regard Bibles as objects of superstition magnifies the misery in which they live and die.

Here is "S. L. Clemens'" response to a Brooklyn librarian's request for "a word from me [that] might persuade his colleagues to keep ... *Tom Sawyer* and *Huckleberry Finn*, on the list of books generally available to children":

> I am greatly troubled by what you say. I wrote *Tom Sawyer* and *Huck Finn* for adults exclusively, and it always distresses me when I find that boys and girls have been allowed access to them. The mind that becomes soiled in youth can never again be washed clean; I know this by my own experience, and to this day I cherish an unappeasable bitterness against the unfaithful guardians of my young life, who not only permitted but compelled me to read an unexpurgated Bible through before I was fifteen years old. None can do that and ever draw a clean sweet breath again this side of the grave.[32]

Brodwin goes on to explain that the frequently sexual and violent "images of sinful passion" on display in the Bible along with the harshness of the god that punishes the least sin can cause a "young boy to feel temptation and guilt before he has sufficiently developed ... to be able to cope" with them. He feels sinful "even before he knows the meaning of sin. Punishment seems cruel, inevitable, and just." The Bible that is supposed to support and guide his moral growth instead intensifies his feelings of guilt "and obsessive need to reform."[33]

Numerous precedents support the theory that the Bible provided Clemens/Mark Twain with literary archetypes for Huck's narrative. In his article on the uses of the Bible in *Huckleberry Finn*, McCullough comments that the allusions to the Bible that he singles out "not only heighten the ironic impact of the novel, but add a further dimension to Twain's characters."[34] Similarly, Randy Cross, who sees Mark Twain using his characters to covertly deny "the divinity of Jesus Christ and the validity of the Bible," suggests that the novel's "biblical references, *both explicit and covert*, are not the childish misunderstandings of an ignorant, fourteen-year-old Huck, but the beliefs of his iconoclastic, forty-eight-year-old creator"[35] (italics added).

Cross's argument raises a problem to which he pays no attention. In fact, both of these archetypalist camps, the critics who point to Clemens' biblical allusions as "reverent" and those who see them as being sarcasms, have mostly ignored each other. If *all* the biblical allusions in the novel represent the author's beliefs, then the most obvious of them, the Mosaic allusions explored by Kenneth Lynn, Daniel Barnes, Billy Collins, and Earl Briden, need to be reconciled with the iconoclastic pattern that Cross indicates, for it is improbable that Clemens, whose contempt for the Bible as a source of moral instruction has been amply documented by Stanley Brodwin, Allison Ensor, Jr., and C. T. Harnesberger, would have made Huck a "Mississippi Moses" unless this structural device provided him with a basis for burlesque and satire. Yet Collins, in his examination of the novel's presentation of the liberation drama of Exodus, extends Lynn's work to the conclusion that Mark Twain uses parallels to Exodus to poke fun at the notion that slavery was the peculiar pet of the deity and adds "the weight of Biblical authority" to make his condemnation of slavery even more powerful.[36] While it is not yet time to take sides in this disagreement, it receives due attention in subsequent chapters of this study.

In the Wilks episode (Chapters XXIV–IX), Mark Twain lampoons both the gullibility of the faithful, who are ready and eager to be taken in by "soul-butter and hogwash," and the pair of rapacious frauds posing as an English parson and his deaf-mute brother, who are only too glad to oblige them. The king's malapropism, "orgies" for "obsequies," brings this satire into clearer focus by highlighting the emotional excesses of these scenes. Kenneth Lynn, pointing out the ironic contrast between "Jim's sorrow and compassion for his deaf-and-dumb daughter" at the conclusion of Chapter XXIII and "the spectacle of the two frauds talking on their hands" at the end of Chapter XXIV, shows why Huck feels "ashamed of the human race":

> The gullible townspeople now seem as subhuman as the crooks who defraud them. As Henry Nash Smith has pointed out, when the townspeople move rapidly up the street to have a look at the newly arrived "parson" and "deaf-mute," Huck likens them to soldiers marching along, thereby calling attention to their regimented minds and lives. A moment later he refers to them as a "gang" which is "trotting along," as if they reminded him of a herd of squealing pigs. The people [...] are now not only associated with, but have actually become, the dirty animals which are the novel's leading symbol of degradation and sordidness.[37]

This symbol, by the way, as will be shown in Chapter III of this study, is also Clemens' symbol for the biblical God and the low origins of His Word (see Chapter Three, Section IV-C).

Although this study of *Huck Finn* does not concur with Collins' conclusions, it does answer his call for a reassessment of the thematic integrity of the novel. Extending the work of Barnes, Briden, Cross, and Quirk as well as Lynn, Collins, Nielson, and McCullough, who have contributed to the conversation about uses of the Bible in the novel, the coming discussion confirms their insights into Clemens' reliance on biblical allusions to structure Huck's narrative, but it finds these allusions to function in a consistently satirical way. The next four chapters attend to the allusions they identify and many others that have escaped detection until now, or that this broad summary has passed over. The conclusion this evidence supports is that Randy Cross knew not how right he was when he attributed the irony of Huck's "burlesque Resurrection" along with *all* of the novel's other biblical allusions, "both explicit and covert," to Huck's "iconoclastic, forty-eight year old creator."

VIII. Of Noah and Sons

In Clemens' view it was undue reverence for the Bible that led to the evils Collins catalogs, not just the misuse of it to prove that slavery was "the peculiar pet of the Deity." Moreover, as Tom Quirk has observed, a covert parallel to the legend of Noah in Chapter IX calls up "the story of Ham, so often cited by the antebellum South as theological justification of the uncharitable institution of slavery." Quirk points out that while "the events in Chapter IX do not strictly parallel the legend of Noah, they are sufficiently close to the biblical story to suggest that the resemblances, and the deviations, were deliberate." Exact parallels include "the birds that deliver a message, the flood, the tame wildlife, and the floating house," but more interesting are Clemens' "clearly ironic modifications of the legend of Noah":

> Noah, after the flood, gets drunk one night and falls asleep naked. His son Ham has the misfortune to see his father unclothed and runs to warn his brothers. The oldest brother, Shem, backs into the tent of Noah and covers his father's shame. When Noah awakes, he is incensed and damns the descendants of Ham [to servitude].

As Quirk observes, there are several traits that pap has in common with Noah, and it is of course pap's corpse that Jim covers in the house of death, which is itself an ironic inversion of the ark of all life that Noah built. The commonalities Quirk notices are that they are both drunkards; they both engage in angry rampages; and they are both supporters of slavery—pap by bigoted support of it and Noah by instituting it. Both are also wrathful characters. In the context Clemens sets up, pap "lies in" for Noah in the "House of Death" episode [see Appendix A], according to Quirk, and "by performing the act of Shem" when Jim "covers the nakedness of Pap," (while Huck, by not looking at the "three days" dead, naked corpse, acts in parallel to both Shem and Japheth, as Quirk might also have noticed), the fugitive slave "demonstrates his humanity, even moral superiority." In the passage from Genesis that Quirk quotes, Shem and Japheth, careful to avoid seeing Noah, cooperate to cover their father's nakedness. Jim's insistence that Huck not look at the naked corpse of his father is another parallel to this biblical text.[38]

"It is suggestive," continues Quirk, "that Pap is both the real father of Huck and, since the lineage of 'servants' can be traced back to Ham, the genealogical father of the slave, Jim." Quirk speculates that "it may have been Twain's original intention to make Jim a 'big brother' to Huck, to have Jim play Shem to Huck's Japheth." This relationship produces further parallels that extend far beyond Chapter IX, for when "Jim builds a wigwam on the raft, ... Huck, like Japheth, 'dwells in the tents' of Jim," and "Jim's humanizing influence 'enlarges' the character of Huck Finn."[39] Furthermore, Quirk finds that "the most significant aspect" of Clemens' allusions to the Deluge is that "it may account for the ensuing voyage down the river" and that "the legend of Noah provides a mythical framework for their escape. The raft becomes a new ark and the Mississippi becomes a moral force that insulates them from a thoroughly wicked world."[40] Thus, in Quirk's view, this "ironic treatment of the story ... becomes a venomous attack on slavery itself and a condemnation of a new, postdiluvian civilization whose initial proclamation was so undemocratic."[41]

Notice, however that while Mark Twain's attack is only on slavery and the civilization that spawned it and then perverted scripture to support it, Clemens attacks this biblical prop for "the peculiar institution": Pap's corpse, which when alive harbored all the worst traits of Noah, drunkenness and wrathfulness, becomes the patriarch Noah in Quirk's reading, so that the allusions he notes point out the moral absurdity of the Bible story that justified the moral absurdity of slavery. Quirk's reading of "The House of Death" episode clearly lends support to the idea that one can read Clemens' biblical allusions at least in part as anti-biblical satire.

IX. Acts, Not Words

Three further biblical allusions demand mention before this chapter ends. Clemens bases his biblical burlesque on both the Old and New Testaments as he attacks the morality of the Bible and the "sivilization" that based both slavery and racism on its teachings. This attack is nowhere more evident than in the closing section, which begins with Huck's voluntary return to society and his faux rebirth as Tom Sawyer, and continues through the boys' burlesque re-enactment of the "Doubting Thomas" episode of St. John and their burlesque performance of the roles of Moses and Aaron in the liberation drama of Exodus that Collins has explored. In Chapter XXXVII of the novel, Hearn notes, Uncle Silas' reference to Acts 17 calls up the Apostle Paul's teaching that "God ... hath made of one blood all nations of men for to dwell upon the face of the earth"; this egalitarian standard flies in the face of preacher Silas' practice of racism and slavery.[42]

As in the climax of the novel, where it is not the reader's approval of the righteousness of Huck's *beliefs*, but the rightness of his acts—in tearing up his note to Miss Watson and setting out to "steal Jim out of slavery again"— that Clemens courts, the author makes clear that it is Silas Phelps' *works*, not his *faith*, that the reader must consider in providing what Wayne Booth refers to as "mature moral judgment, ... far more exhilarating sport than identifying a pun or recognizing the source of an allusion."[43]

X. Chapter Summary: Looking for Huck Finn in the Bulrushers

There is no shortage of precedents to confirm that the Bible's influence on Clemens was profound and that allusions to its creation myth and its account of ancient history up to the time of the early Christian church provided him with material for constructing the plot, characterization, and, to an undetermined extent, the theme(s) of *Adventures of Huckleberry Finn* hidden in the "bulrushers."

The problems a reader encounters as one sets out to explore the impact of these biblical allusions on the meaning of Huck's story stem from the fact that the author's attitude toward the Bible appears to be ambivalent. At times he impresses one as being extremely irreverent, as when Huck and Tom reenact the post-Resurrection encounter of the Apostle Thomas with the risen Christ and the context implies that "Jesus played it on them," as Cross contends,[44] and when Clemens portrays the Bible itself as an idol worshiped by the credulous dupes at the camp-meeting or crushing the last breaths out of Boggs in the Bricksville murder sequence. In other episodes he appears to be making reverent allusion, as Collins concludes, to what some Americans regard as the moral foundation of American culture, as when he includes extensive parallels to Exodus in the opening chapters of the book, throughout the middle section, especially in the feud episode, and in the course of Tom Sawyer's liberation scheme/evasion, as if he were trying to justify the travesty that Tom sets in motion by anchoring its morality in the "moral authority" of "the liberation drama of Exodus," which remains uncritically affirmed by many millions of Christians and Jews to this day.

The resulting confusion of these mixed messages has led to most readers who are even aware of them regarding these allusions as interesting sidelights on the action of the story, but taken together they appear to be a self-contradictory maze of misleading clues to the meaning of the novel as a whole—if it has any coherent message to impart at all, which the "Notice" that functions as its preface overtly, if not covertly, denies. From the literature of *Huck Finn* criticism, there appears to be little evidence that an archetypal reading of Twain's "narrative" attending to biblical parallels can take one far toward solving the problem of coming up with a unified and satisfying reading of the novel as a coherent whole in either thematic or dramatic terms, despite the efforts of Kenneth Lynn, Vaneta Neilson, Earl Briden, and Billy Collins to do so, and of Daniel Barnes, Randy Cross, Joseph McCullough, and Tom Quirk to demonstrate that irony is the keynote of Clemens' biblical themes in *Huck Finn*.

CHAPTER THREE

Catching the Brazen Serpent in Clemens' Net of Allusion
Huckleberry Finn, Pilgrim's Progress, Paradise Lost *and the Bible*

I. Under the Aegis of the Cross

Notice that "a cross" is the "sign" of Tom's gang in Chapter II, a simple graphic for the illiterate as well as the most sacred symbol of Christianity. Here Clemens signals his awareness of the deeper significance in the child's-play at mayhem and murder performed under the sign of the Cross. This symbol could as easily have been an "X," the customary "mark" of illiterates. Most critics have overlooked the significance of Clemens' use of this symbol in commentary on this passage, as if it were inconceivable that the cruelties at which the boys play might have larger religious—rather than just social—significance.

The symbol carved into the rock is a carryover from *Tom Sawyer*, but that does not diminish its force. As a result, no commentary in this study's research base has pointed out the irony of Tom's claiming trademark rights on the Cross as the sign of his robber band,[1] and Tom's games are thus closely associated with the orthodox forms of religion that the author later subjects to scathing satire.

Integral to this episode in the cave is the opening salvo of Mark Twain's satire on Southern-style romanticism, a theme that of course recurs in several episodes of Huck's *Adventures*, most notably here, in Chapter XII, and in Chapters XXXIV–XL. As Hearn points out, this child's-play at crime (under the aegis of the Cross) does foreshadow the actual violence, fraud, and treachery—and religiosity—that Huck will confront later in the story: Tom's games anticipate the horrors that await Huck when he flees from St. Petersburg.[2]

II. Incongruent Parallels

Biblical parallels alone may not convince readers skeptical of this reading because Clemens' burlesque technique necessarily warps the content of episodes beyond moral recognition as he continues his strategy of defamiliarizing these well-known Bible stories. For example, although pap's rebuke to Huck in Chapter V reflects God's rebuke to Adam in Genesis 3 almost sentence-for-sentence, the congruency of these two passages has not until now been pointed out, perhaps because the idea of a god as despicable as Huck's "pap" is too ridiculous or terrifying. He would, and does in the novel, transform the world he rules to hell—one very similar, as W. R. Moses has shown, to Dante's *Inferno* (see Chapter Four, Section IV).

Even more reprehensible is the deity Clemens caricatures from other Bible stories: the bloodthirsty manipulator of Pharaoh's will, for example, who hardens hearts to "get me honor" (see Chapter Three, Section XIX and Chapter Five, Section IV). Whether one accepts Clemens' view of a satanic god or rejects it as too nightmarish or as theologically unsound; whether one agrees with or decries Samuel Clemens' view of religion is finally irrelevant to this study. As a protest against the evils of uncritical reverence not just for scripture but for all forms of moral authority—especially the conscience that is not innate or God-given, but an acquired, imprinted set of cultural norms—*Huckleberry Finn* is a great achievement of literary art. Furthermore, Clemens projects a new vision of the texts he burlesques that may forever temper one's perception of the originals.

Nevertheless, the misprision to which Clemens subjects his sources might leave some unconvinced that the novel's deep structure is sufficiently congruent with that of the Bible to make the novel a burlesque of the stories of the Fall, Cain and Abel, the legend of Noah, Abraham's near-sacrifice of Isaac, the wisdom of Solomon, the vengeance of Samuel the sword-wielding prophet, the doomed friendship of David and Jonathan during King Saul's tragic fall, the career of Moses from the ark of bulrushes to its end just short of the Promised Land, and the Resurrection of Christ.

The biblical allusions that this study has explored thus far contribute to the novel's religious satire and provide a unifying factor that may alter the widespread misconception of *Huckleberry Finn* as a loosely structured or even incoherent work; but its burlesque vision surmounts its biblical sources to come to grips with theology as well as mythology. The double exposure of mythology and history, as will be shown in Chapters Three through Six of this study, is really a triple exposure that superimposes the theology and cosmology of John Milton onto Clemens' portrait of pap and Huck to render much of the book a simultaneous burlesque of both the Bible and *Paradise Lost*.

III. Pap Finn and the God of Genesis

The chief function of pap Finn in the text is to personify the deity Clemens abhorred in the Bible. This comparison between the God of Abraham—who demanded that patriarch's willingness to cut his own son's throat as the measure of his "fear" of God (Genesis 22: 12)—and pap Finn—who in the throes of *delirium tremens* attempts to knife his only son (Chapter VI)—is not made here arbitrarily. The evidence of the text testifies that this was Clemens' conception.

The powerful presence of pap in the opening chapters and his subsequent physical absence is not, as H. N. Smith suggests, an indication that the author originally "had in mind the possibility of involving Pap more elaborately in the course of events. But ... what the angels might have led Pap to do is never revealed."[3] Pap is more elaborately involved than Smith and James Cox, who asserts that "Huck's lineal descendence from Pap removes him from the garden of innocence,"[4] suspect. Both writers overlook pap's function in the novel's religious satire because they do not see that he is a caricature of the Old Testament God. This portrayal of the biblical God anchors Clemens' religious satire.

Consider Huck's first conversation with pap in the novel. This episode in Huck's room at the Widow Douglas' house in Chapter V (which Clemens composed in 1876 as he began the novel) parallels God's confrontation of Adam after Original Sin. Pap comes to Huck as God the Father seeks out Adam. Whereas Adam hides himself in fear, Huck can no longer hide (although he has "hidden" his money by selling it to Judge Thatcher), but he is at first afraid. Both God and pap speak first: God criticizes Adam's sense of nakedness, while pap comments on Huck's "starchy clothes." Both Huck's clothing and Adam's shame evidence sin in the eyes of their inquisitors: "Hast thou eaten of the tree...?" asks God (Gen. 3: 11); Adam, by eating the forbidden fruit, has pretended to godhood (Gen. 3: 5). In pap's view Huck has "put on airs over his own father and let on to be better'n what *he* is." Thus, both have committed sins of pride involving the acquisition of knowledge: Adam's new Moral Sense and Huck's new literacy.

In a rhetorical and substantive parallel, God asks, "Who told thee that thou wast naked?" (Gen. 3: 11), and pap demands, "Who told you you might meddle with such hifalut'n foolishness, hey?" Both Adam and Huck name a woman as the reason for their disobedience; Huck responds, "The widow. She told me"; Adam explains, "The woman ... she gave me of the tree, and I did eat" (Gen. 3: 12). God curses Eve, then Adam (Gen. 3: 16–19); pap threatens in parallel, warning Huck, "I'll learn her how to meddle ... here you're a-swelling yourself up like this. I ain't the man to stand it." Later, pap fulfills his threat to "learn" Huck and the widow by abducting his son from St. Petersburg and forcing him to live in rags, squalor, and physical abuse at a hut in the wilderness along the Illinois shore. Similarly, the God of Genesis evicts Adam and Eve from paradise into the wilderness to punish their disobedience and to prevent their committing further crimes.

Pap's notion of the further crime Huck might commit also resonates with the biblical text when one considers pap's "First thing you know, you'll get religion, too. I never see such a son." For the God of Genesis, the removal of Adam and Eve from Eden is necessary to prevent their eating of the Tree of Life and so becoming immortal (Gen. 3: 22; see Appendix B). For Samuel Clemens, true religion had nothing to do with subservience to a "jealous God" who harshly judges the pettiest shortcomings of his creatures (traits for which the Creator, Clemens maintained, was culpable): the deity pap personifies. In jealous rage at his boy climbing out of the sty he was born into, pap truly reflects the biblical deity Clemens abhorred and derided.

Kenneth Lynn has characterized the hogs of pap's tanyard, Huck's sacrifice, the Grangerford-Shepherdson church, and the streets of Bricksville, along with the metaphorical ones that greet the duke and the king at the beginning of the Wilks sequence, as "the novel's leading symbol of degradation and sordidness."[5] Pap's emotional exclamation in the judge's parlor that his hand "was the hand of a hog" (Chapter V) forges the link between this symbol and Clemens' characterization of the biblical God and the low origins of His Word. Pap's identification as the God of Genesis along with his association with hogs in the tanyard and his self-proclaimed physical identification with them provide the implied authorial commentary that Wayne Booth demands of an author as his chief duty to the reader.

Significantly, when Huck ritually escapes his pursuers in Chapter VII, his masterstroke is the killing of a hog, an act in which Lynn finds the truest expression of Huck's relationship with his father.[6] And so it is, but not just for its psychological validity as Huck's expression of sublimated aggression toward pap. For on the archetypal level, Huck's scapegoating of the wild boar he kills is a ritual deicide that frees him for the time being from the consequences of his birth into a culture that sees itself as fallen and depraved (see Chapter Two, Section VII).

Thus, Cox's assertion that Huck's lineage separates him from the Garden notwithstanding, pap's relationship with Huck *binds* Huck to Eden and *defines* the archetypal ground covered by Huck's adventures. All subsequent references to the novel's ubiquitous hogs and to pap himself reiterate this basic formulation. When Huck strips pap of all his possessions in Chapter VII; when Jim and Huck discuss the morality of borrowing and stealing in Chapter XII; and again when Tom tells Huck that borrowing is stealing in Chapter XXXV, their conversations resonate with the biblical book of Exodus in which God instructs the Israelites to "borrow" from the Egyptians "jewels of silver ... and gold."[7] At the conclusion, when Jim reveals that pap "ain't a-comin' back no mo" because he is dead ("Chapter the Last")—killed, appropriately, soon after Huck's ritual patricide/deicide—the "intense symbolic stature" of pap Finn "in his brief but violent pilgrimage"[8] culminates in the symbolic death of the deity in whose image Clemens conceived pap.

The ending, however, is not the unqualified triumph that pap's death suggests. As Cox maintains, it is conscience that is the real tyrant, and one function of conscience, Clemens implies, is to project gods in the image of human cultures to turn socially conditioned moral codes into revealed moral absolutes. Even before we learn of pap's demise, a new avatar of the Old Testament God has supplanted him. Tom Sawyer emerges from the evasion as the God of the Gilded Age. Through Tom's *deus ex machina* advent in the closing section, his re-enactment of Exodus 1–14, his manipulative treatment of everyone around him, whites and blacks alike, his thirst for kingdom, power, honor, glory, wealth, and bloodshed, his gilded rule of respectability with its emphasis on conformity, duty, and principle—in short, through his *conscientious* behavior—Clemens deifies his mythical All-American boy. His is the kingdom, the power, and the glory (along with the depravity)—not Huck's—at the end of the novel.

IV. Enter Satan

IV-A: Of God, Pap and Satan

Samuel Clemens' ironic pattern of allusion begins in the narrative, as Barnes, Lynn, and Collins have pointed out, with the first chapter's introduction of the Moses motif. It continues through pap's return from down-river. Jim's "hairball oracle" foreshadows pap's dual identification with both God and Satan: "Dey's two angels hoverin' roun' 'bout him. One uv 'em is white en shiny, en t'other one is black" (Chapter IV). The episode in Huck's room at the widow's house, in which Clemens reiterates this black and white contrast between pap's black hair and white skin, parallels God's confrontation of Adam after the Fall.

Although the serpent is missing from the Eden of St. Petersburg, Satan—the Miltonic one—is present. Along with the God of Genesis, Clemens caricatures him in his characterization of pap, preparing the way for the novel's conflation of the Judeo-Christian archetypes of good and evil.

Clemens' familiarity with Milton's epic has been well established by literary scholars. Gary Scharnhorst informs us that in 1858, Clemens "wrote his brother Orion that he considered 'the grandest thing' in it to be 'the Arch-Fiend's terrible energy!' He wrote Olivia Langdon in 1869 that after their marriage they would enjoy together 'the drum-beats of Milton's stately sentences.'" By 1877, however, his attitude toward the poem had shifted, and "he listed *Paradise Lost* among those works he would have burned had they been submitted to him for publication," and in 1879 Clemens "claimed in a letter to Howells that [his brother] Orion had planned to 'write a burlesque' of the epic." Clemens not only had strong feelings about the epic poem, but also, as Scharnhorst adds:

> Certainly, Twain was influenced by *Paradise Lost* in several [...] late works, for he modeled parts of *A Connecticut Yankee* (1889), "Extracts from Adam's Diary" (1893), "The Man That Corrupted Hadleyburg" (1900), and *The Mysterious Stranger* (1916) on the epic, and he proclaimed in 1900 that it was "a work that everybody wants to have read and nobody wants to read."[9]

Pap's first surreptitious visit to the widow's, which Huck describes from the evidence of his distinctive boot prints—marked with a hobnailed cross "to keep off the devil" (Chapter IV)—parallels Satan's approach to the garden of innocence in *Paradise Lost*. Pap's tracks show he came "up from the quarry, stood around the stile a while, and then went on around the garden fence" (Chapter IV). When Milton's Arch-Fiend first comes to Eden, he too departs unnoticed; he too walks uphill to the border of the garden; he too disdains "due entrance."[10] When pap confronts his son in the boy's room, Huck notices the window up and concludes pap "clumb in by the shed." Milton describes Satan's intrusion in similar terms:

> Now to th' ascent of that steep savage Hill
> *Satan* had journey'd on, pensive and slow;
> But further way found none [; ...]
> Due entrance he disdain'd, and in contempt,
> At one slight bound high overleap'd all bound
> Of Hill or highest Wall and sheer within
> Lights on his feet. As when a prowling Wolf,
> Whom hunger drives to seek new haunt for prey,

> Watching where Shepherds pen thir Flocks at eve, [...]
> Leaps o'er the fence with ease into the Fold;
> Or as a Thief bent to unheard the cash
> Of some rich Burgher, whose substantial doors,
> Cross-barr'd and bolted fast, fear no assault,
> In at the window climbs, or o'er the tiles:
> So clomb this first grand Thief into God's fold.[11]

Pap, too, has been driven by hunger "to seek new haunt[s]," and he climbs "in at the window" to "unhoard the cash" of a "rich Burgher" by the name of Huckleberry Finn. As Satan spies on Eden's inhabitants,[12] so pap watches Huck in Chapter V with "his eyes shining through long, tangled, greasy, black hair" "like he was behind vines," as one can imagine Satan spying on Eden. Both pap and Satan are compared to toads,[13] and Clemens' description of pap—"his face ... a white to make a body's flesh crawl," and "his clothes ... just rags"—roughly parallels that of the angels who guard Eden and tell Satan when they discover him there, "Thou resemblest now/ Thy sin and place of doom obscure and foul."[14]

Declares Satan:

> I alone first undertook
> To wing the desolate Abyss, and spy
> This new created World, whereof in Hell
> Fame is not silent, here in hope to find
> Better abode.[15]

Declares pap:

> I've been in town two days, and I hain't heard nothing but about you bein' rich. I heard about it away down the river, too. That's why I come. You git me that money tomorrow—I want it [Chapter V].

Thus both pap Finn and Satan share covetousness as motive, upward direction of travel, stealth and extortion as method, and similarity of appearance. And they account for their presence in Eden/St. Petersburg with parallel frankness and brevity. Moreover, as W. R. Moses suggests and Mark Twain confirms (see Chapter Four, Section IV), "down the river" is hell in the cosmos according to Mark Twain:

> The "nigger trader" was loathed by everybody. He was regarded as a sort of human devil who bought and conveyed poor helpless creatures to hell—for to our whites and blacks alike the southern plantation was simply hell; no milder name could describe it. If the threat to sell an incorrigible slave "down the river" would not reform him, nothing would—his case was past cure.[16]

In this initial confrontation between pap and Huck, Clemens reinforces the dual identification of pap with both God and Satan by contrasting his all-black hair and ghastly white skin, reiterating the contrast between the black and white angels Jim sees "hoverin' 'roun 'bout him." Continuing in this vein, Clemens recounts pap's misadventures in vernacular hyperbole that renders them more comical for their mythical grandiosity.

IV-B: *About Pap*

Most analyses of pap's character focus on his psychological and sociological—indeed, sociopathic—relations with Huck and the community. Valuable though these commentaries are, they largely overlook Huck's father's function in the religious satire of the implied author. From Huck's first mention of pap in Chapter I to his last on the final page, there is an intensity—a "terrible energy"—that makes pap Finn one of the most memorable villains in our literature.

Readings that dismiss Huck's relationship with pap as "sheer melodrama"[17] miss the mark because despite pap's loathsome activities, the "appalling glimpse" Clemens gives "of Pap's inner life"[18] moves one to pity the "poor devil" (Chapter VI). Huck's all-embracing compassion and his admiration for all things extraordinary extend even to his abusive father so that, while the relationship is melodramatic on the level of the implied narrator (whose image as a purveyor of melodrama and conventional morality Clemens cultivated), and who seems to have no clue as to the deeper meanings of the events Huck reports, when viewed from the implied author's perspective Huck's relationship with his pap provokes a response more complex than melodrama can evoke.

Then too, there is an air of mystery and morbidity about the elder Finn. His personal magnetism is both fascinating and repulsive. As H. N. Smith perceives him, "He is in a sense a ghost the first time we see him, for his faceless corpse has been found floating in the river." He reappears in St. Petersburg from the "mysterious underworld" "away down the river,"[19] and the reader's last sight of him is as the abandoned corpse Huck and Jim discover in the floating house (Chapter IX), a scene which Clemens recalls at the close of the book ("Chapter the Last").

Pap's isolation, too, contains something of the anti-heroic. He is a loner—except for Huck and the "two mighty hard looking strangers" with whom he is last seen alive in the story forming an unholy Trinity (as we learn from Mrs. Loftus in Chapter XI)—and who probably murder pap for the money Judge Thatcher gave him to hunt for Huck's killer (Chapter XI). Whether on the river, in St. Petersburg, or in the wilderness on the Illinois shore, pap sees authority as tyranny and plots indomitably, ruthlessly, hopelessly to "git my rights." His goals, of course, are reprehensible, but his "terrible energy" in pursuit of them makes him, paradoxically, a bad man and a wonderful character. Pap's very boot print in the snow calls to mind the Cross and Satan in a symbolic expression that foreshadows the conflict-ridden essence of pap Finn at the outset of his involvement in the plot (Chapter IV).

Pap's burlesque conversion in Chapter V ("Pap Starts in on a New Life"; see Appendix A) adds to the developing religious satire by showing how gullibly the new judge and his household, "gentlemen and ladies all," as pap addresses those gathered to witness his sham reform, seize on his feigned change of heart as "the holiest time on record." The episode is delightful bathos; pap vows tearfully that he has "started in on a new life"; everyone present shakes his hand emotionally, and "the judge's wife, she kissed it":

> Then they tucked the old man into a beautiful room, and in the night some time he got powerful thirsty and clumb out on the porch-roof and slid down a stanchion and traded his new coat for a jug of forty-rod, and clumb back again and had a good old time; and towards daylight he crawled out again, drunk as a fiddler, and rolled off the porch and broke his left arm in two places, and was most froze to death when somebody found him after sun-up. And when they come to look at that spare room they had to take soundings before they could navigate it.
> The judge he felt kind of sore. He said he reckoned a body could reform the old man with a shotgun, maybe, but he didn't know no other way.

IV–C: *Pap's Fall from Grace*

While pap nearly keeps his vow to "die before he'll go back," the humor of Huck's account and its ironic ending mask the seriousness of pap's fall: not just from the roof, but from grace as well. It leaves him, like Milton's Arch-Fiend at the opening of Book I, confounded and prostrate after his expulsion from Heaven and fall through Chaos, an event with which pap's brush with death resonates more strongly when one considers how the paragraph's closing metaphor transforms the spare room in the house of "the new judge" (suggestive of Christ) to Chaos by likening it to a river crossing (see Chapter Three, Section VIII).

The next major phase of Huck's relations with pap takes place in Chapter VI ("Pap Struggles with the Death Angel"; see Appendix A), in which pap abducts Huck and imprisons him in an old log hut on the Illinois shore, the scene of pap's drunken diatribe against the government. Pap's monologue is important not only as social satire on the racial bigotry that permeated Southern society, but more subtly as religious satire. Clemens develops pap's diatribe into a satanic expostulation reiterating the Miltonic motives for Satan's rebellion in Heaven. Pap's major complaint is that "A man can't get his rights in a govment like this"; Satan's ire against Heaven's government is aroused in Milton's epic when

> By Decree
> Another now hath to himself ingross't
> All power, and us eclipst under the name
> Of King anointed.[20]

Pap contrasts his state under the law with that of a free black college professor visiting from Ohio:

> He had on the whitest shirt you ever see [...], and the shiniest hat; and there ain't a man in that town that's got as fine clothes as what he had; and he had a gold watch and chain, and a silver-headed cane—the awfullest old gray-headed nabob in the State.
> The law takes a man worth six thousand dollars and up'ards, and jams him into an old trap of a cabin like this, and lets him go round in clothes that ain't fitten for a hog. [...] Look at my hat—if you call it a hat—but the lid raises up and the rest of it goes down till it's below my chin, and then it ain't rightly a hat at all, but more like my head was shoved up through a jint o' stovepipe. Look at it, says I—such a hat for me to wear—one of the wealthiest men in this town if I could git my rights.

Pap's secessionist rhetoric—"when they told me there was a state in this country where they'd let that nigger vote, I drawed out"—matches the cause of the Southern rebellion, and also Satan's incitement to rebellion in Heaven:

> Who can in reason then or right assume
> Monarchy over such as live by right
> His equals, if in power or splendor less,
> In freedom equals? Or can introduce
> Law and Edict on us, who without law
> Err not? Much less for this to be our Lord,
> And look for adoration to th' abuse
> Of those Imperial Titles which assert
> Our being ordain'd to govern, not to serve?[21]

Pap's ire at the injustice of "Law and Edict," couched in distortions at which the archetypal liar himself might blush, starts him on his tirade:

> Call this a govment! Why just look and see what it's like. Here's the law a-standing ready to take a man's son away from him—a man's own son, which he has had all the trouble and all the anxiety and all the expense of raising. Yes, just as that man has got that son raised at last, and ready to go to work and begin to do suthin' for *him* and give him a rest, the law up and goes for him. And they call that govment!

The issue that Satan seizes is also a matter of the preferment of another over himself in the machinations of unjust government: God's Son has been exalted above the angels, Satan included, just as the "prowling, thieving, infernal, white-shirted free nigger" college professor has been exalted above pap— "one of the wealthiest men in this town if I could git my rights." Moreover, his own son is being preferred to him as the rightful owner of Huck's kingly wealth. Satan's secessionism, too, is matched by pap's: "Sometimes I've a mighty notion to just leave the country for good and all. Yes, and I *told* 'em so; I told old Thatcher so to his face. Lots of 'em heard me, and can tell what I said. Says I, for two cents I'd leave the blamed country and never come a-near it agin. Them's the very words."

And later:

> I says I'll never vote agin. Them's the very words I said; they all heard me; and the country may rot for all of me—I'll never vote agin as long as I live. And to see the cool way of that nigger—why, he wouldn't a give me the road if I hadn't shoved him out o' the way. I says to the people, why ain't this nigger put up at auction and sold?—that's what I want to know. And what do you reckon they said? Why they said he couldn't be sold till he'd been in the State six months, and he hadn't been there that long yet. There, now—that's a specimen. They call that a govment that can't sell a free nigger till he's been in the State six months.

Besides the specific motives—greed for wealth and status, envy and outrage at the "unjust" preferment of another over themselves, jealousy of their presumed rights—that pap and Satan have in common, and besides their similar politics, secessionism and civil war, there is a similar father/son motif to be seen in both works. Satan is furious because God's Son is coming into His property, and Satan's envy is aroused; pap covets Huck's property and is angry because the unjust "govment" is keeping it from him. Earlier, through pap's identification with God, Huck became, by implication, God's son, the heir to the Throne, the possessor of kingly wealth. Now pap as Satan is furious that he can't lay his hands on the Son's wealth, to which he, as the boy's father, has lawful right: "His lawyer said he reckoned he would win his lawsuit and get the money if they ever got started on the trial." Thus, as one continues picking at the threads of pap's argument, *Paradise Lost* continues to unravel. Clemens' strategy of combining archetypes that Milton keeps separate is, ironically, both the mainspring of his novel's satirical mechanism and the cloak that conceals his religious satire.

V. Enter the Death Angel

V-A: "Hell, in My Book..."

An extract from Clemens' letter of 23 March 1878 (during the period in which the first portion of the *Huck Finn* manuscript was pigeonholed) to his brother Orion illustrates the author's attitude and testifies that Clemens was considering just such an artistic method; his letter implies that he did not want Orion to attempt any such literary endeavor as a burlesque of *Paradise Lost*:

> Now look here—I have tried, all these years, to think of some way of "doing" hell, too—& have always had to give it up. Hell, in my book, will not occupy five pages of MS, I judge—it will be only covert hints, I suppose, & quickly dropped. I may end by not even referring to it. And mind you, in my opinion you will find that you can't write up hell so it will stand printing.
>
> Neither Howells nor I believe in hell or the divinity of the Savior—but no matter, the Savior is none the less a sacred Personage & a man should have no desire or disposition to refer to him lightly, profanely, or otherwise than with the profoundest reverence. The only safe thing is not to introduce him or refer to him at all, I suspect. [...]
>
> Go to work & [re-vamp] or re-write it. God only exhibits his thunder-&-lightning at intervals, & so they always command attention. These are God's adjectives. You thunder-&-lighten too much; the reader ceases to get under the bed, by & by.[22]

Despite his cautionary advice to Orion, we now know that Sam Clemens had already written these episodes of the story; as Fred Kaplan reports: "From July to September 1876 he had written 146 of his manuscript pages, chapters 1 to 2½, and 5 to 8½ of [...] *Adventures of Huckleberry Finn*."[23]

The "scant five pages" to which Clemens refers in his letter describe work he had already done on his novel. The emphasis on the wording of the first paragraph of the excerpt from his letter to Orion should fall on the thrice repeated *"you,"* the last of which Clemens himself underlines.[24] The plot of the novel testifies that the man who "should have no desire or disposition to refer to him [the Savior] lightly, profanely, or otherwise than with the profoundest reverence" was Orion Clemens; Sam Clemens was reserving that literary endeavor for himself.

In support of the idea that this mythological displacement was one of his fundamental conceptions as he set out to create Huck's story, consider that Chapters V through VIII½ of the manuscript and the finished novel include: pap's intrusion into Huck's room at the widow's, where he re-enacts God's confrontation with Adam in Genesis 3; pap's "fall from grace"; his abduction of Huck in parallel to God's expulsion of Adam and Eve from Eden (see Appendix B); his re-enactment of Satan's Miltonic diatribe against unjust government in Heaven and his re-enactment of Satan's punishment in Hell after the Fall of Man (see below and Appendix C); pap's personification of Incontinence in the first phase of Huck's tour of Dante's Hell explored by W. R. Moses (see Chapter Four, Section IV); his re-enactment of Satan's confrontation with the Angel of Death at Hell's gate in *Paradise Lost* (see below and Appendix C); the simultaneous burlesque of Abraham's near-sacrifice of Isaac with an implicit parallel to God's own sacrifice of His Son (to whom he does "not ... refer ... at all"; see below); Huck's archetypally multivalent escape from pap and the widow in Chapter VII (see Chapter Three, Section VII); Huck's escape into Chaos (below); and his rebirth as a new Adam in his Jackson's Island Eden (see below and Appendix D). Clemens had written all of these episodes about two years before he wrote his advice to his brother.

In the culminating incident of Chapter VI, the literary archetype of Clemens' text could hardly be more clearly marked unless the author had provided a marginal gloss. The night of pap's drunken diatribe in the cabin where but a moment ago this reading witnessed the scene of Satan's rebellion in Heaven, Huck awakens to awful screaming. Gone now are pap's pride, eloquence, and fury. Witness Samuel Clemens' literary version of Hell:

> I don't know how long I was asleep, but all of a sudden there was an awful scream and I was up. There was pap looking wild, and skipping around every which way and yelling about snakes. He said they was crawling up his legs; and then he would give a jump and scream, and say one had bit him on the cheek—but I couldn't see no snakes. He started and run round and round the cabin, hollering "Take him off! Take him off! He's biting me on the neck!" I never see a man look so wild in the eyes. Pretty soon he was all fagged out, and fell down panting; then he rolled over and over wonderful fast, kicking and grabbing at the air with his hands, and screaming and saying there was devils a-hold of him. He wore out by and by, and laid still a while, moaning.

In composing this passage, Clemens drew heavily (but not exclusively) on the account in *Paradise Lost* X of God's punishment of Satan and his legions following Satan's triumphal return to Hell after his seduction of Eve and, through Eve, Adam.[25] Satan announces his victory; then:

> So having said, awhile he stood, expecting
> Thir universal shout and high applause
> To fill his ear, when contrary he hears,
> On all sides, from innumerable tongues
> A dismal universal hiss, the sound
> Of public scorn; he wondered, but not long
> Had leisure, wond'ring at himself now more;
>   His Visage drawn he felt to sharp and spare,
> His Arms clung to his Ribs, his Legs entwining
> Each other, till supplanted down he fell,
> A monstrous Serpent on his Belly prone,
>   Reluctant, but in vain; a greater power
> Now rul'd him, punisht in the shape he sinn'd
> According to his doom: he would have spoke,
> But hiss for hiss return'd with forked tongue
> To forked tongue; for now were all transform'd
> Alike, to Serpents all, as accessories
> To his bold Riot: dreadful was the din
> Of hissing through the Hall, thick swarming now
> With complicated monsters.[26]

Among the numerous parallels between these two passages (printed in parallel in Appendix C), both pap and Satan, having just delivered speeches, discover themselves beset by swarming serpents, then collapse to writhe as snakes themselves while being tormented by the others writhing about them. Although Satan cannot speak, pap's inarticulate cries and broken sentences indicate that his agony has, like Satan's, been imposed by an external agency: "a greater power" in Satan's case and "the jug" (of spirits) in pap's. And the serpents that share this torment with Satan are, of course, themselves "devils" (see Chapter Four, Section IV-B and Chapter Five, Section XI-A).

Clemens continues playing up the hellish nature of pap's suffering by adding the passage immediately following these parallels to Milton:

> Then he laid stiller, and didn't make a sound. I could hear the owls and wolves away off in the woods, and it seemed terrible still. He was laying over by the corner. By and by he raised up part way and listened, with his head to one side. He says, very low:
>
> "Tramp—tramp—tramp; that's the dead; tramp—tramp—tramp; they're coming after me; but I won't go. Oh, they're here! Don't touch me—don't! hands off—they're cold; let go—Oh, let a poor devil alone!"
>
> Then he went down on all fours and crawled off, begging them to let him alone, and he rolled himself up in his blanket and wallowed in under the old pine table, still a-begging; and then he went to crying. I could hear him through the blanket.

In addition to pap's being tormented by "devils," Huck's hearing owls and wolves (harbingers of death) in the distance and pap hearing the "tramp—tramp—tramp" of the dead coming for him emphasize that this entire scene is set in Hell, and this phase of his agony ends with pap's crying: "Oh, let a poor devil alone!" as his torment continues.

V-B. Of Satan's Blade and Death's Dart

Clemens continues his barely covert account of hell as pap enters a new phase of his agony:

> By and by he rolled out and jumped up on his feet looking wild, and he see me and went for me. He chased me round and round the place with a clasp-knife, calling me the Angel of Death, and saying he would kill me, and then I couldn't come for him no more. I begged, and told him I was only Huck; but he laughed *such* a screechy laugh, and roared and cussed, and kept on chasing me up. Once when I turned short and dodged under his arm he made a grab and got me by the jacket between my shoulders, and I thought I was gone; but I slid out of the jacket quick as lightning and saved myself. Pretty soon he was all tired out, and dropped down with his back against the door, and said he would rest a minute and then kill me. He put his knife under him, and said he would sleep and get strong, and then he would see who was who.
>
> So he dozed off pretty soon. By and by I got the old split-bottom chair and clumb

up as easy as I could, not to make any noise, and got down the gun. I slipped the ramrod down to make sure it was loaded, and then I laid it across the turnip barrel, pointing towards pap, and set down behind it to wait for him to stir. And how slow and still the time did drag along. (end Chapter VI)

When Satan arrives at the gate of Hell in *Paradise Lost*, he challenges its guardian[27]:

> Whence and what are thou, execrable shape,
> That dar'st, though grim and terrible, advance
> Thy miscreated Front athwart my way
> To yonder Gates? through them I mean to pass,
> That be assured, without leave askt of thee:
> Retire, or taste thy folly, and learn by proof,
> Hell-born, not to contend with Spirits of Heav'n.[28]

> Each at the head
> Level'd his deadly aim; thir fatal hands
> No second stroke intend.[29]

> So frown'd the mighty Combatants, that Hell
> Grew darker at thir frown; so matcht they stood;
> For never but once more was either like
> To meet so great a foe.[30]

These terrible combatants, however, never come to blows:

> and now great deeds
> Had been achiev'd, whereof all Hell had rung,
> Had not the Snaky Sorceress that sat
> Fast by Hell-Gate and kept the fatal Key
> Ris'n, and with hideous outcry rush'd between.
> O Father, what intends thy hand,
> Against thy only son? What fury, O Son,
> Possesses thee to bend that mortal Dart
> Against thy Father's head?[31]

This "Snaky Sorceress" turns out to be Sin, Satan's daughter. The "execrable Shape" is Death, Satan's only begotten son (by Sin).[32] Sin warns Satan of Death's power:

> But thou O Father, I forewarn thee, shun
> His deadly arrow; neither vainly hope
> To be invulnerable in those bright Arms,
> Though temper'd heav'nly, for that mortal dint,
> Save he who reigns above, none can resist.[33]

In both the novel and the epic poem, then, Satan, failing to recognize his only son, faces the Death Angel at the gate of Hell intending mortal combat. In neither episode is a blow struck, and both end with the Death

Angel armed with a weapon superior to Satan's blade. Huck's making sure the gun is loaded underscores his intent to kill pap if he has to. And his use of the ramrod instead of—or in addition to—a ball as the load in the gun—a detail that is usually misread as Huck's checking to make sure there is a ball in the barrel of the gun—renders his weapon a "dart" superior to pap's blade.

To Christian sensibilities, pap's character appears simply demonic, but by painting Huck's father's portrait with the intermingled features of both God and Satan, the implied author combines them and thereby negates the moral polarity of Christian cosmology in the novel. In addition, pap's three-personed identity as God, man, and Satan, contrary to Cox's reading, *defines* the archetypal ground on which the action of the novel takes place; this ground, however, is not merely "the garden of innocence"; it is the entire Judeo-Christian cosmos. Clemens' portrait of pap exposes a "jealous God" obsessed with his own power, a man who would murder his own son in an alcoholic rage, and a Satan with just one virtue: the "terrible energy" Clemens admired in the Miltonic fiend.

There is no evidence in the text, however, that Mark Twain conceives of or comprehends this archetypal development; it takes place solely on the level of "THE AUTHOR." Through pap, Clemens superimposes on Huck identities which connect him to the three hierarchies of this religious cosmos: Heaven, Earth, and Hell, thereby identifying Huck with Christ, Adam, and the Angel of Death. By this conflation of archetypes, Clemens symbolically bestows upon Huck the capacity to become morally autonomous. But for Huck to achieve this birthright, he must first grow into something more, archetypally speaking, than *Tom Sawyer's Comrade* (the subtitle of the novel). He must become an adult in order to fulfill his heroic potential. As becomes clear in Chapter Five of this study, Huck's attainment of adulthood is what the climax of the novel is about.

VI. Of Pap, Abraham, Isaac and Huck

There is another dimension of religious satire implicit in Clemens' construction of this episode in which a father attempts to kill his son with a knife, for this motif also parallels the account in Genesis of God's demand that Abraham, the founding patriarch of "His chosen people," sacrifice his only son in a ritual of obedience to demonstrate his complete submission to God's will. Not only does Clemens parallel the willingness of Abraham to slay his only son with a knife, but both episodes lead to an animal sacrifice in the boy's stead: Huck's slaying the hog in the next chapter (VII), and Abraham's sacrifice of the ram he finds at the scene.[34]

Just as the motive and the means are important aspects in the investigation of any homicide, in both stories only the lack of opportunity prevents the would-be slayer from committing the deed. Yes, in the biblical account God calls off the sacrifice as Abraham is about to fulfill his command, and in a related incident the true mother of the infant judged by Solomon reveals herself in response to his judgment, but, as in Jim's treatment of the legend of Solomon in Chapter XIV, where he lambastes that king for his callousness toward the disputed infant, it is the cruel *ideas* of filicide and infanticide rather than the deeds themselves that Clemens' treatment of these episodes from the Bible deplores as threatened acts of insanity (see Chapter Three, Section XIV).

By casting pap as Abraham, willing to sacrifice his son Isaac (Huck) with his knife, Clemens for the first time in the narrative burlesques a biblical story that represents to Clemens the deity's disregard for the lives of children. Imagine Isaac's horror, terror, and confusion as Abraham binds him and lays him on the sacrificial pyre and bares his knife, not impersonally like pap in the throes of *delirium tremens*, which is horrible enough, but with tragic self-awareness and moral clarity that one might call *delirium religions*. Isaac's close call adds a dimension to Clemens' allusions as Huck faces off with pap.

Furthermore, in order to appreciate the fullness of Clemens' religious satire in this passage, it is important to remember that Abraham's willingness to sacrifice his only begotten son prefigures what Clemens came to regard as a theological absurdity: the crucifixion of Christ. Thus while pap as Satan in this scene is in conflict with his son the Death Angel, and pap as Abraham is about to kill his son Isaac, pap as God acts in parallel with the New Testament account of the crucifixion in which, as recorded in St. John 3: 16, God does sacrifice "his only begotten Son" in a living ritual of atonement for the sins of Adam and Eve.

As is often the case in Clemens' masking of his biblical sources for events of the plot, conflation of the source texts serves to blur their outlines. Just as "pap as God" might appear to contradict "pap as Satan" and/or "pap as Abraham" within the same passage, the momentary resonance of pap's attempted murder of Huck with these other well-known episodes of religious lore helps to conceal what it at the same time reveals: Clemens' abhorrence of the biblical God. Alluding to these examples of what he saw as divine callousness toward the lives of only sons must have been especially poignant for Clemens since the death of his own infant son—for which he blamed his own negligence—in 1872.[35]

VII. The Multivalent Irony of Huck's "Great Escape"

In fear for his freedom and his very life, Huck flees the world created in the first six chapters of the novel. For Huck, of course, his get-away is a practical plan, "some way to keep pap and the widow from trying to follow me" (Chapter VII). As Earl F. Briden has shown, Clemens informs Huck's escape plan with folkloric elements of magic and ritual found in the Mississippi Valley in the early 1800s.[36] In addition there are the biblical allusions to the legend of Moses that Collins and Briden have found in the passage. These parallels transform Huck's plot into a covert re-enactment of both Passover and, since Huck stages his own murder and flees for his life, Moses' flight from Egypt after killing an Egyptian slave driver who was beating a Hebrew slave.[37]

Briden's explication of the parallels that link Chapter VII of the novel with the Passover story finds that Huck's escape re-enacts the final plague of the death of the firstborn that led to Pharaoh's decision to release the Hebrews from slavery in Egypt. Parallel elements in these two stories include Huck's fleeing captivity and setting out on "his own liberation drama" and "like Moses making his passage by water" to the wilderness; pap's drunken confusion in mistaking Huck for the Death Angel echoes Exodus 12, in which "God and the Destroyer pass over Egypt, slaying the captors' first-born children and sparing the ritually secured Israelites." Two elements form the keystone of Briden's analogy: "the slaughter of the symbolic pig," which Huck lays bleeding on the cabin floor—providing a clue that he has been murdered—"and Huck's stripping the cabin of 'everything that was worth a cent.'"

In the Bible story, the origin of Passover "likewise has its ritual center in animal sacrifice" and blood smeared about a dwelling. Escaping pap, Huck saves his own life by "losing it," and he wins his freedom "by ritually shedding and distributing the blood of his animal sacrifice." God instructs Moses to tell his Hebrews as they depart from Egypt: "Let every man borrow of his neighbor, and every woman of her neighbor, jewels of silver and jewels of gold." "As a consequence," Briden observes, in departing "they spoiled the Egyptians ... just as Huck despoils Pap."[38] Briden finds that Huck's situation parallels that of Moses not only in these details, but also in the broader frame of reference in which "the Passover rite meant not only the deliverance of his people and himself, but also death to the captor."[39] Moses' escape also begins a long spiritual quest, as does Huck's as he sets out on his own overtly picaresque journey.

The only points to which I take exception in Briden's analysis are his assertions that spoiling the Egyptians is Moses' idea—for Moses merely relays God's instructions to his people[40]—and that pap functions as the Death Angel, whom Huck represents consistently in Chapters VI and VII. In relation to Huck in this re-enactment of the Passover myth, pap retains his standing as the Principal, as he does symbolically throughout the story. Even pap's death, to which the reader is an unwitting witness in Chapter IX, appears to be an indirect consequence of Huck's "magic" in Chapter VII, for Huck's "murder" and disappearance begin the causal chain that leads to pap's murder.

It is also important to notice in this context that Clemens has once again alluded to a biblical example of God's disregard for the lives of children—in this case again—specifically:

> 12 [b] all the first-born in the land of Egypt, both man and beast;
> 29 [b] from the first-born of Pharaoh that sat on his throne unto the first-born of the captive that was in the dungeon; and all the first-born of cattle.
> 30 And Pharaoh rose up in the night, he, and all his servants, and all the Egyptians; and there was a great cry in Egypt; for there was not a house where there was not one dead."[41]

The biblical context of these verses does explain God's rationale for holding the lives of all the Egyptian first-born forfeit due to Pharaoh's refusal to let Moses and his people go, and Clemens' allusions may force one to wonder: What could be the reason for God's callousness towards these babes, innocents (since no one but Pharaoh had any say in the matter), and even the cattle? The Lord explains to Moses:

> 9 And the LORD said unto Moses, Pharaoh shall not hearken unto you; that my wonders may be multiplied in the land of Egypt.
> 10 [b] and the LORD hardened Pharaoh's heart, so that he would not let the children of Israel go out of his land.

Verse 31 informs the reader that after this atrocity, Pharaoh is convinced that his best policy for ridding Egypt of the horrors visited upon him and his people by the Hebrews' God is to let them go:

> 31 And he called for Moses and Aaron by night, and said, Rise up, and get you from among my people, both ye and the children of Israel; and go, serve the LORD, as ye have said.
> 32 Also take your flocks and your herds, as ye have said, and be gone; and bless me also.
> 33 And the Egyptians were urgent upon the people, that they might send them out of the land in haste; for they said, We be all dead men.

But in Chapter 14, God tells Moses again:

> 4 And I will harden Pharaoh's heart, that he shall follow after them; and I will be honored upon Pharaoh, and upon all his host; that the Egyptians may know that I am the LORD. And they did so.

Clemens evidently found this more of a self-indictment than a justification for atrocities that would make any person in the world today a candidate for prosecution for crimes against humanity. Not for the last time in the novel, Clemens gives the reader an example of the biblical God's fondness for mass-slayings of the innocent to punish the "guilty," and the testimony of the LORD himself expunges Pharaoh's own guilt, so in Clemens' view there is only one party left to blame for the barbarities recorded in Exodus: the AUTHOR of the Book.

In regard to its psychological realism, Kenneth Lynn has shown how Huck's slaying a hog that he subconsciously identifies with his father is the truest expression of his relationship with pap[42]; this symbolic act, as we have seen in light of the hog's symbolic identification through pap with the Old Testament God (see Chapter Three, Section III), is also a ritual deicide that frees Huck, temporarily, from the mythic forces brought into play in the opening six chapters (an echo of the six days of creation in Genesis, making this a Sabbath ritual).

Simultaneously, Huck's ritual patricide/deicide is a ritual suicide in which the blood of an animal is shed not only instead of his father's, but also instead of his own. Huck's holding the hog against his breast and mingling his own hair with the beast's blood suggest this identity transfer. As a ritual suicide, Huck's escape bears yet closer examination, for the identity he transfers to the hog he has slain is not only literal but also symbolic; as such this identity transfer takes place on the mythic level of the implied author where Huck may be viewed as his own exorcist ritually repudiating the mythological heritage in which he has been implicated as both Adam and Isaac and the sons of both God and Satan.

In addition, it is worth noting at this point that Huck's escape also parallels the escape of the young child Jesus to Egypt to avoid Herod's attempt to kill him,[43] a parallel reinforced when Clemens again alludes to the passage in St. Matthew that tells this story (Chapter XVII; see Chapter Three, Section XVIII). Collins' discussion of the ways in which the entire novel casts the shore society as Egypt in archetypal terms complements this motif, completes Huck's triune identity in this passage as the young child Jesus as well as a Moses figure, the Death Angel, and the human son of pap. Thus the innocent Huckleberry Finn escapes the mythological cosmos of Judeo-Christianity into an anarchic state (Chaos) in which he can begin to form his own values.

Clemens' tripartite management of viewpoints provides the structure that "preserves the unities" of this multivalent complex of meanings. For the implied narrator, Mark Twain, matters of realism, characterization, and perhaps even the sort of Bible-thumping critics often detect in Twain's allusions to Scripture are concerns. It is necessary here to keep in mind that for Huck, this is all just a practical plan and a natural process. He ascribes no symbolic dimension to this sequence of events, and Clemens leaves it completely up to the reader to assemble all his "covert hints" into a coherent design that makes sense of Mark Twain's narrative and Huck's story.

VIII. Escape into Chaos

Ritually cleansed, Huck falls asleep in his canoe. On awakening he finds himself disoriented in an altered reality where space and time seem expanded:

> When I woke up I didn't know where I was for a minute. I set up and looked around, a little scared. Then I remembered. The river looked miles and miles across. The moon was so bright I could 'a' counted the drift logs that went slipping along, black and still, hundreds of yards out from shore.
> [...]
> I heard one man say it was about three o'clock and he hoped daylight wouldn't wait more than about a week longer.

When Satan escapes from Hell and sets out to cross Chaos, Milton makes clear in Book II that God does not govern this realm:

> a dark
> Illimitable Ocean without bound,
> Without dimension, where length, breadth, and highth
> And time and place are lost, where eldest *Night*
> And *Chaos*, Ancestors of Nature, hold
> Eternal Anarchy.[44]

The first association of the Mississippi with Chaos occurs when Clemens parallels pap's journey up the river to that of Satan across Milton's "desolate abyss" (see Chapter Three, Section IV: A). The dark water imagery and distortions of time and distance in both texts suggest that the great river represents Chaos. Both Satan and Huck experience disorientation upon entering this realm, as the passage above shows in Huck's case and the following in Satan's, as he encounters

> "A vast vacuity. All unawares,
> Flutt'ring his pennons vain, plumb-down he drops

> Ten thousand fadom deep, and to this hour
> Down had been falling, had not by ill chance,
> The strong rebuff of some tumultuous cloud
> Instinct with Fire and Nitre hurried him
> As many miles aloft.[45]

Both passages also follow closely upon the confrontation between Satan and the Death Angel, a relationship reasserted briefly in the novel as pap returns and passes by Huck's canoe "so close I could a reached out the gun and touched him" or shot him, as Huck's choice of implements reiterates that he is prepared to do. But Huck, significantly, is now invisible to pap, and he will remain so to the entire community on Jackson's Island the following day.

Furthermore, Milton writes of Chaos, "Chance governs all"[46]; at the mercy of chance, or "luck," Huck and Jim drift, rather than flee, toward the Phelps farm. As observed above, Clemens parallels pap's ascent from "down the river" to Satan's from Hell through Chaos, and, in Huck's steamboat vernacular, likens the wrecked spare room at the new judge's house to a river crossing to express the chaos that pap had wrought there—*Chaos* indeed. Moreover, when pap tells Huck that he heard about Huck's wealth "away down the river" (hell in the cosmos according to Sam Clemens; see Chapter Three, Section IV-A), this resonance also supports the idea that the river represents Chaos. Considering the river's similarity to Milton's Chaos in these passages, and keeping in mind the emergent pattern of mythological displacement in the novel, one can see that the implied author equates the river with Chaos from the point of pap's advent in St. Petersburg. He continues to do so throughout the novel (see Chapter Four, Section XXI).

Huck's expanded experience of time and space in the above passage occurs within doubled parentheses of sleep and death. His night journey takes him from his awakening in "dead quiet" to his landing on Jackson's Island in "dead water"; there he lies down for "a nap before breakfast" (and with this comment, the seventh chapter ends). As long as Huck abides in Chaos, he remains in a state of moral/archetypal non-being that necessitates his adoption of a new identity at every stage of his journey. James Cox observes of the pattern of death and rebirth in the novel that Huck is "dead" throughout the journey down-river and that he is "reborn" at every turn of the river.[47] More precisely, Huck returns to the womb-like security of Chaos (morally speaking)—where he is able to postpone taking moral responsibility for his actions indefinitely—whenever his renewed involvements in society become too threatening.

IX. Jackson's Island: New Eden for the American Adams

At the opening of Chapter VIII, Huck awakens from his death/sleep, like Adam on the sixth day of creation, in a paradisiacal setting:

> I laid there in the grass and the cool shade thinking about things, and feeling rested and ruther comfortable and satisfied. I could see the sun out at one or two holes, but mostly it was big trees all about, and gloomy in there amongst them. There was freckled places on the ground where the light sifted down through the leaves, and the freckled places swapped about a little, showing there was a little breeze up there. A couple of squirrels set on a limb and jabbered at me very friendly.
> I was powerful lazy and comfortable.

Compare the following passage from Milton's epic, where Adam recounts his own first awakening in Eden to the Angel Raphael:

> As new-waked from soundest sleep,
> Soft on the flowery herb I found me laid
> [...]
> Straight toward Heaven my wond'ring Eyes I turned,
> And gaz'd a while the ample Sky,
> [...] about me round I saw
> Hill, Dale, and shady Woods, and sunny Plains,
> And liquid Lapse of murmuring Streams; by these,
> Creatures that liv'd and mov'd, and walk'd or flew,
> Birds on the branches warbling: all things smil'd;
> With fragrance and with joy my heart o'erflow'd.[48]

The similarities between these two passages are so striking that they require no comment beyond the suggestion that Clemens is reasserting Huck's identification with Adam (see Chapter Three, Section III and Appendix D)—but this time the *unfallen* one.

Huck watches from hiding as the ferryboat searching for his corpse passes by the island with all his social and mythical relations aboard: "Pap, and Judge Thatcher, and Bessie Thatcher, and Jo Harper, and Tom Sawyer, and his old Aunt Polly, and Sid and Mary, and plenty more. Everybody was talking about the murder." For them he is dead, and Huck finds himself alone in his sylvan paradise in freedom like Adam's before the creation of Eve: "I was boss of it; it all belonged to me." Soon, like Adam again, Huck feels "lonesome."[49]

In his exploration of the island he discovers another camp in the woods. Huck's first reaction is fear, and in its description Clemens parallels the creation of Eve from Adam's rib[50]: "it made me feel like a person had cut one of my breaths in two and I only got half, and the short half, too." Of course, the imbedded ironic comment on relations between man and woman only becomes humorous when one appreciates that Clemens is alluding to the creation of the first woman in this passage. Huck soon learns that the camp belongs to Jim, Miss Watson's slave: "I was ever so glad to see Jim. I warn't lonesome now." Thus both Huck and Adam soon bond with companions in their "garden of innocence."

X. "What Comes of Handlin' Snake-Skin"

At first Huck and Jim live in peace on Jackson's Island, until Huck unwittingly and then knowingly violates Jim's superstitious code. The action and the bad luck incurred parallel the biblical account of Original Sin: Huck handles a snakeskin, Jim warns him not to, Huck does it again with the snake he has killed, and judgment follows (Chapter X); God warns Adam and Eve not to eat the fruit of the Tree of Knowledge, Eve is tempted by a serpent to eat the forbidden fruit, eats it and shares it with Adam, and judgment follows. Jim's being bitten on the heel by the rattlesnake and Huck's chopping off its head parallel God's curses upon the serpent and the man: "it shall bruise thy head and thou shalt bruise his heel."[51]

After Jim recovers he says "that handling a snake-skin was such awful bad luck that maybe we hadn't come to the end of it yet." Indeed, the pair again and again blame Huck's mistake for their later misfortunes on the river. After they pass Cairo in the fog and after they lose their canoe, with which they had planned to return up-river, they blame the snakeskin. Later in Chapter XVI (titled "The Rattlesnake-Skin Does Its Work"; see Appendix A) Huck breaks his narration to inform the reader: "Anybody that don't believe yet that it's foolishness to handle a snake-skin, after all that snake-skin done for us, will believe it now, if they read on and see what more it done for us."

For Huck, true to Clemens' management of point of view and literary archetype, this statement is simply a reiteration of his faith in his superstitions, not in any way symbolic. However, Huck and Jim thus blame every misfortune of the raft-journey on Huck's violation of superstition in Chapter X, and that act—along with its consequences—in context parallels the Eden myth and the Doctrine of Total Depravity, an association repeated over and over again in the novel's many references to snakes (see Chapter Five, Section XI-A).

XI. Of Huck, Eve, Adam and Jim

In this episode of the Jackson's Island sequence, Huck's role as the bringer of the curse that results in Jim's being bitten by a rattlesnake and the ensuing misfortunes they experience parallels the role of Eve in the story of the Fall. Like Eve, Huck has not been warned that consorting with serpents (or their vacant skins) is bad luck. Nor does he intentionally cause Jim harm, just as neither Adam nor Eve, in Clemens' view, meant any harm by their transgression of the sole "thou shalt not" in Eden. In Chapter XI of the novel, immediately after the narrative informs us of Huck's violation of superstition and subsequent Tom Sawyer-esque practical joke that results in Jim's injury, Huck puts on a feminine disguise and goes on a spy mission to find out what is going on back in St. Petersburg. His adopting a female persona—the only time in the opening and middle sections of the novel he does so—emphasizes his role as the female actor in the myth that the tenth chapter re-enacts (see Chapter Five, Section XI).

Also in this episode, Jim plays the role of Adam. Previously, in Chapter IX, we have seen the pair of fugitives reenact the legend in which the sons of Noah receive his blessings and curses, making Jim and Huck symbolic brothers. Here in Chapter X we see them portrayed as twin Adams, making both of them types of the new breed of human being called in our national mythology the American Adam. As Henry Nash Smith has written: "According to this powerful cultural image, the Europeans who crossed the Atlantic to settle the North American continent abandoned the complex culture of the Old World, summed up in its written records, in order to make a completely fresh beginning in the New World."[52] By including an African American within this myth Clemens expands it to include Americans of all races, and he reiterates the brotherly bond between them that Tom Quirk has pointed out.[53]

XII. The Curse of the Rattlesnake-Skin and the Depravity Doctrine

Clemens, be it recalled, believed the central feature of the story of the Fall to be "an unsurpassed act of absurd cruelty" on the part of the Creator, since never having seen an example of death, Adam and Eve could not possibly understand the penalty they called down on themselves by their transgression.[54] In the following exchange between Huck and Jim, Jim's forgiving Huck echoes Clemens' judgment that the biblical account of the Fall is the prime example of divine injustice:

> I begun to suspicion something. So did Jim.
> I says:
> > "Maybe we went by Cairo in the fog that night."

He says:

"Doan le's talk about it, Huck. Po' niggers can't have no luck. I awluz 'spected dat rattlesnake-skin warn't done wid its work."

"I wish I'd never seen that snake-skin, Jim—I do wish I'd never laid eyes on it."

"It ain't yo' fault, Huck; you didn' know. Don't you blame yo'self 'bout it" [Chapter XVI].

Jim's forgiving Huck in this passage contrasts with God's cursing Adam, Eve, and even the unwittingly offending serpent in Genesis, which Milton regards as a mere vehicle for the Tempter; yet God curses it anyway.

In the eleventh chapter's final parallel to the Eden myth, Huck sets a decoy-fire on his old camp-site to delay their pursuers. In Genesis 3 God banishes Adam and Eve from the Garden of Eden and places "at the east ... a flaming sword which turned every way."[55] Then the two fugitives take to the raft and slip away in "dead stillness," and the newborn Adams withdraw into Chaos (see Chapter Three, Section VIII).

Huck's and Jim's re-enactment of the Eden myth in the Jackson's Island sequence is a new beginning that leaves them free of the Doctrine of Total Depravity, for Huck's ritual suicide/patricide/deicide in Chapter VII has lifted him out of the religious matrix that condemns humankind in Christian theology. Jim, as a primitive man, is not burdened with a Puritan conscience, and his morality is heart-centered, but Huck remains a child, and he is subject to the censure of his socially imprinted conscience, the collective voice of the community in himself. Not until he frees himself from this psychological bondage—this curse—can he become one whose decisions and acts are not subject to rationalization or moral justification. "Ultimate salvation" in Samuel Clemens' thinking on theology and morality, "is to be set free of the consequences of the fall and to become a god."[56]

Clemens continues to parallel the Eden myth in the milder curse to which Huck and Jim remain subject; bad luck dogs them all the way down the river. This curse is a modulated echo of the depravity doctrine, however, for while it dooms the fugitives' flight to futility from the outset, it inflicts no moral blight; rather, it necessitates growth in Huck. Significantly, their luck changes and the raft-journey ends after Huck decides, "forever," to turn his back on conscience and morality.

XIII. Of Huck's and Jim's Alliance

Chapter VII records Huck's escape from pap and the fictive universe thus far created in the text into Chaos, the amoral realm where he takes refuge whenever the stresses of civilization become intolerable. His sojourn in nature on Jackson's Island reveals his need of companionship, and he finds it in his island Eden in the person of Jim, introduced earlier in Chapters II and IV as a comic "darkey" (as seen through Huck's and Mark Twain's eyes). By now readers know that Huck's limitations distort his perceptions in ways that make his version of the facts unreliable as gauges of the motives and conduct of the adults he encounters. When Huck discovers that he shares the island with Jim, he is delighted: "I warn't lonesome now."

Chapter VIII (half way through which Clemens pigeonholed the manuscript) begins with parallels to *Paradise Lost* that identify Jackson's Island as a natural Eden. Huck and Jim can abide there as twin Adams only as long as the evil racism of the shore does not intrude. Each also plays the role of Eve in the myth: Jim when Clemens parallels the creation of Eve in Huck's discovery of his camp; and Huck when he unwittingly violates Jim's superstition about handling a snakeskin. With Huck's disrespectful practical joke that almost gets Jim killed, this evil does intrude because Huck embodies it, and the curse of the snakeskin dooms their idyll in another parallel to the Eden myth.

Victor Doyno illustrates the care Clemens devoted to refining his rendering of Jim's dialect voice as he recounts his initial flight from slavery in St. Petersburg. There are nine changes on the manuscript page, all of which clarify Jim's pronunciation. The most notable are Clemens' replacements of "whah" for "where," "arter" for "after," "mo' en" for "more'n" (meaning "more than"), and "yuther" for "other."[57] This immersion of the author's mind in Jim's language reflects his increasing interest in Jim's character.[58] In this, the reader's third view of him, he ceases to play the role of the "comic 'darkey'" that has veiled his character previously, and Jim begins to emerge as a person.

At this point in the Jackson's Island sequence, the pattern of mythological displacement has already placed the action in a natural Eden in which Huck has played the role of Adam, and Jim briefly functions as Eve. It would be an error to regard this association as the authorial suggestion of a homo-erotic bond, as Leslie Fiedler has been inclined to do,[59] and readers would be ill-advised to read this in, since it is doubtful Clemens conceived of Jim as a pedophile; rather, this attribution of the feminine role to Jim suggests his potential as a nurturer to the motherless boy as well as the bringer of temptation/Eve to Huck/Adam as he involves Huck in his "immoral" flight to freedom.

Clemens' characterization of Jim shows "his intelligence and resourcefulness," as he anticipates the use of dogs to track him and finds a way to frustrate pursuit by taking to the river; "it's interesting," observes Doyno, "that Twain seems to have first realized the advantages of untraceable raft travel while looking at the world from Jim's point of view.⁶⁰

Chapter IX, the first half of which concludes the 1876 portion of the manuscript, recounts Huck's and Jim's move to a cave on high ground, the "June rise" flood, and the adventure of the floating house, in which Jim identifies pap's body and decides to keep pap's death a secret from Huck. Not coincidentally, it is also at this point in Huck's narrative that Clemens casts the pair as the sons of Noah re-enacting the Bible story seen in the churches of the slaveholders as the cornerstone of the biblical foundation of slavery. His inclusion of this allusion also signals that the brotherly relationship between Huck and Jim is one that has the potential to transcend race in the developing characters of his twin American Adams, and this new beginning makes this allusion to the story of Noah especially appropriate here.

However, the passage resonates with the Bible story of Noah in ways that are uncomplimentary both to the patriarch and to the "sivilization" he founded, commenting sarcastically on the character of the patriarch Noah by pointing out that both Noah and pap Finn are prone to drunkenness and wrathful outbursts. The fact that pap is a corpse at this point suggests that this ancient story has no innate force, but only the vitality lent to it by "superstition" (see Chapter Two, Section VIII).

XIV. Of Huck, Jim and "Sollermun"

The difference between Kenneth Lynn's and Daniel Barnes's perceptions of the significance of the same biblical parallel, as discussed earlier (see Chapter Two, Section I), has far-reaching implications. Lynn, together with the critics who have extended his work, tends much more than Barnes to see such parallels as Bible-thumping on Mark Twain's part. Thus, when Huck and Jim dispute Solomon's wisdom,

> the parenthood problem, like the liberation theme, has been given a deeper moral seriousness through a Biblical association[. ...] The scene is a vital element in the moral pattern of the novel. For Huck, like Solomon, is listening for the voice of truth and the accents of love as a means of identifying the true parent he seeks.⁶¹

This biblical resonance, however, is not without irony. Besides introducing Mark Twain's well-known naturalistic views on the influence of training on individual development and providing a biblical association that gives "the parenthood problem ... a deeper moral seriousness," Chapter XIV presents a biblical analog for the novel's splitting a child in two—albeit only along moral lines—to reveal the ways in which Huck's deformed conscience obstructs the impulses of his sound heart.

When Huck asserts that "you can't learn a nigger to argue," his bigoted question-begging serves to emphasize the merits of Jim's interpretation and the extent to which prejudice—not only racial but intellectual also—prevents the implied reader from recognizing that "de real p'int" of the story of Solomon's wisdom is that king's remarkable callousness toward the life of the infant involved (see Chapter Three, Sections VI, VII and XVI) and the extent to which that insensitivity is—as Jim says—a function of Solomon's upbringing (in the house of King David, his father).

Critics have often read this passage as another instance like the wooden leg joke of Chapter IX where the author is merely exposing both of his heroes to readers' affectionate ridicule by playing on their ignorance. Walter Blair, for instance, dismisses its thematic importance with the comment that "the interlude is minstrel-show stuff which does little to develop the book's theme."[62] On the contrary, this explicit allusion to the legend of Solomon elaborates several themes and shows how Clemens could wield minstrel show humor to serious moral purposes.

Of course, the vernacular text does require us to regard both sides of the dispute as humorous distortions, but Huck's lame defense of Solomon nevertheless serves to emphasize that his *socialization* at the widow's has caused him to shift from taking "no stock in dead people" to taking a lively interest in Solomon. Jim's emphasis on Solomon's inhumanity as a function of training brings Huck's own background into clearer focus. On the one hand his culturally imprinted insensitivity to the plight of the slaves parallels Solomon's alleged attitude toward the infant in the Bible story. His association with Jim, on the other hand, countervails this influence, contributes to his moral growth, and moves him finally to repudiate his conscience in his decision to "*go* to hell" to save Jim.

Thus Clemens uses a biblical analog near the outset of the middle section to introduce an element of literary satire into Huck's narrative, biblical satire strengthened for Victorian readers by Jim's likening Solomon's harem to a "bod'n house," or brothel, as his metaphor hints. There is an even darker side to this metaphor: Hearn points out that it does not occur to Huck that many plantation owners in the South treated their female slaves like harems, and the widespread rape of African American women by their masters is an additional evil of "the peculiar institution" that Clemens subtly suggests (see Chapter Five, Section VII).[63]

This interlude parallels the Bible text to which it broadly alludes in more ways that enhance its seriousness than the one that Lynn and his followers have noticed. Huck's failure to defend Solomon's methods reminds one not only that he is a boy who has been without any mother-love and so cannot refute Jim's unorthodox interpretation of the story, but also, as Hearn notes, that his recent predicament as the object of a custody fight between pap and the Widow Douglas has put him in the same situation as the infant in the Bible story.[64]

The fact that Jim, as a loving father, could never have conceived of Solomon's method for mediating the dispute between the two women buttresses Jim's unorthodox argument. This treatment of the legend serves to emphasize that Huck's socialization has moved him toward an orthodoxy that his relationship with Jim challenges and eventually obliterates. As Hearn also notes, this apparently gratuitous episode emphasizes Twain's point that authentic morality comes only from attending to inner knowing, as Jim demonstrates by his self-reliance in this episode, never from conformity to the external authority of socially imprinted cultural norms, from which Huck argues ineffectually.[65] In this respect, the humor of this episode in Chapter XIV masks its serious implications, not the least of which is to emphasize Huck's orthodox bigotry as a background for his humiliation in Chapter XV, where he commits the social sin of humbling himself "to a nigger." Only against this background can the reader appreciate Huck's contrition as *a* moral turning point in his troubled alliance with Jim.[66] But it is not *the* turning point. Huck remains deeply conflicted about Jim's flight until Chapter XXXI.

Thus the narrative moves from the impenetrable ambiguity of the implied author's initial attitude toward his protagonist and orthodox Christianity in Chapters I–III (see Chapter One, Section III) toward open hostility that associates orthodoxy with bigotry in Huck and warm-hearted humanity with skepticism and a decidedly anti-biblical stance on Jim's part. In other words, "THE AUTHOR" is winning his implicit argument with the implied narrator, Mark Twain, who, in contrast to Clemens, has been using "biblical authority" to ground Huck's adventures in conventional moralism.

As the story continues, the overt religious satire focuses on the particular form of Christianity Miss Watson calls, as Manierre emphasizes, "religion." This religion, the self-righteous and morally rotten branch of Christianity that used scripture to justify slavery, was a respectable satirical target for Mark Twain to chop at nearly twenty years after the Civil War, and, as numerous critics have observed, the novel's *overt* religious and social satire is aimed at antebellum, Southern, Calvinist Christianity. William Gibson, Victor Doyno, Jocelyn Chadwick-Joshua, and Andrew Levy all agree that this satire is neither so parochial nor retrospective as it appears, however; Gibson was one of the first, in 1976, to point out that Jim's imprisonment is a metaphor for the continuing denial of civil rights to the freed slaves long after their official emancipation.[67] So there is a trap for the reader inherent in Clemens' choice of targets. As Mark Twain reveals the deformity of Huck's conscience and persuades the reader to join him in reviling the corrupt form of Christianity in which Huck's conscience has been formed, the implied author sets out to show us that it is not just Miss Watson's "religion" but the Bible itself—"the brazen serpent in the wilderness"—that exerts a pernicious influence on social values.

In view of the ironic multivalence of Clemens' text, Chapter XIV can be read as both irreverent commentary on the Bible text to which it alludes directly and a morally serious association of Huck with Solomon, who, be it recalled, at the beginning of his reign preferred "an understanding heart to judge thy people" to all other gifts God might give him, and so received the "wise and understanding heart" whose insight the story of his judgment on the two women and the disputed infant illustrates.

Thematically, the implicit parallel between the young King Solomon who addressed his God as "but a little child" and Huck, a boy whose heart and conscience are on a collision course and who, at least briefly, will show that he too has acquired a "wise and understanding heart" "to discern between good and bad," as Solomon prays,[68] could hardly be more clearly drawn. The text simultaneously associates Huck with the boy king and the infant he judged, but it does so in an irreverent tone that, like the reference to Moses of Chapter I, reminds us that while Clemens can use the Bible to serious moral purpose and even show reverence for Bible stories whose teachings he found admirable, he does not take it seriously as the divinely inspired Word.

To extend Daniel Barnes' analysis, the *fact* that Huck's situation parallels I Kings is not as important as "the further ironic implications" of this biblical parallel. For the moment of judgment to which Huck's relationship with Jim forces him, the moment in which he obeys the impulse of his "wise and understanding heart" (or "sound heart," as Clemens himself later expressed it) is the moment when he rejects the dictates of his socially informed conscience and fulfills ironically his potential for judging between good and evil with the insight of Solomon and, as will be shown later, the rebelliousness of Satan.

XV. Of Huck and Jim in Conflict

In Chapter X, which recounts Huck's first practical joke on Jim and its evil consequences, Clemens continues to compound all these elements of plot, theme, and archetypes, and his manuscript shows that he did it as he wrote his first draft; his later revisions of the plot were minimal, aside from the passages he later inserted into Chapters XII and XIV, in part to further develop the novel's send-up of romantic fiction, and, of at least equal importance, to further develop its religious satire. This evidence supports the view that until the raft floats past Cairo into slave territory on both sides of the river, Clemens knew exactly what he was doing in isolating a runaway white trash racist boy with a fugitive slave on a raft adrift on the Mississippi.

The issues the pair confronts on Jackson's Island—cast in archetypal terms as Eden (see Chapter Three, Section IX)—center on the theme of racial harmony disrupted by Huck's persistent bigotry, symbolized by the curse of the rattlesnake-skin. It is superstition to be sure that Huck's handling a snakeskin is the source of all the pair's misfortunes on their journey, even as it is also superstition that leads Huck to blame himself for the consequences of his practical joke on Jim, and by extension it is also, Clemens implies, superstition that Eve's consorting with a serpent led to the Fall.

The events of this four-chapter Jackson's Island section of the story continue to expand the religious and social satire undergirding the plot with first Huck's and then Jim's identification as an Adam figure, and they show Clemens' concern with matters that occupied him throughout his life: the injustice and cruelty of a Creator who saw fit to punish the ones He created as if He were not responsible for their nature.

When Jim recovers from his snakebite, Huck goes ashore in feminine disguise (see Chapter Three, Section XI and Chapter Five, Section XI) to discover that slave hunters are bound for the island in search of Jim, and the fugitives suffer banishment from Eden (Huck's second; see Chapter Three, Section IV-A) into the anarchic realm of Chaos. The eleventh chapter appropriately concludes the opening eleven-chapter section of the novel with Huck's intuitive recognition of his bond to Jim: "They're after us!" (the first-person title of Chapter XI; see Appendix A) and Huck's setting a decoy-blaze that parallels the "flaming sword" that guards the way back into Eden in Genesis 4: 24.

The three-chapter series recounting the wrecked steamboat adventure culminates in the biting biblical satire of Jim's criticism of Solomon in Chapter XIV (most of which was interpolated into the manuscript at a late stage of composition)[69] in a passage with many ironic twists that recapitulate and tie together mythic aspects of the story thus far with its conclusion and put Jim (with Clemens) in condemnation of the monarch who conceived of cutting an infant in two to settle a custody dispute; Jim tells Huck:

"de *real* pint is down furder—its down deeper. It lays in de way Sollermun was raised. You take a man dat's got on'y one er two chillen; is dat man gwyne to be waseful o' chillen? No, he ain't; he can't 'ford it. But you take a man dat's got 'bout five million chillen runnin' roun' de house an it's diffunt. *He* as soon chop a chile in two as a cat. Dey's plenty mo'. A chile er two, mo'er less, warn't no consekens to Sollermun, dad fetch him!"

The interlude concludes with Huck, Jim having out-reasoned him twice, concluding, "I see it warn't no use wasting words—you can't learn a nigger to argue. So I quit." Huck falls back on pap's bigotry to prop up his self-esteem, and once again Clemens reminds us that Huck is a racist.

Huck's debate-defeat motivates his second abortive practical joke on Jim in XV, where he convinces Jim that their separation in fog has been a dream. Jim's famous rebuke of Huck following Huck's fooling him comprises one of Doyno's two-page selections of facsimiles from Clemens' manuscript. Here, the revision touches up the dialect and, as Doyno points out, invests Jim with "more dignity, a sharper memory, and more self-control ... and intensity."[70]

While Huck's transformation in his regard for Jim is usually seen as the pivotal moment in this exchange, it is equally important to note that this is a profound shift for Jim as well. From the outset of their alliance, Jim has been courting Huck's co-operation by every means at his disposal, but his fatherly regard for Huck—and, probably, his being fed up with Huck's recent hijinks—now move him to correct the boy.

Clemens' revision of Jim's response to Huck's punch line—"what does *these* things stand for?"—expresses Jim's mental process: After a long pause he repeats Huck's question and answers it in a tone that slaves don't take with masters: "I's gwyne to tell you." And after indirectly calling Huck white trash—another step out of "his place"—he absents himself. Jim would of course know the risk he is taking here of alienating Huck, but the effect of Jim's words is to bind Huck more strongly to Jim. And his genuine concern for Huck's welfare also reminds readers that Jim's responsibility to take care of Huck originates with his keeping pap's death a secret, presumably so that Huck wouldn't decide to go home. This scene provides another example of how hard readers have found it to perceive Clemens' development of Jim's character through the distorting window of Huck's point of view.

The low comedy of Huck's practical joke turns in part on the idea that reality is non-symbolic. Abstractions rarely occur to him. Hence when he observes that Jim has feelings, and "cares just as much about his people as white folks does for their'n," he concludes, *as he sets these incidents down on paper* (notice the shift in narrative tense from past to present): "It don't seem natural, but I reckon it's so" (Chapter XXIII). It does not occur to him to base on this observation the generalization that all people of color have the same feelings as white people have. For Huck, Jim is just an exception to the rule of white supremacy that he has been trained to believe.

Chapter XVI throws Huck's growing anxiety and ambivalence toward Jim into bold relief as the slave hunters provide Huck with the perfect opportunity to get right with his conscience and betray Jim. But he discovers he "warn't man enough" to do it and instead fools the slave hunters into thinking there is small pox aboard the raft. Shortly afterward, the fugitives discover they have passed the mouth of the Ohio River and lost their canoe. They blame the curse of the rattlesnake-skin for all their bad luck, reminding the reader that this curse echoes the Depravity Doctrine (see Chapter Three, Section XII). The chapter concludes with the wreck of the raft, the pair's separation, and Huck's arrival at the Grangerford farm. The 1876–79 portion of the manuscript concludes with Huck and Buck Grangerford talking about the feud in Chapter XVIII.[71]

Even Clemens' deletion of the famous Raftmen's Passage from this section of the story has the effect of keeping the narration focused narrowly on the developing relationship between Huck and Jim. Huck thus encounters the slave hunters almost immediately after humbling himself to Jim in the previous chapter, while the memory of it is fresh in the reader's mind as well as Huck's own. In this sense, Chapters XIV to XVI describe a power struggle between the pair in which Huck repeatedly tries to assert his superiority while Jim works to guide Huck and win his respect and support for his flight to freedom. The Raftmen's Passage had no place in this pattern of characterization, dramatic conflict, and thematic development, so Clemens transplanted it. His inclusion of it in Chapter III of *Life on the Mississippi* in 1883 as he was finishing *Huck Finn* shows that he was looking for someplace else to publish it, and he did so in a way that made it a short story that would promote advance interest in his new novel.

XVI. Of Huck and "Solomon, David and the Rest of the Sacred Brotherhood"

More recent work than Barnes', focusing on texts other than those dealing with Moses and Solomon, supports his observation that Old Testament parallels help to structure the novel (see Chapter Two, Section I). Veneta Nielson has shown that there is much in the description of Colonel Grangerford and his sons and the friendship of Huck with Buck Grangerford that recalls the Old Testament story of Saul, his son Jonathan, young David, and the prophet Samuel: "This episode is a parable," asserts Neilson, in which the feud involving Saul Grangerford reflects the feud of the biblical King Saul with the young David who succeeded him. The turning point of the story of the fall of Saul and his sons, Nielson recalls, while garbling the details of the story as it is recorded in I Samuel 15, is Saul's failure to "carry out the command of the Lord and smite the Amalek, because he remembered their kindness to Israel. He was compelled finally to slay the people, but could not kill Agag, nor the sheep, oxen, cattle, and lambs. Then Samuel himself 'hewed Agag in pieces before the Lord in Gilgal' and chose David, still a boy, instead of Saul."[72]

It was the Kenites whom Saul spared for their kindness. God's vengeance targeted the Amalekites, led by Agag, and Saul did "smite them" in response to—but not full compliance with—Samuel's command:

> 3 Now go and smite Amalek, and utterly destroy all that they have, and spare them not; but slay both man and woman, infant and suckling, ox and sheep, camel and ass.

But, contrary to "my commandments," the Lord tells Samuel, Saul did not also cause the slaughter of

> 9 ... the best of the sheep, and of the oxen, and of the fatlings, and the lambs, and all *that was* good, and would not utterly destroy them: but every thing *that was* vile and refuse, that they destroyed utterly.[73]

In other words, Saul disobediently let his force plunder the foe, and "he took Agag, the king of the Amalekites, alive." The only reason suggested in this text for sparing Agag, after Saul "utterly destroyed all the people with the edge of the sword," given at the end of the previous chapter, is Saul's practice of taking "any strong ... or valiant man unto him" to serve in his ongoing wars against the Philistines.[74] Gory details aside, both stories conclude with the deaths of Saul and his three sons and the mourning of the friend of the youngest: David's lament for Jonathan in II Samuel 1 and Huck's powerfully understated grieving for Buck at the close of Chapter XVIII.

While Nielson finds that "[t]o read the story of the feud as a parable of the biblical story ... is to glimpse the vision which overpowers Clemens' attacks on the formal stereotypes he too often misnamed religion,"[75] she observes the "savagery" of the prophet Samuel, whose God had no mercy even on innocent women and infants, and who, overcome with *delirium religions*, "hewed Agag in pieces before the Lord in Gilgal," not in the heat of battle, but in cold blood (see Chapter Three, Section VI).

Compared to the prophet Samuel, ISIS and the ayatollahs of the modern-day Middle East and their Western invaders are a liberal lot, "mild as Sunday-school," as are the leaders of Israel and Syria and Myanmar and all the contemporary perpetrators of self-righteous genocidal or internecine wars, who can thump this Bible text—or ones like it in other religions' scriptures, whatever the creed—in justification of *their* crimes, not to mention those of 19th and 20th century Christian despots and imperialistic purveyors of "holy war" around the world—whom Mark Twain branded "The Blessings Of Civilization Trust."[76] Fanaticism usually finds its justification in some scripture or another; that's why Clemens commented, "Plainly God never knew anything about human beings, or he would not have trusted the idiots with so dangerous a thing as a Bible."[77]

"But," continues Nielson—somewhat illogically, in view of the actual Samuel portrayed in the Bible—"behind the most terrible stories of the cruelty or depravity of man are the faces of their prophets who seem to have faith that something is about to improve, and that the improvement is in the basic nature of man." Her wishful projection onto Clemens of reverence for the acts of his biblical namesake provides yet another example of the tendency of archetypal critics to conflate "THE AUTHOR's" moral ideas with those of the stories to which he alludes in constructing his "parables."

There is much to recommend Nielson's suggestion that Clemens had this biblical source in mind as he composed the feud chapters, and that "his delving and dredging for timeless values sets Clemens among those who are called religious writers." Nielson's effort to discover Clemens' reverence for anything in the Bible story save the strong bond of friendship between David and Jonathan is more than a bit strained, however, not least because it is out of character for Clemens, but mainly because it is not so much *man's* cruelty and depravity to which his art directs our attention as it is the prophet Samuel's and his God's cruelty and depravity. For it was He who directed the genocide against Amalek: "man and woman, infant and suckling, oxen and sheep, camels and asses." And He directed His prophet's sword- or axe-strokes as Samuel "hewed Agag in pieces." And He required the deaths of Jonathan and the brothers of David's guiltless friend and of the army they led—as well as King Saul's death—to punish Saul for his disobedient refusal to destroy "with the edge of the sword" King Agag and his people's good livestock along with *all* of his people and the rest of their possessions. In this "land of echoes," as Andrew Levy calls modern-day America, these echoes too reverberate in the news.

In Nielson's own judgment: "The senseless paradoxes and ironies of depraved cultures, even the horrors [...] Mark Twain described in 'To the Person Sitting in Darkness,' are not more savage than Samuel in Gilgal." As long as the world reveres gods like the prophet Samuel's, Clemens' parable suggests, nothing, certainly not "the basic nature of man," is about to improve.

"Errors," concludes Nielson, "are not in the voices of prophets. Errors are in the ears of the deaf, the hearts of the unhearkening."[78] Amen.

In reply to a Brooklyn librarian's appeal to Mark Twain, Paine reports:

> When it became known that a public library in Brooklyn had banished *Huck Finn & Tom Sawyer* from the children's room, presided over by a young woman of rather severe morals [...,] one of the librarians, Asa Don Dickenson, who had vigorously voted against the decree, wrote privately of the matter. Clemens [...] replied:
>
> DEAR SIR,—I am greatly troubled by what you say. I wrote *Tom Sawyer* & *Huck Finn* for adults exclusively, & it always distresses me when I find that boys & girls have been allowed access to them. The mind that becomes soiled in youth can never be washed clean. I know this by my own experience, & and to this day I cherish an unappeasable bitterness against the unfaithful guardians of my young life, who not only permitted but compelled me to read an unexpurgated Bible through before I was 15 years old. None can do that and ever draw a clean, sweet breath again this side of the grave. Ask that young lady—she will tell you so.
>
> Most honestly do *I wish that I could say a softening word or two in defense of Huck's character since you wish it, but really, in my opinion, it is no better than those of Solomon, David, & the rest of the sacred brotherhood.*
>
> *If there is an unexpurgated* [Bible?] *in the Children's Department, won't you please help that young woman remove Tom & Huck from that questionable companionship?*
>   Sincerely yours,   S. L. CLEMENS [italics added][79]

Obviously, there is a word missing from Clemens' final paragraph after the word "unexpurgated." This missing word must be "Bible," it being the only one that makes sense in this context.

The variations between Clemens' versions of these mytho-historical stories and the Bible's throw the disgust with which the author viewed the Bible's "pernicious influence"[80] into bold relief. "How long will people's awful cruelty to one another endure?" is an implicit concern of the novel, as Nielson's analysis of the feud episode has shown. For as long, Clemens implies, as well-meaning people continue to revere scriptural archetypes for anti-social behavior. Should we exonerate the prophet because he was "only following orders"? As we shall soon see, the road to hell can be paved with intentions derived from bad preachments.

XVII. Of Cain and Abel

If we admit these parallels, how are we to avoid judging the biblical conflicts to which Collins and Nielson refer as being moral absurdities equivalent to the Shepherdson-Grangerford Feud? Hearn notes a general parallel to the story of Cain and Abel and the first murder in the Bible, but he connects the meaning of the feuding clans' names only with the long competition on the

American frontier between farmers and herders.[81] Range wars may have been in the back of Clemens' mind, but of much greater concern to him on the mythological level of the story is the conflict between the *first farmer* and the *first herder*. For some forgotten sin of Cain's, Abel's burnt offering of flesh proved more pleasing to the nostrils of the Almighty than Cain's vegetables. To the extent that the feud is a war between "regular Old Testament" families (Nielson's phrase[82]), shepherds vs. farmers, and has its origin in a lawsuit whose grounds and outcome have been forgotten—just as the specific sin that rendered Cain's sacrifice unacceptable to God has been long forgotten—Clemens burlesques this Bible story as well as those discussed above.

A significant difference between Clemens' parable and the Bible's version of this story is that in the biblical story it is the farmer who kills his herder brother, while in *Huck Finn*'s version the reverse is true: the "herders" slay the "farmers" (as in the older, Babylonian version of this myth from which Joseph Campbell traced the biblical version found in Genesis 4: 1–15),[83] and Cain, the farmer, winds up accursed and marked for his protection.

The curse on Cain is relevant to the plot of the novel, for when God condemns Cain to be "a fugitive and a vagabond ... in the earth," Cain fears for his life and protests, "every one that findeth me shall slay me," and God "set a mark upon Cain, lest any finding him should kill him."[84] Some racists claimed that the "mark of Cain" was a black skin, as Clemens likely knew, and the fact that Jim, as the innocent bearer of this mark, winds up as "a fugitive and a vagabond" in the plot of the novel sounds further biblical echoes in Clemens' redaction of this myth.

What is important is not the exclusive or exact delineation of any one biblical text, but the *resonance* of Huck's narration of the feud with three of the Old Testament myths by which the Shepherdsons and Grangerfords live and die, all of which were familiar to Samuel Clemens and his readers and all of which involve bloodshed for which Clemens imputes the blame to the biblical God.

Resonance gives the writer the ability to recall these legends and the power to enrich the text with deeper implications than its narrators know. The impact of a derivative text on the myth it dramatizes takes place at least subliminally for the reader whose imagination and world-view are structured by that myth, according to structuralism. This interaction between texts is a major factor contributing to a reader's "intuitive apprehension" (Booth, see Chapter One, Section III) of a work. This feature of Clemens' literary artistry may help us to understand why so many different contingents of American society have found this novel offensive.

XVIII. Of Saul and Rachel Grangerford

Chapter XVI ends the raft voyage for the time being and takes Huck into his sojourn with the clan headed by Saul and Rachel Grangerford. The first thing we learn about this patriarch and his wife are their given names, and we read each only once. Saul is named for King Saul, whom the prophet Samuel deposed in the Bible story alluded to in this episode, and Rachel for the bereaved mother in Jeremiah's prophecy, named in St. Matthew 2: 18:

> In Ramah was there a voice heard, lamentation and weeping, and great mourning,
> Rachel, weeping for her children,
> And would not be comforted
> Because they are not.

Clemens signals from the outset that this clan is destined for destruction. As W. R. Moses has shown, this encounter begins the next phase of Huck's tour of *The Inferno*, and in this second circle of Hell abide the violent sinners.[85] It would be interesting to observe whether these two names were added as foreshadowing in one of Twain's 1880s revisions, or if he already knew in advance of his composition of the rest of Chapter XVIII what would come of Huck's stay with them, for these names are internal evidence that Clemens knew from the time he assigned them that Rachel would mourn her children and that Saul and his sons were doomed.

XIX. Of Huck and Moses

In a further explanation for the role switch between Cain the farmer and Abel the herder, Collins, in his discussion of the significance of the names of the feuding clans, briefly parallels the feud to the triumph of Joseph the shepherd's sons (Shepherdsons, i.e., the Hebrew people) over the grangers of the Nile Valley.[86] In fact, there is more to recommend the idea that Clemens intended elements in the feud episode to parallel the Bible text Collins cites than his explication reveals. He observes that Buck's riddling allusion to Exodus marks this as an episode in which Huck, Mark Twain's "Mississippi Moses," has arrived in a house in which the law of "an eye for an eye and a tooth for a tooth" rules: "an unenlightened pre–Christian" society in which the core teachings of the New Testament have no sway"[87]—not when it comes to matters of family honor and a blood feud. Collins finds Colonel Grangerford "the arch-typical Southern Colonel" who, as the aristocratic lord of a plantation and its population of slaves, is, along with his entire family, a proper target for the re-enactment of the Passover (the second in the novel; see Chapter Three, Section VII).[88]

Collins's argument becomes yet more persuasive when one considers Mark Twain's fondness of pointing out the biblical deity's habit of punishing the guilty by slaughtering whole families—and especially first-born sons. Since the vendetta claims the lives of not just the first born, but *all* the males of Saul's household including Buck, the youngest of them, Collins concludes, "where Twain's Moses passes, severe judgment indeed falls upon the Egyptians."[89]

Collins's case could be further reinforced by recalling that Colonel Grangerford's patrician status links him with the aristocratic Widow Douglas, who, as Barnes points out, identifies herself with Pharaoh's compassionate daughter who adopted the infant Moses, when the widow selects Moses in the ark of bulrushes as the text for Huck's first household devotional lesson in Chapter I (see Appendix A, Chapter Two, Section II, and Chapter Five, Section IV). Huck's last sight of Buck Grangerford and his cousin resonates structurally with the Mosaic motif running through the text, for in their last view of the host of Pharaoh that pursued the Israelites out of Egypt and into the Red Sea, "the children of Israel … saw the Egyptians dead upon the seashore"[90] just as Huck, near the end of Chapter XVIII, leaves Buck and his cousin lying dead on the river-shore. What differentiates the novel's view of "Egyptian" warriors' death by water from the Bible's, of course, is the contrast between Huck's—and the reader's—shock and dismay, and the Israelites'—and reverent Bible reader's—"shock and awe" at the power of God.

Collins' argument reiterates and extends Lynn's insights as a basis for claiming that Clemens' treatment of "the escape theme of the book of Exodus" makes "the whole novel … more structurally and thematically coherent than readers have perceived it to be."[91] As Collins views him, Huck Finn is a Moses figure whose adventures begin in a barrel instead of a basket of rushes and end in prospect of the Territory instead of the Promised Land. And Clemens' condemnation of society becomes even more evident, in Collins view, as Clemens adds "*the weight of biblical authority*" (italics added) to his case against slavery.[92]

To explain Mark Twain's choice of Bible texts to thump, Collins points out that most African Americans regarded the legend of Moses as the clearest biblical support for the anti-slavery cause.[93] They believed this in spite of the fact that the Mosaic "holy ordinance" instituting slavery among the Israelites, recorded in Exodus 21, was another biblical prop by which white Christian masters and pastors justified the system by which they deprived African Americans of human dignity and rights.[94] Being held captive with illiteracy an enforced aspect—by both custom and law—of their condition, the slaves were not accountable for their confusion about the Bible's actual content.

Collins gives background for his reading by observing the important role of "signs" and portents in the religious life of American slaves and the Hebrew people in Egypt, and he asserts that the whites in the novel "are heathen and Egyptian" to the extent that they rely on religion to support slavery. Huck, Collins writes, does not know that biblical teachings supporting slavery stand in for the religion of Egypt "represented in the Bible by Pharaoh with his priests and magicians": "Although Huck does not learn this on the raft trip, *he does recognize the paradox of morality at odds with religion* and eventually announces his famous decision to go to hell rather than betray Jim" (italics added).[95] While the reader may well recognize this paradox, I find, with David Burg, that there is nothing in the text to suggest that Huck ever attains the intellectual sophistication to recognize a paradoxical relationship between morality and religious teachings[96]; in fact, as this study has pointed out repeatedly, a basic characteristic of Huck's personality is his commitment to the actual and his obliviousness to the abstract; however, Collins asserts, the proof is in the text for "the discerning reader ... to discover Huck Finn in the bulrushes for himself."[97]

Collins next gets down to the business of showing how the novel's three major parts elaborate their biblical theme and of unmasking Moses *alias* Huckleberry Finn. The opening section, which ends with the beginning of the raft voyage, establishes "the hypocrisy of religion used to justify slavery" as Clemens parallels Huck's adventures to the legend of Moses. In the middle section, which he sees ending with the king's selling Jim to Silas Phelps, Collins observes society's perversion of religion and its moral effects: modern "plagues" corresponding to the biblical ones. He finds that the conclusion of this "Moses analogy" in the last section with its numerous parallels to Exodus completes this pattern of biblical allusions.[98]

There is much to recommend Collins's careful tracing of this biblical analog for Huck's *Adventures,* and within the subtextual bounds of the implied narrator's argument, Collins' interpretation is valid; it is clearly the implied narrator's intention to dignify Huck's quest with these Mosaic allusions, but ultimately, and especially in his treatment of the conclusion, Collins fails to recognize the extent to which Clemens' treatment of the Mosaic theme contributes to his satire on a "sivilization" that reveres the Bible as the capital moral authority. Thus when this critic opines that whether Clemens parallels or merely parodies Exodus, as in the Phelps farm sequence, the author's allusions should be taken seriously,[99] Collins overlooks Clemens' iconoclastic attitude toward the biblical archetypes of episodes in order to make the case for the novel's being based structurally and thematically on the story of Exodus and the moral authority of the Bible.

One might more accurately state the case: Whether he merely parallels or parodies a Bible story in an immediate context, Clemens' ultimate purpose was burlesque, to evoke from the reader the kind of laughter that "can blow a colossal humbug to rags and atoms at a blast"[100] (see Chapter Five, Section IV).

Even in the Passover parallel Earl Briden discloses in the ritualism of Huck's escape from pap and the Widow Douglas there is underlying satire. On a serious level, Huck's ritual escape, by associating him with the legend of Moses, emphasizes the inevitability of his return to struggle yet again with those who seek his life. We may flee, suggests Clemens, but freedom flies before us until we have mastered the circumstances that restrict our liberty and prod us to flight in the first place. Moses fled Egypt after killing a servant of Pharaoh who was abusing a Jewish slave.[101] Ironically, Huck also commits a symbolic homicide at the outset of his flight, but his victim is Huckleberry Finn, the child of a society to which he no longer wishes to belong. Moses' flight to avoid prosecution becomes Huck's tragicomic avoidance of persecution in "the land of milk and honey," the American Eden/Egypt of St. Petersburg (see Chapter Three, Section VII).

Or consider the mixture of reverence and lust with which the townspeople of the Wilks episode gaze at "twenty elegant little piles" of "yaller-boys," three hundred gold dollars in each, set before them by the king and the duke: "Everybody looked hungry at it, and licked their chops" (Chapter XXV). Their attitude constitutes the true idolatry of the Egypt of the West, despite Collins's assertion that in the novel, there is no confrontation between the forces of righteous religion and those of idolatry.[102] In a sense he is right, for in Clemens' view these forces are almost one and the same, but Huck does indeed confront the force of idolatry—including the materialistic modern variety—when the duke and king display six thousand dollars in gold to the Wilks family's neighbors. Here, however, the moment of biblical resonance, serious enough in context, becomes a satirical jab at the materialistic values of the Gilded Age. Other examples of idolatry, of course, are the attitude of Bible-olatrists in the camp-meeting and Boggs-Sherburn episodes toward "the brazen serpent in the wilderness" (Chapters XX and XXI)—another allusion to the story of Moses.

From beginning to end, the Mosaic parallels catalogued by biblical exegetes like Lynn, Briden, Nielson, and Collins further the religious satire of *Huckleberry Finn*, as do the biblical allusions noticed by Barnes, Cross, and Quirk, who recognize the irony of the parallels they trace. Sometimes Clemens directs his ironic thrust at the reader through the ingénue narrator, whose failure to recognize the fundamentally religious character of his situation gives rise to conflicting explications. Sometimes Clemens undercuts the conventional morality of the implied narrator, making Mark Twain's Bible thumping ring hollow; sometimes the joke is on Huck himself, as Barnes points out. But the implied author's razor-irony is always poised in the background. And Clemens surely knew that besides the story of Ham in Genesis, another biblical prop for slavery was Moses' provision for slavery among the Israelites, because he alludes to this provision in the biblical laws governing slavery earlier in the book (see Chapter Two, Section VI).

The irony of Clemens' American Moses fleeing from "sivilization" into the wilderness is hardly complimentary to America's self-image as the Promised Land. Huck's initial rejection of Moses along with the Widow Douglas' relatively enlightened piety, Tom Sawyer's respectability, and pap's brutality constitutes *Huck's* blanket rejection of the social and religious milieu of prewar Southern culture. As Huck progresses on his journey south, the mythic setting of his experience thrusts northward as well, in concert with Col. Sherburn's denunciation of the common man, both Northerner and Southerner (Chapter XXII), so that one must consider Huck's final decision to "light out for the Territory ahead of the rest" against the universal background of its mythic context. Lynn, Collins, Neilson, and Briden have in part revealed the extent to which that context is biblical, but, except as concerns Southern culture before the war, they have generally failed to perceive the extent to which it is satirical.

XX. Chapter Three Summary: "THE AUTHOR's" Concept

In Fred Kaplan's chronology of the composition of *Huck Finn*, he notes, "Between November 1879 and March 1880," Clemens wrote "more than another 200 [pages], chapters 18½ to 21 and the prefatory 'Notice.'"[103] These chapters span the horrific violence of the conclusion of the feud episode; the advent of the duke and the king, pap's priests; the camp-meeting where Huck encounters Bible-olatry and the king's religious fraud; and Col. Sherburn's murder of Boggs in Bricksville, where the Bible again figures as an idol of healing and agent of death. Huck personifies Moses and David in the feud section, and Clemens recreates the first murder in the Bible in his treatment of the Grangerford-Shepherdson feud. This episode, as W. R. Moses reveals, marks Huck's arrival at the second level of his tour of Dante's Hell (see Chapter Two, Section V and Chapter Four, Section IV). Finally, having repeatedly crossed the line between irreverence and blasphemy so many times that religious satire had become his predominant theme in the manuscript, Clemens drafted the "Notice" that warns the reader not to take Huck's tale "too seriously" (see Chapter Six, Section II and III). And his first paragraph in Chapter I makes it clear, along with his initial identification of Huck as a Moses figure in Chapter I, that in prospect of the covert satire he was about to create, Clemens was careful to distance himself as far as possible from the implications of Huck's *Adventures*.

All of the commentary discussed so far—even the insights of critics with whose conclusions this discussion does not agree—lines up as support for the assertion that satire aimed primarily at Bible based religion is never far from the author's mind as Huck recounts his life in St. Petersburg, his abduction by his father, his escape to Jackson's Island, and his tenuous alliance with Jim. Throughout the first two sections of the novel the text provides mounting evidence, consisting mainly of parallels to *Paradise Lost*, *Pilgrim's Progress*, and the Bible, that Clemens' consistent intention is to create a veiled commentary on the shortcomings of Judeo-Christian mythology as a basis for morality.

Huck morphs from Moses to Adam / Christ/ Death Angel, to Isaac about to be sacrificed, to Christ, back to Moses, to ritual suicide/patricide/deicide (Chapters I–VI), to corpse, to new-created Adam, to Noah's son Japheth, to Eve (as the bringer of temptation/fall/banishment to Jim/Adam in the rattlesnake episode on Jackson's Island), to cherubim guarding Eden, to Solomon, to the child he judged, to David, and back to Moses once more— all during the course of the first eighteen chapters. And Saul and Rachel Grangerford's unwitting and catastrophic personification of biblical models emphasizes the dangerous moral complacency that results from their peculiar brand of self-righteousness. Taken together in the context of our consideration of tripartite point of view, these allusions and many more to come constitute the "pattern in the carpet" that unifies Huck's episodic narration and transforms it into Clemens' coherent work of art.

In addition, the author's allusions to *Paradise Lost* in his characterization of both pap and Huck and in his depiction of the river as Chaos introduces a previously undetected dimension of this pattern, one that broadens the scope of his religious satire and intensifies its criticism of the puritan worldview. The intermingled features of God, man, and Satan in his characterization of pap Finn, and of Christ, Adam, and the Angel of Death in Huck's "self-portrait" testify to Clemens' preoccupation with this anti-biblical, anti-Miltonic theme. And his identification of the Mississippi River with Milton's Chaos provides a moral womb out of which his white American Adam can be born and born again until Huck outgrows his need of this amoral refuge from the consequences of his "immoral and criminal" alliance with Jim.

CHAPTER FOUR

To *Vilify* "the Ways of God to Men"
Huck Finn, Pilgrim's Progress, The Inferno *and* Paradise Lost

I. A Little Social Background

Samuel Langhorne Clemens was a product of the American Frontier, that no-man's-land suspended between the genteel East and the Wild West. In his lifetime the pastoral romance of the American Eden was rewritten into the bewildering sound and fury of the Industrial Revolution while the Civil War assured the industrial states of almost exclusive political and economic domination of the Union for many years to come. In *Adventures of Huckleberry Finn* Clemens sets out to explore the causes of the problems his America was facing.

Typical of his era, he sought some of the answers in the conflict between conventional, mythologically and theologically based moralism and his own philosophical blend of naturalism and Christian Idealism. Whether or not Clemens believed the myths he discovered lurking in the shadows laying for Huck under the guise of conscience is less important than the fact that in the radical vision of the novel, Clemens rips the beard off the God of the Bible to expose a satanic deity.

Biblical satire, however, is not the whole picture he gives us in *Adventures of Huckleberry Finn*. There is another layer of satire that he subordinates to it to explore a related threat to the progress of the American republic: that is, the ever-present danger to our democracy of the corrupting influence of European style aristocracy. By the early 1880s Clemens had already spent more than two years abroad, and the impressions he brought back from his time in Europe and the Middle East in 1869 and from Europe, where he and his family toured Germany, Switzerland, Italy, France, and England for sixteen months in 1879 and 1880,[1] combined with his lifelong observation of the corrosive effects on Americans' character of their fascination with the trappings of nobility and aristocracy, convinced him of the real danger to the body politic that this trend posed.

He recounts how in his own family an "American Claimant" to an English earldom wasted his life dreaming of reclaiming his title and lands:

> And the Colonel [Lampton] always spoke with studied and courtly deference of the Claimant of his day,—a second cousin of his,—and referred to him with entire seriousness as "the Earl." "The Earl" was a man of parts, and might have accomplished something for himself but for the calamitous accident of his birth. He was a Kentuckian, and a well meaning man; but he had no money, and no time to earn any; for all his time was taken up in trying to get me, and the others of the tribe, to furnish him a capital to fight his claim through the House of Lords with. He had all the documents, all the proofs; he knew he could win. And so he dreamed his life away, always in poverty, sometimes in actual want, and died at last, far from home, and was buried from a hospital by strangers who did not know he was an earl, for he did not look it. That poor fellow used to sign his letters "Durham," and in them he would find fault with me for voting the Republican ticket, for the reason that it was unaristocratic, and by consequence un-Lamptonian. And presently along would come a letter from some red-hot Virginian son of my other branch and abuse me bitterly for the same vote—on the ground that the Republican was an aristocratic party and it was not becoming in the descendant of a regicide to train with that kind of animals. And so I used to almost wish I hadn't had any ancestors, they were so much trouble to me.[2]

A thorough exploration of Clemens' political philosophy would take up at least a volume in itself, and anyone acquainted with his writings knows that the subject of democracy and meritocracy vs. hereditary aristocracy takes up a good deal of space in many of his works, as it does in *Huckleberry Finn*. In *Huck Finn* he parallels the Southern system of plantation aristocracy and hereditary, divine-right slavery to the European article, implying that there is only a difference of degree—not kind—between the two. This is what his satire of romantic literature is about in the novel, for he felt that the aristocratic pretensions of Americans had led and could continue to lead to the undermining of the democratic spirit and the independence of the American people. The two greatest dangers to human progress and liberty, in his view, are a hereditary aristocracy and an Established Church. In the novel, ironically, the condition of *hereditary slavery* contributes to this trend. Like the north and south poles of a magnet, the conditions of slavery and aristocracy in the novel represent paired manifestations of the same dynamic—regardless of whether the hereditary condition is at the top or the bottom of the social hierarchy.

Elements of this satire include his implicit criticism of the aristocratic pretensions of leading citizens of the shore communities like the Widow

Douglas, the Grangerfords, Colonel Sherburn, and Silas Phelps. And his portrayal of the duke and the king—unaristocratic frauds, to be sure—but morally indistinguishable, as Huck observes, "from the real kind" (Chapter XXIII), furthers his attack on aristocracy. It is no coincidence that in their biggest scam, these royal frauds pose as English clerics, for their threefold imposture—as royalty, as clerics, and as Englishmen—emblemizes the complicity of aristocracy and religion in perpetuating all forms of slavery, including the actual kind along with metaphorical ones like Tom Sawyer's subservience to the authority of books and the righteousness of tradition. Of course, this satire culminates in the closing chapters in Tom Sawyer's evasion, in which his aristocratic pretenses make a mockery of everything that has gone before.

When one views Clemens' era through the lenses he provides, one can begin to see how an economic conflict between the industrial North and the agrarian South could be pursued into bloody combat to the strains of *The Battle Hymn of the Republic*, and how racism came to be re-institutionalized, despite the moral rhetoric of Abolitionism, under the guise of implementation of the Emancipation Proclamation and the 13th, 14th, and 15th Amendments: All was justified morally by the postulates of conscience, the "infallible voice" of the deity within.

II. Heart vs. Conscience

Harold Kolb contends that Mark Twain could not write another *Huckleberry Finn* because he had stopped believing in the instinctive virtue that distinguishes Huck's character.[3] But as H. N. Smith has shown, Clemens' discovery of Huck's "capacity for love"—not the intuitive ethics that he rejected in Lecky's *History of European Morals*,[4] but the Christ-like, ego-transcending commitment to helping Jim—was the discovery that gave tragicomic depth to the novel in the first place and that provided the basis for the heart-versus-conscience dialectic at the core of the book's argument.[5] Clemens' untiring exploration of the capacity of the human heart to love against all odds is the humanizing element that tempers his satirical vision and prevents his work from becoming what he thought Swift's to be: "void of every tender grace, every kindly, humanizing element[;] what a bare, glittering iceberg is mere intellectual greatness,—& such was Swift's."[6]

As noted previously, James Cox contends that "the radical vernacular vision" of *Huckleberry Finn* is an attack on conscience itself, not just on the perversion of Christian doctrine that justified slavery in the prewar South, but on the "higher" or "inner" conscience that guided America into the twentieth century.[7] And it is that. But this generalization, while true to Clemens' radical vision and to the theme of religious satire, is but a dipperful of the novel's full argument. Much of what Clemens had to say he could only present symbolically because what the author believed to be true he also believed he could dramatize only indirectly, subtly, with the ironic artistry that enabled him "to conceal my frenzy from the reader."[8] Boldly to equate the biblical God with swine and Satan might well, as Clemens knew it would, have bewildered, outraged, and alienated his audience.

And if the real meaning of the novel had been recognized during his life, he might have suffered *all* of the terrible consequences about which he warns the reader in his "Notice" (see Chapter Six, Section III). But to create a new version of the mythology that shaped Western civilization, an antithetical version that would co-exist with the Bible and, Clemens may have hoped, help to undermine the authority of the Book beneath the level of conscious recognition in his audience—that was the feat of subversion that he achieved in pitting Huck's love for Jim against his biblically informed conscience.

III. *Pilgrim's Progress* and Huck's Regress

This study frequently characterizes the allusiveness of Clemens' literary artistry as ironic. While the author lifts ideas and whole episodes from sources in Christian literature, his context reverses the moral polarity of his sources, as Franklin Rogers has explained,[9] so that, as Harold Bloom theorizes, the finished work becomes an intentional misreading, or "misprision," of the works from which it derives.[10] To avoid confusing the antithetical ideology of Clemens' derivative plot with that of the texts to which he alludes, this study resorts to the term *ironic allusion* to characterize Clemens' moral inversions and negations of his literary archetypes.

For example, Alfred Bendixen's comparison of Huck to Bunyan's Christian—to whom Huck calls our attention in Chapter XVII—illustrates such an ironic allusion. Bendixen's reading reveals that broad similarities of style and plot break down when Huck's crucial decision to reject the world ends in his opting for hell not heaven. Furthermore, a fundamental difference between Christian and Huck is that between a pilgrim and a picaro: Bunyan's hero "has a specific goal—he leaves his family and home to seek Heaven" while Mark Twain's anti-hero "really has no specific goal—he is running away from something"—his family and home—"not towards anything," and he "drifts more than he travels." Both, however, "are outcasts whose moral superiority is based on a rejection of civilization's values, on a flight from society"[11] (see Chapter Four, Sections XVIII and XIX, and Chapter Five, Section III).

As Bendixen might have added, the fact that Huck is fleeing *from* St. Petersburg while Christian is moving *towards* the New World theocracy of the Puritans suggests further significant historical and philosophical differences between Bunyan's pilgrim and Clemens' fugitive, differences that Clemens makes explicit in *Captain Stormfield's Visit to Heaven*.[12] Perhaps Clemens' most succinct expression of his feelings for Bunyan's theology is his comment, "And as for the *Bostonians*, I would rather be damned to John Bunyan's heaven than read that."[13] Bendixen's insight into the similarities between *Huck Finn* and *Pilgrim's Progress* clearly implies that the adventures of Clemens' lonesome picaro are irreverent variations on Bunyan's devout theme.

It is hardly consonant with Clemens' views or his overall treatment of the Bible in his novel to claim, as Lynn and Collins have done, that the thematic key to the unity of the novel is the liberation drama of Exodus, which relies for its moral authority on the very God Mark Twain "tried to drop ... into a candle," as Nielson aptly puts it.[14] Nor, on the other hand, have the commentators who have noticed some of the religious satire and Bible parallels summarized above done more than dip into the novel here and there to discover pieces of a puzzle that, when fully assembled, portrays the God of the Bible as all the most venomous things Mark Twain says about Him and His religions in his later, overt religious satires like *Letters from the Earth*. Huck, as Bendixen has suggested, is Clemens' version of Bunyan's Christian—and a very lonely one at that. The climactic choice he makes for damnation does take him straight to hell—that is, back to the society of Bible-olatrists he has been fleeing.

IV. Going Through Hell

IV-A: Moses Discovers Huck Finn *in* The Inferno

Clemens had more than biblical parody in mind when he created the structure that makes religious satire the undergirding structure and overarching theme of *Huckleberry Finn*. In his extended comparison between the moral vision *Huckleberry Finn* manifests and that of Dante's *Inferno*, W. R. Moses has observed some striking parallels between these two works. Although he declines even to speculate on the question of direct influence, "the pattern of evil" Moses detects in both works persuasively suggests that an exploration of the degrees of human depravity was very much on Clemens' mind as he composed the last half of the first section and the entire middle section of the novel. Each stage of the journey downriver is a descent that parallels and consecutively corresponds to a phase of Dante's infernal vision in that it brings Huck into confrontation with ever-more-profound corruption of specific kinds.[15]

Finding pap to be "the personification of incontinence," Moses calls him "a spendthrift," "indiscriminately drunken," and "sullenly or frantically wrathful." And Moses declares that that while pap's abuse endangers Huck's life, his attack in Chapter VI is "not directed at Huck as a personality." Moses emphasizes that morally and psychologically the impersonal aspect of pap's attack on Huck relieves its viciousness.

Next Moses observes that violence—especially the "violence against neighbors" for which Dante provides a special place in Hell's second level—finds its epitome in the Shepherdson-Grangerford feud. Although Huck encounters plenty of violence elsewhere in his travels, the feud is "an exchange of witless murders," as Moses characterizes them, that ends in the massacre of the Grangerfords that nearly includes Huck, who would have died "as a person—anonymous, but recognized to be human"—guilty of aiding Buck and his cousin. In addition to this more profound threat to his survival, he also suffers the emotional violence of seeing his friend Buck gunned down. Moses calls Buck's murder "a trauma from which Huck can never fully recover"; in another of his rare asides to the reader, Huck comments: "I wish I hadn't ever come ashore that night to see such things. I ain't ever going to get shut of them—lots of times I dream about them" (Chapter XVIII). Observing that Huck mentions no such persistent nightmares about pap, Moses asserts: "The strain increases with the degree of evil encountered." Jim, who functions as Huck's protector and guide out of this circle of Hell, plays the role of Dante's Virgil in this life-threatening situation.

Set free of the feud, Huck almost immediately encounters Fraud in the persons of the duke and the king, fraud that brings on yet more violence. These confidence men live by "lying, hypocrisy, and theft" taking advantage of whomever they can as they drift from scam to scam. Their career through the middle section of the story epitomizes Fraud in Dante's scheme. First they defraud their hosts on the raft by posing as royalty; then the people of Pokeville and the camp-meeting as the duke poses as the new printer for the town and steals from both the print shop and its customers while the king makes a killing as a freshly converted pirate; then the people of Bricksville, where they pose as itinerant actors; then as an English parson and his deaf-mute brother as they attempt to steal the orphaned Wilks girls' fortune and sell their slaves into perdition; and finally Huck and Jim again as they steal what they believe to be Huck's slave and betray Jim.

"Their vicious attempt to defraud the girls causes Huck to suffer both deep moral disgust and severe emotional pain," writes Moses, and he quotes another of Huck's asides: "I can't ever get it out of my memory, the sight of them poor miserable girls and niggers hanging around each other's necks and crying" (Chapter XXVII). And Huck's sense of peril increases again: "This was the most awful trouble and the most dangersome I ever was in, and I was kinder stunned" (Chapter XXVIII). This fraud endangers Huck's life again, neither as a figment of pap's deranged imagination nor as an unknown associate of the Shepherdsons' enemy, but this time as an active and willing "partner in villainy"; and so the threat is most intensely immediate and personal as Huck is dragged in the iron grip of a "Goliar" named Hines to the graveyard (Chapter XXIX). The frauds' final and greatest treachery reduces Huck "to the lowest spiritual point" he suffers. Though his loyalty to Jim overwhelms his conscience, and Huck decides to steal Jim "out of slavery again" (Chapter XXXI), Moses observes that "the price he pays is a sense of alienation both from society and from God": "All right, then, I'll *go* to hell."

With Jim's disappearance, Moses sees Huck's tour of *The Inferno* ended: "Unless he encounters the arch-fiend in person, he can go no deeper."[16] But Huck does go deeper. The climax in Chapter XXXI culminates in Huck's identification with Clemens' Adamic Satan, thus formally completing his tour of Dante's Hell *to its nadir*. Huck does not just *meet* Satan; he *becomes* the Arch-Rebel. At that point in his narrative he emerges from Chaos for the last time, abandoning his moral refuge with a wholehearted and whole-*headed* commitment to Jim and to "wickedness" (see Chapter Four, Section XVIII).

While Moses is concerned only with the congruency of Dante's and Clemens' visions and carefully avoids claiming direct influence,[17] Alan Gribben has shown that Clemens' library contained several copies of *The Inferno*, two of which date from the 1860s. His known references to the Italian poet begin in 1869 and imply a lifelong familiarity with *The Divine Comedy* that had grown to "reverence" by 1905.[18]

Furthermore, in his commentary on Mark Twain's *A Curious Dream*, W. G. Marshall finds that allusions to "certain sections of the *Inferno* ... establish the central theme of avarice and ... allow Twain to make devastating statements about man's inability to transcend a purely materialistic frame of reference or to rise above a hellishly intense craving for opulence." *A Curious Dream* was first published in 1870, fourteen years prior to the first publication of *Huckleberry Finn*. In documenting the intentionality of the parallels he has discovered, without an appreciation of which the story amounts to "mere creampuffery," as Marshall phrases it, he points to Thomas Werge's discussion of similar parallels in *The Man That Corrupted Hadleyburg*.[19]

As Werge reads *Hadleyburg*, "The inhabitants of the sixth *bolgia* of the eighth circle of the *Inferno* and the town of Hadleyburg are identical in their morally perverted and grotesque forms."[20] In view of these two articles on Clemens' short fiction and of his possession of and recurrent references to Dante's work, it is very likely that the parallels Moses perceives as a link between the raft voyage of *Huckleberry Finn* and the dream vision of Dante are more than a merely coincidental feature of the universality of both works, as Moses characterizes them.

IV-B: Infernal Allusions

Further substantive parallels between these two texts include incidents in which Clemens borrows from the Italian poet's plot in order to elaborate his religious satire. These allusions indicate the source of his structural allusions to *The Inferno*. Pap's punishment in being transformed to "a monstrous Serpent on his Belly prone" in Chapter VI simultaneously parallels the punishment of Satan in Milton and the description in Dante of the punishment of Agnello Brunelleschi in the seventh gulf of the third circle of Hell, where the various classes of fraud find eternal retribution; Agnello's transformation to a serpent in Canto XXV may be a source for Satan's in Book X of Milton's epic, but since Clemens alludes to both poets at other points, it is fair to speculate that he is aware of both in his narration of pap's parallel punishment for the crimes he commits, including fraud, in his "brief but violent pilgrimage" (as James Cox characterizes his career through the novel).[21] When he first awakens Huck, "yelling about snakes," pap cries out that one is "biting him on the cheek." Dante observes Agnello, the victim of his six-legged monster-serpent: The beast springs upon him, intertwining its limbs with his "while deep in either cheek / He fleshed his fangs."[22] The demon and Agnello's soul then transform into each other as "both shapes ... assume / The other's substance"[23]; pap collapses to writhe on the dirt floor "kicking and grabbing at the air in his hands." Pap embodies not only Incontinence, but also Violence and Fraud in his attempts to rob and kill Huck, befitting his role as divine fiend, and his punishment in being robbed and murdered fits his crimes.

Hearn lists several possible but uncertain sources for the king's performance of "'The King's Camelopard,' or 'The Royal Nonesuch.'" The antics of the king onstage are sketchily revealed:

The king come a-prancing out on all fours, naked; and he was painted all over, ring-streaked-and-striped, all sorts of colors, as splendid as a rainbow. And—but never mind the rest of his outfit; it was just wild but it was awful funny. [...] Well, it would a-made a cow laugh to see the shines that old idiot cut.

Since the king is the very personification of Fraud, the following passage from Dante's Canto XVII is relevant to the king's capering in addition to the mostly obscene models Hearn reports, several of which involve burning candles inserted into the caperer's elevated posterior[24]: The poet Virgil, Dante's guide through Hell, summons the monster demon Geryon (Fraud):

> My guide address'd,
> And beckon'd him, that he should come to shore,
> Near to the stony causeway's utmost edge.
> Forthwith that image vile of Fraud appear'd,
> His head and upper part exposed on land,
> But laid not on the shore his bestial train.
> His face the semblance of a just man's wore,
> So kind and gracious was its outward cheer;
> The rest was serpent all: [...] the back and breast,
> And either side, were painted o'er with nodes
> And orbits. Colors variegated more
> Nor Turks nor Tartars e'er on cloth of state
> With interchangeable embroidery wove,
> [...]
> So on the rim, that fenced the sand with rock,
> Sat perch'd the fiend of evil. In the void
> Glancing, his tail upturn'd its venomous fork,
> With sting like a scorpion's arm'd.[25]

It is conceivable that Dante's description of the demon Fraud in this passage provided another source for Clemens' characterization of the king, one morally far more serious and thematically more relevant to the developing religious satire than the capers Hearn discusses.

Comparison of these two texts turns up several parallels in Clemens' and Dante's descriptions, for the king, too, can put on "the semblance of a just man's" face; both have associations with serpents—Geryon, the monster the poet describes, physically, the king morally and in his recent scam at the camp-meeting, where "the brazen serpent" looms large; and both are "painted o'er" with brightly colored patterns. Dante's fiend being armed with a scorpion's sting perhaps completes the parallels with oblique confirmation that the king, as Hearn speculates, has a lighted candle inserted into his anus.

It is also important to note here that Geryon at Virgil's bidding bears Dante and his guide down into the penultimate depth of Hell, where all sorts of fraud find retribution, and it is the king most of all who carries Huck and

Jim into the incidents that elaborate on the theme of Fraud and its retribution.

With regard to the idolatry of the Egypt of the West, there is yet another relevant passage in *The Inferno*, Canto XVII, which confirms that there is no difference between the worship of gold and any other form of idolatry, in the poet's view. When Dante encounters Pope Nicholas V, damned for simony, he addresses him without pity: "Of gold and silver ye have made your god, / Differing wherein from the idolater, / But that he worships one, a hundred ye?" When Huck observes the people in the Wilks parlor staring at Peter's gold, he sees them in a bestial state typical of the novel's portrayal of the damned: "Everybody looked hungry at it and licked their chops" (Chapter XXV). In light of Dante's rebuke of this pope—who like the king is a predator posing as a prelate—one can see Clemens' point more clearly (see Chapter Four, Section XV).

In Canto XXI, Dante observes the punishment of peculators, men who were in life "'barterers: of 'no' / For lucre there an 'ay' is quickly made.'"[26] The fate of these condemned souls, whose treachery in life was "to traffic the interests of the public for their own private advantage,"[27] is to swim in boiling pitch forever. Not coincidentally, Huck's last sight of the royal frauds is of them drenched with tar and covered with feathers, ridden on a rail, about to be tossed into the river (Chapter XXXIII)—about as close as Clemens could get to having his peculators suffer the same doom as Dante's.

In at least a broad sense, in the context of these allusions to *The Inferno*, Jim's character as well as these others derives from Clemens' modeling this series of episodes—from pap's advent to the final exit of the duke and the king—on Dante's plot and characters. Jim's role as Huck's protector and guide resonates strongly with the relationship between Dante, the narrator of *The Inferno*, and Virgil, his guide and protector throughout his tour of Hell. Consider Virgil's mission statement in Canto I:

> I, for thy profit pondering, now devise
> That thou mayst follow me; and I, thy guide,
> Will lead thee hence through an eternal space,
> Where thou shalt hear despairing shrieks, and see
> Spirits of old tormented, who invoke
> A second death; and those next view, who dwell
> Content in fire, for that they hope to come,
> Whene'er the time may be, among the blest,
> Into whose regions if thou then desire
> To ascend, a spirit worthier than I
> Must lead thee, in whose charge, when I depart,
> Thou shalt be left: for that Almighty King,

> Who reigns above, a rebel to his law
> Adjudges me; and therefore hath decreed
> That, to his city, none through me should come.[28]

The mission of Virgil certainly resonates with the role of Jim in relation to Huck, even though there is no single passage in the text that appears to be modeled on this speech.

In Clemens' allusive context, however, there are some close parallels to be observed. Like Virgil, who "ponders for [Dante's] profit," Jim looks out for Huck's benefit in many ways. Huck's growth is a function of his bond with Jim, and the fugitive slave becomes a father figure to the boy. Jim keeps Huck safe—even saves his life by getting him out of the feud—at several points in the narrative. At the beginning of the raft voyage, as they set out into Chaos on the river (see Chapter Three, Section VIII and Chapter Four, Section XXI), Jim accompanies Huck into "an eternal space," and during the journey, as Moses' insights show, Huck spends a great deal of his time in the one to which the poet refers here. In the novel's versions of Hell, Huck does indeed hear "despairing shrieks," and sees living and dying men "tormented." Although it is not clearly Clemens' intention, it may have been part of his conception of the plot to make the Phelps farm an analog of Purgatory, to which Virgil refers in the next few lines.

More importantly, the final six lines of his statement to Dante reflect poignantly on Jim and Huck. This portion of Virgil's comment states his outlaw status as one born before the birth of Christ and foretells the separation of the two poets should Dante desire to enter the city of "that Almighty King." To Clemens, this sort of "luck of the draw" access to Heaven based on date of birth must have seemed a laughable injustice completely in character for the biblical God he derides throughout the novel.

This passage suggests that the outcome of the journey will be the separation of Jim from Huck due in part to Jim's status as an African American, whether "free" or enslaved, in a society whose "law/ Adjudges" him unworthy of the rights of citizenship. And, of course, Jim's status as a fugitive slave makes him "a rebel" against the law of divine right slavery on which the society of the novel is founded.

The debt to Dante that W. R. Moses has revealed in his exploration of parallels between Huck's progress—more precisely, regress—down the river is an additional aspect of Clemens' religious vision that broadens and deepens its scope, advancing his religious satire by showing how the agents of evil either exploit the credulous faithful, as is the case with pap, the duke, and the king, or the religiously faithful use their religion to justify barbarous behavior, like the feuding clans, the participants in the camp meeting, the lynch-mobs, and most of all, the slaveholders. The explicit comparisons Clemens invites between the progress of his fugitive from the New World theocracy of the Puritans' American heirs and the *Progress* of John Bunyan's pilgrim is another strand in this structural and thematic pattern in the design of the novel (see Chapter Four, Section III).

V. Back to the Raft

Clemens returned to the MS in 1879 with a renewed sense of purpose.[29] It must have troubled him, as it has troubled some critics, that after the feud chapters, Huck and Jim could not just go on drifting down the river floating ever farther from Jim's goal. When they set out again it is presumably still Jim's hope to find or buy a canoe so that they can start back north. That is what Jim, at least, planned to do after losing the canoe in Chapter XVI ("The Rattlesnake-Skin Does Its Work"; see Appendix A). After "two or three days and nights went by," Huck reports his finding a canoe and immediately taking it up a creek to forage for berries. There he encounters the two anonymous scoundrels whom we come to know as the duke and the king (Chapter XIX). They always take Huck along when they go ashore so that Huck and Jim cannot escape them while they are gone, and so, plausibly, the southward voyage continues to the Phelps farm.

When he chose to continue the raft voyage, Clemens must have realized that Huck and Jim have a long way to go before Huck completes his moral education: his flight to moral autonomy. Clemens intends that the reader grasp this undergirding and over-arching theme of the book, the boy's heart's rebellion against his "deformed conscience" and his victory over its depraved values, subliminally, at least. As Jim puts it in his futile attempt to teach Huck to think critically, "de *real* pint is furder down—down deeper" (Chapter XIV) than the social satire and the developing characterization of Huck, and even than the working out of Jim's flight to freedom, because Jim's liberation is a function of their bond. Even though Huck's commitment to Jim is not what gets Jim to the Phelps farm, their journey together does, and without Huck, and once, almost, because of Huck, Jim could have been captured almost anywhere along the way. The purpose of the voyage for Huck is his moral education and flight to autonomy—freedom from his conscience based on his innate goodness—concepts he could never articulate even if they occurred to him. This theme—"the moral of the story"—reveals the implied author's purpose in having the pair resume the raft voyage and continue their sojourn in Chaos.

Because Tom Sawyer is coming with the news of Miss Watson's recent demise and her deathbed manumission of Jim, his arrival at the Phelps farm ironically fulfills the fugitive slave's flight to the qualified freedom Jim attains. Without his flight, she would have either willed him to her sister or sold him, and although she might have regretted it, there is nothing she could have done about it. In this sense, Jim's flight does in fact lead actively to his liberation, contrary to the claims of a host of critics that the entire journey has been pointless because pap is dead and Jim is free for most of their trip.[30]

Miss Watson, as Tom says, has been dead for two months, and although one cannot calculate the exact duration of the raft voyage because Huck gives us few temporal markers along the way, except for the raft voyage beginning on the "June rise" and the ripening of watermelons in the gardens of the Phelps slaves after it ends; so we can only surmise that she died shortly after Jim fled while her "shame" (Chapter XLII) at having meant to sell him was fresh on her Calvinist conscience, a circumstance that would help to explain her forgiving him and setting him free in her will in her hope and fear for her own salvation.

Furthermore, if, as many in the village believed, Jim were Huck's killer (Chapter XI), her actions would have made her indirectly responsible for Huck's death, since Jim fled her shameful treatment of him, and Huck's death at the hands of her chattel would have implicated her morally in his murder. Jim's manumission in this light becomes a last gasp effort to repudiate her responsibility for Huck's death—a distant echo, perhaps, of Pontius Pilate's hand washing. Such are the intricate machinations of conscience. Therefore, without their flight it is doubtful that either Huck or Jim could have achieved what freedom they do attain, and this is especially true of Huck. For both of them, an important purpose of the journey has been their discovery of each other's loyalty and trustworthiness: their final achievement of real friendship despite their racial difference.

In the course of their continued flight, Clemens continues his exploration of the religious and social milieu of ante-bellum Southern culture, but he continues to anchor the episodes he presents in the mythology on which *all* of America's social mores were founded. His critique of the religious underpinnings of Western culture thereby becomes all-inclusive, extending north even as his twin fugitives drift ever farther south.

VI. Rehabilitating Miss Watson

Critics have made too much, by the way, of Miss Watson's mean spirit. True, she is not a sympathetic character, and her decision to sell Jim down the river is evil, but we see her only through the eyes of a feral boy who sees her as harsh and cold, and to whom she represents the worst impositions of "sivilization." However, her "learnin' me my book" is no mean achievement. In this respect, Miss Watson and the widow work a "hard cop/soft cop" routine on Huck that renders him literate in "three or four months" (Chapter IV). That is very effective teaching over a very short term.

In the end, Miss Watson's deathbed manumission of Jim redeems her hard-heartedness toward him, an act one can well imagine her performing, although most readers have disagreed with this analysis of her character, as she faces the Judgment Day with Huck's death and her attempted damnation of Jim on her conscience and her fear of hell on her mind. Her detractors have underappreciated her toughness and dedication to her duty to Huck because the reader knows her only through the eyes of a feral child and those of critics who apparently have no guilt about their past and no fear of the hereafter.

VII. Of Piracy and Fraud

The crime spree that begins with the advent of the two frauds in Chapter XIX commences immediately. They dispossess Huck and Jim of their wigwam and take over the raft, acts of piracy that the king's fraud at the camp-meeting underscores. The duke and the king introduce themselves to one another as nameless rogues, but there is an obvious degree of moral difference between the two. The duke's specialty is "most anything that ain't work." The king is a religious fraud who bilks people of their money under the guise of preaching and pretended conversions: "Preachin's my line, too, and workin' camp-meetin's and missionaryin' around," he says (Chapter XIX).

The king, who is at least morally related to one of Chaucer's rogue prelates, is the more degraded of the pair, and Clemens suggests the comparison in this exchange by making the king's speech lower class in its heavier dialect, which Clemens accented by eliding terminal "g's" on the king's progressive verb endings, such as "missionaryin'." His appearance is also more degenerate than the duke's, whom Jim later finds to be "a tolerble likely man, in some ways," while also saying of the king, "dis one do *smell* like de nation ["euphemism for damnation"], Huck"[31] (Chapter XXIII). Jim's simile is apt, in view of the king's being the personification of monster demon Geryon in Dante's *Inferno* (see Chapter Four, Section IV-B).

Clemens revised this passage heavily for the first edition. In the *Comprehensive Edition*, Doyno substitutes the manuscript text for that of the first

Four. To Vilify *"the Ways of God to Men"* 131

edition, remarking that as the two con men exchange boastful introductions, the king comments on Christians' greater willingness to donate money "for the most distant heathens." Commenting that this satire would have been offensive to many of Clemens' readers, Doyno suggests that the author revised the king's account of himself, which resonates with pap's false conversion for similar motives in Chapter V, to tone down its irreverent implications. In the king's "conversion" from (actual) piracy and in his later imposture of an English parson in the Wilks scam, Clemens' satire targets the king's duped victims—less controversial objectives than "Gospel work," which offers opportunities for scams that target revivals, camp-meetings, "occupying" for preachers, and missionarying.[32]

Doyno disregards the fact that while toning down the king's resumé, Clemens embellishes the duke's in the first edition text, making clearer that fraud is the shared calling of the pair and that the main differences between them are age, education, and the degrees of their depravity. Thus readers are left with a regrettable textual quandary in which Clemens' clearest vision of these rogues is available neither in the manuscript text nor in the first (or any other) edition (see Appendix E). Combining the first edition and manuscript texts (following the more elaborate first edition text (italicized) for the duke, followed by the king's self characterization from the manuscript, produces the following exchange:

> The duke: *"Jour printer; by trade; do a little in patent medicines; theatre-actor—tragedy, you know; take a turn at mesmerism and phrenology when there's a chance; teach singing-geography school for a change; sling a lecture sometimes—oh,* I do lots of things—most anything that comes handy, so it ain't work. What's your lay?"[33]
>
> The king: "Gospil-work, mainly—most any kind of gospil work: boosting revivals along, or getting 'em up; working camp meetings; 'occupying' for a preacher that wants to take a week's rest; and missionarying. Thar's more money in missionarying than the others; folks will plank out cash for the heathen mighty free, if you only locate your heathen fur enough off. I've took in as much as seventeen dollars at one grist for the pore benighted Goojoos—invented 'em myself—located 'em away up just back of the north pole. Seeing that that worked so good, I kind of strained myself, next time, and located some in a comet, expecting to jest simply bust the community—but it warn't a go. They wouldn't ante a red—and I come mighty near getting ducked, too."[34]

This ordering of Clemens' variant texts has the effect of more strongly foreshadowing the moral descent that occurs as the raft drifts ever deeper into the depths of Dante's hellish vision, from pap's Incontinence; through the warlike Violence of the feud; through Violence and Sloth and Fraud in the lazy towns of Pokeville and Bricksville; through more serious Fraud in the Wilks episode and Treachery leading up to the climax; and finally to its bottom-most depth, where Huck overcomes his conscience and undergoes his satanic rebirth with his resolve to "*go* to hell." The irony is, of course, that he has been going there every time he has stepped ashore since his abduction in Chapter VI (see Chapter Three, Section V and Chapter Four, Section IV and XVIII).

This descent traces the moral arc of the first two sections of the narrative through Chapter XXXI. This observation emphasizes the point that from the moral perspective of "THE AUTHOR," this arrangement of texts, his later version of the duke and his original conception of the king, conforms most closely to the thematic pattern being observed here. These variants are fascinating for what they reveal about both the themes of the narrative and the consideration Clemens gave to arriving at the first edition text. Here, as it does at many points that Doyno indicates, the effect of Clemens' final revision of the manuscript is to soften its *overt* religious satire, but at several points, one of which is coming up next, his revisions rhetorically intensify its *covert* religious satire.

VIII. In the Lair of the Brazen Serpent

Again in Chapter XX Doyno interpolates Clemens' much more extravagantly satirical and racially charged manuscript version of the camp-meeting episode into the first edition text.[35] His comments reveal that Clemens drew details of this passage in large measure from Johnson Jones Hooper's sketch "The Captain Attends a Camp-Meeting."[36] Here, Doyno points out another source-text for *Adventures of Huckleberry Finn*. As is repeatedly pointed out elsewhere in this study's commentaries on other literary archetypes, this passage provides yet another example of what Franklin Rogers has declared to be Clemens' "necessarily conscious" borrowing (see Introduction, Section VII). And as we have seen many times over, in Clemens' hands the source-texts he uses become "mere foundations on which he erects a structure of incident, character axis, and theme all his own."[37]

Whether he was transmuting low comedy to high art, as he does with Hooper, or transmuting high art to humor and satire, as in his treatment of Milton, it is always necessary to keep the thematic import of the original in mind as well as its structural characteristics so that in recognizing the source one does not fall victim to the temptation to project the moral ideas of that source onto Clemens' text. As is the case with Milton and Bunyan, Clemens often reverses the moral polarity of his sources, transforming his allusions into the implicit parody of literary burlesque (see Chapter Three, Section III and Chapter Four, Section III).

Four. To Vilify "the Ways of God to Men" 133

The differences between the manuscript version of the camp meeting and the first edition begin with Huck's arrival at the meeting ground in a passage expurgated from the published text (first edition text italicized):

> *The first shed we come to, the preacher was lining out a hymn. He lined out two lines; everybody sung it*—roared it out, they did, in a most rousing way:
>
> "Am I a soldier of the cross,
> A follower of the Lamb,"—
>
> —then the preacher lined-out the next two:
>
> "And shall I fear to own his cause, Or blush to speak his name?"
>
> —*And so on. The people woke up more and more, and sung louder and louder; and towards the end, some begun to groan, and some begun to shout. Then the preacher begun to preach.*[38]

This passage leads into Huck's reporting the preacher's sermon. Compare the published text's milder treatment of the scene:

> *The first shed we come to the preacher was lining out a hymn. He lined out two lines, everybody sung it, and it was kind of grand to hear it, there was so many of them and they done it in such a rousing way; then he lined out two more for them to sing—and so on. The people woke up more and more and sung louder and louder; and towards the end some begun to groan and some begun to shout. Then the preacher begun to preach.*[39]

Gone from the revised version is the bestial roaring of the hymn, along with its words—words that ask a question to which the scene that follows seems to require the answer: Absolutely! Evidently the author did not wish for his readers to draw this conclusion *consciously*. His milder and more empathetic treatment of this scene in revision shows that Clemens felt it contributed too strongly to the overt religious satire of the passage in the same way that a headline strengthens an article. Also noteworthy in Clemens' revision is Huck's positive response to the singing in the published passage: "it was kind of grand to hear it." During Clemens' extensive editing of this episode, he made Huck's narration more sympathetic, as he did here with Huck's response to the singing.

It is at the camp-meeting that the preacher holds up his open Bible and shouts to the congregation: "It's the brazen serpent in the wilderness! Look upon it and live!" The effect of Clemens' revisions of the paragraph containing the preacher's exclamation is to intensify its rhetorical impact. Compare the following extracts from the narrative, the first from the manuscript, the second from the first edition (italicized):

> The preacher begun to preach, and he warmed up, right away, and went a-weaving first to one side of his platform and then t'other, then a-leaning down over the front of it, with his arms and his body a-going it all the time, and sing-songing his words out with all his might and main, so you could a heard him a mile; and every now and

then he would hold up his open Bible, and kind of pass it around this way and that, shouting, "It's the brazen serpent in the wilderness—ah! look upon it and live—ah!" And people would sing out, "Glo-o-*ree!*—A-a-*men!*" and so on, and next he would lay the Bible down and weave about the platform, and work back to the Bible again, pretty soon, and fetch it a bang with his fist and shout—"Here it is! the rock of salvation—ah!" And so he went a-raging, and the people groaning and crying, and jumping up and hugging one another, and *Amens* was popping off everywhere. Every little while he would preach right *at* people that he saw was stirred up.[40]

> Then the preacher begun to preach; and in earnest, too; and went weaving first to one side of the platform and then the other, and then a leaning down over the front of it, with his arms and his body going all the time, and shouting his words out with all his might; and every now and then he would hold up his Bible and spread it open, and kind of pass it around this way and that, shouting, "It's the brazen serpent in the wilderness! Look upon it and live!" And people would shout out, "Glory!—A-a-men!" And so he went on, and the people groaning and crying and saying amen.[41]

The greater economy of Clemens' first edition text sharpens the focus of his narration onto this brazen serpent-idol, the Bible, which here and in the next episode functions as a symbol for the power of superstition and ignorance in the lives of the people Huck encounters along the river. This direct association of the Bible with the degradation that Huck observes is an aspect of Clemens' religious satire that he intensifies by deleting much of the superfluous social satire surrounding the preacher's exclamation and diminishing the emphasis on the religious frenzy of the scene while tightening the passage's focus on the Bible by placing it at the rhetorical climax of the paragraph.

Huck's diction becomes more restrained as well: "Warmed up" becomes "*in earnest*"; "a-weaving" becomes "*weaving*"; "t'other" changes to "*the other*"; "body a-going it" shrinks to "*body going all.*" Clemens alters "sing-songing" to "*shouting,*" "might and main" to "*might,*" and the preacher's "ahs" disappear along with the less controversial second half of his pronouncement, "Here it is! the rock of salvation—ah!" Huck's "went a-raging" diminishes to "*went on,*" and Clemens cuts the people's "groaning and crying, and jumping ... and hugging" out completely. "*Amens* was popping off everywhere" changes to the more dignified "*people would shout out, "Glory!—A-a-men!"*—transforming the scene from a carnival with fireworks to a more dignified worship service. Toward publication Clemens must have realized that if he wanted to include the sacred book in this passage, he would have to tone it down, and in so doing, he managed at the same time to augment its satirical effect with regard to "the brazen serpent in the wilderness."

As Doyno reveals, the people at whom the preacher begins to preach directly include a woman who "corresponds to Hooper's character": "a fat nigger wench, about forty." After changing "wench" to "woman," he later dropped this incident altogether.[42] Of course, the alteration of "wench" to

Four. To Vilify "the Ways of God to Men"

"woman" would have produced a second exception to the rule in the novel of never referring to an African American as a human being (see Chapter Six, Section V).

Clemens deleted the first half of the following paragraph in revision. In it, the preacher addresses this woman. The part of the passage that survives in the first edition is italicized (from "O, Come"); words italicized in both passages are underlined in the first edition text; variations in the responses of the congregation are indicated by their enclosure in square brackets for the manuscript and parentheses for the first edition text. The paragraph concludes with variant phrasings following "oh, enter":

> "The sperrit's a workin' in you brother—don't shake him off—ah—Now is the accepted time—ah! [A-a-*men*] The devil's holt is weakenin' on you sister—shake him loose, shake him loose—ah! One more shake and the vict'ry's won—ah! [*Come down, Lord!*] Hell's a-burning, the kingdom's a-coming—ah!—one more shake and your chains is broke—ah! [*Glory hal-lelujah!*] *O, come to the mourner's bench! Come, black with sin!* [A*men*!] *come, sick and sore!* [A*men*!] *come, lame and halt and blind!* (a*men*!)⁴³ *come, pore and needy, sunk in shame!* [A-a-*men*!] *come, all that's worn and soiled and suffering* ["g" elided in MS]! *—come with a broken spirit! come with a contrite heart! come in your rags and sin and dirt! the waters that cleanse is free, the door of heaven stands open—oh, enter in and be at rest!* into the everlasting rest!" [A-a-*men*! Glo-o-ry! glory! Come down Lord!] (a-a-*men*! glory, glory hallelujah!)

As Victor Doyno notes, the preacher's exhortation, "One more shake, sister, one more shake and the chains is broke," might cause this woman—especially in the throes of *delirium religions*—to feel she is being liberated from slavery, and, for the first time in her life, mistakenly believe that her liberation is at hand. In this state of confusion, she could forgive her oppressors and join them in celebration. Of course, the whites repulse her joyful overtures.⁴⁴

The manuscript version of the camp meeting includes another incident that did not make the cut into the first edition at all. This passage has racial implications that heighten the social and religious satire of the episode (the lead-in from the published text is italicized, and the revised version of the passage, also italicized, follows the manuscript version):

> *Folks got up, everywhere in the crowd, and worked their way, just by main force, to the mourner's bench with the tears* a-pouring down their faces, and folks hugging them and crying over them all the way. And it was worse than ever *when all the mourners had got up there to the front benches* in a gang. They hugged one another, and shouted, and *flung themselves down on the straw,* and wallowed around, *just plum crazy and wild.* One fat nigger woman about forty, was the worst. The white mourners couldn't fend her off, no way—fast as one would get loose, she'd tackle the next one, and smother him. Next, down she went in the straw, along with the rest, and wallowed around, clawing dirt and shouting glory hallelujah same as they did.⁴⁵

> ... tears running down their faces; and when all the mourners had got up there to the front benches in a crowd, they sung and shouted and flung themselves down on the straw, just crazy and wild.[46]

The more detailed and outrageous out-takes are revealing. Note that the mourners arrive at the benches "in a gang" like a herd of squealing pigs. This bestial image reinforces the "roaring" of the hymn previously and anticipates the (repeated) "wallowing" and "clawing dirt" that follow. In their religious delirium these people degrade themselves to the condition of swine in a sty, and in this image Clemens reiterates one of the central motifs of his religious satire; this identification of the "mourners" with hogs echoes the identification of God with the hogs of pap's tanyard; pap himself, whose hand "was the hand of a hog"; Huck's ritual suicide/patricide/deicide, where he transfers his mythological identities to a scape-hog; the afternoon denizens of the Shepherdson-Grangerford church; the streets of Bricksville, where loafers and hogs share the muddy main street; and the citizens of the Wilks episode, who follow the newly arrived duke and king "trotting along in a gang" (see Chapter Three, Section III A).

Calling the bestial condition of these mourners degraded is understatement. Yet in "the lowest deep" of Hell they sink into "a lower deep still,"[47] experiencing revulsion at the embraces of a slave woman. Mark Twain summed up his opinion of religion when he wrote: "The Moral Sense ... differentiates man from beast ... and sets him *below* the beast ... since he is always foul-minded and guilty and the beast always clean-minded and innocent."[48]

Chapter Three, section V of this study, "Hell in My Book," shows how Clemens imports two key passages from *Paradise Lost* into the novel. In this passage, he again alludes to one of them, the one in which all hell breaks loose in Pandaemonium, Satan's capital in Hell, and the host of fallen angels who have gathered to hear him boast of his recent victory in Eden are all transformed to serpents that writhe on the floor and make a "din" of universal hissing, "Punish't in the shape he [Satan] sinned." Here the mourners transform into hogs and their inarticulate groaning and crying does give voice to their suffering, but it is clear that these are the prostrate writhings and the clamor of the damned, and Clemens inverts their celebration of "salvation" into his description of their damnation.

These deletions and revisions, including the hymn-singing, the preacher's sermon, the crowd's responses, the treatment of the details from Hooper's story, and many details of Huck's observations and descriptions have the cumulative effect of diminishing the social satire of this episode both to make it less offensive to "genteel" readers and—of equal importance—to protect

Huck from seeming cold and unsympathetic in his observations of and reactions to people in the throes of *delirium religions*. At the same time Clemens retains and even sharpens his religious satire. In the end, the first edition version shows almost as clearly as the manuscript that the ignorance, gullibility, superstition, emotional excess, and reverent awe of their "brazen serpent" idol, all of which the participants bring to the camp meeting with them, set them up to be degraded and defrauded (see Chapter Three, Sections III–V).

In Doyno's and Hearn's opinions, Clemens' first version of this episode would have outraged his contemporary audience so that he was forced to tone it down for propriety's sake,[49] but what was unacceptable then would today be regarded as riotous fun in some quarters, and if the author were writing now, he might well prefer to resurrect his original treatment of the episode.[50] This statement clearly articulates an aspect of this remarkable text pointed out earlier: Along with its tripartite characterization of its persona, narrator, and author (see Chapter One, Section I—VI), it defines its *implied reader* as well.

Clemens was revising not only for his audience, but also with an eye to Huck's characterization. Insofar as these changes sharpen his religious satire, the author would most likely retain the revisions he made; to the extent that reinstating the manuscript text's at-times rather cold-blooded, satirical tone would undermine Huck's standing as a sympathetic narrator, whose innocence and compassion lend his vision moral authority, the author would doubtless let these revisions stand as well. Obviously, the characteristics of the reading public have evolved since the 1880s, but Huck Finn is *still* the empathetic, compassionate, good-hearted boy he was back then.

In the king's fraudulent story there are many similar revisions: deletions of expressions of emotional excess, of physical contact, of specifically religious language like "got religion," "saved," "set my soul afire and saved it from that other fire that burns for everlasting—glory hallelujah!" The substitutions of milder expressions and general boiling down of the king's false testimony portraying himself as a newly converted pirate make it shorter and lend it a more humorous tone, ending the episode on a more comic, less satirical note. In this instance, Clemens might well have preferred the manuscript version.

IX. The Brazen Serpent Makes a Kill

Like a great constrictor, "the brazen serpent" crushes the last breaths out of the dying Boggs when it is placed there "by some thoughtful idiot" in

Bricksville, an Arkansas town replete with mud and loafers and hogs and lorded over by the "aristocratic" Colonel Sherburn, a cold-blooded murderer brave enough to face down a lynch mob as he voices his contempt for the common man (Chapter XXI–XXII). There the duke and king continue their career of fraud with the three-night performance of The Royal Nonesuch (see Chapter Four, Section IV-B).

"The brazen serpent" provides Clemens with a particularly apt symbol for his attitude toward the Bible, since it combines the serpent—the bestial archetype of the tempter in Eden compounded with the depravity doctrine that the curse of the snakeskin emblemizes (see Chapter Three, Section X and Chapter Five, Section XI)—with the Book the preacher "fetches a bang with his fist" as the source of salvation. In Chapter V Clemens conflates the features of God and Satan in his description and characterization of pap Finn (see Chapter Three, Section III and IV A and C). In Chapter XX he does the same thing with the Bible itself, merging these moral archetypes into a single image that conflates and thereby negates their moral force. When viewed as an idol, the Bible itself becomes Clemens' symbol of divine depravity. At the camp-meeting the king is able to defraud the congregation with an absurd tale that resonates vaguely with the New Testament parable of the prodigal son, and in Bricksville, Boggs' death agony is more horrifying because the weight of the huge Bible on his bleeding breast crushes out the last gasps of his life.

Commenting on the childhood experience on which he drew in writing this latter episode—William Owsley's shooting of Sam Smarr on a street not far from the Clemens family home in Hannibal—Clemens comments in Mark Twain's *Autobiography*:

> The shooting down of poor old Smarr in the main street at noonday supplied me with some more dreams; and in them I always saw again the grotesque closing picture— the great family Bible spread open on the profane old man's breast by some thoughtful idiot, and rising and sinking to the labored breathings, and adding the torture of its leaden weight to the dying struggles. We are curiously made. In all the throng of gaping and sympathetic onlookers there was not one with common sense enough to perceive that an anvil would have been in better taste there than the Bible, less open to sarcastic criticism, and swifter in its atrocious work. In my nightmares I gasped and struggled for breath under the crush of that vast book for many a night.[51]

Stanley Brodwin's analysis of Samuel Clemens' attitude toward the Bible establishes Clemens' motive for attacking the Bible in *Huckleberry Finn*. Clemens' marginalia in Lecky's *History of European Morals* (1869), which, according to Walter Blair, may date from the period of *Huckleberry Finn*'s writing,[52] include the comment: "Plainly God never knew anything about human beings, or he would not have trusted the idiots with so dangerous a thing as a Bible."[53]

Observing the "curious kind of brute logic in Mark Twain's views about the Bible," Brodwin writes that the nineteenth century was one in which biblical authority shaped "the social order, morality, and even the most intangible aspects of civilization," and he suggests that "to a perceptive man" of that era, "there would be no escape from the problem that the Bible had ... created more suffering than good." Calling attention to "religious wars," "bigotry and hatred" fomented by different interpretations of scriptural texts, and the use of the Bible to sanctify interfaith persecution and racist chattel slavery, Brodwin observes "the stark fact" that the Christian religion and the Bible "had failed to effect a morally better world." It would be easy, he suggests, for a thoughtful contemporary observer like Sam Clemens to "conclude that the Bible was 'dangerous.'"[54]

X. The 1883–84 Completion of the MS: From Old Testament to New

Although Clemens thought in 1880 that *Huck Finn* was almost ready for publication,[55] he discovered that he had a long way to go before he had fully explored its deepest themes and resolved Huck's moral conflict. By 1883 he had come to see his way forward through to Huck's climactic rebirth as the innocent Adam/Satan/Christ and into the massive literary and biblical burlesque of the Phelps farm sequence.

Chapter XXII ("Why the Lynching Bee Failed"; see Appendix A) contains Col. Sherburn's tongue-lashing of the lynch mob that shows up in his yard, and it is significant that his address to the crowd looks beyond the local setting of the novel to observe that "the average man's a coward":

> In the North he lets anybody walk over him that wants to, and goes home and prays for a humble spirit to bear it. In the South one man, all by himself, has stopped a stage full of men in the daytime and robbed the lot. [...] Why don't your juries hang murderers? Because they're afraid the man's friends will shoot them in the back in the dark—and it's just what they *would* do.

While Clemens puts Sherburn's contemptuous tirade in the mouth of a cold-blooded murderer who delivers the example of the cowardice of Southern jurors as a threat rather than a sociological observation to the lynch mob that has come to "string him up," there can be little doubt that some of Sherburn's words speak for Sam Clemens' convictions, and that the novel in which he speaks is an extended parable of human nature as Clemens observed it, both North and South, not just a satire on antebellum Southern culture. This incident provides a fitting introduction to both the religious and social themes of the final section, so it is no wonder that Clemens puts it into the mouth of an unsympathetic character like Sherburn, for doing so is in keeping with his strategy of keeping a firewall of irony between himself and his audience.

In Chapter XXIII, Huck and Jim discuss the "orneriness of kings" in a humorous passage reminiscent of their discussion of Solomon and the French language in Chapter XIV, one that shows Huck's distorted knowledge of history, presumably acquired from his schooling, his reading, and Tom Sawyer, during the "three or four months" of his adoption by the widow. This passage concludes, "What was the use to tell Jim these warn't real kings and dukes? It wouldn't a done no good; and besides, it was just as I said; you couldn't tell them from the real kind"; this is a key point in Clemens' parallel satire against the corrupting influence of hereditary aristocracy (see Chapter Four, Section I).

XI. Of "De Lord God Amighty"

Chapter XXIII concludes with Jim's homesickness and guilt about his daughter's affliction:

> "Oh, Huck, I bust out a-cryin' en grab her up in my arms en say, 'Oh, de po' little thing! de Lord God Amighty fogive po' ole Jim, kaze he never gwyne to fogive hisseff as long's he live!' Oh, she was plumb deef en dumb, Huck, plumb deef en dumb—en I'd ben a treat'n her so!"

This authentic expression of sincere religious sentiment dispels the fog of hypocrisy and emotional excess that Clemens has been attacking with relentless satire on the pernicious influence of conventional religion up until this point. Out of Jim's mouth, these words ring true. But also, notice that "Lord" is rendered conventionally, not as "Lawd" which would be more consistent with Jim's dialect (as Clemens reproduces it in his notebook dialog redacted in this study's preface). The impact of Clemens' choice of spellings on the reader is to increase the impression of seriousness that Jim's statement makes, since there is almost always an element of humor in dialect spelling. On the margin of the manuscript Clemens wrote of the phrase "De Lord God Amighty": "This expression shall not be changed"[56] (see Introduction, Section III and Chapter Six, Section V). Evidently he had given it close consideration.

XII. Of King Noah and "Old Leviticus"

Chapters XXIV–XXIX of the novel recount the Wilks episode. Hearn documents several of Clemens' revisions that shed light on his creative process and his thinking about the themes he was developing as he composed the last half of the novel. In Chapter XXIV, Huck describes the king dressed up for his role as a counterfeit English parson (the first edition text is italicized, deletions in parentheses, and revisions in normal type):

> *The king he allowed he would drop over t'other village, without any plan, but just trust in Providence to lead him the profitable way—meaning the devil, I reckon. We had all bought store clothes where we stopped last; and now the king put his'n on, and he told me to put mine on. I done it, of course.* (But it was because I had to, not because I wanted to.) *The king's duds was all black, and he did look real swell and starchy. I never knowed how clothes could change a body before. Why, before, he looked like the orneriest old rip that ever was; but now when he'd take off his new white beaver and make a bow and do a smile, he looked that grand and good and pious that you'd say he had walked right out of the* (Bible.) *ark, and maybe was old Leviticus himself.*[57]

Hearn notes that Clemens deleted Huck's remark on being required to dress up.[58] Of course, this comment is in character for Huck, since one of the things he "don't take no stock in" is clothes, and it is summer in the South, now. But there is an added layer of meaning in his comment: Huck is being compelled to go along with whatever the king has in store for him, and he can't find a way out, much as he couldn't find a way out of pap's cabin earlier in the book. This resonance between the king and pap reinforces the meaning of Huck's comment about trusting in Providence/the devil: Clemens' scheme portrays them as being all one. This edit is puzzling because Clemens makes it clear that Huck and Jim do want to escape from the royal frauds, both at the end of the Wilks episode and in Chapter XXXI. Perhaps he did not want Huck to become too resentful of the frauds too soon; as long as he finds them entertaining, he is willing to go along with them, and as soon as they go away, he will again confront the problem of what to do about Jim.

In the manuscript, Huck's description of the king reads: "you'd say he had walked right out of the Bible." Clemens' revision heightens the humor of Huck's comment, owing to the ignorance it reflects of "who's who" in the Old Testament. Hearn suggests that the king's looking like a preacher causes Huck to seek biblical terms with which to characterize him, but he mixes up the story of Noah with the title of the third book of Moses; "the reference to the Ark was an afterthought."[59]

This garbling of biblical texts points to the vagueness of Huck's knowledge of what the Bible actually says, challenges the reader to fill in the blanks, and at the same time it connects the king with the Ark in a repetition of the association of the raft journey with Noah's voyage in Chapter IX. This identification of the king with Noah, which is actually underscored by Huck's mistake because it forces the reader to supply the correct name oneself, equates the king with pap, whom we last saw as a corpse "lying in" for Noah in the "House of Death" (see Chapter Two, Section VIII and Appendix A). This motif draws attention to the biblical justifications for slavery that provided a religious prop for "the peculiar institution." At the same time, by inviting the reader to laugh at Huck's ignorance, and removing the name of the sacred book from this passage, Clemens makes these points, injects humor into the incident, and avoids offending Bible-olatrists while doing so.

Furthermore, his reference to Leviticus carries serious satirical import in regard to religion, for Leviticus is not the name of a biblical character, but the title of the third book of the Old Testament, and the theme of that book, as the following biblical head note reveals, is relevant to this fictional situation in which a con artist is about to impersonate a parson:

> NAME
> The title of this book in our English Bible is derived from the Greek and Latin versions referring to the Levites in their priestly responsibilities. It is primarily devoted to the ministry of the priests and the religion of Israel.
>
> PURPOSE
> The contents of Leviticus imply devine [sic] revelation given at Mount Sinai. Fifty-four times the phrase occurs "God said." [...] It [the book] contains the instruction for offerings, the institution of the priesthood, laws of holy living and the feasts and seasons observed by God's holy nation.[60]

While the king is a rapacious imposter whose moral degeneracy receives emphasis from this allusion to the mission of the Hebrew priesthood, Clemens' satire here has a further dimension. For the king, whose profession is religious fraud, is the authentic priest of the hog god/devil personified by pap Finn. And, in Clemens' inverse perspective, pap, as shown earlier, is Clemens' faithful representation of the biblical deity (see Chapter Three, Section III). By implication, then, the king in his dereliction and degeneracy faithfully represents the role of religion in this society: conning the faithful and condemning them to endless suffering for the enrichment of those who are supposed to provide for their physical and spiritual well-being.

In a further instance of intratextual resonance, this brief incident recurs as Huck recounts Tom Sawyer's arrival at the Phelps farm, dressed in his store clothes and a hat that he handles with style, prepared with a false identity, bound to perpetrate fraud (see Chapter Five, Section VI).

As the king begins his parson imposture at the start of the Wilks episode (Chapters XXIV–XXIX), a highly significant sequence involving him in a triple fraud, his previous association with pap through Noah and "old Leviticus" confers on him simultaneous standing as false divine right king, pretended Englishman, and now evil divine, all in one thoroughly corrupt three-personed individual.

XIII. Of Lechers, Blasphemy, and Huck's Innocence

In Chapter XXV Hearn notes that Clemens played down the lecherous aspect of the king's behavior toward girls and young women; in the manuscript, as Ferguson points out, "the king and the duke were considerably more lecherous in the first draft of the novel":

> Soon as he could, the king shook the hare-lip, and sampled Susan, which was better looking. After the king had kissed Mary Jane fourteen or fifteen times, he give the duke a show, and tapered off on the others.[61]

The first edition text reads:

> The king he spread his arms and Mary Jane she jumped for them, and the hare-lip jumped for the duke, and there they <u>had</u> it!

Hearn points out two further instances in the Wilks episode where Clemens revised or did not revise this trait out of his twin rogues. Making their characters less offensive sexually focuses the reader's attention on what is even more deeply evil in these two, epitomized in the king's recurrent religious frauds.

Also in Chapter XXV, a small revision, the substitution of "sky" (in the published text) for "throne" (MS) shows Clemens' care to avoid offending readers' religious sensibilities—an index of just how revolutionary his religious satire was in contemporary society and how important to him it was to keep that satire covert and maintain plausible deniability if any critic should penetrate his firewall of irony; comments Hearn: "Originally 'the throne' [of God] (MS)," but Clemens once again blunts the satire by substituting "sky," probably to avoid striking too irreverent a tone, as Hearn speculates,[62] but possibly to preserve Huck's literal-minded narration as well. Since the Throne is not visible, and he tends to regard the real as what he can see, this projection of theism is somewhat out of character and so points to the author as the one pulling Huck's strings here. Nevertheless, this unfortunate revision also uncouples the association of earthly thrones occupied by divine-right monarchs—whom Clemens equates with the duke and the king—with the Throne occupied by the ultimate Monarch, whom Clemens equates with pap Finn (see Chapter Three, Section III).

In the same passage in Chapter XXV, another one-word revision, the substitution of "woman" for "heifer (MS)," again to eliminate "crude" and "demeaning" language,[63] reduces the satiric impact of Huck's description of the scene in the Wilks parlor preceding the funeral of Peter Wilks. Here is this passage as it reads in the manuscript (in parentheses) and first edition (italicized):

> *Well ... it worked the crowd like you never see anything like it, and so everybody broke down and went to sobbing right out loud—the poor girls, too; and every woman, nearly, went up to the girls, without saying a word, and kissed them, solemn, on the forehead, and then put their hand on their head, and looked up towards the* (throne) *sky, with the tears running down, and* (then let go) *then busted out and went off sobbing and swabbing, and give the next* (heifer) *woman a show. I never see anything so disgusting.*[64]

Not only does the manuscript intensify the satire, but it also recalls the motif we have seen associated with the influence of religion several times before in the novel: the transformation of human beings to beasts by the language with which Huck describes their religious excesses. Transformations to hogs are the main examples of this motif, but here we empathize with Huck's disgust at this scene of so much posturing and pretense more strongly when he remarks of the women that their gaze goes up to the Throne of God, and that in his view they seem like a herd of cows, all facing in the same direction and acting alike, as Huck's conversation with Judith Loftus in Chapter XI illustrates. But Clemens' desire to have Huck always appear as a sympathetic character—never as harshly satirical except when condemning an evil character like the king—again moved the author to make this change.

The delicate nature of the task Clemens sets for himself is frequently evident in his revisions, which tend to strengthen Huck's sympathetic status as a good hearted narrator whose disgust at the hypocrisy and posturing he observes carries moral weight, and to divert *overt* religious satire away from the Bible and the faithful into a focus on the ways religion can be used by scoundrels for deceit and fraud. This essentially social satire scrupulously avoids criticism of sacred doctrine, religious institutions, sincere religious sentiment, and religion itself. However, this satire on religious mores is only the tip of the of the iceberg, the great mass of which consists of direct, repeated attacks on the Bible itself and the God it portrays and their "pernicious influence" on society.

XIV. The King's Speech

Perhaps it galled Clemens to make many of these changes that vitiated the satire he had made, but in some places—the sermon at the camp-meeting, for instance—his revision has the effect of preserving Huck's goodheartedness: Clemens effectively mutes some of Huck's critical comments, making him seem more sympathetic and innocent, while requiring the reader to see what Huck does not say, but Clemens manages to reveal anyway. One reason for the author's extensive revisions of the camp-meeting episode is that too often in those scenes of *delirium religions,* the narration comes off as intentionally satirical instead of naïve. When Clemens noticed that his inspiration as a satirist had overwhelmed the narrative voice of his persona— leaving a hole in his firewall of irony—he toned down the overt satire, closed the hole, and preserved Huck's naiveté.

On the other hand, his revision of the king's speech, which the manuscript renders in direct discourse a little later in this episode in Chapter XXV, exhibits masterful sharpening of the satire as he revised it for publication. Compare the manuscript text to the first edition (italicized):

"Friends, good friends of the diseased, and ourn too, I trust—it's a sore trial to lose him, and a sore trial to miss seeing of him alive, after the wearisome long journey of four thousand mile; but it's a trial that's sweetened and sanctified to us by this dear sympathy and those holy tears; and so, out of our hearts we thank you, for out of our mouths we cannot, words being too weak and cold. May you find sech friends and sech sympathy, yourselves when your own time of trial comes, and may this affliction be softened to you as ourn is today, by the soothing ba'm of earthly love and the healing of heavenly grace. Amen" (MS).[65]

Well, by-and-by the king he gets up and comes forward a little, and works himself up and slobbers out a speech, all full of tears and flapdoodle about its being a sore trial for him and his poor brother to lose the diseased, and to miss seeing diseased alive, after the long journey of four thousand mile, but it's a trial that's sweetened and sanctified to us by this dear sympathy and these holy tears, and so he thanks them out of his heart and out of his brother's heart, because out of their mouths they can't, words being too weak and cold, and all that kind of rot and slush, till it was just sickening; and then he blubbers out a pious goody-goody Amen, and turns himself loose and goes to crying fit to bust.

Janet McKay's stylistic analysis of the published version of the king's speech ("Tears and Flapdoodle") yields insight into Mark Twain's humor and Clemens' satiric strategy and artistic accomplishment. McKay observes that Huck's run-on sentence masks Clemens' use of both indirect and direct discourse. This loosely coordinated, "cumulative sentence," in which Clemens switches from Huck's emotional perspective on the king's pretentious manner and words, to quoting the con man, and then back to Huck's response to the king's hypocritical bombast, contributes to the overall effect of reinforcing the reader's perception of Huck as being verbally unsophisticated, even as he very effectively portrays the king as contemptible. The author's handling of Huck's style frames the king's speech in the narrator's revulsion, and Huck's outrage at the phony preacher's posturing drives home Clemens' satire on the ways people use pious rhetoric for self-serving and immoral purposes.

Contrasts between Huck's voice and "the bombastic posturing of the King," according to McKay—along with Clemens' handling of personal pronouns—distinguish the narrator's words from the king's, as "disdain" colors Huck's word choices, and the verb phrases "turns … loose, … slobbers out, … and … blubbers out" express "Huck's scorn for the king's histrionics." Adding to the contrasts between Huck's narration and his quotation of the king, McKay identifies "vernacular constructions," and "lexical choices" typical of Huck's style, including, for example, tautology ("the king he") and "flapdoodle" and "goody-goody"; these elements, which do not occur in the king's rhetoric, heighten the contrast between the styles of the two speakers in this sentence. Huck's or the king's twice-uttered malapropism, "diseased" for "deceased," prepares for Huck's calling the king's act "sickening," compounding the implied author's commentary on this scene. Huck's natural, unrefined style serves semantically to express what McKay calls his "persistent skepticism about people who try [or pretend] to be good by 'sivilized' standards."

In contrast to the style of Huck's narration, the portion of the king's speech parenthesized within the narrator's run-on sentence consists of a display of pretentiously pious words focusing the reader's attention on the king's and his listeners' exaggerated show of grief: "to lose the diseased, and to miss seeing diseased alive, after the long journey of four thousand mile, but it's a trial that's sweetened and sanctified to us by this dear sympathy and these holy tears"; thus Huck's descriptive phrase "rot and slush" connects his narration to juxtaposed scenes where all of the mourners put on overwrought expressions of "genteel mourning" (e.g., the neighbor women, whose copy-heifer behavior and weeping Huck finds "disgusting"); McKay points out that Huck's vernacular effectively captures "the mental and physical sogginess of the scene."

The emotional impact of this "sobbing and swabbing" contrasts to Huck's own understated responses to sad situations earlier in the story, as McKay also notices. Instances of this emotional reserve include his terse narration of his face-off with pap in Chapter VI, his passing sorrow for the gang trapped aboard the foundered *Walter Scott* in Chapter XII, and his brief shedding of tears for Buck Grangerford in Chapter XVIII. This contrast is the product of Clemens' rhetoric, and in this passage the impression that Huck's naïve narration makes on the reader is a function of the contrasting styles of the two speakers.

Huck's colorful vernacular rhetoric and sincere emotional stance provide the author's primary means to achieving what McKay calls his "powerful indictment" of "pretended or misguided piety," which H. N. Smith has indicated as one of the novel's principal satirical themes: (see Chapter Two, Section II). "However," McKay comments, Clemens' stretching for "the maximum satiric effect" led him to reach beyond relatively simple ironic contrasts between the king and the narrator: "Huck's scathing denunciation becomes the angle from which we view the sham and adds to his moral authority. Outrage reinforces satire." McKay's incisive and much more extensive analysis of the king's speech concludes that Huck's deceptively simple style "comes to represent honesty in a dishonest world."[66]

Ferguson observes that "every phrase in the draft is carried over into the final text," as Hearn notes, "but the indirect reporting, by implying compression from much greater length, immeasurably heightens the effect."[67] Clemens' editing," notes Hearn, did drop one phrase for propriety's sake: "'earthly love,' a term usually applied to carnal desire."[68] Nevertheless, his revision is actually longer by about a dozen words than the manuscript version.

When Clemens puts this redaction of the king's speech into Huck's mouth, he feels free to let Huck comment on his own feelings about it because Huck is reacting to the villain of the episode and stands on solid moral and emotional ground in reviling the king; in earlier scenes his disgusted comments on the conduct of the faithful believers—no matter how degraded their conduct at the camp-meeting and funeral—would have seemed both blasphemous and heartless. Now it is the king's hypocrisy, which readers *would* find offensive along with Huck, that Clemens reviles.

Huck's indignation at the king's posturing and his outrage at the victimization of the Wilks sisters prepare him—and the reader—emotionally and morally—for the dangerous and chivalrous escapade on which he is about to embark: stealing "the king's plunder" (see Appendix A) and rescuing three damsels in distress and their slaves. This is the first time in the story that Huck plans and acts heroically, and it comes close to costing him his life. But his action bears fruit; he rescues the girls, restores their inheritance, and, although the swindlers escape and continue to victimize Huck and Jim, he does have the satisfaction of having prevented much greater harm to the Wilks sisters and their slaves while escaping dangers to himself and Jim. And by making this risky stand for morality in this episode, Huck has gone back on his decision to "do [right or wrong] whatever come handiest at the time" that provisionally solved his moral dilemma over helping Jim escape (Chapter XVI); his manipulation of everybody around him is hardly the easiest way out of this situation, and when his plans unravel, his efforts put him into mortal danger.

XV. Six Grand in "Yaller-Boys"

A little later on in Chapter XXV, the frauds lay their hands on the Wilks sisters' five thousand seven hundred dollar inheritance, and add their own money to bring the sum to an even six thousand, for appearance's sake. The manuscript shows that Clemens gave consideration to the amount of money involved, and Hearn speculates that the larger sums Clemens considered while he was arriving at the total of six thousand were excessive, and so Clemens cut the amount of the Wilks sisters' inheritance in the manuscript on grounds of realism.[69]

No one in this study's research base has pointed out that six thousand is exactly the sum of Huck's own fortune at the start of the novel, and he is the only one present who does not covet this pile of money: "When we got up stairs, everybody gathered around the table, and the king he counted it and stacked it up, three hundred dollars in a pile—twenty elegant little piles. Everybody looked hungry at it, and licked their chops" (Chapter XXV).

While everybody else gazes at the money, Huck looks at their faces, not just at the gold. One of Huck's endearing qualities is that money has no hold on him; he is not subject to its allure and does not experience the greed that motivates so many of the people around him. The worship of gold is another form of idolatry that transforms human beings into beasts in the novel, as Clemens shows again in this scene, where their money-lust makes them look like hungry dogs licking their chops (see Chapter Four, Section IV-B).

When he flees this town, he leaves *another* six thousand dollar fortune in his wake. The fact that money—especially these two identical, large amounts of money—brings him more trouble and danger than security and satisfaction actually makes money a burden to Huck that restricts his freedom and attracts unwanted attention. The only other significant sums he mentions having in the text are the eight dollars in silver he and Jim find in Chapter X and the forty dollars given to him by the slave hunters in Chapter XVI, which he shares equally with Jim. The fact that Huck is immune to money-lust makes him an ideal observer of the materialistic society Clemens satirizes.

When the duke and king get the money, the king comments, "Thish yer comes of trust'n to Providence. It's the best way, in the long run. I've tried 'em all, and ther' ain't no better way" (Chapter XXV). Hearn comments that this kind of "cynical blasphemy" characterizes Simon Suggs in Hooper's 1845 model for Clemens' camp-meeting in another allusive echo of *Adventures of Captain Simon Suggs*; Clemens, in Hearn's view, "boosted the cynicism" of the king's comment by putting it into the mouth of this contemptible imposter. Noting that the author was familiar with the ways that people tend to distort religious precepts for their selfish advantage, Hearn quotes Mark Twain: "The Christian's Bible is a drug-store. Its contents remain the same; but the medical practice changes."[70]

The king's repeated mention of this "trusting to Providence" motto in chapters XXIV and XXV evidently make an impression on Huck, for when he comes to the Phelps farm in Chapter XXXII he goes along "without a plan," trusting "to Providence to put the right words in my head." In this sense, his apprenticeship with the swindlers pays off (see Chapter Four, Section XX).

XVI. The Hog-King

Farther along in this same chapter, Dr. Robinson warns the Wilks girls that "the ignorant tramp, with his idiotic Greek and Hebrew," is a fraud. In the manuscript, as Hearn points out, Dr. Robinson reviles "the ignorant hog, with his putrid and idiotic Greek and Hebrew."[71] Here again we find the hog motif applied this time to the king, who as a fraudulent king, Englishman, and clergyman as well as an actual con man is a true devotee of the hog-god/devil who rules religion in Huck's world. Pap Finn, of course, is the incarnation of this god/fiend in the novel (see Chapter Three, Section III and IV A and C). Clemens again applies this motif to the king at the opening of Chapter 26 of the manuscript when Huck comments on the prospect of sleeping with him: "Maybe he could [stand it], but I couldn't a stood him, only I was long used to sleeping with the other kind of hogs."[72] Hearn comments that Clemens "scrapped this delicious bit of sarcasm" for plot considerations.[73]

Clemens scrupulously purged all references to the king as a hog from the published text and toned down his application of bestial imagery to the king especially. When Huck describes the king as putting "out his paw" to greet Dr. Robinson in the manuscript, Clemens revises "paw" to "flapper," which, as Doyno points out, is also "a slang word that means *hand* as well as *flipper*,"[74] implying that Huck feels there is something fishy about him. When Huck comments on the king's greed in Chapter XXVIII, "I never see such a giraff as that king for wanting to swallow *everything*," Clemens retains the image.⁷⁵ In one of the few revisions that *attribute* a bestial image to the royal frauds, Clemens makes a one-word change in the following passage from Chapter XXVIII (first edition text italicized):

> "I got to travel with them a while longer, whether I want to or not—druther not tell you why—and although this town would get me out of their (hands) *claws if you was to blow on them, I'd be all right, but ther'd be another person that you don't know about who'd be in awful trouble."*

This revision renders the royal, reverend frauds "bestial and threatening."⁷⁶

As Huck finds himself confronted with the anomaly of the truth being "better, and actuly *safer*, than a lie," Huck describes Mary Jane Wilks' reaction to his having "mouth[ed] off once too often," revealing that the girls' lamented slaves will return inside of two weeks (Chapter XXVIII). Huck's truly chivalrous loyalty to the sisters, along with his crush on Mary Jane—revealed with charming irony in his praise of her beauty and "sand"—prompts him to betray the frauds. As he considers what he should do, he is baffled by the strange quandary in which he finds himself, and in the end he acts on his "dangerous" impulse to tell the truth. Among the revisions on his manuscript page is the brilliantly incongruous insertion of the simile describing Mary Jane: *"looking kinder happy, and eased up, like a person that's had a tooth pulled out."*

Huck's admiration of Mary Jane's beauty and spirit comprises another important dimension of his own characterization, for it makes him seem much more human and vulnerable as he falls in love for the first time, an indicator that he is on the verge of growing up (see Chapter Five, Section XIII). Moreover, her promise to pray for him as she goes out of his life touches him deeply and reminds the reader, as does Jim's appeal to "de Lord God Amighty," that not all of religious sentiment is hypocrisy and sham, even as his aside to the reader as he narrates this encounter prepares us for Huck's climactic commitment to "wickedness" (see Chapter Four, Sections XVIII and XIX):

> *No, I hain't ever seen her since; but I reckon I've thought of her a many and a many a million times, and of her saying she would pray for me; and if ever I'd a thought it would do any good for me to pray for her, (I'm dum'd [damned]) blamed if I wouldn't a done it or bust.*⁷⁷

In Chapter 28, after Huck gets Mary Jane's sisters to cooperate with his scheme, Clemens' manuscript (in normal type) reads: "*'All right,'* they said, *and cleared out to lay for their* (cussed) *uncles,* (and give them the love and the kisses, and tell the old principal hog) *and tell them the message.* Clemens deleted "cussed" and "old principal hog" and substituted "and tell them the message."⁷⁸ Again at the end of the Wilks episode (Chapter XXX), when the duke and king accuse each other of having tried to steal the entire take, the manuscript version of the duke's accusation reads "hog" where the published bestial metaphor reads "ostrich."[79] Unfortunately, in editing out all of these references to the king as a hog, Clemens dropped this motif completely from the Wilks episode. Perhaps he feared that it was becoming so prominent a feature of the story that it would alert readers to his having intentionally satirized a sacred subject, even though this "man of the cloth" is a vicious imposter; or perhaps he was more concerned with toning down the overt satire. In any case, from the camp meeting on, he consistently edited out all direct references to people as hogs. The only one he kept is the implication that the crowd that greets the royal frauds in Chapter XXIV resembles a "gang" of pigs, as H. N. Smith and Lynn infer (see Chapter Two, Section II); otherwise he struck out these swinish images even at the cost of vividness of imagery and sharpness of sarcastic wit in his characterization of the king, especially.

An additional word choice of Huck's deserves mention here. In Chapter XXXI Huck's penultimate view of the king provides the last example of Huck describing the king through bestial imagery; Huck happens on the duke while he is tracing Jim and recalls seeing "*the king in that* (gin-mill) *doggery, yesterday.*" Doyno points out that Clemens substituted "doggery" twice for "gin-mill" in the episode.[80] Clemens' choice of words here is particularly apt in consideration of two further motifs in the text: by likening the king to a dog in this last scene before the two rogues are tarred, feathered, and ridden on a rail—in their final, all too real bestial transformation to "a couple of monstrous big soldier-plumes" (Chapter XXXIII)—which, of course, were made of ostrich feathers—we see the king being baited and stripped of his ill-gotten "forty dirty dollars" by the loafers there, and Clemens recalls the scene of the dog-baiting by the loafers of Bricksville in Chapter XXI, thus foreshadowing the king's coming punishment along with the duke. In addition, Huck's final bestial simile for the pair obliquely recalls the duke's reviling the king after the final fiasco of the Wilks sequence: "I never see such an old ostrich for wanting to gobble everything."

Moreover, in the archetypal scheme of allusion to Dante's *Inferno*, this last view of the king, who personifies Fraud and now Treachery, puts him on a par with the denizens of the last circle. There Brutus, Cassius, and Judas—the latter of whom Huck mentions as he remarks of Mary Jane, "She had the grit to pray for Judas if she took the notion" (Chapter XXVIII)—are forever gnawed in the triple maws of Lucifer (see Chapter Four, Section IV-A).[81] In light of the king's having just betrayed Jim, whom Clemens elevates to the status of a Christ figure (see Chapter Five, Section IX and Chapter Six, Section

V), he is morally equivalent to Judas, and by thus likening the "doggery" to the deepest pit in Hell, this scene sets the stage for Huck's great debate, in which he becomes Samuel Clemens' Adamic Satan (see Chapter Four, Section XVIII and XIX).

XVII. Laying the Rattlesnake-Skin to Rest

The fullness of Clemens' religious satire in *Huckleberry Finn* is not to be grasped without a working knowledge of *Paradise Lost* and the career of Satan in that epic. Extensive parallels, some of which we have already explored, show that Clemens drew on Milton's epic in order to structure the novel and deride the epic poet's effort to "justify the ways of God to men" (see Appendix B, C, D, and F).[82] A central concern of the religious satire of *Huckleberry Finn* is to *vilify* the ways of God—the God of the Bible, *Pilgrim's Progress,* Dante's *Inferno,* and *Paradise Lost*—to "the damned human race."

Since the Bible is also the principal source for *Paradise Lost*, more biblical burlesque becomes apparent as one explores the Miltonic derivation of *Huckleberry Finn*, as shown in Chapter Three of this study. In Clemens' portrayal of pap Finn, he reduces the stories of God and Satan in his sources to a single absurdity. Conflation prevails where one would normally expect differentiation (see Chapter Three, Section II), and some of the biblical parallels we have not yet examined make sense—that is, in Clemens' inverted moral perspective, nonsense—only when one sees them going hand-in-hand with Milton's archetypes of evil, as is the case with pap Finn and "the brazen serpent."

Through Clemens' misprision of the numerous biblical and Miltonic texts to which he alludes, he creates a covert archetypal context for Huck's realistic narrative that causes it to resonate in a well-read, Christian reader's imagination with all of the writings listed above. Two of these stories were especially evocative in the nineteenth century: the myths of the American Adam as protagonist of the American Dream in the American Eden/Promised Land, and of the Civil War as a variation on the theme of "Let my people go." Beneath the biblical allusions, even more deeply concealed in the archetypal substructure, lies a pattern of allusions to *Paradise Lost*. The identification of pap as the avatar of God and Satan (see Chapter Three, Section III, IV and V); of Huck as Christ, the Death Angel, and Adam; and of the river as Chaos initiates this pattern and comments sarcastically on Judeo-Christian religion (see Chapter Three, Section V, VIII and IX).

This misprision is wholly consonant with the author's later characterizations of Satan that identify biblically informed conscience (which Clemens/

Mark Twain reviled as "the Moral Sense ... which differentiates man from beast and sets him ... below the beast"[83]) as the strongest force of evil in the novel. In Chapter XXXI Huck's "Great Debate" mirrors the form of a similar confrontation between Milton's Satan and *his* conscience, but Clemens inverts the puritan's moral logic. Huck's victory over his own conscience enables him at last to align himself fully with Jim's quest for freedom, while that of Milton's Satan leads to his self-dedication to evil and to the corruption of humanity. Huck's moral victory, in the novel's religious satire, thus sets him forever free from the Doctrine of Total Depravity emblemized by the curse of the rattlesnake skin (see Chapter Three, Section XII). Transcending conscience enables him to go back to the world he has been trying to escape to attempt an act of compassion that defies that society's—and his own conscience's—depraved values.

Clemens bases the evasion on the popular Mosaic text, the liberation of Israel from Egyptian bondage, to reveal the incompatibility of Huck's humane values and Jim's dignity with the roles they must play in society. Seen in context, the final chapters provide neither the "Jim's debasement nor Huck's suppression" (Kolb)[84] nor his "sad initiation" (Cox)[85] from which he emerges as an "empiricist member of society" (Manierre).[86] Rather, the conclusion leaves Huck free of the obligation to continue wearing the archetypal guises society has forced on him and to revert to the one adult archetypal role to which he has freely—albeit unwittingly—aspired: the Arch-Rebel who at last wholeheartedly rejects "sivilization" in his decision to "light out."

XVIII. Huckleberry Satan: The "Lower Deep" in Huck's "Great Debate"

Huck Finn is incapable of controlling events without moral autonomy. Therefore, he must choose between the dictates of his "deformed conscience" and the impulses of his "sound heart," as Samuel Clemens succinctly expressed the central conflict of the novel. According to Huck's conscience, Jim is immoral, for a slave's "virtue" is a function of his obedience and loyalty to his owner. Huck's legal and moral "duty" is clear: Huck must turn Jim in. But the fugitive slave is also, unbeknownst to him, his friend and brother, as well as his surrogate father. Unable though Huck is to consciously acknowledge Jim's full humanity, he cannot bring himself to betray Jim. When he misses a chance to do so he observes, "I warn't *man* enough" (Chapter XVI, italics added).

Huck cannot *think* of Jim as a *man*, either—a human being whose birthright is freedom—for the heart is mute. He can only feel "sick" at the prospect of breaking his promise not to betray Jim (his promise of Chapter VIII), of which Jim reminds him as he shoves off "all in a sweat to tell" in Chapter XVI. At fifty yards distance, Jim's "Dah you goes, de ole true Huck, de on'y white genlman dat ever kep' his promise to ole Jim" "took the tuck all out of me."

Huck avoids choosing and doesn't "bother no more about it," seeing that "it's troublesome to do right and ain't no trouble to do wrong, and the wages is just the same." This temporary resolution of his moral dilemma sees him through to the Wilks episode, in which his disgust and indignation at the perfidy of the royal frauds moves him to risk everything to do what is right by helping the three orphan girls and their slaves. But "the wages of sin is death,"[87] as is written in the New Testament, and on the journey downstream as they voyage in Chaos, Huck commutes into Hell with each visit ashore as he continues his moral education. In Chapter XXXI circumstances force Huck to take a permanent stand on his moral issue—not on whether slavery is right or wrong—but on whether or not to continue helping Jim to escape it. Although his conscience sees it as a choice between salvation and damnation—life or death—Huck's "sound heart," strengthened by his love for Jim, overrules his "deformed conscience," bringing the raft voyage and the curse of the rattlesnake skin to an end (see Chapter Three, Section X and XII).

As James Cox has so aptly observed, the structure of *Huckleberry Finn is* a trap that lures the sympathetic reader into "fatal approval" of Huck's moral decision. How fatal that approval is, however, has not yet been fully revealed, despite the waves of critical ink that have washed over the debate between Huck's conscience and heart. Numerous critics have claimed that the climax is Huck's moment—and Mark Twain's moment—of moral transfiguration, the moment readers have been waiting for since the opening chapters set up the reader to expect a conversion drama, the story of a "poor lost lamb," as the widow calls Huck in Chapter I, coming home to God. In this respect, Huck's rebirth in Chapter XXXI fulfills his identification with the Savior in his willingness to "lay down his life for his friend."[88] Huck's "passion" alone on the raft is his Gethsemane, and his resolve to save Jim marks his retrieval of his identity as Christ, which he cast off in his ritual escape from society in Chapter VII (see Chapter Three, Section VII).

The implied narrator's ironic inversion of Huck's moral language, in context, only enhances the satisfaction that most readers of this persuasion derive from the climax. However, as Norris Yates has observed, the passage contains religious elements that can unsettle one's confidence in the climax as a conversion drama narrated with charming irony. Yates finds that Huck's apparent conversion "is only the prelude to a counter-conversion,"[89] in that it bears remarkable similarity to "recorded conversions out of or away from religious life."[90] Huck, concludes Yates, appears to have been converted to something, but to what—since "he shows no special desire to love God or to achieve union with Him; Christ is not even mentioned; [and] Satan too as an anthropomorphic force [seems to be] absent from his reflections"—Yates finds not at all clear:

> No two conversion cases are exactly alike, and Huck's conversion is lacking in several elements found in many. [...] Nevertheless Huck's experience [...] may be viewed either as an incomplete conversion followed by backsliding or as a counter-conversion which turns out to be permanent. By presenting part of Huck's moral growth within the pattern of a religious phenomenon that was widespread in rural America, and in a sense, by turning that pattern upside-down, Mark Twain supplied ingredients in the irony of the novel which deserve closer attention.[91]

By extending Yates' work to give "closer attention" to the ironic ingredients of the climax, we can once again reconcile contradictory views of this passage by considering the author's ironic management of point of view and literary archetype.

Huck's "Great Debate" is in fact one of Clemens' most subtle and powerful literary burlesques, a moment in Huck's narrative when Clemens discharges all the mythic pressures that have been building up through the development of archetypal material in a mighty guffaw that he apparently hoped might demonstrate the power of laughter over "a colossal humbug."

To fully appreciate the impact of the climax, one must understand it—in its context of combined biblical and Miltonic satire—as the arrival of Clemens' fugitive from the New World theocracy of the puritans at his opting for hell, not heaven (in contrast to Bunyan's Christian; see Chapter Four, Section III). But there is much more to it than that: As we are about to see, Huck's Great Debate with his conscience is also an intricate burlesque in which Huck's climactic monologue re-dramatizes Satan's once-famous debate with his own conscience on Mount Nephates in Book IV of *Paradise Lost*. In the bizarre view of Mr. Clemens, Huck's posture is in contrast to the implied narrator's moralism by its essential anti-morality; in overturning Huck's conscience Clemens discovered Satan to be the only poetic and mythological alternative to God, and so Huck Finn becomes the first avatar of the "Adamic Satan" figure into which Clemens eventually transformed Mark Twain (see Chapter Two, Section VII and Chapter Four, Section VIII).

In Chapter XXXI of the novel, the logic, sequence, and substance of Huck's internal debate mirror those of Satan, also fresh out of Chaos, in a wholly congruent counter-conversion at the beginning of Book IV (The passages are printed in parallel in Appendix F to facilitate comparison). Since both Satan and Huck Finn are "nigh the birth" of a "dire attempt,"[92] and since the conversion factor in Huck's experience is inherently a rebirth metaphor, both passages imply that their protagonists are being born again, or converted. "Conscience wakes despair" in Satan as "horror and doubt / Distract his troubl'd thoughts," and he confesses "all his [God's] good prov'd ill in me, / And wrought but malice"[93]; the more Huck thinks about his situation, "the more my conscience went to grinding me," and he suffers the conviction that "my wickedness was being watched all the time from up there in Heaven, whilst I was stealing a poor old woman's nigger that hadn't ever done me no harm" (Notice the ambiguous reference of "that" in Huck's sentence to both "old woman"—to which Huck means it to refer—and "nigger"—to which it refers grammatically and emotionally).

As both Satan and Huck face responsibility for sin, each tries plea-bargaining and blames fate: Satan wishes he had been born lower, but recognizes that it wouldn't have made any difference: "Other Powers as great / Fell not"; Huck seeks an excuse in his low birth: "I was brung up wicked, and so I warn't so much to blame." Satan acknowledges he had "free Will and Power to stand,"[94] and Huck, contemplating his "miserable [Satan's word] doings," remembers the Sunday school he avoided where "they'd a learnt you ... that people that acts as I'd been acting about that nigger goes to everlasting fire." Each thus sees his sin as an act freely willed. Huck's fear of hell mirrors Satan's recognition,

> Against his [God's] thy will
> Chose freely what it now so justly rues.
> Me miserable! which way shall I fly
> Infinite wrath, and infinite despair?
> Which way I fly is Hell; myself am Hell;
> And in the lowest deep a lower deep
> Still threat'ning to devour me opens wide,
> To which the Hell I suffer seems a Heaven.[95]

Each thus accepts damnation as the just consequence of his sin. Both Satan and Huck next look at their chances for pardon. Satan's:

> O, then, at last relent: is there no place
> For Repentance, none for Pardon left?"[96]

matches Huck's:

> I about made up my mind to pray, and see if I couldn't try to quit being the kind of a boy I was and be better. So I kneeled down."

Satan sees no way left:

> but by submission; and that word
> *Disdain* forbids me, and my dread of shame
> Among the Spirits beneath.[97]

For Huck, too "dread of shame" is a precipitating factor in his counter-conversion:

> It would get all around that Huck Finn helped a nigger to get his freedom; and if I was ever to see anybody from that town again I'd be ready to get down and lick his boots for shame."

Trying to "pray a lie," Huck discovers "away inside of me I was holding onto the biggest one [sin] of all."

Satan considers:

> Ay me, they ["the Spirits beneath"] little know
> How dearly I abide that boast [that he would "subdue th' Omnipotent"] so vain,
> Under what torments inwardly I groan;
> While they adore me on the Throne of Hell,
> With Diadem and Sceptre high advanc'd
> The lower still I fall, only Supreme
> In misery; such joy Ambition finds.
> But say I could repent, and could obtain
> By Act of Grace, my former state; how soon
> Would highth recall high thoughts, how soon unsay
> What feign'd submission swore; ease would recant
> Vows made in pain, as violent and void.[98]

Huck, "living his ritual," as James Cox has phrased it, and feigning submission, discovers "You Can't Pray a Lie" (see Appendix A); so then he writes the letter to Miss Watson and immediately feels "good and all washed clean of sin for the first time I had ever felt so in my life, and I knowed I could pray now." "Ease," however, recalls memories of the raft journey and fond thoughts of Jim and how he "said I was the best friend old Jim ever had in the world, and the *only* one he's got now; and then I happened to look around and see that paper." Soon indeed Huck recants his vow to reform by tearing up the letter; reflects Satan, as his soliloquy continues:

> For never can true reconcilement grow
> Where wounds of deadly hate have pierc'd so deep.
> Which would but lead to worse relapse,
> And heavier fall[99]:

The sight of the letter hurts Huck to his heart. But Huck's wound is not of hate but love. Satan's "dread of shame / Among the Spirits beneath," matched at the outset of Huck's counter-conversion by his similar dread of shame should he ever meet anybody from St. Petersburg again, is finally outmatched by Huck's loyalty to Jim, and both Satan and Huck arrive at the same conclusions.

Having purchased "Short intermission, bought with double smart,"[100] Huck concludes

"All right then, I'll *go* to hell."

Satan seals his rebellion with the rhetorically milder formulation:

> This knows my Punisher; therefore as far
> From granting hee, as I from begging peace."[101]

By thinking "no more about reforming," putting "the whole thing out of my head," and resolving to "take up wickedness again," Huck echoes Satan's farewell:

> So farewell Hope, and with Hope farewell Fear,
> Farewell Remorse: all Good to me is lost;
> Evil be thou my Good."[102]

Finally, Clemens mirrors Satan's vow to hold "Divided Empire with Heav'n's King"[103] in Huck's plan to "steal Jim out of slavery again." Clemens frames Huck's moral victory in a satanic rebirth that marks his attainment of adult, heroic stature with devastating irony that stands the moral archetypes (God and Satan) of Judeo-Christian religion on their conflated ears.

In addition to Yates' valuable commentary above, two further critiques of this climactic passage call for comment at this juncture. The first of these is Janet Holmgren McKay's incisive stylistic analysis of Clemens' handling of point of view in this passage, in which she finds that Clemens "does some violence to Huck's character" by having him engage in this internal debate, the style of which "demonstrates the tensions between the implied author, narrator, and character [!]."

"Stock religious phrases," observes McKay, "compete with constructions and lexical choices the reader has come to associate with Huck." McKay suggests that "by incorporating his conscience's voice into Huck's own discourse," the author commits "a contradiction of his character[;] ... Huck's preoccupation with religion and his concern for society's judgment ... mark the intrusion of the authorial personality."[104]

McKay is partly right. At this point in the narration, the tensions among the implied author, implied narrator, and narrative persona break the discourse into separate streams marked by Huck's uncharacteristic expression, as McKay notices but cannot fully explain because she does not know what the reader now can see: Clemens models Huck's debate on Milton's satanic soliloquy, and the change in Huck's language gently directs attention to this authorial intrusion (see Introduction, Section VI and Chapter One, Sections III and IV).

Part II of Huck's tri-partite narration, the portion subtitled "short intermission, bought with double smart" (see Appendix F), restores the narration of Huck's reverie to his customary linguistic patterns as he recapitulates his voyage with Jim: "Huck's memory of Jim ... determines his ultimate change of heart"; in part three of his debate, Huck, "no longer thinking in terms of his conscience":

> happened to look around and see that paper.
> It was a close place. I took it up, and held it in my hand. I was a-trembling, because I'd got to decide, forever, betwixt two things, and I knowed it. I studied a minute, sort of holding my breath, and then says to myself:
> "All right, then, I'll *go* to hell"—and tore it up.

McKay observes that while his narration "dramatizes a painful moral lesson," Huck expresses the conclusion reached by his "sound heart" "in words dictated by his conscience." Thus, concludes McKay: "The authorial personality eclipses the character he has developed, and subsequent developments in the novel (the "slapstick" shenanigans of Jim's rescue) seem to confirm ... that Twain has lost touch with Huck's voice and personality." Again, McKay has no way to account for this apparent breakdown in sustaining Huck's characteristic voice other than stylistic consideration, and so here she reaches the limit of utility of the critical tool she brings to bear on Huck's Great Debate: "Huck's character growth comes ... through the reminiscences which counteract the external forces of society. And they are external to Huck despite the fact that Twain presents them as part of Huck's discourse."[105]

From the perspective of Sam Clemens, it is not "losing touch with Huck's voice," but *in part* the overriding importance of fulfilling his novel's thematic and stylistic demands that moves the author to violate the customary sound of Huck's voice, here at what readers can now fully appreciate to be the moral climax of the story in Huck's rebirth as Satan. George Carrington, however, asserts in regard to the climax, "It helps to see chapter 31 ... as a record put down with no grasp of what it means (and, from Twain's side, without much attention to the decorum of point of view)."[106]

Only with regard to the points of view of the narrator and implied narrator is his reading strategy helpful; it is a tactic that blinds the reader to the meaning of this passage from the standpoint of the implied author, whose ironic treatment of Huck's moral crisis reveals the underlying moral quandary that Huck resolves. The authorial intrusion that Cox, McKay, and Carrington detect in the rhetoric of the climax underscores the insertion into this passage of Clemens' Miltonic burlesque, which prepares the way not for senseless "slapstick shenanigans" but for the biblical burlesque of Exodus 1–14 and other Bible texts to which Tom Sawyer's antics give rise in the closing section of the novel (as will be shown in Chapter Five of this study).

There is a further, at least equally important explanation for Huck's shift to the more active, aggressive language patterns of Tom Sawyer at the end of this scene; for in his identification with both Christ and Satan, Huck arrives at the dawn of his manhood. He is no longer a child for whom the passive and negative vernacular speech characteristics that have marked his style remain appropriate, so it is not Mark Twain who "loses touch with Huck's voice and personality"; it is Huck Finn himself who has outgrown his charming, childish ways. At the dawn of his manhood, it is time to "put away childish things."[107] From this point on, although Tom's advent reasserts the social matrix of the opening of the novel, Huck remains dedicated to and actively pursues Jim's liberation.

XIX. Hell-Bound

Hearn notes that Huck's climactic wrestling match with his conscience is a passage that Clemens revised and expanded extensively. For most readers, Clemens' violation of Huck's point of view here passes unnoticed in this, one of the most famous scenes in American literature. His burlesque is not evident in his original conception of the climax; Hearn points out that Clemens revised the passage extensively, adding almost 150 words and making its tone "more serious and earnest." Clemens' revisions to part three of Huck's debate transformed it from a "return to the tone of the opening of the novel" into "the classic argument of civil disobedience against conventional morality in nineteenth-century American fiction."[108]

At what point it occurred to the author to base Huck's struggle on Milton's account will never be known, but probably he saw his opportunity early on and wrote the first draft without consulting the text of *Paradise Lost*, then went back and rewrote the passage with Milton's epic at his elbow. The pattern of allusion throughout the opening section, where Clemens casts pap as Milton's Satan and Huck as his son the Death Angel, and Clemens' reiteration of the scene in Pandaemonium at the camp-meeting in the manuscript version of that episode (see Chapter Three, Section V-A and C and Chapter Four, Section VIII), along with the Chaos motif (see Chapter Three, Section VIII) suggest that Huck's climactic re-enactment of Satan's soliloquy was not an afterthought, but a burlesque that was fundamental to Clemens' conception of both the theme of religious satire and Huck's development as a mythic character.

By ritually submerging Huck's three-personed identity as the sons of God, man, and Satan—Christ, Adam, and The Death Angel—in the river (Chaos) during his escape in Chapter VII, Clemens frames the purpose of Huck's quest for moral autonomy in archetypal terms (see Chapter Three, Section VII). The design of the novel therefore demands that Huck's achievement of his goal also find expression in fulfillment of this pattern. Furthermore, the events leading up to Huck's decision to "*go to hell*" indicate that if a confrontation with Satan is to eventuate from Huck's descending tour of Hell, as W. R. Moses has characterized Huck's journey (see Chapter Four, Section IV), this is the moment at which it must occur. For these reasons, Huck has been hell-bound for thirty chapters when he arrives at the climax of his commitment to Jim.

XX. The Con Artists' Apprentice

One of the important *motifs* of Huck's story—and Mark Twain's realist fiction—is manipulation among the characters: from the widow's and Tom Sawyer's well-intentioned manipulation of Huck in trying to make him a respectable member of society; through pap's feigned conversion to get control of Huck's fortune; through Huck faking his own murder; through Jim's concealment of pap's death; through Huck's attempts to fool Jim in order to assert his own superiority; through Huck's assumption of various identities in order to control situations; through Sophia Grangerford's use of Huck to communicate with her lover; through the slaves' ruses to bring Huck to Jim; through Huck's five-way con of the Wilks sisters and the royal frauds in order to save the girls and send their predators to justice while assuring his own escape and Jim's; through the increasingly depraved scams perpetrated by the royal frauds; through Tom's concealing Jim's manumission in order to make Huck and Jim his pawns and wreak havoc on the domestic peace of the Phelpses: From beginning to end the plot of *Huckleberry Finn* consists of one long string of scams.

It is no coincidence that in this context, the duke and the king play a large and pivotal role, for they are professionals at manipulation, a pair of moral derelicts who cruise the river towns in an endless quest for the next crowd of suckers to take advantage of, and in their first adventure at Pokeville the king demonstrates his superiority to the duke by raking in almost eighty-eight dollars to the duke's nine-fifty (Chapter XX). Obviously, religious fraud is the most lucrative field for confidence games in the novel, and after the duke one-ups the king with the Royal Nonesuch, taking the Bricksville crowd for four hundred sixty-five dollars (Chapter XXIII), the king reasserts his superiority in the Wilks episode with, if only briefly, an almost five thousand, seven hundred dollar take with more projected.

Huck, who is as often on the receiving end of these schemes as on the giving end, is an impressionable and intelligent lad, and he fosters his native talent by observation and practice. If we observe his growth in the arts of manipulation, we can see that he grows by leaps and bounds as he drifts with Jim and the duke and king toward the Phelps farm. Of course, one of his best ploys is his first in the novel, his feigned murder at pap's hut, whereby he escapes. But this scheme only involves imaginative scene setting, not interaction with other human beings (Chapter VII), and his next two efforts are not so successful: his practical joke with the dead snake that almost gets Jim killed (Chapter X) and his attempt to persuade Judith Loftus that he is a girl. She is skeptical of his second story as well, and even gives him some instruction in the fine art of feigning, for after all, he appears only to be the runaway he is, and her main concern is to help him on his way after having had her fun with him (Chapter XI).

Huck does better with the boatman at the ferry-landing, picking up information on the fly that enables him to con the ferryman into trying to save the outlaws on the *Walter Scott*, but his attempt to help them could have gotten the ferryman into trouble, had it succeeded, so it was not well considered (Chapter XII). After his humiliating failure to assert his superiority to Jim (Chapter XV), he does better with the slave hunters: not only fooling them and saving Jim, but also turning a forty-dollar profit in this more delicate, if inadvertent, "dodge" (Chapter XVI).

Huck has talent, and when the royal frauds come aboard he gets the opportunity to study under masters who have neither conscience nor morals. Under their tutelage he learns such valuable lessons as these: having "all the fools in town" on your side will net "a big enough majority in any town" (Chapter XXVI), but "over-reaching don't pay" (the title of Chapter XXVIII; see Appendix A), and "trust'n' to Providence"—even if it means "the devil," as Huck reckons it does in Chapter XXIII, is "the best way, in the long run," as the king declares in Chapter XXV, "The King Turns Parson" (Huck's title for this chapter; see Appendix A). Another lesson Huck learns from the king at the end of the Wilks scam is not to get fooled into overconfidence by your own role-playing, nor to trust *too much* to Providence. By the end of Chapter XXVIII, Huck is close to completing his own masterpiece of manipulation, now that "Dead Peter Has His Gold" (see Appendix A):

> Everything was all right now. The girls wouldn't say nothing because they wanted to go to England, and the king and the duke would ruther Mary Jane was off working for

the auction than around in reach of Doctor Robinson. I felt very good; I judged I had done it pretty neat—I reckoned Tom Sawyer couldn't 'a' done it no neater himself. Of course he would 'a' throwed more style into it, but I can't do that very handy, not being brung up to it.

Huck has learned about all that the royal, reverend frauds have to teach him, and he has also learned a lesson that appears to be beyond these nameless rogues: There is nothing like a healthy measure of truth to make your victims believe in you:

> I went to studying it out. I says to myself, I reckon a body that ups and tells the truth when he is in a tight place is taking considerable many resks, though I ain't had no experience and can't say for certain, but it looks so to me, anyway; and yet here's a case where I'm blest if it don't look to me like the truth is better and actuly *safer* than a lie. I must lay it by in my mind and think it over some time or other, it's so kind of strange and unregular. I never see nothing like it. Well, l says to myself at last, I'm a-going to chance it; I'll up and tell the truth this time, though it does seem most like setting down on a kag of powder and touching it off just to see where you'll go to. Then I says:
> "Miss Mary Jane, is there any place out of town a little ways where you could go and stay three or four days?"

Huck's apprenticeship with the royal frauds is coming to an end, here. There remains one important lesson, however: Huck underestimates their depravity:

> After all this long journey and after all we'd done for them scoundrels, here it was all come to nothing, everything all busted up and ruined, because they could have the heart to serve Jim such a trick as that and make him a slave again all his life, and amongst strangers, too, for forty dirty dollars [Chapter XXXI].

Actually, from their point of view, it is Huck they have disserved, since they believe that Jim is Huck's property that they have stolen. But Huck is not to be faulted for missing that point, initially. Nevertheless, that is what they think, and when he accidentally encounters the duke Huck confronts him with a story—made up on the spot—that he had thought:

> "They've got into trouble and had to leave; and they've took my nigger, which is the only nigger I've got in the world, and now I'm in a strange country, and ain't got no property no more, nor nothing, and no way to make my living'; so I set down and cried. I slept in the woods all night. But what *did* become of the raft, then?—and Jim—poor Jim!"

The duke answers in kind—that is, with half-truth:

> "Blamed if I know—that is, what's become of the raft. That old fool had made a trade and got forty dollars, and when we found him in the doggery the loafers had matched half-dollars with him and got every cent but what he'd spent for whisky; and when I got him home late last night and found the raft gone, we said, 'that little rascal has stole our raft and shook us, and run off down the river.'"

"I wouldn't shake my *nigger*, would I?—the only nigger I had in the world, and the only property."

"We never thought of that. Fact is, I reckon we'd come to consider him *our* nigger; yes, we did consider him so—goodness knows we had trouble enough for him [...] And I've pegged along ever since, dry as a powder-horn. Where's that ten cents? Give it here."

Just like pap in Chapter V the duke focuses on the dime Huck fictitiously reports having earned, and demands it. Huck continues conning him with another lie invented on the fly to win his sympathy, and gives him ten cents. Then the duke overreaches, underestimating his opponent:

The next minute he whirls on me and says:
"Do you reckon that nigger would blow on us? [...] "
"How can he blow? Hain't he run off?"
"No! That old fool sold him, and never divided with me, and the money's gone."

The duke is obviously lying about the king having sold Jim without his knowing, because leading up to this episode he and the king were conspiring secretly in their desperation for money, and Huck and Jim had sensed trouble coming. Huck doesn't reveal that he knows this and maintains his "wounded child" act:

"*Sold* him?" I says, and begun to cry, "why, he was *my* nigger, and that was my money. Where is he?—I want my nigger."
"Well you can't *get* your nigger, that's all—so dry up your blubbering. Looky here—do you think *you'd* venture to blow on us—"
He stopped but I never see the duke look so ugly out of his eyes before.

The duke's "*Looky here,*" in this context, echoes pap's identical expression in Huck's room at the widow's in Chapter V, emphasizing the duke's moral equivalence with pap, the hog-god/devil who would stop at nothing to get what he wants. Here, the duke, whom Jim sees as "a tolerble likely man" in Chapter XXIII, reveals that as a developing character, he has degraded himself considerably in the interim, having found "his true father" in the king as Huck has found his in Jim.[109] Clemens makes this father-son motif explicit when the four fugitives reunite on the raft after the Wilks episode in Chapter XXX, and the pair blame each other for stealing the gold and the duke declares angrily, "I never see such an old ostrich for wanting to gobble everything—and I a-trusting you all the time, like you was my own father."

Huck continues:

I went on a-whimpering, and says:
"I don't want to blow on nobody; and I ain't got no time to blow, nohow; I got to turn out and find my nigger."
He looked kinder bothered, and stood there with his bills fluttering on his arm, thinking, and wrinkling up his forehead. At last he says:

"I'll tell you something. We got to be here three days. If you'll promise you won't blow, and won't let the nigger blow, I'll tell you where to find him."

Huck's act has had its intended effect on the duke at this point; Huck is not seeking information, he is angling for orders, and he has convinced the duke that he doesn't know where Jim is so that the duke can try to manipulate him into staying out of the way while the con men work their next scam. The duke offers him a deal, and it is exactly what Huck wants; so far, this game of wits has been fairly evenly matched. Now the duke tips his hand:

> So I promised, and he says:
> "A farmer by the name of Silas Ph—" and then he stopped. You see, he started to tell me the truth, but when he stopped that way and begun to study and think again, I reckoned he was changing his mind. And so he was. He wouldn't trust me; he wanted to make sure of having me out of the way the whole three days.

One could quote from this passage further to show how nimbly Huck plays the duke. But it is already clear that Clemens' point is that the student has surpassed his teachers. Huck plays the duke for a sucker:

> "That was the order I wanted, and that was the one I played for. I wanted to be left free to work my plans.
> "So clear out," he says; "and you can tell Mr. Foster whatever you want to" [Chapter XXXII].

Before Huck gets to Jim, the fugitive slave does "blow" on the frauds, and despite Huck's characteristically compassionate attempt to warn them (Chapter XXXIII), they fall victim to the rude justice of that time and place (see Chapter Four, Section IV-B).

In Chapter XXXI, before his "counter-conversion" that has so preoccupied—and baffled—commentators, Huck learns from a chance encounter where Jim is and who has him. Huck's gathering information from a local and then using that information to advance his agenda echoes the king's strategy in Chapter XXIII. His chance encounter with the duke informs him of nothing but the real danger to him that the royal rogues represent.

After he resolves to help Jim, he sets out for the Phelps farm to "get the lay of the land": "According to my plan, I was going to turn up there from the village, not from below." Here, just as pap, in parallel to Satan, arrived from "down the river" to spy out the widow's place unobserved before climbing in through Huck's window to confront his son (Chapter IV), Huck spies on the Phelps farm "from below," like Satan spying on Eden in *Paradise Lost* (see Chapter Three, Section IV A), before openly arriving in Chapter XXXII, in which he reports: "I went right along, not fixing up any particular plan but just trusting to Providence to put the right words in my mouth when the time come; for I'd noticed that Providence always did put the right words in my mouth if I left it alone."

Of course, Huck's words here echo the king's in Chapters XXIV and XXV, and although he does not recognize it this time, the implication, as with the king, is that he is relying on "the devil" as much as divine providence. The previous episodes recounting his unexpected encounter with the duke, and its successful outcome, and before that his manipulation of the Wilks affair to the benefit of the sisters (which worked, although not as he planned), has built up his confidence and prepared him for his next scam.

XXI. Abandoning Chaos: The End of the Journey

Reflecting his decisive abandonment of Chaos at the end of Chapter XXXI, Huck leaves the raft on an island like the one where he and Jim found it. His canoe, like the one that made his escape possible when it was given to him by the river, he returns weighted down with rocks in a verbal echo of the sack of rocks that he dropped into the river in the course of his escape from pap and the widow. Clemens also reverses Huck's direction of movement within a similar time frame. In Chapter VII Huck sets out from the shore and reaches Jackson's Island just before dawn; in Chapter XXXI he sets out from the island and reaches the shore just before dawn as if no time had elapsed between these two passages. By reversing events of Huck's flight, Clemens signals that the Adam/Christ/Satan figure born out of Chaos is about to be reborn into the mythological matrix he escaped through his ritual suicide (see Chapter Three, Section VII). Huck is ready to return to society. He has completed his tour of *The Inferno* as a moral free agent (see Chapter Four, Section IV), and his "rebirth" as Tom Sawyer in the following chapter fulfills rather than disrupts this pattern of return.

Another point at which Mark Twain's "congeries of claptrap" plot[110] has struck readers as being extremely implausible is Huck's mistaken identity as Tom Sawyer in Chapter XXXII; and so it is, in terms of realism; however, when one considers that on the mythic level Huck has been voyaging in Chaos, a dimensionless realm of dreamtime where "chance governs all," it should not surprise anyone so much to discover that his voyage has taken him nowhere any more than it should be startling after a dream to awaken in the same bed one fell asleep in. The real journey has taken place in Chaos— in Huck's character development—and that is where Clemens places his emphasis by returning Huck to the very social matrix he escaped in Chapter VII (see Chapter Three, Section VIII).

Huck's real triumph is his achievement of adulthood and moral freedom. Although still outwardly a boy, his long initiation has brought him to the dawn of his manhood. Jim's eventual revelation of pap's death reaffirms that Huck has come of age. Appropriately, Clemens dissolves Huck's ties to society through pap, Tom Sawyer, Jim, and Aunt Sally and Uncle Silas Phelps. At last, Huck is free to navigate his own way in the world. His next step, whatever it might be, will be his own.

This freedom is Huck's ultimate triumph; having transcended his conscience, whatever he does next will be a self-determined act that others still enmeshed in the webs of religious superstition and social conformity spun by "the damned human race" will be powerless to control. As we are about to see, the final stage of the novel's covert religious satire lands him back in the world, completes his disillusionment, and sets him free. Huck's quest for manhood and freedom has succeeded.

XXII. Chapter Summary: Inspirations from 1879 to 1883

As Mark Twain tells readers in Chapter III of *Life on the Mississippi* (1883), in his introduction to the "Raftmen's Passage" that he excised from the section of the manuscript recounting the first phase of the raft voyage, *Huck Finn* is a book that he had been working on "in fits and starts for the last five or six years, and might possibly finish in another five or six more."[111] This comment, of course, needs to be taken with more than a grain of salt, since it and the portion of the story it introduces can be regarded as thinly veiled advertising marketing his next book, which was to be *Adventures of Huckleberry Finn* (1884). Nevertheless, it does contain more than a grain of truth to be consumed along with the salt.

As F. Kaplan has detailed, Clemens began the novel in 1876 with most of the first eight and a half chapters. He resumed work on it in the winter of 1879–'80, completing most of chapters eighteen through twenty-one, pigeonholed it again and finished it in 1883–'84. Other commentaries, such as V. Doyno's account, do not contradict this timeline, and we know from the evidence of the author's working manuscript that paper and ink testify to his having composed the novel in these three major phases with the story proceeding for the most part consecutively, with a few interpolations—parts of Chapters IV, XII, and XIV, for example, that Clemens inserted as he revised.

It has also been established that he wrote the portions of the story not specifically accounted for in this timeline—chapters IX-B—XVII and XXII—?—between these three major phases of composition. "Fits and starts" seems like a fair description of the process Clemens went through in writing *Huck Finn*, and it is safe to assume that while his "tank was refilling" between-times, he gave the novel a good deal of thought and evidently wrote some of it, too, for scholars acknowledge that *by* 1879 he had completed Chapters I through the first half of XVIII, and that *by* 1883 he had written some of the last half of the book; but the exact timeline appears to be uncertain, and the creative, conceptual timeline is unknown. So pontifications about his having "had no idea about where his book was heading" from commentators who themselves don't know where it was coming from or going to should also be taken with a liberal dose of salt.

That being said, it is evident from the episodes covered in this chapter and the previous one that Clemens began Huck's "autobiography" with a clear sense of direction and purpose: to burlesque Bible stories that he found to be objectionable as archetypes for a morally just society—especially those of the Old Testament. The 1876–1880 portions of the novel relentlessly burlesque Genesis, Exodus, I and II Samuel, and I Kings; and, through Clemens' allusions to Milton and Bunyan, they undermine the notions that the biblical God is just and that the Bible is divinely inspired.

Instead, Clemens portrays the God of the Bible as being cruel, vicious, immoral, and intemperate as is pap Finn—no different in kind from Milton's Satan—who meets his doom naked in a whore's house, where he is shot in the back by one of his fellows of the trinity in which he is last seen alive. And Clemens portrays great patriarchs, Adam, Abraham, Noah, Moses, Saul, David, Solomon and the prophet Samuel, as a "sacred brotherhood" of delusional servants of a depraved Master, whose followers in Huck's world manifest the curse of the Depravity Doctrine in their lives day in and day out, as their idolatrous attitudes toward the sacred Book and money "preforeordestinate" them to do.

As the book thus far must have appeared to its author around 1880, when scholars say that he thought it almost finished, there was not that much more to it than a thoroughgoing burlesque of Old Testament stories buttressed with allusions to *Paradise Lost*. And while Clemens had kept his burlesque of sacred literature covert, there may have been a fair chance in his day, when scholars and the reading public were well versed in Bible lore and book length literary burlesque was near the zenith of its popularity as a comic art form, that his blasphemous parody would be detected. Pigeonholing it may have been his only sensible option until he could figure out how to publish the story without getting caught.

Four. To Vilify "the Ways of God to Men"

Not only this danger, but also the evolving moral seriousness of the book—its tragic aspects—were on his mind as well. He ended the second phase of composition—the pre-1879 portion of the narrative—just as the feud is about to explode and the raft voyage to resume in Chapter XVIII. Knowing the time of his naming Saul and Rachel Grangerford would tell scholars how much he knew about their impending doom when he again set the manuscript aside at some time prior to the end of 1879, when, his tank having refilled, he finished Chapter XVIII and added XIX-XXI.[112]

However much he may have known of the outcome of the feud episode, his return to the great river and the pressure to finish *Life on the Mississippi* in 1882-83 intervened and forced him to allow his tank time to refill. His reunion with his former master-pilot Horace Bixby on that re-acquaintance with the river and the society it transected may have rekindled his interest in burlesquing Shakespeare; this possibility is suggested by his later recalling the recitation of long passages of the bard's plays humorously interlarded with profane nautical coaching by pilot George Ealer to his "cub" Sam Clemens at the wheel. Wherever the inspiration came from, it appears that Clemens came to the realization that the way to further conceal his blasphemy was to bury it in a welter of purely literary burlesque that would distract readers from his more fundamental religious satire. From Chapter XVIII on to the end of *Huck Finn*, this strategy is evident first in his burlesque of *Romeo and Juliet* at the end of the feud episode, then of *Hamlet* and *Macbeth* in the duke's rendition of Hamlet's soliloquy in Chapter XXI, and next of *King Lear* in the Wilks episode, where, as Doyno has pointed out, Clemens' parody of that play becomes more extensive and thematically significant,[113] as does his treatment of Hamlet, as is also mentioned in the Introduction to this study (see Introduction, Section IV).

Religious satire in all of these episodes, however, remains Clemens' primary concern. This theme is evident in the incongruous parallels to the *Progress* of Bunyan's Christian. One can see it in the structural congruency of Clemens' exploration of the nature and degrees of evil to Dante's; in the contortions of conscience implied in Miss Watson's manumission of Jim; in the king's advent as the avatar of Fraud and his relentless targeting of the credulous faithful for his own monetary gain; and in Huck's observations at the camp-meeting, with its introduction of the brazen serpent as Clemens' symbol for "the pernicious influence" of religion and the Bible. Clemens continues hammering at sacred icons as Boggs expires beneath the crushing weight of a Bible in the next chapter; and as the text conflates the king's character with those of Noah, Aaron the Levite, and pap Finn in the king's next religious fraud leading into the Wilks episode. There, Clemens provides biting social satire on raw materialism overlaid with religious posturing and pretense as the townspeople dramatize the effects of this toxic amalgam of self-righteous assurance and idolatry of gold.

Huck's climactic rebirth recalls every archetypal identification—as the sons of God and Satan, especially—that he cast off as he escaped into Chaos, and Clemens underscores the structural conclusion to the raft journey and Huck's abandonment of the moral womb of Chaos with inverse parallels to Huck's escape from pap and the widow, a motif that bridges the opening, middle, and closing sections of the story. As the middle section ends, Clemens emphasizes his theme of religious satire in Huck's identification as both Christ and Satan as he achieves moral autonomy—the implicit goal of his unacknowledged quest.

Yet Clemens does not portray all religious experience as evil. In Jim's anguished cry for "de Lord God Amighty's" forgiveness and in Mary Jane Wilks' promise to pray for Huck, the author provides examples of the positive side of sincere religious feeling to express his characters' best instincts. In view of her effect on Huck, it is possible that Clemens conceived Mary Jane as his Beatrice in the series of allusions to *The Inferno* that becomes a vital structural component of the middle section.

Throughout this 1879 to 1883 section one can observe in Clemens' revisions the process of his composition, his weighing and balancing of the competing demands of characterization, audience, and theme as he strove—in his revision of the king's speech, for example—to attain the maximum satirical effects while preserving Huck's status as a naïve and sympathetic picaro with no clue to the meaning of the events he witnesses and reports, and to maintain also "THE AUTHOR's" firewall of ironic distance from the implications of Huck's narrative.

Clemens clearly conceived of the concluding evasion engineered by Tom Sawyer as, in part, a distraction from what was really on his mind as he pits Huck and Jim against the forces of their world represented by Tom's inane "authorities," as the next chapter argues, but the religious satire that undergirds the closing section ultimately unifies the novel thematically while enhancing its topical relevance and its dramatic integrity.

CHAPTER FIVE

"Dark, Deep-Laid Plans"
The Evasion as Religious Satire

I. Going (Back) to Hell

For Samuel Clemens, the association of "down the river" with hell was an inevitable consequence of his boyhood in Missouri. As he tells us in a memorial essay about his mother: "to our whites and blacks alike the Southern plantation was simply hell; no milder name could describe it."[1] Bernard DeVoto knew not how great a compliment he paid to Samuel Clemens' art when he wrote of the evasion "In the whole reach of the English novel, there is no more abrupt or more chilling descent."[2] James Cox opines that Huck arrives in hell "within five minutes of reading-time" after his decision to go there.[3]

Beneath the satire on Southern chivalry long and mistakenly regarded as the primary target of the evasion's satire, the covert biblical satire of the conclusion lampoons a society founded on the moral authority of the Bible; it exposes what Clemens regarded as the pernicious influence of biblical religion on Western culture; and it pillories the biblical God. An abrupt—if not chilling—descent is precisely what Clemens was aiming for in having Tom and Huck set Jim free "by the Book."

II. Locking the "Echo Chamber" and Hiding the Key

As Huck prepares for his solo re-entry into the society of the shore, the manuscript has him putting on "some old, rough clothes" appropriate to his new identity as Satan emerging from Chaos on his mission to corrupt "this new World"[4]—like pap Finn at the boy's room in the widow's house.[5]

As Victor Doyno comments, "Twain's creative imagination is extraordinarily repetitive, creating a book which resembles an intratextual echo chamber."[6] As one can see in this reiteration of the scene in Chapter V where pap's first appearance parallels Satan's entry into the garden of innocence and the angels criticize his appearance: "Thou resemblest now thy Sin and Place of Doom obscure and foul"[7] (see Chapter Three, Section IV-A), Clemens keeps the echoes reverberating, tying together the opening and closing sections with repetition of archetypal motif and variation of situation so that whether actions are taken for good purposes or evil, the masks that his characters must assume to play their roles in the unfolding, covert drama are the same.

This echoic character of the narrative manifests immediately in the Phelps Farm sequence as Huck finds himself cast into the role of Tom Sawyer and Tom arrives to assume the character of his brother Sid. Thus—even as they reprise their relationship from the opening of the novel—like the duke and the king, the boys pose as "false brothers" plotting to commit "crimes" during the closing section, and the first of these is fraud.[8]

In Chapter XXXII, in anticipation of Tom's arrival at the Phelps home, Huck goes to head off his friend and prevent him from blowing Huck's cover. This transitional passage, between Huck's "rebirth" as Tom Sawyer and the recognition scene in which Clemens sets up their initial encounter in the concluding section as a burlesque Resurrection, shows Huck continuing to take decisive action on his mission to free Jim.

These false brothers at the same time pose on the archetypal level as Moses and Aaron, the biblical brothers who were instrumental in freeing the Israelites from Egyptian bondage, thus reasserting the Moses motif that Clemens elaborates in the opening and middle sections of the narrative. Furthermore, Huck, cast in the role of Clemens' Adamic Satan, functions as moral antipode to Tom, whose shenanigans resonate with the plan of the God of Exodus to free His chosen people. And Huck as Christ, acting out of his compassionate, self-sacrificial commitment to Jim, embodies the values without system that countervail Tom Sawyer's principled value system based on conformity and authoritarianism: Tom's are the values of the dominant culture, and he represents those values as the incarnation of Aaron, founder of the Hebrew priesthood and the first high priest in Leviticus (see Chapter Four, Section XII).

III. The Burlesque Resurrection of Huckleberry Finn

Clemens implies his rejection of New as well as Old Testament mythology during the Phelps farm sequence in an incident that has been the subject of commentary by Frank Baldanza, Billy Collins, and Randy Cross. When Tom and Huck reunite in Chapter XXXIII, each of these critics has found that the text calls to mind—resonates with—a moment of Bible myth. For Collins, Huck and Tom become Moses and Aaron preparing to set Israel free. For Baldanza, Tom becomes "Doubting Thomas," the Apostle who refused to believe in the Resurrection until he had touched Jesus' wounds and satisfied himself that his Lord was not a ghost. While Baldanza himself sees no broad contextual significance in the parallel, no need to emphasize Huck's role as a Christ figure,[9] Cross interprets this parallel as Mark Twain's specific denial of the Resurrection. He finds this episode to be a parody of the story related in St. John 20: 24–28 and portrays Huck as Christ and Tom Sawyer as the Apostle Thomas who doubted Christ's return from the grave. At first, Huck's appearance beside the road frightens Tom, who mistakes him for a ghost:

> I says "Hold on!" and it [the wagon] stopped alongside, and his mouth opened up like a trunk and stayed so; and he swallowed two or three times like a person that's got a dry throat and then says:
> "I hain't ever done you no harm. You know that. So, then, what you want to come back and ha'nt *me* for?"
> I says:
> "I hain't come back—I hain't been *gone.*"

Here, writes Cross, "Twain covertly reflects Christ's death, burial, and resurrection."

> He says:
> "Don't you play nothing on me, because I wouldn't on you. Honest Injun, you ain't a ghost?"
> "Honest Injun, I ain't," I says.
> "[...] Looky here, warn't you ever murdered *at all?*"

"With Huck's answer," asserts Cross, "Twain again denies the divinity of Jesus Christ":

> "No, I warn't ever murdered at all—I played it on them. You come in here and feel of me if you don't believe me. So he done it; and it satisfied him" [Chapter 33].

Cross invites readers, "Compare Twain's parody with the exchange between Jesus and Thomas in St. John 20: 27–28":

> 27 Then saith he to Thomas, Reach hither thy finger, and behold my hands; and reach hither thy hand, and thrust it into my side: and be not faithless, but believing.
> 28 And Thomas answered and said unto him, My Lord and my God.

Cross concludes, "The parallels between the two stories are significant. Twain did not believe Jesus to be divine, and he considered the story of Jesus' death, burial, and resurrection to be nothing more than that—a story. To Twain, Jesus 'played it on them.'"[10]

Only in terms of Clemens' management of viewpoint can we reconcile these three critics' divergent explications. The concept of resonance introduced earlier (see Chapter Three, Section XVII) enables one to entertain the suggestion that none of them is wrong, that the same passage calls up two moments of Bible myth, simultaneously identifying Huck with Moses and the risen Christ while denying the resurrection of Jesus (see letter to Orion Clemens, Chapter Three, Section V-A).

Prior to his taking refuge in Chaos in Chapter VII by means of his ritual suicide/patricide/deicide, Huck, as the son of pap—whose symbolic identity spans Heaven, Earth, and Hell (see Chapter Three, Section III-VII)—bears the complementary filial identities of Adam Christ (the second Adam), Huck/Moses/Isaac, and The Death Angel (see Chapter Three, Section VII). It is appropriate that once he emerges from Chaos and returns to his world, he should resume symbolic standing in each of these dimensions. And since by sacrificing his hope of salvation—in his own understanding—he has quite literally laid down his life to save Jim's, thereby earning the status of a Christ figure; while on the human level his being reborn as Tom Sawyer/Moses gives him a new identity by which he can make his way in society; and at the same time his becoming the Satan figure he embodies at the climax, Huck fulfills his mythic destiny to live simultaneously in all three realms—in other words, to transcend morality and achieve moral autonomy.

It is therefore important to realize that the burlesque Resurrection of Huckleberry Finn is a feature of his adventures that is both appropriate and necessary to the fulfillment of the implied author's thematic patterning and archetypal development of Huck's story. The foregoing discussion of point of view makes it possible to assert that at the same time Mark Twain plays another of his "moral aces" by identifying his "saintly child in conflict with a corrupt society" with the risen Christ (a synthesis of the views of Kolb and Baldanza) Clemens trumps Mark Twain's ace by transforming this moment to a burlesque Resurrection that denies Christ's own. Only when one sees how the text manifests the inherent tension between the conventional moralism of the implied narrator and the "radical vision" (Kolb and Cox; see Chapter One, Section VII-C) of the implied author can one embrace all of the implications Baldanza, Collins, and Cross reveal.

Furthermore, Huck's decision to help Jim rather than betray him or simply abandon him is to prefer hell to salvation. Apropos of his identification with the risen Christ, by sacrificing his respectability in Tom's eyes Huck embodies one of the highest ideals taught by Christianity even as he reveals to Tom what only the day before he would have been ready to "get down and lick his boots for shame" to admit, thus reaffirming his "satanic" defeat of his conscience. Only thus can one comprehend all the terms of the novel's paradoxical vision and begin to make sense of the monstrous incongruities of the cosmos according to Samuel Clemens.

IV. Stealing Jim "by the Book"

George Carrington asserts that in view of the author's scrupulously maintained distance as Huck relates his affairs to the reader, it is useless to seek in the text evidence of how Mark Twain wishes us to regard his narrator, so by authorial default the reader must make whatever one can or will of Huck's narrative.[11] Carrington, who prefers tragicomic novels to comic ones, therefore argues for a tragicomic reading that focuses on dramatic unity rather than thematic integrity. His argument articulates an assumption that has been a stumbling block for numerous critics: "Huck is, after all, the projection of a writer who was knowledgeable about the smaller techniques of storytelling but notoriously inarticulate about the deeper meanings of his most serious work."[12]

According to Carrington's theory—indeed, most readings of the evasion—the freedom of expression Mark Twain won by turning the telling of his story over to Huck Finn cost the author his ability to realize the thematic potential of his material. Thus, in the closing section, when Huck appears to abdicate initiative to Tom Sawyer, Mark Twain is powerless to stop him because he himself had previously surrendered control to Huck. As this school of thought regards the conclusion, the evasion reflects Twain's unwillingness to face the tragic implications of the raft-journey and supports an estimate of his art as welling out of his unconscious mind onto the printed page with minimal interference from the self-conscious artist (see Introduction, Section I).

Huck's point of view, however strongly it commands attention, must not absorb all of our attention if we are to discover the meaning—*vis-à-vis* "THE AUTHOR"—of his story. As in the opening section where, as this study has shown, Clemens disarms the reader by distancing himself from Huck's heretical digressions on Moses and prayer (see Chapter One, Section III and Chapter Two, Section II); and as in the middle section, where the Bible and the "sacred brotherhood" of Old Testament heroes and their God come under the implied condemnation of Clemens while Huck and Mark Twain remain oblivious; even so in reading the conclusion, one must attend to Clemens' scrupulous management of viewpoint and be prepared to recognize in derivative aspects of the narrative, in its treatment of the liberation theme of Exodus and in its fulfillment of Huck's resolve to "*go* to hell" for Jim, the presence of "THE AUTHOR" as the controlling and unifying consciousness that makes the Phelps farm sequence the inevitable destination of the raft journey.

While the first-person narrator *is* a distancing device, that is not to say that Clemens employs it as a means of depriving the reader of "guidance" altogether, as Carrington contends.[13] As argued in this study's first chapter, which discusses point of view, Clemens at the outset gives us not merely Huck's perspective, but those of an implied narrator (Mark Twain) and an implied author (Clemens) most of the time. Each of these three levels of discourse in the closing section conforms to its own logic: From Huck's pragmatic point of view, his deference to Tom Sawyer makes complete sense. Aside from his supposed dependency on Tom, Huck *knows* (albeit mistakenly) that Tom's duty is to unmask him and foil his plan to steal Jim:

> Well, one thing was dead sure; and that was, that Tom Sawyer was in earnest and was actuly going to help steal that nigger out of slavery. That was the thing that was too many for me. Here was a boy that was respectable, and well brung up; and had a character to lose; and folks at home that had characters; and he was bright and not ignorant; and not mean, but kind; and yet here he was, without any more pride, or rightness, or feeling, than to stoop to this business, and make himself a shame, and his family a shame, before everybody. I *couldn't* understand it, no way at all. It was outrageous, and I knowed I ought to just up and tell him so; and so be his true friend, and let him quit the thing right where he was, and save himself. And I *did* start to tell him; but he shut me up, and says:
> "Don't you reckon I know what I'm about? Don't I generly know what I'm about?"
> "Yes."
> "Didn't I *say* I was going to help steal the nigger?"
> "Yes."
> "*Well* then."
> That's all he said, and that's all I said. It warn't no use to say any more; because when he said he'd do a thing, he always done it. But *I* couldn't make out how he was willing to go into this thing; so I just let it go, and never bothered no more about it. If he was bound to have it so, *I* couldn't help it [Chapter XXXIV].

Huck must humor Tom no matter what he eventually comes to think of his comrade's methods and purposes. Huck has no choice but to go along with whatever Tom says because he does not know Tom's secret: Jim is already legally free. Tom intentionally withholds this fact from Huck to secure his cooperation (Chapter XXXIII), just as Jim has withheld from Huck the fact that the corpse they discovered in the floating house in Chapter IX was the body of pap.

There is an interesting parallel between Huck's interview with the duke in Chapter XXXII and his conversation with Tom in XXXIII. Both the duke and Tom behave in the same way, starting to speak the truth and then rethinking their position and substituting a lie. Huck catches the duke's lie, but he falls for Tom's inexplicable promise to help him steal Jim:

> I says:
> "All right; but wait a minute. There's one more thing—a thing that *nobody* don't know but me. And that is, there's a nigger here that I'm a-trying to steal out of slavery, and his name is *Jim*—old Miss Watson's Jim."
> He says:
> "What! Why Jim is—"
> He stopped and went to studying. I says:
> "*I* know what you'll say. You'll say it's dirty, low-down business; but what if it is? *I*'m low-down; and I'm a-going to steal him, and I want you to keep mum and not let on. Will you?"
> His eye lit up, and he says:
> "I'll *help* you steal him!" [Chapter XXXIII].

Noticing this repetition with variation can help the reader to see that Tom is withholding information in order to control the situation, and to appreciate that, in a sense, Tom the boy is both father to the duke and the true heir to pap Finn (see Chapter Four, Section XII and Chapter Five, Section VI).

Accepting the inevitable, Huck makes himself at home with the Phelps family and puts his trust in Tom's promise to help him. If he seems insensitive to Jim's plight as the victim of Tom's abuse, let it not be forgotten that for Huck, he and Tom are all that stands between Jim and a far worse fate. Jim's suffering at Tom's hands is trivial compared with what awaits a runaway slave "down the river," and Jim, too, although Huck reports "he said he wouldn't ever be a prisoner again, not for a salary" (Chapter XXXVI), accepts the abuse he receives with gratitude for the hope of rescue it offers.

From the point of view of Mark Twain, the implied narrator, the evasion resurrects the ghosts of Moses, Aaron, Pharaoh, and the children of Israel in fulfillment of the novel's reenactment of the liberation drama of Exodus, as Collins has observed (see Chapter Three, Section XIX). The elements of this parallel have long been recognized, but its place in the satirical scheme of the novel has not been noticed. If one considers Mark Twain's mythological displacements an attempt to dignify the machinations Tom Sawyer sets in motion, as has Collins, I must still part company with him at his assertion that this technique makes a profound difference, for what good is technical virtuosity on an untuned instrument? All it can accomplish is to make fools of the implied narrator and those who applaud his performance. This is another example of Mark Twain functioning as Sam Clemens' straight man in this text (see Chapter One, Section VI-A).

To all Collins's deductions regarding the biblical analog of the evasion, readers disenchanted with the concluding section's burlesque of the flight to freedom must respond: So what? Mark Twain's victimization of Jim is still in poor taste, overlong, and the classic example of Mark Twain's greatest flaw as a novelist, his irresistible impulse to burlesque even his own best work in an ill-timed play for the belly laugh. Disenchanted readers are not likely to be moved to applaud the conclusion because it is based on the moral authority of the Bible; they are more likely to resent it as an ill-conceived attempt to dignify vulgarity by sprinkling it with holy water.

Of course, there are other motifs in the implied narrator's conclusion that claim a good deal more of the casual reader's notice: the extended satire on Tom's literary models, for example, which has elicited a chorus of groans from readers who consider Tom's antics not merely ridiculous, but at best insensitive and at worst, cruel. Although Victor Doyno has shown that this section works aesthetically and thematically to fulfill the demands of Mark Twain's literary and social satire,[14] it is the dramatic aspects of the absurd evasion that generations of readers and critics have found disappointing.

For Mark Twain the realist, however, once Tom Sawyer had taken control of the plot to set Jim free, there was no recourse but to report how he sets about it. The main objection to the novel's conclusion has been that Mark Twain allows Tom Sawyer to put in an appearance at all. That decision, however, lay not in the province of the implied narrator, but of Samuel Clemens, who produced this closing burlesque as an artist writing first of all to please himself: "I shall *like* it," he wrote of the novel in an 1883 letter to W. D. Howells, "whether anybody else does or not."[15]

One thing the author must have liked about it is that in *Huckleberry Finn* he had created a structure complex enough to let him have his say even as he appeared to stand remote from his fictive world. The fact that Mark Twain's Bible thumping rings hollow locates the entry into the implied author's religious satire at the conclusion. Most readers, Clemens judged, would be content to laugh at Mark Twain's ending, and the popularity of the evasion in his own day testifies to the accuracy of his judgment. For those perceptive enough to frown at Tom Sawyer's antics, he created a more elaborate joke whose butt is Mark Twain and Tom Sawyer and all who accept the evasion as good clean fun.

This satire challenges the moral authority of the God of the Bible and the God of the Gilded Age. By combining a topical satire on Reconstruction with religious satire, Clemens ascribes the corruption of society to the perversity of its "superstitions." The first step toward seeing this satiric strategy in operation is to review Mark Twain's retelling of the liberation drama of Exodus in the closing section.

Billy G. Collins has identified most of the parallels between Exodus 1–14 and the conclusion of *Huck Finn*. As he points out, Huck approaches the Phelps farm without a plan, "trusting to Providence to put the right words in my mouth" (Chapter XXXII). In Exodus God sends Moses to Egypt to free Israel,[16] and He tells Moses "I shall teach thee what thou shalt say."[17] Thus, Huck's "trusting to Providence to put the right words in my mouth" as he approaches the Phelps place is one of the first of these parallels (Chapter XXXII), even as it echoes the king's pronouncement that "trust'n' to Providence is the best way." Later, Tom Sawyer joins Huck and they pose as brothers while working to "free" Jim. Moses' brother Aaron joins him, and they work together to free Israel.[18] Collins observes that the evasion's warnings and plagues closely parallel Exodus,[19] but like most Bible readers he passes over a puzzling aspect of the Bible story that Clemens emphasizes in order to transform his version of the legend of Moses to burlesque. Exodus (7–11) states repeatedly that the plagues were inflicted on Egypt not because Israel was helpless, but because God hardened Pharaoh's heart. God repeats His intention as the story concludes, and He explains His motive:

> 17 And I, behold, I will harden the hearts of the Egyptians, [...] and I will get me honor upon Pharaoh, and upon all his host, upon his chariots, and upon his horsemen.
> 18 And the Egyptians shall know that I *am* the Lord, when I have gotten me honor upon Pharaoh[. ...]
> 30 Thus the Lord saved Israel that day out of the hand of the Egyptians; and Israel saw the Egyptians dead upon the seashore.[20] (See Chapter Three, Section XIX)

As Tom conceives it, the purpose of the evasion is *not* to free Jim, for Tom knows Jim is already legally free. For him as for the God of Exodus, the purpose of a "magnificent" escape is to get fame and honor. Tom complains to Huck, "You got to invent all the difficulties," but sees more "honor" to be gained that way (Chapter XXXV). Both Tom and the biblical God see honor to be gained from inventing difficulties and manipulating the wills of those whose "duty it is," as Tom says, to oppose them. In Chapter XXXIX Tom and Huck carelessly unleash plagues of rats and snakes in the Phelps home while doing so intentionally in Jim's cell. Tom's pseudo-rites, unbeknownst to him, mock the Bible. His mention of a "torchlight procession" (Chapter XXXV) recalls that the Lord guides Israel out of Egypt "by night in a pillar of fire,"[21] and the boys' thefts of household goods, especially silverware, remind us that God, through Moses, told the Hebrews to "borrow" from their Egyptian neighbors "jewels of silver, and jewels of gold" (see Chapter Three, Section VII).

As the evasion approaches its climax, Tom begins his campaign of "non-namous letters." It proves most effective: "I never see a family in such a sweat," reports Huck. Tom's purpose in sending the letters, like God's in causing the Egyptians to pursue Israel, is to prevent "'there being nobody nor nothing to interfere with us, and so after all our hard work this escape'll go off perfectly flat.'" As in Huck's telling metaphor, the Phelps's home is "full of ghosts, laying for them behind everything" (Chapter XXXIX). For Huck, these are just the phantasms of fear; for Clemens, these ghosts are the archetypal figures hovering in the background of Huck's narration.

The evasion, as a covert parody of a well-known Bible story, fuses the realistic "river vs. shore" level of the plot with the archetypally developed theme of heart vs. conscience, lifting the novel's indictment of society out of the implied narrator's provincial social and literary satire/morality play into the implied author's universal satire on the civilization that founded its morality on Bible myths. Implicit rejections of Judeo-Christian mythology as a guide to humane behavior come early and late in the closing section.

V. Of Huck, Satan and Christ

"Covert," in the context of this discussion, suggests that Clemens (as the letter to Orion Clemens cited in Chapter Three, Section V-A substantiates) has cloaked his mockery of biblical mythology in an overtly realist narrative and has structured the novel to resonate in the reader's imagination with the biblically informed Moral Sense that Clemens believed to be the root of the evils of Western civilization. By keeping his burlesque beneath the level of the narrators' and reader's awareness, Clemens avoids offending readers' biblically based beliefs even as he kicks the props of mythology from under Huck's conscience and moves him toward the heart-centered, amoral attitude that prompts him to go to hell for Jim.

This shift results in Huck's identification with Satan—shocking to Christian sensibility, but perhaps less so when one realizes that Clemens' "Adamic Satan" (Brodwin; see Chapter Two, Section VII and Chapter Four, Section VIII) embraces the highest Christian ideals in his decision to "love thy neighbor" and "lay down his life for his friend." As A. Ensor remarks, "In Twain's view the only significant message of the Bible was that taught by Christ; one must love his fellow man"[22]; and as Brodwin describes the Mark Twain-Satan connection: "The grand irony is that, in order to succeed ['in teaching man the nature of man's evil'], as Mark Twain tried to do through his art,

Satan must reincarnate the blithely indifferent, amoral attitudes of unfallen Adam."[23]

Compare Huck's attitude in the following excerpt from Chapter XXXVI:

> "*Now* you're *talking!*" I says; "your head gets leveler and leveler all the time, Tom Sawyer," I says. "Picks is the thing, moral or no moral; and as for me, I don't care shucks for the morality of it, nohow. When I start in to steal a nigger, or a watermelon, or a Sunday-school book, I ain't no ways particular how it's done so it's done. What I want is my nigger; or what I want is my watermelon, or what I want is my Sunday-school book; and if a pick's the handiest thing, that's the thing I'm a-going to dig that nigger or that watermelon or that Sunday-school book out with; and I don't give a dead rat what the authorities thinks about it nuther."

Notice that Huck couldn't care less about Tom's still incomprehensible agenda and that he still objectifies slaves along with watermelons and Sunday-school books. There has been no shift in his conscious regard for slaves as property, and Clemens gives us no hint here or elsewhere that Huck has made any value judgment against slavery. Far from it; his repeated use of "my" when he clearly means "somebody else's" emphasizes the amorality of his thinking: "blithely indifferent," indeed.

The first of the revisions to the Phelps farm sequence that Hearn notes is a wording change in Chapter XXXIV: Clemens substituted the expression "mild as goose milk" for Tom's "mild as Sunday School,"[24] and Hearn explains that the manuscript simile is more fitting, since it refers back to the attack on the Sunday school picnic that Tom Sawyer and his gang perpetrated in Chapter III; but avoiding any expression that even hinted at blasphemy evidently prompted this revision.[25] Hearn also notes that an almost identical revision in Chapter XXXV substitutes Tom's "infant-schooliest ways" for the more sarcastic "Sunday-schooliest ways" in Tom's put-down of Huck's pragmatic approach to stealing Jim.[26] These changes fit the general pattern of Clemens' revisions that remove overt religious satire—even at the expense of other thematic concerns. Also, the "echoic" effects of such word choices are cumulative; by eliminating a few reverberations of his irreverent theme Clemens effectively modulated the volume of this satire, not its pitch or tone.

In another note, Hearn comments, "It seems obvious that at this point in the story Twain had no idea where the novel was heading."[27] Conflating the points of view of the implied author and implied narrator has misled many readers to this conclusion. Yet the closing section makes complete sense, and it fulfills—with complex precision and a clear sense of purpose and design—the three distinct sets of thematic concerns implicit in the three points of view from which Huck's story is told.

VI. Of Tom's Grandfather's Ram

When Tom arrives at the Phelps farm, Huck describes him approaching the house in fascinating terms:

> He lays over the yaller fever, for interest, when he does come. Tom was over the stile and starting for the house; the wagon was spinning up the road for the village, and we was all bunched in the front door. Tom had his store clothes on, and an audience—and that was always nuts for Tom Sawyer. In them circumstances it warn't no trouble to him to throw in an amount of style that was suitable. He warn't a boy to meeky along up that yard like a sheep; no, he come ca'm and important, like the ram.

In Huck's first sentence of the paragraph, Tom's arrival calls to mind the arrival of a plague, as in Exodus (see Chapter Three, Section XIX); like the king in Chapter XXIV he arrives with his store clothes on, prepared to perpetrate a fraud, and in this costume, like the king again, he performs an act for his audience, throwing in "style"; finally, in a telling metaphor, he is transformed into "the ram"—an interesting choice of beast, since the ram has several archetypal associations: For one, it is the sacrificial animal Abraham found at the scene of his near-sacrifice of Isaac, another echo connecting Huck's escape with its parody in the closing burlesque (see Chapter Three, Section VI).

> When he got afront of us, he lifts his hat ever so gracious and dainty, like it was the lid of a box that had butterflies asleep in it and he didn't want to disturb them, and says:
> "Mr. Archibald Nichols, I presume?"

Like the king in Chapter XXIV, dressed in his "store clothes" and sporting a "new white beaver" that he doffs "with a bow ... and ... a smile" that make him look "grand and good and pious" (see Chapter Four, Section XII), Tom arrives prepared with information from a local (his driver, most likely), poses as "a stranger from Hicksville, Ohio, and his name was William Thompson—and he made another bow." These echoes associate Tom with the king and foreshadow his role in the closing section's covert religious satire.

There is yet more resonance between these two passages. In Chapter XXIV Huck says of the king's appearance, "you'd say he had walked right out of the ark, and maybe was old Leviticus himself." As mentioned previously, this association of the priestly tribe of Levites had its ministerial origin with Moses, who called upon his brother Aaron to be the founder of the priesthood of Israel in Exodus 28: 1. In the parody of Exodus implicit in the concluding section, Tom's role includes his identification as this same brother of Moses with whom Huck unwittingly associates the king (see Chapter Four, Section XII).

The ram to which Huck's simile compares Tom is also the sign of Ares/ Mars, the Greco-Roman god of war, and Tom will initiate unrest and instigate a shooting (his own) in the course of the evasion. Not coincidentally, Jim consistently addresses Tom in the closing section as "Mars Tom"—of course meaning "master"—but he might—with even greater verisimilitude—have addressed Tom as "Massah," thus ironically associating Tom with the Messiah he is not. But Clemens selects the form "Mars" with good reason, as Tom occupies center stage about to "afront" this entire family, and the echoes here in the closing section keep reverberating, thundering "like empty barrels rolling down stairs, where it's long stairs and they bounce a good deal" (Chapter IX).

Furthermore, in Chapter XXXIII absent-minded Silas tells Sally when he finds one of her missing spoons in his pocket, that he "was a-studying over my text in Acts Seventeen before breakfast, and I reckon I put it in there, not noticing." The setting of Acts 17: 22 ff. is "in the midst of Mars' hill" in Athens, where the Apostle Paul preaches the equality of all people in the eyes of "THE UNKNOWN GOD." This teaching, too, is something that Silas Phelps is "not noticing." Not only was Clemens aware of the significance of Mars as the god for whom this Athenian hill was named, but he also repeatedly associates Tom with Mars or his symbol, the ram, from his advent in and throughout the Phelps farm sequence.

And speaking of thunderous reverberations, the trumpets used to bring down the walls of Jericho in Joshua 6 were made from the horns of rams, which were clearly very important in the bestiary of the ancient Hebrews. Finally, Tom's transformation to a potentially dangerous beast marks his place in the archetypal scheme of the book as an avatar, like pap (who in this sense is Tom's grandfather, and the king, in the same sense his father, making Tom "his grandfather's ram") of the corrupting power of religion aligned with Bible mythology, which is precisely what Tom's arrogant and duplicitous scheme for stealing Jim (from himself) manifests as Tom Sawyer steps, "ca'm and important," with a bow and a doff of his hat and a smile, into his role as the God of the Gilded Age.

VII. Of Aunt Sally and Uncle Silas

In Chapter XXXVI, Jim tells Tom that Uncle Silas "come in every day to pray with him, and Aunt Sally come in to see if he was comfortable and had plenty to eat, and both of them was kind as they could be." Hearn reports that Twain considered portraying Uncle Silas as torn about "what to do with

Jim: The farmer-preacher 'wishes he would escape—if it warn't wrong, he'd set him free—but it's a gushy generosity with another man's property.'"[28]

It is important to recognize that it is racism and the institution of slavery that blinds Silas and all his fellow slaveholders to the plight of every one of their chattels. Here Clemens provides another illustration of the way slavery had the effect of stultifying the humanity of everyone, but only as regards the slaves. Otherwise, the Southern slaveholders were not often hard-hearted, and were in Clemens' view no different from people everywhere (see Preface, Section V, quotations 1 and 2).

Clemens also provides evidence for another aspect of Silas' bigotry and hypocrisy through Huck's description of the scene in Chapter XXXVII where the boys' thefts drive Aunt Sally to distraction:

> "Missus" comes a young yaller wench, "dey's a brass cannelstick miss'n."
> "Cler out from here, you hussy, er I'll take a skillet to ye!" [reacts Aunt Sally].

Hearn notes that "young yaller wench" denotes "A young mulatto woman, the result of miscegenation often through the master himself; light-skinned female slaves were usually domestic servants who attended the mistress and her children."[29]

In a note to Chapter XXII Hearn writes that Clemens was aware of the meaning of "wench." While he worked on the Hannibal *Courier*, his employer owned a woman slave cook with a daughter who attracted the attentions of his co-worker, fellow apprentice Steve Wilkins. The situation was distressing to the girl's mother, who was worried that the young white man would rape her daughter.[30] Mark Twain later commented, "She quite well understood that by the customs of slaveholding communities it was Steve's right to make love to [rape] that girl if he wanted to."[31]

In an earlier passage in Chapter XIV, where Huck and Jim discuss Solomon and his harem (see Chapter Three, Section XIV), Hearn notes that Huck misses the irony here that "Southern plantations were often run like harems, with nighttime visits by the masters to the slave quarters."[32]

Given all this information, one might speculate that Aunt Sally's angry reaction to the "young yaller wench" telling her about the missing candlestick is more than just the last straw in a series of upsetting disappearances. Since Huck seems blissfully ignorant of sexual matters, his use of the term "wench" can presumably be attributed to his having heard others use it, and it does fit the pattern mentioned earlier in this study of whites referring to African Americans by terms that recognize the least degree of their humanity (see Chapter Six, Section V). Nevertheless, Clemens' awareness of the connotation of "wench," the girl's mulatto complexion, her presence in the Phelps household, Uncle Silas' age, which makes it conceivable that he is her father if not her lover, and Aunt Sally's disproportionate anger toward her, calling her "hussy"—with connotations of "saucy, mischievous, and immoral"[33]—and threatening her physically with a cast iron skillet—all suggest that Tom's aunt is enduring more provocation here than Huck is aware of.

Moreover, this incident is an ironic inversion of the one Clemens recounts from his apprentice days (above); there, the slave girl's mother is alarmed at the threat of her daughter's rape by a white man who is young, penniless, and single, while in the novel the wife of an older and prosperous white man may be angered by the attractiveness of the enslaved girl to her husband, whose chattel she is. Even the missing, phallic brass candlestick is suggestive of Clemens intending an oblique reference to the sexually abusive customs to which "the peculiar institution" gave rise: gross and widespread abuses of human rights and dignity by whites, even those who did not own slaves, like young Wilkins. And it is Huck, who like the young Sam Clemens, innocently finds the situation entertaining. Whether "saintly" Uncle Silas is guilty of this particular abuse or not, his owning this young, mixed-race woman—and its implications for his wife—makes him a party morally to every such abuse.

VIII. The Acts of Silas Phelps

Although Huck presents an affectionate and admiring portrait of Silas Phelps, Clemens shows the more discerning reader a dark side of his character of which Huck, at least, is unaware. Once again in this concluding section of the story, Clemens challenges the reader to "fill in the blanks" in Huck's narration from one's own "wider experience," as John Lindberg has proposed (see Chapter One, Section I). Here is Huck's sympathetic take on Uncle Silas:

> He was the innocentest, best old soul I ever see. But it warn't surprising; because he warn't only just a farmer, he was a preacher, too, and had a little one-horse log church down back of the plantation, which he built it himself at his own expense, for a church and school-house, and never charged nothing for his preaching, and it was worth it, too. There was plenty other farmer-preachers like that, and done the same way, down South [Chapter XXXIII].

Clearly, *Huck* finds no fault with Silas; Mark Twain's ironic inversion of Huck's meaning—"and it was worth it, too"—injects humor into the comment and hints that the implied author and narrator *do* find fault with something in the old man's character and actions. Of course, Silas' being a typical Southern farmer-preacher-schoolmaster points up the complicity of religion and education in perpetuating the system of plantation culture, and the uncounted population of the Phelps farm includes its labor force of human chattels whose constant presence in the background of Huck's narration—and sometimes the foreground also—opens Huck's assessment of the character of Silas Phelps to question.

Since Huck finds no fault with this systemic evil, it is no wonder he is blind to Tom's uncle's moral failings, but that doesn't mean the author expects the reader to buy into Huck's viewpoint exclusively. Once again, Clemens relies on the reader's ability—or lack thereof—to provide what Wayne Booth refers to as "mature moral judgment … more exhilarating sport than identifying the source of an allusion or deciphering a pun" (see Chapter One, Section III). The above passage underscores both Huck's and preacher Phelps' moral blindness to the inhumanity of the social system in which Silas participates as farmer, educator, and pastor.

Uncle Silas' reading in Acts 17 in Chapter XXXVII directs the reader's attention to a biblical text that does undermine Silas' righteous standing as a slave-owning preacher. The text addresses him personally, since his biblical namesake is the Apostle Paul's companion in incidents around this chapter, in which Paul teaches the following doctrine:

> 22 Then Paul stood in the midst of Mars' hill, and said, Ye men of Athens, I perceive that in all things ye are too superstitious.
>
> 23 For as I passed by, and beheld your devotions, I found an altar with this inscription, TO THE UNKNOWN GOD, Whom therefore ye worship, him declare I unto you.
>
> 24 God that made the world and all things therein, seeing that he is Lord of heaven and earth, dwelleth not in temples made with hands;
>
> 25 Neither is worshiped with men's hands, as though he needed any thing, seeing he giveth to all life, and breath, and all things;
>
> 26 And hath made of one blood all nations of men for to dwell on all the face of the earth, and hath determined the times before appointed, and the bounds of their habitation;
>
> 27 That they should seek the Lord, if haply they might feel after him, and find him, though he be not far from every one of us:
>
> 28 For in him we live, and move, and have our being; as certain also of your own poets have said, For we are also his offspring.

Here Clemens gives us in the words of Paul, the leading theologian of the New Testament, in a text that emphasizes the equality of all people in the eyes of their Creator, a standard by which slavery could not stand save through the denial of the humanity of the slaves.

Yet every day Silas goes to the hut where he holds Jim prisoner to pray with him, as Jim tells Tom in the previous chapter, raising the question, how can Silas square his religion with his behavior as a slave owner? Is his attention to Jim's religious life just a cynical ruse by which to foster slaves' superstition and reinforce the power of the slave owners over their "soulless" chattels? Or is this self-contradictory behavior just the nth degree of hypocrisy? As Hearn remarks in pointing out the irony of Silas ministering to Jim while treating him like a sub-human, "Property rights win over human rights again"; by making "good-natured Uncle Silas" careless of Jim's fate, Clemens dramatizes the contradiction of a generally kind man who cannot perceive the humanity or appreciate the suffering of the slaves he owns and oversees, despite his being a preacher who is familiar with the New Testament.[34]

IX. Of Jim and the Doctor

Doyno points out that comparison of Clemens' working manuscript with the first edition text reveals that in Chapter XLI the revision makes Tom appear more foolish and stresses Jim's readiness to assist the doctor, thus enlisting reader sympathy for Jim by emphasizing his compassion for Tom and his bravery.[35]

Of course, Jim's act is indeed brave. By stepping forward he is sacrificing not only his freedom but also, probably, his very life (see Chapter Six, Section V). This act makes Jim a Christ figure in a completely positive sense. Chapter XLII is entitled in some later editions "Why They Didn't Hang Jim" (see Appendix A). It is not necessary for Jim to suffer the utmost consequence of his selfless act in order that his self-sacrifice for his tormentor's "salvation" entitle him to this supreme moral standing.

Despite the numerous studies of *Huck Finn* that reveal biblical allusions embedded in the closing section (see Chapter Five, Section III and IV), Doyno asserts, "The Phelps episode does not have many explicit references to religion."[36] This is a point on which this reading of the novel radically diverges from his. In my view, the deepest meaning of the Phelps farm sequence is its significance as religious satire—to which the abundant literary satire on Tom's "authorities" and the authority of literacy itself are subordinate. For although it is the illiteracy of the slaves that helps to perpetuate some of the abuses Clemens exposes, their ignorance also insulates them from some of the morally corrosive effects of the culture of literacy and corrupt religiosity that perverts Tom Sawyer's play, as Doyno makes clear. At the source of that toxic brew of authoritarianism, self-righteous arrogance, cupidity, deceitfulness, and treachery, as Tom's re-enactment of God's role in Exodus 1–14 reveals, lies the ultimate literary/moral authority of the Western world: the Bible.

The Sacred Book thus stands alone as the ultimate target of the social satire based on Jim's imprisonment and Tom's and the Phelpses' abusive treatment of Jim. Religious satire underlies all of the rest of Mark Twain's literary satire and explains how well meaning people like the slaveholders can justify their evil institutions and deeds on biblical grounds. This explanation also comprehends what Andrew Levy sees as the endless recycling that Clemens observed in history, for which the echoic structure of the novel becomes a metaphor as situations change but their dynamics remain the same over and over, world without end.

X. "Discovering Kingdom-Come"

An 1883 or '84 insertion into the portion of the novel written, apparently, between 1876 and 1879 elaborates on Huck's adventure with Jim and a gang of thieves and would-be murderers aboard the *Walter Scott* in Chapter XII. Doyno comments that the insertion supports his view of Clemens' thematic goal of making his satire throughout the story target Tom Sawyer, "who recklessly attempts to duplicate European literary adventures in real life." Doyno finds it "intriguing" that Clemens puts a mixture of "nationalistic and religious concerns" into Huck's account of his attempt to emulate Tom's "recklessness [and] yearning for adventure": "And wouldn't he throw style into it?—wouldn't he spread himself, nor nothing? Why, you'd think it was Christopher Columbus discovering Kingdom-Come."[37]

In the closing section, it is precisely "Kingdom-Come" that Tom's overtly romantic mischief discloses, and the text of the manuscript bears witness that the author intends that Tom Sawyer's evasion, with its burlesque of the biblical escape story of Exodus underlying its burlesque of romantic escape fiction and its parody of the novel's plot, should cast Tom as the heir to pap Finn. When he penned this insert into the portion of the manuscript begun in 1876, Clemens was tying together disparate parts of the manuscript to underscore and elaborate their common themes, including religious and subordinate social/literary satire.

XI. The Brazen Serpent Swallows Its Tale

XI-A: The Serpent Motif

There is another motif in *Huck Finn* to which "the brazen serpent in the wilderness" draws our attention: from pap's satanic advent in Chapter V—

inherently a serpent metaphor; through the scene of pap's torment as he suffers Satan's punishment as "a monstrous Serpent on his Belly prone" in Hell (Chapter VI); through Huck's being led by "a good-sized snake" to Jim's camp on Jackson's Island (Chapter VIII), which, apropos of its status as Eden has no shortage of snakes; through Huck's handling the snakeskin that brings "bad luck" (Chapter X); through his putting a dead rattlesnake in Jim's bedding and Jim's being bitten by one that joined "its mate" there (Chapter X: "What Comes of Handlin' Snake-Skin); through Huck and Jim blaming the curse of the snakeskin for all the troubles they endure throughout the raft voyage (Chapter XVI: "The Rattlesnake-Skin Does Its Work"; see Appendix A); through the lead-up to Huck's reunion with Jim shortly before the climax of the feud episode, where Huck's personal slave Jack takes him into the swamp to guide him to "a whole stack o' water-moccasins" that turns out to be Jim (Chapter XVIII); through the camp-meeting where the brazen serpent figures large and the mourners who throw themselves down in the straw—in the manuscript, anyway—act out for the second time in the story the account in *Paradise Lost* of the punishment of Satan and his legions in Hell after the Fall; through the king's identification as the monster serpent Geryon (Fraud) in Hell in the Royal Nonesuch (see Chapter Four, Section IV-B); through the boys' strewing garter snakes throughout the Phelps home and Jim's log cabin/cell after Jim refuses to accept a rattlesnake as a pet (Chapters XXXVIII and XXXIX): Huck's *Adventures* are crawling with snakes.

This serpent-motif serves several purposes. Of course, on the archetypal level of the implied author, these snakes are one-and-all a reminder of the serpent-tempter in Eden; they stand for Huck's ongoing temptation in his alliance with Jim—whether to betray him (a moral crime) or help him (a legal and moral one in this fictive society)—up until Chapter XXXI. They remind the reader also of the pervasive racism of the society Huck, Jim, and Tom personify, for Huck's disastrous practical joke in Chapter X is motivated by his desire to "have some fun" at his black companion's expense, like Tom Sawyer in Chapter II. And their superstitious calculation that all their bad luck is attributable to Huck's violation of Jim's belief echoes the Depravity Doctrine, the effect of Original Sin.

For Jim, as they float south on the raft, Huck's racist attitudes represent another aspect of the snakeskin curse: Like the pet rattlesnake Tom offers him, Huck is a perilous companion who is as likely to betray Jim as to befriend him until Chapter XXXI. And Tom's reviving this serpent motif in the evasion ties him into this pattern of repetition and variation. Tom's association with harmless garter snakes underscores the inauthenticity of his escape plan and at the same time associates him with the serpent symbol. The image that symbolizes Clemens' conflation of the bestial emblem of the Tempter with the moral authority of the Bible is "the brazen serpent."

XI-B: *The Glaring Travesty*

Many readers have complained that *Huckleberry Finn* ends in a burlesque of its own plot. From Leo Marx to Bernard DeVoto to Franklin Rogers, critics have deplored the ways in which Mark Twain subjects Huck and Jim to Tom's ridiculous and cruel antics in an ill-timed play for the belly laugh. Marx protested that "to take seriously what happens at the Phelps farm is to take lightly the entire downstream journey"; DeVoto claimed that the evasion constitutes the most "abrupt and chilling descent" in "the whole reach of the English novel" (see Introduction, Section I)[38]; Rogers declares that the "entire final section represents an admission of defeat in the attempt to give the book a coherent form. The book is essentially a structural failure because the travelers reach no physical goal..., and during the evasion Huck fails to act in accordance with the instinctive humanity which characterizes his relations with Jim during the journey."[39] Many similar analyses concur with these inadequate readings.

Although this study does not support the conclusions they reach about the meaning of this self-burlesque, these critics put their fingers on an important dimension of Tom's and Mark Twain's intrigue. For what Tom and the implied narrator engineer is quite a thorough parody of Huck's and Jim's flight with an overlay of style meant to bring it up to Tom's "educated" standards. Victor Doyno notices the contrast between Huck's ingenious and spontaneous plan of escape in Chapter VII and Tom's imitation of romantic escape fiction. This contrast, he proposes, is clearly deliberate, since both escapes feature "identical... details of sawing a hole in a cabin wall which is hidden by a cloth."[40] Actually, the boys do not saw a hole in the wall of the cabin where Jim is imprisoned, although they do conceal the hole they dig under it as Doyno points out.

Furthermore, among many parallels between the evasion and Huck's and Jim's flight are Tom's mistaking Huck for a ghost just as Jim did (Chapter VIII), and Huck's request that Tom promise "not to tell" when he informs Tom of his mission to steal Jim, just as Jim extracted a similar promise from Huck (Chapter VIII). Tom keeps Jim's manumission by Miss Watson a secret just as Jim kept pap's death a secret ("Chapter the Last"). Allusions to the story of Moses are a prominent archetypal feature of both Huck's escape and Jim's imprisonment. Both episodes deal with imprisonment in a log cabin. When Huck suggests sawing Jim out of the hut, "the way I done before I was murdered, that time," Tom approves of the idea, and then one-ups it with his plan to dig Jim out with "case knives" (Chapter XXXIV). Tom's projected path of flight once they get Jim out is resumption of the raft voyage to which Huck's and Jim's escapes led ("Chapter the Last"). In a parallel to Huck's thefts of provisions, in the course of the evasion Tom insists on stealing—Huck calls it borrowing, in accord with pap's custom, but Tom corrects him, thereby clarifying the Bible's word-choice—three knives, a spoon, a brass candlestick, a sheet, a shirt, a spoon, a brass warming pan, a large grindstone, one of Aunt Sally's dresses, and a slave-girl's frock, as well as tin plates stolen from the slaves—all on Jim's behalf; during his own escape from pap Huck took everything his father had. Huck finds "an old rusty saw-blade under ... weatherboarding" like the one he found and used to escape pap's hut (Chapters VI and XXXV), and he proposes that they use it on Jim's bed leg, but Tom won't have it. Tom requires Jim to use his own blood for ink (Chapter XXXVI); Huck used the blood of the hog he killed as a substitute for his own (Chapter VII). Tom insists on sawing the bed leg in play to free Jim's chain; Huck sawed out of his confinement for real. After Jim refuses to accept a rattlesnake as a pet, Tom settles for garter snakes with buttons affixed to their tails (Chapter XXXVIII); Jim found a real rattlesnake in his bedding after Huck planted a dead one there, and it did bite him (Chapter X). In an echo of Chapter VII's Passover allusions, "we stuck a picture which Tom drew in blood, of a skull and crossbones, on the front door; and next night another one of a coffin, on the back door (Chapter XXXIX). And at the conclusion of Tom's preparation for the evasion, he has Huck put on a frock to deliver his "nonnamous letter"; in Chapter XI Huck went ashore in a dress on his spy mission; and Jim escapes in one of Aunt Sally's dresses, reminding readers of their having played the role of Eve to each other's Adam in the Jackson's Island sequence. Pursuit by dogs, a danger that Jim wisely avoided in his own escape, is also a prominent feature of the evasion.

Not all of these parallels are within Tom's control, of course. In making the evasion a burlesque of Huck's own escape, Clemens uses Mark Twain's literary burlesque and his parody of the novel's plot to draw our attention to the arti- and superficiality of the completely bogus escape that Tom engineers for Jim. The contrast to the authenticity of Huck's own elaborate and profoundly multivalent escape could not be more painfully marked or boldly highlighted. The most important contrast between Huck's adventures and Tom's evasion is that while Huck's adventures are all in earnest (even the practical jokes), Tom's are in game, and heartless. Tom's inability to appreciate the difference gives us clear insight into his character, which Clemens weighs, measures, and finds wanting, as have readers to the present day.

Doyno's more thorough and insightful discussion of some of the repeated motifs pointed out above, along with others not noticed here, supports this study's general assertion that the inherent burlesque of the plot of the novel that is observable in the closing section is not accidental nor an inharmonious descent into pointless self-parody,[41] but rather an aspect of the coherent design of the novel that is essential to its meaning as religious satire: satire exposing the basic conflict between Huck's compassionate pragmatism and Tom's conscientious, egotistical conformity.

Tom's imitations of Huck, whose real life adventures he no doubt envies and tries hard to out-do, and Clemens' exploration of Tom's character as the new avatar of the biblical deity in the novel, the racist heir to pap Finn, make it clear that Clemens stands behind all of Tom's nonsense knowing full well what both of his narrators and Tom—and he himself—are up to. Through all Tom's hijinks Huck *never once* loses sight of his goal of freeing Jim; nor, for that matter, does he enthusiastically join in Tom's pretenses; for Huck they are clearly nothing more than a means to his own end: stealing Jim. If a pick would work better, he'd use one, and does. Tom is in it for glory, and by getting shot during the escape he actually does out-do Huck's feigned murder in his own mind, which is what he really cares about, although, once again, Huck is oblivious to Tom's ulterior motives.

The importance of being entertaining was always on Sam Clemens' mind, and he knew his audience far better than we ever can. On his *Twins of Genius* tour with George Washington Cable, he revised passages from the evasion for public reading, and evidently they went over well (Hearn notes numerous revisions for these performances in his notes to the text). As Andrew Levy reports, Mark Twain entertained his audiences with "parody after parody, code after code." His "references to freeing a black man who was already free"; the "eighty years" Tom imagines it taking to free Jim—"so like the eighty years between the American Revolution and the Emancipation Proclamation"; and the "forty dollars" Tom pays to Jim" sounds "an echo of the forty years in wandering spent by the biblical Israelites … and the forty acres and a mule promised and then not delivered to freed slaves after the War." And then Clemens added dogs: "He even added a passage where dogs are [turned] loose on Jim." The dogs were a reminder to "many readers" of the ones "patrolling [convict] work camps, as they had patrolled plantation borders before the war":

> It was as if Cable's cause—prison reform—was Twain's own, but on the sly. When combined with the familiar jargon of convict-lease with which he laced the evasion sequence—words like "shackles," "guards," "prisoner"—those dogs in pursuit didn't quite give away the politics. But they made it a little harder to laugh without the ghost of those politics shaping the laugh.[42]

The parody of Huck's and Jim's own escapes that Clemens embeds into the evasion is in large measure part of his characterization of Tom Sawyer, who is not the same Tom Huck and the reader have known in the past any more than Huck is the same Huck. Adolescent boys change fast, and that is an eternal verity. At the end of *The Adventures of Tom Sawyer*, Mark Twain comments: "The story could not go much further without becoming the history of a *man*. When one writes a novel about grown people, he knows exactly where to stop—that is, with a marriage, but when he writes of juveniles, he must stop where he best can."

Doyno comments that Clemens "artistic intuition" that Tom was not the right boy to follow into manhood is borne out in the closing chapters of *Huck Finn*, where Tom represents many of the worst evils of contemporary society: "Tom dramatizes a particular kind of moral corruption, a combination of subservience to his authorities and absolute, arrogant, disregard for his companions."[43]

Tom's and Mark Twain's parody of Huck's and Jim's flight contributes to the reader-distraction with which Clemens masks the deeper meaning of Huck's tale, drawing attention away from its religious satire by focusing it on the glaring travesty that Mark Twain engineers through Tom's aping of romantic escape fiction and of Huck's and Jim's escapes and of the collapse of Reconstruction. Indeed, it is what Mark Twain refers to as "the superior glare of something in the body of the burlesque itself," in which "the moral of the burlesque—if its object be to enforce a truth—escapes notice" (see Preface, Section V, final quotation).[44]

The purpose of this glaring travesty that Tom Sawyer and Mark Twain and Sam Clemens contrive is in one respect the opposite of the technique described in the above quotation: Clemens intentionally distracts the reader from his underlying biblical burlesque and religious satire by concealing it within the "extraneous interest" of his literary satire and his parody of almost everything that has led up to Tom's hijacking of the plot. Only by looking past the travesty can we see into the concealed meanings of the closing section of Huck's story.

Huck's rejection of the moral system that sustains slavery and racism at the climax of the novel and throughout its concluding section does not render him a colorblind opponent of these evils. It only prepares the way for social transformation commensurate with his moral transformation. As history testifies, moral leaps may give rise to social change that is not always of the *quantum* kind; it has taken over seven generations for our society to get from the collapse of Reconstruction to Black Lives Matter, and the painful truth that the affirmational name of this movement challenges is that black lives still don't matter any more than the fictive dead black man Huck invents to invest his lie to Aunt Sally in Chapter XXXII with realism.

But this paradoxical strain in Huck's character does not diminish his moral stature; it just leaves a long way to go before he becomes what Clemens attempted to make Mark Twain become. Huck's moral quantum leap, like Satan's passage through Chaos in *Paradise Lost*, establishes a bridge between his world (Hell) and ours—a bridge that the fictional Mark Twain/Adam/Christ/Satan did ultimately cross, as Brodwin has shown, and America is still crossing. Huck's choice to "steal Jim out of slavery again" (Chapter XXXI) is a commitment to devote his soul to this lone black Christ figure who endures the whole Passion of "his people" and to reject all he has learned from his pap, the avatar of racist evil. His commitment establishes that bridge from the hell of our past to the hope for our future and the possibility of racial reconciliation. In *Adventures of Huckleberry Finn* Clemens solved the problem of where to end the tale by Huck's embracing Jim as his true father and becoming a whole man.

XII. Reconciling Antithetical Critiques 3.0: Embellishing the Travesty

By referring to Clemens' manuscript text, students of the novel can observe the process of composition and revision that produced the novel and from that observation draw some conclusions about what kind of book Clemens thought he was writing, as Victor Doyno and Michael Patrick Hearn and De Lancey Ferguson have demonstrated. It is not only the intention of this chapter to validate Doyno's thesis that anti-literary, anti–European, anti-authoritarian satire comprises a profound level of the novel's motive, moral, and plot, but also, and more importantly, to extend his insight into the themes and literary artistry he observes in his genetic explication of the novel and the manuscript.

This study is greatly indebted to his work for revealing the extent to which the implied narrator does succeed in posing as the ultimate authority for the meaning of the book, and its intention is to demonstrate that an additional genetic explication of Clemens' novel in light of his manuscript is possible and that such a reading validates both Doyno's explication and this one, yielding a more comprehensive critique of Clemens/Mark Twain's bewilderingly complex and polyvalent text. As is the case with James M. Cox and Harold Kolb and with Kenneth Lynn and Daniel Barnes, only by discovering how antithetical perspectives on the thematic development of the text can be reconciled and revealed to be mutually complementary can students of the novel approach a comprehensive appreciation of its complexity and meaning. It is not a case of either/or, but a proposal of both/and that this study sets forth.

Victor Doyno sees the closing satire on romantic escape fiction as "de real p'int" of Clemens' satire; I see it as the "glaring travesty" that distracts the attention of the reader from the underlying pattern of "echoes" that anchors the text in biblical, Dantean, and Miltonic literary archetypes and religious satire. In this respect, this study extends Doyno's insights into Clemens' use of literary sources, for it reveals that even within the extensive burlesque of fiction that Tom instigates in the closing section, the undergirding burlesque of religious literature is Clemens' fundamental concern.

Like Huck, whose insensitivity to the ways in which his *Adventures* manifest Clemens' mythic paradigm—on which Western culture is based—destines him to live his rituals (see Chapter One, Section VII-B), Clemens guides the reader toward the realization that unless one takes responsibility for one's own, culturally projected mythology that contributes to the perpetuation of the formative myths shaping the collective unconscious of our culture, the recycling of our history is as certain as the doom of the Grangerford clan (see Chapter Three, Section XVI).[45] This reality is why history repeats itself and the issues facing our society today are fundamentally the same as those with which Clemens' America was grappling.[46] "Tom," as Doyno suggests, exemplifies a special sort of "moral corruption" that blends subservience to what he regards as "authorities" with "absolute, arrogant, disregard" for his comrades.[47] We see a lot of that sort of corruption in both our domestic and international relations to this very day.

XIII. Questions about Huck's Growth

At the end of the novel Huck Finn stands at a crossroads. He can return to St. Petersburg and reclaim his wealth (or remain with the Phelps family, which amounts to the same thing), or he can "light out ... ahead of the rest," turning his back on another six-thousand dollar pile of "yaller-boys" (see Chapter Four, Section XV) and the security he has been offered. His only unqualified victory is that he now has the freedom to choose. "What," Clemens' art asks of the reader, "would *you* do? What should Huck do?" To answer these questions, the reader must look into his own heart and conscience, always a constructive exercise, and rethink some very basic questions about the relationship between the individual, society, and God. There are no easy answers.

Huck *says* he will turn his back on "sivilization." Can one take his decision seriously? If not, then despite Huck's closing assertion that "there's nothing more to write," the book ends on either a moral cliffhanger or a note of derisive irony. Clemens gives us at least three more instances that reflect a change in Huck's attitude toward Tom during and after the evasion. Victor Doyno has done much to dispel the mistaken reading embraced by many critics that sees Huck acting as Tom Sawyer's lackey and enthusiastically playing along with Tom's antics.[48] This change in their relationship suggests that Huck is now able to distinguish his own agenda from Tom's, and that this capacity enables him to move into a new matrix of individuality, one that does not contain Tom Sawyer as a demigod to follow blindly.

Consider, for example, Huck's sarcastic remark (apparently lost on Tom): "'If it ain't unregular and irreligious to sejest it,' I says, 'there's an old rusty saw blade around yonder.'" Tom simply comments "'It ain't no use to try to learn you nothing, Huck,'" and insists on making the saw blade for sawing the leg off Jim's bed from a spoon (Chapter XXXV). Irony, be it remembered, has not been Huck's long suit. By allowing him a touch of it now, Clemens may be signaling that Huck has begun to recognize his own superiority to Tom and has outgrown the dependency relation to his "comrade" that the subtitle of the novel emphasizes. Again in Chapter XXXVI, Huck reacts sarcastically to Tom's plan to smuggle things into the hut in the pockets of Aunt Sally and Uncle Silas: "'Don't do nothing of the kind, it's one of the most jack-ass ideas I ever struck.'"

Again when Huck asks Tom in "Chapter the Last" what his plans were had the evasion succeeded, Tom says:

> What he had planned from the start, if we got Jim out all safe, was for us to run him down the river on the raft, and have adventures plumb to the mouth of the river, and then tell him about his being free, and take him back up home on a steamboat, in style, and pay him for his lost time, and write word ahead and get out all the niggers around, and have them waltz him into town with a torchlight procession and a brass band, and then he would be a hero, and so would we.

"But," concludes Huck, "I reckoned it was about as well the way it was." If we allow Huck another stroke of irony here, then "about as well" means, as it assuredly does for the implied author and the reader: far better. This is hardly the admiration Huck expresses earlier for Tom's ability to "spread himself." Nor is it the boyish enthusiasm with which H. N. Smith imagines Huck greeting Tom's plan[49]: "Le's all three slide out of here one of these nights and get an outfit, and go for howling adventures amongst the Injuns, over in the Territory, for a couple of weeks or two."

Huck replies, "All right, that suits me." He goes on to say that pap has probably drunk up all his money by now, but his agreement is hardly enthusiastic, and his final comment in the last chapter is "I reckon I got to light out ... ahead of the rest"—the rest, in context, meaning Tom and perhaps Jim—who else is there? And, it should be noted, "light out" is a particularly appropriate expression for the first incarnation of Samuel Clemens' Adamic Satan, whose other name is Lucifer, which means "Bearer of Light."

So the author does at least hint that Huck has grown up, but unless these whispers refer to growth that has already taken place, they are insufficient demonstrations of Huck's maturity and independence from Tom to warrant the assertion that he has outgrown his need and desire for "him and me to be together" (Chapter I). As discussed in Chapter Four of this study, Huck's identification with Satan marks his attainment of adult moral stature, and throughout the closing eleven-chapter section he continues to be identified with biblical adults: Moses and Christ. Only on the realist surface of the narration does he appear at all to remain a child, and as the discussion of the evolution of Huck's language style over the course of the last part of the novel demonstrates, signs of maturation are evident there, too (see Chapter Four, Section XVIII). This implicit commentary on the seriousness of his intention to "light out" is further evidence that such a view of Huck is indeed what the implied author conveys and that we *can* take Huck's final plan at face value. But in order to fully understand the religious satire of the conclusion, the subordinate social satire of Clemens' argument demands closer attention.

XIV. The Conclusion as Triple Exposure: Myth, Literature, and History

As William Gibson first observed, slavery by 1885 had become "a metaphor for the continued denial of civil rights to America's black citizenry" (see Introduction, Section IV).[50] The evasion, with its long postponement of the liberation it is supposed to effect, is a fictional reflection of the actual collapse of Reconstruction inasmuch as Jim's legal status as a "free cretur," as Tom calls him in Chapter XLII—note that no one in this fictive world of racists ever refers to Jim as a man (see Chapter Six, Section V)—has been persistently obscured by the machinations of whites (the "Tom Sawyers" of that day) who hold political and economic power. In Chadwick-Joshua's words:

> Jim completes the realistic and rather dark picture of the progress and promise of Reconstruction. Jim universally represents the southern ex-slave whose future and

anticipated quality of life are at best questionable—given the pervasive economic, social, and political conditions in the South during the late 1880s.[51]

In this respect, too, then, Clemens' conclusion thematically transcends its setting to come to grips with a central moral problem of the post–Reconstruction era, the betrayal of the Emancipation Proclamation that postponed real implementation of the 13th, 14th and 15th Amendments indefinitely.

This aspect of the concluding section fulfills Leo Marx's demand that a novelist reveal "painful truths" to his audience, for the fate of Jim is the fate of every African American man. At the close of the novel the freed slave has progressed but one step out of bondage in all the miles he has traveled with Huck: Jim owns himself. His family, however, is still in bondage, and he has nowhere to go except to flee the slave states before his six months are up and he is once again sold (a law of this fictive world, at least in Jim's home state; see Chapter Three, Section V-A). The conclusion leaves Jim on the horns of a dilemma that goes beyond the dramatic scope of the novel. True to history, Clemens leaves Jim's dilemma unresolved.

When Huck reflects on Jim's heroism in sacrificing himself to save Tom, "I knowed he was white inside" (Chapter XL), many readers have been content to regard this slur on the spiritual worth of African Americans as Mark Twain's ironic way of expressing praise for Jim through Huck and as Huck's final acknowledgment of Jim's humanity. But further consideration of Huck's attitude leads one to notice the racist bedrock underlying Huck's point of view as truly as his notorious response to Aunt Sally's asking if an exploded steamboat cylinder-head hurt anybody: "'No'm. Killed a nigger'" (Chapter XXXII).

While Chadwick-Joshua finds that Huck is feigning this racism as he lies to Aunt Sally, I think that it is at least equally valid—and consistent with his rejection of the humanity of African Americans everywhere else in the text—to conclude that at the end of the book, Huck's racist mindset is as unchanged as his conviction that helping Jim escape was "wicked." And there is no aside to the reader from Huck disavowing the attitude that he expresses in his lie to Aunt Sally or even hinting that he is just telling her what she expects to hear from a proper Southern boy. While Clemens' having her echo Huck's denial of black people's humanity no doubt emphasizes his meaning, as Chadwick-Joshua points out,[52] it is a meaning that Huck never questions before or after this incident. And Clemens struck Huck's ultimate acknowledgment of Jim's humanity from the final chapter of the manuscript: "You're a free man now" never made it into print.[53]

This static dimension of Huck's mental character shows the gulf that separates Huck from his creator. What, after all, makes Jim so great a character is the converse of Huck's praise: Jim is a black *man*—one of the first convincing ones in American literature, and probably the first avatar of the African American Adam/Christ in American fiction (see Chapter Six, Section V). It would have been better for Mark Twain to have killed Jim and preserved his dignity, some say, than to subject him to the humiliations of the evasion. And it would be better to stop reading "where Nigger Jim is stolen from the boys [sic]" complained Ernest Hemingway; "the rest is just cheating."[54] But what way could Clemens choose to represent the fate of African Americans that would better serve his implied criticism of a culture in which even sophisticated readers could pass over an insult to Jim like Huck's calling him "white inside"—what later came to be referred to contemptuously as "an Oreo Cookie"—what better way than by re-immersing Huck and Jim in society at the conclusion and allowing the social consequences of racism to reveal themselves thorough Huck's utterly naïve narration? And what more hopeful sign could Clemens offer to all Americans than that we have the likes of Jim in our midst?

Furthermore, by arranging the evasion not only as a topical satire on the post–Reconstruction era and an intricate burlesque of the romantic escape fiction and European history with which Tom Sawyer's infatuation knows no bounds, but also as a re-dramatization of Israel's liberation from Egyptian captivity, the implied author creates a triple exposure in which the outlines of these three violent epochs of myth and history, separated by a gulf of thousands of years, merge into one another. He implies that the forces shaping these three moments are the same. Here we come to the real point of the novel's biblical satire, and it is not merely to ridicule and deride the Bible in a fit of puerile iconoclasm. Clemens' concern, long misunderstood, is more deeply felt and reasoned than that. The final act of the novel employs the example of these three widely separated historical epochs to argue that in Bible times and in our own, history and literature are shaped by myth, informed by the fictions humankind invents to formulate social reality. As Andrew Levy comments:

> Mistaking a dark comedy about how history goes round for a parable about how it goes forward is a classic American mistake. Writing in the aftermath of the Civil War, surveying all that blood and treasure spent to free slaves, and then Reconstruction collapsing, convict-lease, the rise of the Klan, Jim Crow, lynchings—Mark Twain eventually dedicated *Huck Finn* to the proposition that, contra Lincoln, there was no new birth of freedom.[55]

Like the Shepherdson-Grangerford Feud, which must remind readers of the War Between the States in its pitting neighbors against each other in mortal combat, even as it recalls the Old Testament stories of Cain and Abel, of Moses and Pharaoh, and of the prophet Samuel, Saul, David, and Jonathan (see Chapter Three, Sections XVI, XVII and XIX), the conclusion declares the moral bankruptcy of the biblically informed conscience that Clemens believed had guided Western civilization into dire straits.

XV. Chapter Summary: Going the Whole Hog

From Chapter XXXII on to the end of the story, Clemens recapitulates many of the events and motifs that lead up to Huck's "counter-conversion" at the climax. These repetitions function on each of the three levels of point of view to say something different about where the two fugitives' flight has landed them. For Huck, who is as always blind to the implications of his adventures, the only meaning evident in the concluding travesty at the Phelps farm is that only in continued flight can he hope to avoid the impositions of "sivilization"; having "been there before," over and over again, he recognizes that he has to choose between Tom's way and the by-way that leads to the Territory, where he can escape the restrictions of "the authorities." Huck does not even recognize that Tom, in his envy of Huck, has connived to set in motion a parody of his own real-life adventures. As he sees it, his choice is clear: to "light out ... ahead of the rest."

From Mark Twain's point of view, there are many points of literary burlesque that heighten the comic aspects of the closing sequence. Topical, social satire aims at both political and religious targets: the hypocrisy of slaveholders, as exemplified by Silas Phelps especially, being chief among these, along with the unwitting impersonation by both Huck and Tom of the biblical brothers Moses and Aaron setting out to liberate Jim, who represents in this context the Hebrew tribes held captive in Egypt. This biblical burlesque, for those who have noticed it, has appeared to be an effort on Mark Twain's part to dignify Tom's antics with a humorous but essentially reverent underpinning of "biblical authority" that renders Tom's absurd machinations morally acceptable to an audience convinced of the unquestionable morality of biblical authority, which Samuel Clemens flatly rejected.

As can be seen in Huck's "burlesque Resurrection," these biblical parallels appear to be subject to a range of interpretations, from semi-serious as Baldanza regards them in his recognition of the parallels and dismissal of them as being thematically unnecessary, but worth noting, to Cross's insistence that the inherent irony of this parody of the Doubting Thomas episode in St. John's Gospel constitutes Mark Twain's denial of the divinity of Jesus Christ, a case in point of his consistently iconoclastic attitude toward the Bible throughout the book (see Five III). These critics, as has been seen several times before in this study, are actually following the divergent lines of argument of the implied narrator and the implied author. Baldanza follows Mark Twain's vision of Huck as having emerged from his climactic debate with conscience as a no-longer-lost lamb who has discovered the "higher morality" that aligns his with the reader's beliefs in a fixed code of "enlightened" ethics. Cross, on the other hand, tunes in to Clemens' biblical burlesque and sees the episode of Huck's and Tom's reunion in Chapter XXXII in the "blasphemous" light of the implied author's religious satire.

Along with its reiteration of the Moses motif that Clemens and Twain re-introduce at the outset of this closing section, the burlesque Resurrection episode affirms Huck's actual attainment of Christlike stature in Clemens' scheme even as it stands the reality of the Resurrection in doubt, while from Twain's angle of view it seeks to dignify Tom by making him an apostle of Huck's Christlike mission to liberate Jim. Of course, as his later machinations make clear, he is nothing of the sort. As the biblical Aaron, modest Moses' spokesman, he is responsible for setting in motion the sequence of events that complicates and delays Jim's liberation and aligns Tom with the social, political, and religious collusion that frustrated the intent of the Thirteenth Amendment and Reconstruction, resulting in a long, painful, and still unresolved race-conflict in American society.

As the evasion's burlesque of Exodus unfolds, Clemens makes it clear that Tom has displaced pap Finn in the role of divinity, and Tom's motives in his unwitting re-enactment of the biblical liberation drama mirror those of the God of Exodus: Tom's power-thirst and hunger for honor and glory inflict suffering on all concerned, and they reveal what Clemens regarded as moral failings on the part of God in those episodes of Bible lore, making the God of the Bible a cosmic extension of Tom Sawyer, whose actions echo those of the duke and the king as he re-enters the narrative and quite literally discovers "Kingdom-Come."

Still the naïve narrator, Huck is aware of none of this, and he accepts and admires Aunt Sally and Uncle Silas for what they appear to him to be; nevertheless, Clemens makes it clear that their hypocrisy as slaveholding Christians does not square with egalitarian teachings of the New Testament any more than did the wholesale rape of enslaved women, a human rights abuse that was widespread in the antebellum South, whether or not Silas Phelps acts it out.

On top of the biblical burlesque and parody Clemens overlays a thorough burlesque of his own plot that from Mark Twain's point of view heightens (or fails to heighten) the comedy of the conclusion, while from Clemens' standpoint it reveals Tom's inferiority to Huck, his poverty of imagination, and his egoism. Despite Huck's extended protestation of Tom's good character as he attempts to dissuade his friend from helping him steal Jim, it is clear that Huck doesn't really know Tom anymore and cannot see through his pretense of acting in Jim's interest.

Tom's attempt to re-enact scenes from his reading in real life comprises another level of Clemens/Twain's literary satire that is of secondary concern to this study as the glaring travesty that obstructs the reader's view of what is really happening. Of primary concern is the way the author's burlesque of both Old and New Testament texts imputes the blame for some of the worst moral failings seen in the novel to the putative Author of Holy Writ. This theme emphasizes the complementary nature of myth, literature, and history, viewing them as inseparable elements of a greater whole.

This study views that complex dream/story/reality as "the whole hog" that Clemens has Huck take on as his adventures carry him into conflict with society on all of these levels. While he does emerge victorious, he also winds up very much alone, as mythic heroes inevitably do. Nevertheless, his victory over conscience extricates him from the rut of blind conformity to social, political, and religious authority to which the likes of Tom Sawyer will always be subject.

CHAPTER SIX

Author-Real Intention
Huckleberry Finn *as Religious Satire*

I. Of *Huck Finn* as "Humorous Monologue"

Chapter One of this study begins with John Lindberg's sound analysis of *Huckleberry Finn* as an application of its author's storytelling technique to a book-length story. This approach leads Lindberg to view Mark Twain's prefatory "Notice" in three ways. Stylistically, it divests the author "of all mediation with the reader but Huck." In Clemens' rhetorical strategy, the "Notice" serves as "a device to prevent the reader from bowdlerizing the tale with ... didactic interpretations." Ultimately, its purpose is "to force the reader to heed the voice of the child."

From Lindberg's perspective on the story, this is again insightful interpretation that shows the author's desire to "combine his love for the humorous monologuist [*sic*] ... with his love for children": Mark Twain having thus divested himself of "all mediation with the reader" and circumvented "the impatient sophistication of the listener," he preserves Huck's innocence within the many roles that the people he encounters force upon him.

Lindberg's analysis of Clemens' "Notice" concludes that it challenges the reader to validate Huck's dubious perceptions from his limited perspective. Without "motive" except for survival, without "moral" except for "human bonds defying human bondage," and without "plot" except for a "humorous monologuist seeming to lose his way,"[1] Clemens' storytelling method in *Huck Finn* succeeds, in this critic's view, because it is true to Huck. Lindberg does not drop one sonorous "Clemens" into his text to signify that he has somehow penetrated the implied author's veil of anonymity and is about to reveal him to the reader. And he never burdens his insights with conclusions they will not bear and speculations that must collapse in the next gust of criticism.

Lindberg's essay gives a sound and sensible explanation of the story from the perspectives of its narrator and implied narrator, Huck Finn and Mark Twain. Lindberg's reading does not account for the point of view of the implied author, nor does it need to. That, however, is the purpose of this study, and without contradicting Lindberg, one can hold that there is yet another layer of meaning inherent in "THE AUTHOR's" "Notice": that of Samuel Clemens, the implied author to whose point of view we have been attending for several chapters, now.

II. "THE AUTHOR" Explains

The Mark Twain quotation that ends the Preface to this study is perhaps the closest the author comes to an explanation of his burlesque technique in *Huck Finn*: "One can deliver a satire with telling force through the insidious medium of a travesty, if he is careful not to overwhelm the satire with the extraneous interest of the travesty, and so bury it from the reader's sight and leave him a joked and defrauded victim, when the honest intent was to add to either his knowledge or his wisdom."[2]

In *Huckleberry Finn*, however, Clemens *purposely* overwhelms the satire on the Judeo-Christian worldview—the truth he was most deeply interested in enforcing—with the glaring travesty—especially that of the evasion—in part as a distraction to divert readers' attention (for obvious reasons; see Preface II) from the whole of the truth he intended to enforce. In other words, he intentionally concealed his meaning so well that it has *always* escaped readers' notice. But what of the "nub" or "moral tagged on at the bottom" that "is the key of the whole thing and the only important paragraph"? It appears that if he included such a key, the author of *Huck Finn* must have hidden it under the mat, at least, because the enigmatic conclusion of the novel offers readers *no* explanation of its motive, moral, and plot.

Yet he does provide just such a key that, if hidden at all, is hidden in plain sight. But to find and use this key the reader must *read* it, not just parse out its words into a sentence or two before turning up his nose at it, but exercise one's wit to a degree to which few in this culture of sound bites and text messages are accustomed. Evidently, he regarded it as a duty to the reader to provide it because without the key, it would be impossible for the work to enforce its *intended* knowledge or wisdom, leaving the reader not just blinkered, but "a joked and defrauded victim." Where did he hide this key? At the top.

III. "Thou Shalt Not...": The "Nub" from "THE AUTHOR"

> NOTICE
>
> *Persons attempting to find a motive in this narrative will be prosecuted; persons attempting to find a moral in it will be banished; persons attempting to find a plot in it will be shot.*
>
> BY ORDER OF THE AUTHOR,
> *Per G. G., Chief of Ordnance.*

In the final analysis, unless one can accept the idea of Samuel Clemens being a conscious and meticulous literary artist, biographical evidence supporting the theory presented here would be no more persuasive than even a line-by-line deconstruction of *Adventures of Huckleberry Finn* because, ultimately, it would be only another reader response (see One II). However, the first biblical and Miltonic allusions in the text—its opening words—strongly support the proposition that all of the others *are* intentional.

When "THE AUTHOR" warns that dire consequences await those "attempting" to discover "motive," "moral," or "plot" in "this narrative," he no more denies their existence than a Keep Out sign denies the existence of land beyond. Certainly the tone of the "Notice" is ironic; Mark Twain once pointed out that its humor is a function of its essential irony. "The kernel" of its meaning, he writes, "is ... the public must not take us too seriously. If we remove that kernel we remove the life-principle, and the preface is a corpse."[3] And he no doubt expected it to do precisely what it ostensibly prohibits. But the joke is neither so small nor so obvious, for the "Notice" provides both rhetorical and substantial clues to the novel's meaning. It is in fact trebly ironic, for its language suggests verbal irony; its structural allusion to the Bible and *Paradise Lost* is satiric; and its full meaning renders the "Notice" not a pretended but a real threat. In short, this brief text is the "nub" of *Huckleberry Finn*.

If one is to embrace the theory that Clemens structured his masterpiece to be a covert parody of the Eden and Egypt of the Bible, a satire on the theology and cosmology of John Milton, and an inversion of the "Moral Sense" designed to undermine readers' faith in what Clemens saw as their at-once cherished and self-damning superstitions, it is fair to demand evidence of this intention *in the text*. Whether the "Notice" is a denial of seriousness or a serious warning that the reader disregards at his or her own peril, one must trespass first to find out which it is. The "Notice" is an instance of the sort of "necessarily conscious borrowing" that Franklin Rogers has found to be characteristic of Clemens' burlesque technique.[4]

Samuel Clemens' prefatory warning parallels the very aspects of the Eden myth with which Mark Twain most vehemently found fault. Satan, making Twain's opinion clear in *Letters from the Earth*, observes, "As you perceive, the only person responsible ... [for Adam's and Eve's fall] escaped; not only escaped, but became the executioner of the innocent." In Brodwin's words, "For Mark Twain, their fall is inevitable, but it is also an unsurpassed act of absurd cruelty" on the part of the Creator.[5] The prefatory "Notice" mirrors not only in its ironic effect, but also in its form, substance, and capriciousness what Clemens saw as the intolerable commandment that God gives Adam and Eve in both Genesis and *Paradise Lost*:

> But of the tree of the knowledge of good and evil, thou shalt not eat of it: for in the day that thou eatest thereof thou shalt surely die. (Gen. 2: 17)

> But of the Tree whose operation brings
> Knowledge of good and ill [...]
> Remember what I warn thee, shun to taste,
> And shun the bitter consequence: for know,
> The day thou eat'st thereof, my sole command
> Transgrest, inevitably thou shalt die.[6]

The rhetorical pattern in both of these texts consists of a triad of indication, prohibition, and warning; similarly, Clemens' "Notice" consists of a triad of indication compounded with implied prohibition, and the same three warnings: "Persons attempting to find a motive in this narrative will be prosecuted; persons attempting to find a moral in it will be banished; persons attempting to find a plot in it will be shot."

The triple use of "attempting," with its root form "tempt," serves the treble purpose of reminding one of the Temptation, inviting and challenging one to do precisely what the "Notice" ostensibly forbids, and suggesting that that was the effect of God's warning to Adam and Eve. In *Letters from the Earth*, Satan/Mark Twain expresses the untenability of the situation of Adam and Eve in the Garden: "The serpent said the forbidden fruit would store their vacant minds with knowledge. So they ate it, which was quite natural, for man is so made that he eagerly wants to know."[7]

Or, as *Pudd'nhead Wilson's New Calendar* puts it: "Adam was but human—this explains it all. He did not want the apple for the apple's sake, he wanted it only because it was forbidden. The mistake was in not forbidding the serpent; then he would have eaten the serpent."[8]

Prosecution, banishment, and death, as the "Notice" reminds readers, were the price "our Grand Parents"[9] paid. Moreover, that which the "Notice" forbids, like its biblical and Miltonic counterparts again, is a form of knowledge: the recognition of motive, moral, and plot—in short, meaning—in

Huck's narrative. If one is to take "THE AUTHOR" at his word, then, he has something to say to a thinking reader that is as world shattering as the doctrines of the Fall and Total Depravity on which the biblical and Miltonic views of history and morality are founded.

"BY ORDER OF THE AUTHOR" is precisely the rationale given for the prohibition in Genesis and *Paradise Lost*. When in Milton's epic the newly created Adam asks his Creator's name, he addresses God as "Author" and "Author of this Universe."[10] In the droll voice of Mark Twain, his uncomprehending "humorous narrator," Samuel Clemens clearly implies in the "Notice" what the novel—his fictive universe—is about, and he does so in the primary manner in which it makes its meaning clear: through biblical and Miltonic burlesque. Clemens' art demands that the reader see that the Moral Sense is not divinely instilled but acquired through socialization; likewise, his recognition of cosmic absurdity is the liberation Clemens offers at the end of his career in "young Satan's" farewell to Theodor at the end of *The Mysterious Stranger*:

> Strange! [...] that you should not have suspected that your universe and its contents were only dreams, visions, fiction! Strange, because they are so frankly and hysterically insane—like all dreams: a God who could make good children as easily as bad, yet preferred to make bad ones; who could have made every one of them happy, yet never made a single happy one; who made them prize their bitter life, yet stingily cut it short; [...] who mouths justice and invented hell—mouths mercy and invented hell—mouths Golden Rules, and forgiveness multiplied by seventy times seven, and invented hell; who mouths morals to other people and has none himself; who frowns upon crimes, yet commits them all; who tries [...] to shuffle the responsibility for man's acts upon man, instead of placing it where it honorably belongs, upon himself; and finally, with altogether divine obtuseness, invites this poor, abused slave to worship him![11]

"Per G. G., Chief of Ordnance," puts the message of the "Notice" into the context of a relationship between "THE AUTHOR" and his agent G. G., perhaps General Grant or George Griffin, Clemens' butler at Hartford—or both—perhaps no more than an inconsequential official whose concern with the true meaning of the "Notice" is as limited as Huck Finn's awareness of the significance and meaning of his adventures. But this agent's title reflects military rank, and this reference to the American war machine that shed the blood of tens of thousands of our citizens between the time of the novel's setting and that of its publication should remind readers that the worldviews of the texts Clemens burlesques here provide the fountainhead of and justification for the rivers of blood shed in wars incited by sanctified greed, self-righteousness, nationalism, and religious fanaticism on both sides.

Victor Doyno's comments on the revisions Clemens made to the "Notice" lend support to this explication; "the use in the final version of two semicolons to link the three independent clauses indicates that Twain felt he had, by

1884, created a unified work, with three parallel warnings." Had he "chosen to use three distinct sentences, ... he would have been signaling a grouping of three separable concerns." These observations show that this seemingly offhand, humorous "Notice" is something Clemens devoted as much careful attention to as he gave to the various dialects in the body of the work. His late addition of "moral" between "motive" and "plot" does place morality at the center of the warning, as Doyno observes.[12] What is more, it brings the tripartite structure of the Notice into parallel with its biblical and Miltonic models; and "banished" puts the idea of permanent exile or ostracism for a moral transgression into the warning as well. Furthermore, Doyno's comments on Clemens' punctuation support the view that the single-sentence structure of the "Notice" causes it to reflect its structurally similar models in form as well as content. And as F. Kaplan reports, the "Notice" was integral to Clemens' early conception of the novel; he first drafted it before pigeonholing the manuscript in March of 1880, after his second major phase of composition had carried the story from "chapters 18½ to 21."[13]

Nor is it mere coincidence that all three of these texts—the "Notice" and the warnings in *Paradise Lost* and in Genesis—are tripartite, especially Clemens' and Milton's, since the "Three-in-One" structure is the cornerstone of Christian theology. In Clemens' case, he may also be signaling to the reader that "THE AUTHOR" is the ultimate authority of the text—that he is the god of this microcosm, and that he is manifest in three "persons": Huck, Mark Twain, and Samuel Clemens.

Regarding Clemens' substitution of the word "narrative" for "book," Hearn points out that this word-choice emphasizes Jim's role in the story, for "narrative" became a generic term for writings by fugitives from slavery telling the stories of their flight.[14] Regarding Jim, this "narrative" is indeed about a slave's flight to freedom (see Chapter Six, Section V); regarding Huck, it is about a boy's flight from slavery to a depraved moral system to his authentic rejection of revealed moral absolutes and his achievement of moral autonomy and real freedom (see Chapter Four, Section XVIII).

Doyno comments further, "To a Northerner," the "Notice" with its military format might appear to mock military discipline, suggesting that taking the book seriously amounts to "disorderly conduct." But there was "a different kind of resentment" in the South toward such notices. Because both armies had used land mines during the war, and of course much more widely in the South, where most of the fighting took place, people there were "furious about the devastating effects of unexpected underground explosions." Clemens may have chosen "'Chief of Ordnance' ... because it implies ... general authority over explosive dangers."[15]

These aspects of the "Notice" point again to Clemens' careful composition and revision of this brief text. The fact that it bears up under such close scrutiny and yields up so many insights into its meaning and its relation to the book it begins is itself evidence that Clemens knew what he was doing almost every step of his way. And Doyno's comments on "disorderly conduct" and on the dangers of "underground explosions" are a telling metaphor for the subtextual religious satire of the narrative.

IV. Of the Art of Literary Burlesque

Henry Nash Smith has written about "the vernacular tradition" that Mark Twain fathered in American literature, and he points to both Sherwood Anderson and Ernest Hemingway as prominent followers of Twain's pioneering work. Although "different from one another," both Anderson and Hemingway "illustrate the consequences of the tendency toward primitivism" that Smith finds to be "implicit in *Huckleberry Finn*." He goes on to say that this "vernacular style greatly limited the power" of all of these writers to cope with abstract thought and contributed to an anti-intellectual trend in American letters. Turning their backs on "the Western European literary tradition" may have liberated them, in Smith's view, to explore and "conquer new territory," but only at the "wasteful" sacrifice of "the accumulated experience of the past": "Like the actual pioneer, he [Mark Twain] had to pay a high price for his conquest of new territory and his debt was entailed upon his heirs."[16]

At this point in this study, it is fair to say that while Mark Twain's heirs may indeed have incurred this debt by abandoning the school of literary burlesque, loss of the accumulated experience of the past and the abstractions to which it had given rise was one form of poverty Clemens himself never suffered. The work of Franklin Rogers shows time and time again that Clemens built his primitivist plots and vernacular characters using the recycled structures of classic European and religious literature rearranged in reaction to works the thematic bent of which he rejected—like *Paradise Lost* and the Bible—and in imitation of ones he admired—Dante' *Inferno*, for instance (see Chapter Four, Section IV)—frequently taking the techniques he learned from the Southwestern humorists—Hooper, for example (see Chapter Four, Section VIII)—and elevating them to higher artistic purposes (see Chapter Seven, Section XVI).

This transformation of literary burlesque from low comedy to high art is nowhere more evident than in *Huck Finn*, where he lampoons *Paradise Lost* and the Bible and pillories their God, while, without a hint of irony, building a large portion of his plot, characterization, and theme—especially in the middle section—out of structure borrowed from Dante's *Inferno* (see Chapter Four, Section IV). And his allusions to a wide range of other writers, including extensive burlesque of Shakespeare (see Introduction, Section III), the appreciation of which is indispensible to understanding the book, lends credibility to the notion that if one were to cut out all of the literary burlesque of *Huck Finn*, one would still have it almost entire, but in pieces. And Jim, one of Clemens' greatest vernacular characterizations, is no exception to this principle of his artistry.

V. About Jim

This study has so far looked precious little at how Jim figures in the religious satire of *Huckleberry Finn*. It has taken a long time to get to this question, and it is worth an answer. Critics have made the case that Jim is, if not the true hero, then at least the co-hero of the novel. In Chadwick-Joshua's character assessment:

> Consider the constellation of his virtues: his sense of honor, ethics, loyalty, indomitable faith in the nuclear family (a faith that extends into guardianship of Huck Finn), masterful ability to manipulate language, sturdy sense of duty, grasp of the deep meaning of friendship, clear perception of himself as a man, unintimidating wisdom, desire to be self-reliant, and conscious awareness of taking risks. These traits are the marks of a hero.[17]

John Bassett has observed that the adult characters of the novel are prototypes for who Huck and Tom might become, and that by the end of the novel neither boy has made a "promising transformation."[18] Interesting. What about Jim? Hasn't he become the male role model Huck has so sorely lacked? As Lionel Trilling, Kenneth Lynn, and, most recently, Jocelyn Chadwick-Joshua have suggested, Jim is the true father Huck has sought.[19] In his identification with Adam, Jim shares fully as the new man in the new American Eden, and his becoming an Adam figure underscores the dignity that fits him for this role. So Clemens makes clear that race is no barrier to Jim in the archetypal scheme of the novel.

In addition to his identification with Adam fulfilling the curse on the serpent in Chapter X (see Chapter Three, Section XII), Clemens projects other biblical identities onto Jim: his roles as both Shem and Ham, the sons of Noah, the latter of whom was cursed to servitude in the portion of the legend re-enacted in Chapter IX (see Chapter Two, Section VIII); the representative of "the children of Israel" captive in the American Egypt (see Chapter Five, Section IV); the bearer of "the mark of Cain," doomed to be "a fugitive and a vagabond" (see Chapter Three, Section XVII); and as a Christ figure, when he willingly sacrifices his hope of freedom—and probably his life—to save Tom (see Chapter Five, Section IX).

Without Jim, of course, there could be no *Adventures of Huckleberry Finn*; there could be only a naturalistic novel about a rich, white trash racist son of the town drunk worthy of Theodore Dreiser. No matter how good a heart Huck has, it is the soul-rending conflict over Jim's quest for freedom that gives impetus and interest to the plot. There is one adult character that the above comment about "promising transformations" omits from consideration, and that one is the father figure whom Huck finally emulates: Jim. As Chadwick-Joshua writes, Huck's "wisdom derives from his bond with Jim. ... Huck, now more a son of Jim than of Pap, is true to his and Jim's humanity outside the law."[20]

Furthermore, Jim sets a powerful moral example of a man doing all he can to advance himself and his family while harming no one if he can avoid it—except when he takes just vengeance on the duke and king in Chapter XXXIII—and he sets his personal interests aside—even at risk of his own life, if need be—in loyalty to his "fren's." The final example of this in the novel comes when he sacrifices his remaining hope of freedom to help Tom in Chapter XL. The seriousness of the consequences is underscored in the first-person chapter titles by Clemens' titling the next-to-last chapter: "Why They Didn't Hang Jim" (see Appendix A). And he would rather, perhaps, have used the word, "Lynch." At the end of the book, whatever promise Huck shows is largely due to Jim's influence.

Jim plays another role in the religious satire of the novel as the voice of common sense and parental love when Huck tries to educate him about the wisdom of Solomon in Chapter XIV. Here, as in the conversation between two Negro deckhands redacted in this study's Preface, the subject of African American illiteracy—"de law o' de Souf" (see Preface, Section II)—provides a cloak for opinions Jim expresses that challenge the conventional interpretation of this Bible story as the supreme demonstration of Solomon's wisdom (see Chapter Three, Section XIV). "Minstrel show stuff" for sure, but it's hard to argue with his logic, at which Huck fails utterly, especially in light of Jim's status as a devoted father whose entire family is always in danger of being split—indeed doomed to it—by their "righteous" owners, and of Huck's own status as a motherless waif. Nevertheless, Jim lets the evils of the day suffice, and never complains, although he rarely has occasion not to do so.

As a *man*, Jim stands head and shoulders above all the other characters in moral stature. Careful readers perceive this even through the racist filter of Huck's narration. Of course, that's why so many readers find his ill-deserved maltreatment by Tom extremely distasteful. If it were the duke or the king in that hut, they wouldn't have this problem. Jim is different, though; he deserves respect. Jim deserves freedom. And Huck's deserving freedom is contingent on his loyalty and service to Jim, because Jim is his only worthy male role model.

Now, how does all this figure in the development of Clemens' religious satire? Does it not strike a note of irony that the moral avatar of this narrative is an illiterate fugitive slave—the lowest of the low in this fictive world?— and not an idealized characterization, either, but a lifelike human being. Clemens makes Jim's character more than a little hard to get at, of course, because we see him only through the eyes of a thoroughly brain-washed, ignorant, and early-on, almost completely thoughtless *boy* (see Chapter One, Section I); furthermore, we get all of our insight into his real personality and character only when he is alone with Huck, when he drops the slave act he must play before all other whites, including "Mars Tom."

John Lindberg points out the distortion Huck's point of view causes and investigates its impact on the reader, who experiences the story only through Huck's eyes, ears, and reflections; this narrator's "limitations ... leave many blanks for the reader to fill in."[21] As a result of Huck's limited reliability as a clear window into his world, readers have been only too willing to let their estimate of Jim's character be overwhelmed by the distorting effect of Huck's perception, not to mention the reader's own cultural biases, be what they may (see Chapter Three, Sections XIII and XV).

Many apologists for *Huckleberry Finn* have made much of Huck's friendship with Jim and Huck's transcendent recognition of Jim's humanity in the course of the story. Nothing of the kind happens in the novel. Huck is a dyed-in-the-wool racist from Chapter I through "Chapter the Last." He never gets over it completely. Although he does make emotional and moral progress toward the recognition of Jim as a person, his belief is that Jim is not fully human, but that through some trick of the powers that be, Jim is "white inside" (Chapter XL)—what later came to be referred to contemptuously as an "Oreo Cookie." Yet while this is a story told from the point of view of a racist, it is not a racist book, but a book about racism, the supreme evil of this fictive world.

The low comedy of Huck's practical joke on Jim in Chapter XV turns in part on the idea that reality in non-symbolic. Abstractions rarely occur to Huck. When he observes that Jim has feelings, and when he sees that Jim "cares just as much about his people as white folks does for their'n," he concludes in an aside to the reader, as he writes his story while waiting for Tom's wound to heal, "It don't seem natural, but I reckon it's so" (Chapter XXIII). Even *then*, it does not occur to him to base on this observation the generalization that all people of color have the same feelings as white people have. Instead he simply reflects his training: "It don't seem natural." For Huck, Jim is just an exception to the rule of white supremacy that he has been trained to believe.

Huck's use, by the way, of "people" here to refer to slaves is the only instance of the use in their regard of this or any other generically human term that occurs in the book. In the manuscript, in Chapter the Last, which, being un-numbered, functions as an epilog in the structure of the novel, Huck's statement to Jim that "you're a free man now" is the first and only instance in the novel of *any* white person referring directly to Jim, or any other particular person of color, free or enslaved, as a *man*. The only other, if it bears counting, is the slave hunters' asking Huck "Is your man white or black?" (Chapter XVI). In Chapter XXVIII, Huck actually conceives as a lie his guarded reference to Jim as a "person" as he convinces Mary Jane Wilks to co-operate with his plan to expose the duke and king. But it is a falsehood that reveals a deeper truth: Huck has unconsciously begun to appreciate Jim as a person.

Ultimately, Huck comes to the conclusion that settles the matter to his satisfaction: Jim "was white inside" (Chapter XL). Clemens' scrupulous avoidance of using generically human words like "man" or "woman," "person" or "people," or even "friend," a neutral term with less implication of humanity, in reference to African Americans, has not been noticed in any of the wide range of commentary in this study's research base; yet it is remarkable, because it highlights the racist assumption that black people are sub-human, and it helps us to understand the 214 re-iterations of the n-word in the text, though not to applaud them.

Jim's famous rebuke of Huck and the white boy's humbling himself to the fugitive slave in Chapter XV stand as a turning point in their relationship, but they do not commit Huck to a fundamental shift in his view of Jim beyond the revelation that Jim has feelings. The importance of Huck's dawning perception of Jim's essential humanity in this passage has little-noted historical background that should be horrifying to both races: Victor Doyno points out that an important justification of the institution of slavery was the idea that Negroes did not possess souls,[22] and therefore could not feel as deeply as white people do. If to have a soul essentially means to be fully human, then it is fair to say that Huck's disregard for Jim's feelings arises from his racist assumption that a slave would not have such feelings, being incapable of emotional injury—no doubt a comforting thought to supporters of "the peculiar institution." Indeed, Huck persistently refers to Jim as "nigger" because he is incapable of thinking of Jim as his friend or as a man.

In all the passages where the word "friend" characterizes their relationship, it is Jim who uses it, as he does in his rebuke for the second time in the narrative; Huck never calls Jim his friend or a man—not once. The closest he comes to even thinking of Jim as his friend occurs in Chapter XXXI where he internally echoes Jim's use of it toward him. Otherwise, he refers affectionately to his companion as "old Jim" or "my old Jim," endearments one could apply as easily to a beast. Huck never uses the word "man" to refer to Jim, either. For these reasons, to deny Huck's racist beliefs is to distort his character and to underestimate his monumental moral achievement in choosing the dictates of his heart over those of his conscience. Chadwick-Joshua's more nuanced reading demands consideration in this context, however:

> I disagree with Twain opponents who assert that Huck's calling Jim "white" shows his racism. [...] Huck can never look at another individual of African American descent without being affected by his experience of Jim as well as the other African Americans he encounters in this novel. Is he a racist? No. Can we presume that a long course of development will have to take place before his voice no longer shows its southern origin? Sadly, yes. Twain is a realist.[23]

Nevertheless, Huck Finn's 215 iterations of the n-word encapsulate the racist doctrine that African Americans are not fully human. That is one reason why this word has come to be so offensive today. These facts account for the necessity in this realist satire of the author's use of this increasingly offensive term: it is necessary in the satirical scheme of the novel to point up the institutionalized inhumanity of which slavery is Mark Twain's main case in point; it is necessary to an understanding of Huck's character as a product of his "association and training"; and it is necessary for a measure of comprehension of Jim's situation as a slave and his yearning for freedom and dignity. Verisimilitude is the least of Clemens' motives for his free use of what has since become a six-letter four-letter word. Were he writing today, he probably would have been more sparing in his use of this word because its force has intensified dramatically over time, but he could not expunge it from the novel without undermining its thematic integrity. As Chadwick-Joshua comments, "To have avoided using 'nigger,' 'hell,' and 'poor white trash' would have been a denial, a lie, that would have undermined the novel's power to move readers to frustration at Jim's physical situation."[24]

Neither Mark Twain nor Samuel Clemens ever referred to the co-hero of *Huck Finn*, in print anyway, as "Nigger Jim." The earliest occurrence of this ugly and demeaning epithet (as far as I know) is in Alfred Bigelow Paine's 1912 biography,[25] and it appears to have caught on from there; perhaps Paine was only echoing what may then have been a common misnomer, but this name gained popular currency well into the 20th century, so that when Ernest

Hemingway made his notorious declaration that everything that happens "after Nigger Jim is stolen from the boys [sic] is just cheating," he encapsulated in three misreadings what it took an archive of critical commentary to express during the intervening decades and beyond.

So let's start at the beginning: in Chapter II, where Huck, with Tom, first encounters Jim in the novel. Keep in mind, however, that they are most likely already familiar with each other, since we know that Huck frequented the slave quarters, and was known there; also, he is fully informed of the change in Jim's status after the boys' "close encounter" with Jim in the second chapter, which suggests that he continues to socialize there after the incident he narrates. Jim is also Miss Watson's slave at Huck's home with the Widow Douglas. And we know from Chapter XXIII that Jim has "never been away from home before," so that it stands to reason that Huck has had other dealings with Jim in the past. Also, when Jim first meets Huck on Jackson's Island, the runaway slave mistakes Huck for a ghost, like Tom in Chapter XXXII, and Jim pleads with Huck's ghost, "You go en git in de river ag'in, whah you b'longs, en doan' do nuffn to Ole Jim, 'at 'uz alwuz yo' fren'" (Chapter VIII). This is the first instance of Jim calling Huck "fren," and it suggests that they have known each other a long time.

Huck/Mark Twain portrays Jim in Chapter II as a comically dumb "darkey" soliloquizing in dialect on the noises he hears in the night, then being fooled by the clever, manipulative Tom Sawyer. Of course it's possible that Jim notices the boys hiding and is just having a little innocent fun at their expense before pretending to fall asleep, but the indisputable outcome is, he suffers no harm and comes out of the transaction a nickel richer (imagine a nickel with some *buying power*). Then he gets more than his nickel's worth in enhanced status among his peers by turning it into an object of superstition, which one may find laughable, given the secret of its source and the absurdity of Jim's story, but which resonates with later events of the plot, like the Pokeville camp meeting and the murder of Boggs in Chapters XX and XXI, where it is the Bible that figures as just such a talisman as Jim's nickel, "the brazen serpent in the wilderness" (see Chapter Four, Section VIII). So who tricks whom in this confidence game of musical chairs?

We next meet Jim in Chapter IV to discover that he also serves his community of fellow slaves as a fortune-teller. Jim tells Huck what turns out to be a most prescient fortune, one that foreshadows pap's primary archetypal role in Clemens' thematic development of the story, but on the surface it is ambiguous and inconclusive, as most of us expect divinations to be, which is also a sign of Jim's skill at this sideline. In addition, he tricks Huck out of a perfectly negotiable counterfeit quarter in the transaction. Five more nickels for Jim.

This is not exploitation, for Huck is now a rich white kid, and the quarter *is* counterfeit; Jim is only human (and a slave), and that's a point worth making at this stage of plot development, for the word that most effectively expresses his standing in this "fictive" society is "nigger": in other words, for all intents and purposes, "not fully human."

It is not until Chapter VIII that Huck and Jim meet again on Jackson's Island (chapter title: "I Spare Miss Watson's Jim" [see Appendix A]). Slaves were not permitted to have birthdays or surnames. Slaves and dogs were referred to by a single given name and further identified by their owners' names (according to Mark Twain's footnote in Chapter X of *Tom Sawyer*). The distortion of his character that results from our seeing him through the distorting lens of Huck's point of view has impeded discussion of Jim's role. Clemens knew a lot about Huck's personality when he began the book, but he discovered Jim's in the process of composition.[26]

Were Jim the narrator, how different a text this book would be! Everything shifts with point of view, *every* thing. Although he accompanies Huck for the entire thousand-mile journey, Jim figures in only about half of the twenty chapters that recount the raft voyage (XII, "Better Let Blame Well Alone"—XXXI, "You Can't Pray a Lie" [see Appendix A]). Clemens manipulates viewpoint to explore the effects of racism on both Huck and the reader—for the text also defines the implied *reader* of this novel (see Chapter Four, Section VIII).

Clemens' assessment of his audience was exactly right; few whites took offense at its most offensive parts (not for the right reasons, anyway), and most people laughed at some of its most troubling passages (particularly Chapters XXXIV–XL, which recount the evasion). Later, Huck's movement from his early attitudes toward the slave is reflected in his title for Chapter XV, "Fooling Poor Old Jim" (see Appendix A). In the dialects Clemens replicates, both adjectives here function as endearments; Jim similarly addresses Huck as "de good ole Huck." In Chapter VIII Huck gives his promise not to turn Jim in as a runaway. Huck gives it impulsively, thoughtlessly, boyishly: "I warn't ever going back there, anyway. ... I was glad to have Jim for company. I warn't lonesome, now."

Of course, the emphasized facts of their meeting include: (a) Jim belongs to a member of Huck's recent household and therefore is well known to him; (b) Huck sees Jim primarily as "nigger," not worthy of respect—especially as a fugitive slave; and (c) Huck sees himself, pretty much by default, as the one in control of the situation. Huck is exactly wrong, as it turns out, in both of the latter assumptions. It takes the rest of the novel for us to comprehend just how worthy of respect Jim is, but as for control of the situation, he seizes it immediately by refusing to tell Huck how he has come to be on the island until Huck promises not to tell his secret. After all, Jim is the adult in the situation, and he gets that (although the reader may not); and he also gets that Huck must be petted and coaxed to follow Jim's lead and to keep his promise, because Jim knows how boys—especially white ones—are. It's his business to know all there is for slaves to know about whites and how to deal with them.

Realistically, Jim has to be considering his options here, and they are few and none is without risk that increases his peril. Cannily, he opts for the best of them: forming an alliance with Huck. Huck's socialization makes him assume he is in charge, but Jim's superior maturity and experience are what save the boy from the flood that arrives in Chapter IX as Jim quickly takes Huck under his wing, ingratiating himself to the white boy and enlisting his help in escaping from slavery (see Chapter Three, Section XVIII). This and other aspects of Jim's character make him a developing character even as he remains a static one in Huck's eyes, for Huck can't see Jim's humanity through the color of his skin.

This obstacle to *seeing* Jim as a dynamic character is a major contributing factor misleading readers into concluding that this is a racist book rather than a book about racism. Readers' failure to transcend the point of view of Huck Finn, who *is* a dyed-in-the-wool racist, has created confusion and discord over the racial attitudes embedded in the text. This feature of Huck's narrative is another facet of the social satire that elevates it out of the prewar South into the post–Reconstruction era when segregation and oppression became the sealed fate of America's former slaves and their heirs for generations to come, and up to the present day.

As mentioned earlier, Jim plays the role of Adam in Clemens' dramatization of the fulfillment of God's judgment on Adam and the serpent in Chapter X, and this is the third identification of Jim with a personal biblical prototype. This identification clarifies Clemens' conception of his African American hero. Jim, as Adam, pays the price for Huck's transgression even though he had nothing to do with handling the snakeskin. Jim's snakebite simply confirms his dread of anyone handling snakeskin around him. The snake biting him on the heel and Huck's chopping off the snake's head mirror God's curse on the serpent: "Thou shalt bruise his heel and he will bruise thy head"[27] (see Chapter Three, Sections IX–XII).

Clemens' portrayal of his African American Adam through the lens of his white racist narrator presents readers with a challenge to provide "mature moral judgment"[28] at which most have failed. Far from coming across as a comic "'darkey'"[29] or a childish, tragic victim of slavery and authorial abuse,

Jim emerges from this analysis as a complex, self-defined character who seizes control of his destiny when he can and deals with adversity with courage, intelligence, patience, maturity, and wisdom when he can't.

Ron Powers has suggested that Clemens' butler at Hartford, George Griffin, provided him with one model for Jim's character, and that the penultimate line of the author's "Notice," "Per G. G., Chief of Ordnance," cryptically acknowledges this debt; Griffin's personality displays many of the characteristics imputed to Jim here. Once, when Clemens' wife Olivia fired Griffin only to encounter him the next day still in the Clemenses' service, he responded to her asking him, "George, didn't I discharge you yesterday?" with "Yes, Mis' Clemens, but I knew you couldn't get along without me, so I thought I'd better stay awhile."[30] Griffin's skill at managing household relations, as Ron Powers relates, endeared him to the writer:

> Griffin was an intelligent and forceful man, politically opinionated but graced with a sense of diplomacy: he softened Clemens's tirades as he relayed the gist of his employer's opinions to others, and served as the peacemaker among the hired help. Clemens deeply admired the man, and probably transported some of his strength of character to the persona of Jim.[31]

Besides their move to a high cave as spring thunderstorms and the "June rise" approach, Jim learns something in the next chapter that cements his influence over all that follows: knowledge he withholds from Huck. With this information, Huck could move back to town and go on reveling in Tom Sawyer's paradise. He could grow up rich and respected—even own slaves of his own. Jim knows how to give Huck this kind of freedom, and his withholding it smells a little suspicious, *don't it?* "Moral avatar" indeed! Jim puts Huck's rosy future—and Huck's very life—in jeopardy for what? Just to save his own black skin!

That's one way to look at Jim's keeping from Huck the immensely important fact that the corpse they discover in "The House of Death" (see Appendix A) is none other than pap Finn himself, the very abusive, murderous father whose outrageous actions precipitated Huck's flight. And unlike Jim, Huck hasn't burned any bridges. He would get a hero's welcome in St. Petersburg, especially if he were to return Miss Watson's escaped "property" on his return. Jim's keeping from Huck the fact that pap is dead is a prominent feature of his strategy that Huck never puts together even at the end of the story. That Jim essentially cons Huck into joining his flight is an under-appreciated aspect of his characterization. As John Seelye comments: "Given the universal mendacity that percolates through the book, can Jim remain a stainless figure of integrity?" Most readers, according to Seelye, "assume that Jim has kept Pap's death a secret in order to protect Huck's feelings, but Jim never explains his silence, and he certainly knows that Huck has few tender feelings toward his father." In fact, in view of Huck's having fled from pap's custody, and the likelihood of his going back as soon as the danger is past, "it is difficult any longer to regard the bond between Huck and Jim as perfect." Suggesting that the twin fugitives' society is "a pastoral parody," Seelye asks if it is not just "the pairing of a self-interested league no different in kind only degree from the compact between the two scoundrels who take refuge on the raft also."[32]

Had Huck known of his father's death, would he have accompanied Jim on his flight to freedom? Pap is the only character from his past Huck refers to repeatedly during the journey south. He mentions Tom Sawyer twice, once before boarding the *Walter Scott*—in a revision penned after the rest of the story was finished—and once in Chapter XXVIII, when he is conning the Wilks sisters into co-operating with his plan to escape from the duke and king while restoring their stolen fortune and family, and he mentions the widow a time or two as well, but generally, he lives in the present. Pap, however, abides with him, and it is primarily pap he is fleeing. Knowing of pap's demise would be another game changer, and Jim tells him only when his own freedom is secure. It's not hard to see why.

As Samuel Clemens would probably point out again, here, Jim *is* only human—and therefore self-interested—and "nothing worse could be said of him." By concealing pap's identity, he secures a white ally in his flight to freedom—what an asset!—although, as an ally, Huck is at best a frenemy; their tenuous alliance from Chapter VIII–XVI ("The Rattlesnake Skin Does Its Work"; see Appendix A) rests on nothing more than Huck's need of company, his boyish, impulsive promise, and Jim's deception. Were he a different sort, he could kill Huck and dispose of the body without any chance of getting caught, and the problem of what to do about Huck would be solved. Surely we could come up with lots of reasons why Jim should take Huck under his wing. But Jim is a pragmatist, and one of his watchwords is "Better let blame well alone" (Huck's title of Chapter XII; see Appendix A); and Huck's self-interest is countervailed by his own, from his point of view.

Even though his involving Huck in an "abolitionist plot" endangers Huck, if he returns Huck to the town his own prospects—and his family's—would be doomed because Huck's conscience would assert itself, he would forget his promise, and he would most likely turn the fugitive slave in. Instead, Huck embraces Jim as a fellow-fugitive, and when he finds out slave hunters are coming to the island, he warns Jim, "They're after us!" (Huck's title of Chapter XI; see Appendix A), and the raft voyage begins.

The enjoyment of their loot from the *Walter Scott* gives rise to their discussion of the wisdom of Solomon discussed earlier. Jim's personal take on

Solomon has rarely been taken seriously by readers, not because it is without merit, but apparently because it would be unjustifiably offensive to equate King Solomon with Brigham Young, the contemporary paragon of polygamy, or to suggest that any of the "Sacred Brotherhood" should have less than reverence for the life of a child. That is Jim's point. Mark Twain's putting it in the mouth of a comic "darkey" does not invalidate but only veils it. Jim shows familiarity with the story, and so one can't just dismiss his unorthodox take on it as "ignorance," especially since Jim gives voice to Clemens' own religious skepticism (see Chapter Three, Section XIV).

In Chapter XV ("Fooling Poor Old Jim"; see Appendix A), Clemens uses the fog that he remembered so well from his boyhood and piloting days to advance the plot past its destination thus far: the junction of the Mississippi and Ohio rivers at Cairo, Illinois. But the subject of the chapter is the relationship between its twin protagonists, and its most memorable outcome is the closing exchange between the white boy and the black man who has taken responsibility for Huck's welfare—as he is morally obliged to do, having drawn Huck, by subterfuge, into his flight to freedom.

Jim masters the situation. So primal is he that readers rarely question his motives, and so "simple" that one rarely analyzes his methods. But Jim's put-down of Huck is, from a psychological perspective, so spot-on that it brings about a transformation in Huck's perception of him: "Trash is what people is dat puts dirt on de head o dey frien's en' makes 'em ashamed." Huck is already well aware of his white trash status in society (hence his notorious admiration of Tom Sawyer), but Jim puts a different spin on the term, one that goes to Huck's heart. While Huck accompanies Jim toward legal freedom, Jim leads Huck toward moral freedom (see Chapter Three, Section XV).

But Huck is still conflicted because he is still a racist scion of a racist society; for him, "nigger" is not a pejorative term, only a denotative one. And counting the black man as a friend does not occur to him. It takes until Chapter XXXI for their relationship to deepen into mutual, de facto friendship. In Chapter XVI, when Huck encounters the slave hunters, he has just set out from the raft to betray Jim. As they approach him and ask him "Is your man black, or white?" he finds himself not "*man* enough" (italics added) to tell the truth.

What breaks his resolve to tell at this opportunity to "do the right thing"? Jim's monolog of excitement at his nearness to freedom has a chilling effect on Huck at first:

> It most froze me to hear such talk. He wouldn't ever dared to talk such talk in his life before. Just see what a difference it made in him the minute he judged he was about free. It was according to the old saying, "give a nigger an inch and he'll take an ell."

Thinks I, this is what comes of me not thinking. Here was this nigger which I had as good as helped run away, coming right out flat-footed and saying he would steal his children—children that belonged to a man I didn't even know; a man that hadn't ever done me no harm.

Huck's failure to share Jim's enthusiasm could sound a cautionary note to Jim, who is usually perceived as naively unobservant in his failure to notice Huck's mood. As his "fren'" shoves off to go turn him in, Jim turns his effusion of gratitude on Huck:

"Pooty soon I'll be a-shout'n for joy, en I'll say, it's all on accounts of Huck; I's a free man, en I couldn't ever ben free ef it hadn' ben for Huck; Huck done it. Jim won't ever forget you, Huck; you's de bes' fren' Jim's ever had; an' you's de *only* fren' ol' Jim's got now."

As Huck paddles off on his mission of betrayal, Jim, risking being overheard and detected by the approaching skiff, calls out to Huck from the raft: "Dah you goes, de ole true Huck; de on'y white genlean dat ever kep' his promise to old Jim."

Why does Jim make these exclamations of praise and gratitude to Huck at the risk of his freedom? Could it be that his speech, at least in part, is motivated by the contrary of what he says? Only the reader's perception of Jim, coming as it does through the distorting lens of Huck's point of view, prevents one from reading this exchange as an attempt at persuasion on Jim's part, motivated by his realization that Huck is *not* aligned with his agenda. What, short of threats and force, which Jim never uses (except for the pathetic incident he confesses to Huck involving his deaf daughter in Chapter XXIII), might secure Huck's support but praise, gratitude, and kindness?

His parting call rings not only with affection and gratitude but also with his awareness that Huck is likely to be at a turning point in their alliance. His final words emphasize his regarding Huck as white (and therefore not to be trusted), and remind Huck of his specific promise not to turn Jim in—even calling on Huck to act as a gentleman, not the "trash" he called Huck the previous morning. Clemens' cutting out the long "Raftmen's Passage" where Huck boards a passing cargo-raft may have had the effect of juxtaposing these two passages very closely.

This is not to question Jim's sincerity, but only his innocence of understanding and manipulative intent. His continued praise of Huck's cleverness when Huck returns to the raft, "Dat was de smartest dodge!" expresses his appreciation of Huck's skill at deception and manipulation. One can scarcely appreciate talents in others that are lacking in one's own character.

In this episode, Huck assumes that Jim is unaware of just how close a call he has had, and most readers, it seems, have unthinkingly bought into that assumption. Yet everything Jim has said and done in this sequence supports the reading that he is acutely aware of Huck's internal conflict and doing all he can to woo Huck over to his cause. Again here, as in Chapter XV where Jim obliquely but effectively suggests that he is Huck's friend—not just a temporary traveling companion—when he tells Huck, "Trash is what people is dat puts dirt on de head er dey fren's," Jim closes his persuasive effort by implying that he and Huck are subject to the laws and duties of friendship, the first of which is loyalty. Knowing that Huck is blind to his humanity, Jim nevertheless appeals to Huck's humanity—his heart—and it works.

During the parts of the middle section where Jim plays an active role in the plot, his primary function on the level of character development is to move Huck from his initial "pap Finn stance" on race to the point where he is willing to give up his hope of salvation for his black comrade. In this sense, Jim's bringing the gospel of racial equality to Huck makes him nothing less than a Christ figure in his own right—even without his being lynched in the penultimate chapter.

In these interactions—and especially in the Phelps farm section—Jim adopts the almost passive-aggressive stance slaves had to adopt toward whites as one of the few tools of persuasion at their disposal. Jim's combination of strategic accuracy with abundant sincerity in his dealings with Huck reveals a much greater awareness and understanding of the dynamics of their relationship than he generally gets credit for having.

Notice also that it is only Jim who refers to Huck as "fren." Huck never refers to Jim as his friend. Even at the climax, where his decision to go to hell hinges on his memory of Jim calling him "the only friend he's got now" (Chapter XXXI. "You Can't Pray a Lie"; see Appendix A), he is only recalling Jim's words, but his recollection reveals that he has internalized the attitude of loyalty that friendship evokes. It would take only one more permutation of Huck's thought for him to arrive at the simple declaration, "I'm the only friend he's got." But Huck never gets there, although that is the perception on which he acts.

His encounter with the slave hunters marks the beginning of Huck's whole*hearted* support for Jim's flight. Wholehearted, but not whole-*headed*; Huck remains deeply conflicted until Chapter XXXI. This wavering loyalty is what Jim has to deal with for the duration of the raft voyage, and he is at constant pains to keep Huck on his side, petting, praising, comforting, protecting, and confiding in Huck in ways that gradually bring Huck to *feel* Jim's humanity, even though he can't intellectualize it.

Surely, Jim is genuinely compassionate toward Huck. But the fact is that Jim is in a perilous dilemma: a fugitive slave with a runaway white boy on his hands. So it happens that the raft journey begins with Jim pulling most of the strings that move the plot forward, and continues with Jim constantly courting Huck's cooperation and loyalty. In this sense, Huck *is* the rattlesnake in Jim's bed, and the black man must always ingratiate himself to the white boy. When Huck's final crisis of loyalty comes in Chapter XXXI, he reminisces:

> Somehow I couldn't seem to strike no places to harden me against him, but only the other kind. I'd see him standing my watch on top of his'n, stead of calling me, so I could go on sleeping; and see him how glad he was when I come back out of the fog; and when I come to him again in the swamp, up there where the feud was; and suchlike times; and would always call me honey, and pet me, and do everything he could think of for me, and how good he always was; and at last I struck the time I saved him by telling the men we had small-pox aboard, and he was so grateful, and said I was the best friend old Jim ever had in the world, and the *only* one he's got now.

Clemens never reveals whether Jim's behavior toward Huck is strategic or solely the expression of his almost incredible good nature, but it is most likely a canny combination of both. This reading is consistent with Clemens' oft-expressed opinion that everyone of every race, creed, or color is primarily motivated by self-interest, "a desire for the greater content of spirit."[33]

While the feud chapters shelve the problem of Huck's conflicted relations with Jim, they broaden the scope of Clemens' indictment of a society based on biblically derived mores and drive Huck back into the novel's primary subject: the growth of a relationship of mutual trust and caring between a fugitive slave and a white racist runaway. In Chapter XVIII Jim rescues Huck. The Shepherdsons would likely have swept him up in their vendetta against the Grangerfords or left him to sink or swim on his own. Either way, Jim would bear the responsibility for Huck's fate because he conned Huck into undertaking the journey. Jim isn't just fleeing slavery; he's protecting Huck; that's what makes him the father figure to Huck that Kenneth Lynn and Jocelyn Chadwick-Joshua have persuasively portrayed his being. This role as Huck's protector and guide is also consistent with his role as Dante's guide, the poet Virgil, in the novel's re-enactment of the tour of Hell that the two poets undertake in *The Inferno* (see Chapter Four, Section IV).

When Huck discovers Jim in the swamp, his exclamation, "By jings, it was my old Jim!" reveals a change in his attitude toward Jim: the fugitive slave is no longer "Miss Watson's Jim, "or "old Jim"; now he has become "my" old Jim, creating the impression that while Jim may be his unacknowledged friend, Huck has shifted to regarding him as his own property (Chapter XVIII). When the duke tells Huck in Chapter XXXI, "we'd come to consider him *our* nigger; yes we did consider him so—goodness knows we had trouble enough for him," the duke feigns what appears to be the same mental process that leads Huck to exclaim "my" when Jim unexpectedly appears before him in the swamp.

Jim's ambivalent relations with Huck may help to explain his puzzling behavior in continuing the raft journey once they are back together. He needs to travel against the current now, and the raft only moves south; so why, readers have wondered, would a realist writer resume a pointless voyage? It's a valid question. One explanation is that Jim still has no canoe, their projected means of returning north, so he is doing his best to optimize his chances of acquiring one and also sees the events of the day as a means of securing Huck's renewed complicity in his flight.

A black man alone in a canoe headed north would be more noticeable and suspicious than a white boy and his slave. Charming the still-conflicted Huck back to the raft may be Jim's best hope of enlisting him for the long paddle upstream back to Illinois. Jim has invested in restoring the raft and provisioning it, but he can't possibly see it as anything but an escape from the swamp he is trapped in, and the local market for canoes among the Grangerford slaves appears to be non-existent, because Jim would have bought one if he could have, and he didn't. As it turns out, both Jim and Huck need to make a quick exit and leave no tracks. So, plausibly at least, the voyage resumes.

Early one morning two or three days later, in the next chapter (XIX, "The Duke and the Dauphin Come Aboard"; see Appendix A), Huck finds a canoe and immediately goes exploring. Although he doesn't say so, he must know that his find is a game changer. The lack of a canoe has been all, practically speaking, that has prolonged the raft trip—that is, from Jim's point of view. Huck has been perfectly content to be back with Jim on their floating Eden. And he would apparently be content to continue drifting away from their supposed destination with *his* Jim and postpone paddling north indefinitely. And he finds the means to do it right after as he finds the canoe.

With the duke and the king in control, Clemens again shelves Jim's quest and pursues his own ends: his exploration of the social and religious dynamics of this fictive world and by implication born of Clemens' continuing allusions to religious writings, our own. The advent of these twin reprobates sets in motion a crime spree that gives rise to scathing social and religious satire.

The twin fugitives, however, continue their alliance in the background and continue to deepen their relationship. At the close of Chapter XXIII, Huck observes Jim's sadness; he knows that Jim is "low and homesick" without asking. Huck's comment that Jim "was often moaning and mourning that way, nights, when he judged I was asleep, and saying "Po' little 'Lizabeth! po' little Johnny! it's mighty hard; I spec' I ain't ever gwyne to see you no mo', no mo'!" moves Huck to reflect, in another of his rare asides, "He was a mighty good nigger, Jim was."

Jim also provides a moral touchstone for Huck's disgust at the king's and duke's antics pretending to be a parson and his deaf-mute brother in the next chapters, as Lynn has observed in pointing out that the ironic contrast between "Jim's sorrow and compassion for his deaf-and-dumb daughter" at the conclusion of Chapter XXIII and "the spectacle of the two frauds talking on their hands" at the end of Chapter XXIV shows why Huck feels "ashamed of the human race."[34]

Jim goes into hiding/captivity for the duration of the Wilks episode, and he surfaces only briefly at the close of Chapters XXIX and XXX before the king sells him to Silas Phelps "for forty dirty dollars," a price that resonates with the "thirty pieces of silver" that Judas received for his betrayal of Jesus as well as the "forty years wandering" and the "forty acres and a mule" with which Andrew Levy associates it.[35] Clemens confirms his identification with Christ in Chapter XLII when Jim, risking his life, sacrifices his freedom to help save Tom. In the context of Chapter XXXI this incident confirms Huck's arrival in the depth of Hell where abide Brutus and Cassius and Judas and Lucifer in Dante's scheme (see Chapter Four, Section IV).

From Jackson's Island on to the end of the book, Jim's identification with Adam helps to characterize him: He is the African American Adam, equipped with all the mental, physical, and moral attributes (and lacking only the legal ones) needed to make his way in the world. And being illiterate and black, he is not burdened by the cultural baggage under which Huck, his white mythical counterpart, labors. During the evasion he continues, by his simple presence in the story, to provide a moral standard by which to judge Tom's evasion, much as he does during the Wilks scam earlier through the contrasts Clemens draws between the authentic Jim and the royal imposters, to whom Tom is morally related quite closely (see Chapter Five, Section VI). Thus, archetypally, Jim and Huck are yet another pair of twins in the oft-twained cosmos of Samuel Clemens: biracial twins who prefigure the color-blind future that is America's ultimate hope for an end to the racism that this novel dramatizes and anatomizes so profoundly.

Victor Doyno observes of the conclusion that philosophers have projected a moral society as one in which its designers could "with equanimity" occupy any position. For a moment, such a society exists in the novel after Tom has been wounded, when Huck and Jim perceive, "almost as if they were one person," how Tom's wound changes their situation. Their accord is immediate, and "Huck trusts both Jim and the situation enough to ask Jim to express it":

> So he says:
>
> "Well, den, dis is de way it look to *me*, Huck. Ef it wuz *him* dat, 'uz bein' sot free, en one er de boys wuz to git shot, would he say, 'Go on en save me, nemmine 'bout a doctor for to save dis one?' Is dat like Mars Tom Sawyer? Would he say dat? You *bet* he wouldn't! *Well* den—is *Jim* gwyne to say it? No, sah—I doan' budge a step out'n dis place, 'dout a *doctor*; not ef it's forty year!" [Chapter XL].

The pair of fugitives thus creates "a small society, an inclusive triad," of compassion and trust in which each one might occupy the place of any other with confidence of being treated morally. And "Jim's gentle, considerate phrasing even attributes some dignity to Tom."[36] And, of course, forty years is the period of time the biblical Hebrews spent wandering with Moses in the desert after their escape from Egypt.

Ultimately, these twin Adams become twin Christ figures, although at the end of the story neither of them has a well-defined future. Huck, like his prototype Moses, ends his story in prospect of the Promised Land. Jim, like Adam, is left to find his own way in a conflicted historical era that contemporary readers knew would culminate in the Civil War and Reconstruction (which ended about 1877), and modern readers know, a century-and-a-third later, has culminated in the ongoing aftermath of American race-based slavery.

VI. Chapter Summary: *Huckleberry Finn* as Organic Art

The purpose of this study thus far has been to show that it is possible to read *Adventures of Huckleberry Finn* as an organic and intelligible work of art. The structural paradigm developed along the way does help to reconcile diverse readings of the novel—even the notorious disagreement between the "approving formalists and disapproving moralists" reviewed in the introduction to this study (see Sections I and V). At the core of this argument are two complementary conceptions of Samuel Clemens' literary technique. The first, his management of point of view, enables one to appreciate fully the multivalent irony of the complexes of attitudes and ideology personified by Huck Finn, Mark Twain, and Samuel Clemens. The fact that the book's themes frequently appear to be at war with one another, an aspect of Clemens' art that has long bewildered readers, testifies amply to the appropriateness of a reading strategy attuned to both irony and the hypothesis of threefold rather than twofold point of view set forth in this study's first chapter.

The second part of this reading strategy has been to focus on the literary archetypes of the narrative. Through a recognition of the conflict between Mark Twain and Samuel Clemens in the text, a conflict made manifest in the moral logic of the archetypal material Clemens works into the novel beneath the level of the implied narrator's viewpoint, readers can reconcile diverse critical perspectives by seeing how each contributes on one of the three levels of viewpoint to a full technical and thematic appreciation of the work.

In support of this approach, this study has introduced a fair amount of new textual evidence to show that the primary concern of the implied author in constructing this narrative is to define the nature and function of conscience and to propose humane amorality as the only viable alternative to the corrupting influence of the archetypes of "revealed" morality on human behavior and social institutions. It has also attempted to show that many of the contradictory readings of the novel extant in criticism can be reconciled with one another by seeing how each contributes to a clearer understanding of the text on one or another of the levels of viewpoint that Clemens elaborates (see, for example, Chapter One, Sections I and VII, Chapter Two, Section I, and Chapter Five, Section XII).

The principal theme that emerges from a full consideration of this material is that of religious satire through which Clemens attributes the evils of the society he lampoons (both South and North) to the depravity of its mythology. It is not merely coincidence that the most horrifying scenes to which we are exposed are acts in good faith with the perverted teachings of some form of Bible-based religion, for the author is at pains to show that the satanic hog-god personified by pap Finn is one with the Author of Conscience and Hell in the Bible, *The Inferno* and *Paradise Lost*.

The "Notice," the "Explanatory," and Chapters I–VI lay the groundwork for this satire by establishing threefold point of view: introducing Huck as a picaro who has no idea that his narrative has any meaning at all; Mark Twain as an unreliable narrator who attempts to dignify Huck's adventures by identifying him with Moses, the biblical liberator; and "THE AUTHOR" as a remote literary artist whose point of view is cloaked in a double layer of irony. Huck's comments on religion and prayer, irreverent though they are, simply establish the limitations of his perspective and expose him to the implied narrator's and the reader's mild ridicule. Jim's introduction portrays him as the comic "darkey" he must play in order to survive in this fictive world and does play throughout most of the twenty-two chapters of the framing sections of the book that bracket the raft voyage. Only while he is alone with Huck, in the relatively egalitarian relationship they share on the raft, do we come to know Jim as a man and to appreciate him as the moral standard by which we can measure the hypocrisy, bigotry, and cupidity of the rest of this story's cast of characters, including, to some extent, Huck Finn himself, especially in Clemens' exploration of the evils of fundamentalism and racism.

The events of Chapters I to VI rapidly weave a mythological backdrop in which the widow, Huck, and pap variously figure as stand-ins for Pharaoh's daughter and the child Moses (the widow and Huck in Chapter I); Milton's Satan in prospect of Eden (pap in Chapter IV); God confronting Adam in Eden (pap and Huck in Chapter V); Milton's Satan "confounded' and prostrate in Hell (pap in Chapter V), and then damned and confronting his son the Death Angel (pap and Huck in Chapter VI); and finally as Milton's Satan and Christ (pap and Huck, respectively, in Chapter VI). In addition to these archetypal developments, Clemens works in allusions to the legend of Abraham and Isaac in an incident that burlesques this Bible story by comparing Abraham's willingness to kill his child to pap's crazed attempt to murder Huck. And by extension this biblical prefiguring of the Crucifixion makes God the Father's sacrifice of *His* only begotten son a moral absurdity equivalent to pap's attempt on Huck's life. The motif of the Mississippi as Milton's Chaos introduced in Chapters V to VII supports pap's identification with Satan in this mythological backdrop and provides a realm into which Huck (as Moses, Adam, Isaac, Christ, and the Death Angel) can flee. In his ritual escape from pap Huck symbolically kills himself—ritually immersing all these identities in the river (Chapter VII). This act leads to his escape into Chaos (Chapter VII) and Huck's awakening as Adam in a natural Eden on Jackson's Island (Chapter VIII).

Without a god to judge him, Huck lives in amoral bliss—aside from his loneliness, which reminds the reader of Adam's before the creation of Eve—until Jim joins him in this Eden (Chapter VIII). Then Clemens introduces the archetypal motif of the legend of Noah, in which Huck and Jim become the heirs of Noah: Shem, Ham, and Japheth, brothers in building a new world on the ruins of the old after the Deluge (Chapter IX). Their fall, when it comes, parallels the Eden myth by casting Huck as Eve and Jim as Adam, and by introducing the serpent motif (the purpose of which many have questioned) as an integral part of the novel's design (Chapter X).

This motif serves as a recurring reminder of the potential for brotherly caring between the two disrupted by Huck's racist mind-set; it emblemizes the Depravity Doctrine, which declares that all people are depraved heirs to guilt for the sin of Adam and Eve; and it reminds readers that the serpent is the symbol of Satan—evil's presence in this American Eden/Promised Land (Chapters IX-X). Until Huck gets his own values straight, he is fully committed neither to the values of the island nor to those of the shore (Chapters XI to XXX).

The archetype of the serpent is appropriate here, for it serves symbolically to reiterate the connection between Eden and Jackson's Island and to emphasize Huck's ongoing temptation. Clemens transforms Huck's world to Judeo-Christian myth throughout his tour of Dante's Hell that spans the middle section. At stake in his journey is the power of the snakeskin to hold sway over the outcome of Huck's quest and Jim's. It is his ultimate commitment to Jim in Chapter XXXI that lays this serpent to rest.

Clemens makes no effort to convince the reader that Huck's belief in the curse of the snakeskin is groundless. Rather, he uses it to symbolize the complex of absurd superstitions that he portrays biblical religion embodying. His argument indicts the Bible itself as an idol regarded with superstitious awe, "the brazen serpent in the wilderness." And the fact that the snakeskin that brings Huck and Jim all their bad luck is a dead husk shed by a living serpent expresses to the reader that for the implied author, this insane religion, aside from the commandment "to love ... thy neighbor as thyself," is an empty, dead thing as well, like pap's corpse, with no vital force beyond what credence lends it.

Huck reports that the "ornery preaching" he hears at the Shepherdson-Grangerford church, "was all about brotherly love"—exactly what is lacking in this congregation—and that while on their way home, "they all talked it over ..., and had such a powerful lot to say about faith and good works and free grace and preforeordestination, and I don't know what all, that it did seem to me to be one of the roughest Sundays I had run across yet" (Chapter XVIII). All their theological mumbo-jumbo, Clemens implies, is just another empty snakeskin that the Grangerfords handle at their own peril and which hastens their self-predestined and foreordained destruction.

Clemens' concern with showing whence Huck's conscience derives never abates for long. Against the background of the Dante-esque tour of Hell that spans Chapters V–XXXI, the author stacks biblical vignettes one on another. These include his ironic allusion to the legend of Abraham and Isaac in Chapter VI, along with his implicit simultaneous allusion to the crucifixion; his satire on Noah and slavery in Chapter IX; the parody of Exodus 11: 2 inherent in Huck's discussion of "borrowing" in Chapter XII; the serpent motif of Chapters X, XVI, and XX, in the last of which the Bible itself comes to be portrayed as "the brazen serpent"; the multivalent burlesque of the legend of Solomon in Chapter XIV; the multiple redaction of the legends of Cain and Abel, of David and Jonathan, of Saul and the prophet Samuel, and of the victory of Moses over Pharaoh's army, elements of all of which critics have seen in Chapters XVII and XVIII where Huck recounts the Grangerford-Shepherdson feud.

Then comes the advent of the duke and the king, divine right monarchs of pap Finn's "kind," as Huck swiftly pegs them (Chapter XIX), a pair of "devils" (Chapter XXVI) who know how to exploit the ignorance, superstition, credulity, cruelty, and idolatry prevalent in this Egypt of the West. It is important to remember at this juncture that Huck's "pap"—always spelled with a lower case initial "p" as the word "god" is always spelled with an upper case initial "G" when used as the Deity's name—another inversion that underscores his role in the developing religious satire—is symbolically the hog-god and the devil, divine right ruler of heaven and hell. The duke and even more so the king are, symbolically, pap's regents and priests, and the havoc they wreak in the little towns along the river advances Clemens' religious satire at every turn.

There quickly follow Huck's accounts of the camp meeting—where the Bible is equated with an idol—"the brazen serpent"—an image that reiterates Clemens' combination of his serpent-motif with the god symbolized by the Bible just as he had earlier combined God and Satan in the person of pap—and then the Boggs-Sherburn insanity in Bricksville, where Bible-olatry gives rise to nightmare scenes (Chapter XX–XXI).

In the over-next chapter the royal frauds perform "The Royal Nonesuch," in which the king's costume of paint and, most likely, a lighted candle stuck into his anus, parallels the appearance of the monster demon Fraud in Dante's *Inferno*, a burlesque incident that confirms, as do other elements of Clemens' artistry, that much of Huck's interaction with shore society in the middle section of the story takes place in Hell, a motif that Clemens introduces with the advent of pap in St. Petersburg in Chapter V.

In their most depraved escapade (from the standpoint of scale, anyway) the rogues attempt to bilk the Wilks sisters of their inheritance and sell their slaves, separating the family and selling the mother down the river (to hell) in preparation for the girls' projected move to England with them (Chapter XXIV to XXIX). Here, Clemens reveals the materialistic values of a nominally Christian, hyper-religious society in its idolatry of gold, and Huck leaves another six-thousand dollar fortune in his wake.

As is the case throughout the twenty chapters (Chapters XII to XXXI) of the novel comprising the raft-journey, the implied author and implied narrator appear to be less at odds than in the framing chapters set in and around St. Petersburg (Chapter I–XI) and at or near the Phelps farm (Chapter XXXII to XLII). Two sections of eleven numbered chapters each—more than half the novel, even without counting the epilog "Chapter the Last"—thus bracket the raft-journey and explore the relationship of Clemens' American Adams with the religiously deformed society that Huck ultimately rejects.

This structural symmetry helps to emphasize both that there is undergirding structure in this overtly formless narrative and that there is thematic importance to these framing sections. As the implied author's parallels to Dante's *Inferno* make clear, however, what the implied narrator, Mark Twain, apparently intends as parochial, social satire dedicated to kicking the dead horses of antebellum Southern aristocracy, religion, and slavery twenty years after the Civil War, Clemens transforms to a universal parable of the nature and degrees of evil. Thus the pattern of religious satire that critics of *Mark Twain's* novel have found to be a secondary concern, subordinated to social satire critical of the antebellum South, emerges as a primary theme critical of the Judeo-Christian worldview when the reader views the work as the expression of its implied author, Samuel Clemens.

When Huck achieves his supreme moment of compassion in Chapter XXXI, the climax of the narrative provides the climax of Clemens' religious satire as well: Huck's conversion drama culminates in his rebirth as the Adamic Satan/Christ figure into which Clemens later transformed Mark Twain. The episode is almost a line-by-line burlesque of Milton, a classic example of the high art of literary burlesque as practiced by Samuel Clemens (see Appendix F). The function of this burlesque is to reverse the moral polarity of Judeo-Christian mythology, obliging the approving reader to approve Satan's rebellion against the injustice of the God Clemens perceived in the works he burlesques, principally *Paradise Lost, Pilgrim's Progress,* and the Bible. At the same time, this episode is the culminating event of Huck's tour of Dante's Hell, at the nadir of which the poet found Lucifer ("the light bearer") whom Huck emulates again in the penultimate sentence of the book with his decision to "light out."

After his climactic commitment to Jim, which redeems Huck from the sin of hypocrisy that he confronts in his climactic debate with his conscience, where he tries to "pray a lie," Huck ritually ends the raft journey by reenacting his original flight in reverse: leaving the raft on an island, sinking his canoe, abandoning Chaos, and returning to "sivilization" (Chapter XXXI). Next he is reborn as Tom Sawyer, the risen Christ, and Moses meeting his agent-brother Aaron to set out on their mission of emancipation (Chapter XXXII to XXXIII). His identity as Tom is temporary, unlike his identification with Christ, which he has earned by suffering a spiritual death for Jim. Huck is no longer a child, mythologically speaking, and the farcical events of the concluding section are not, from the implied author's point of view, child's play.

With Tom Sawyer—the *deus ex machina*—"God out of the machinery" indeed—a new avatar of the biblical deity enters the picture. Tom's evasion provides three perspectives on the closing section. It burlesques Huck's own flight to freedom by removing his profound moral conflict and indecisiveness (much like Hamlet's) and substituting Tom's manufactured obstacles to Jim's escape. Echoing the theme of "Let my people go" that gave biblical impetus to the anti-slavery movement, Mark Twain, the implied narrator, presents a Moses figure opposing the superior force of the oppressor in a mythical Emancipation Proclamation. From Clemens' perspective, it is a parody of Exodus 1–14 that points up absurdities in the Bible story while linking the biblical past to the historical present to show how religion can become a template for history. Clemens attributes the blame for the evils of the present to the mythology on which he patterns them.

From Huck's perspective, his provisional rebirth as Tom puts him in a role where he can be at ease—with both his still-present but now impotent conscience and his continuing commitment to Jim—in the Neverland of the childhood he never had. The celebrated lonesomeness of Huckleberry Finn is really the longing of an abandoned child for his absent parents. So when Huck finds himself a comfortable berth in the bosom of the Phelpses, where peace and plenty reign, who should begrudge him the enjoyment of it while it lasts? Even if he is still in hell, he has ascended from worse. Not that he has much choice—Huck is personally and mythically bound to Tom even though they are moral worlds apart. To survive in Tom's world, he and Jim must obey Tom's rules, the rules of "the authorities."

The ultimate authority for the evasion, in the plan of the implied author, is the bloodstained history of Moses. What Clemens has in mind is a conclusion that attacks the Bible as the source of the greatest moral failures on both sides of the Mason-Dixon Line, subordinating social satire to the religious satire that underlies all three sections of the novel to provide its primary unifying theme. Clemens makes clear to the reader attentive to his allusions what motivates Tom. The extensive parallels between the evasion and Exodus make it abundantly clear that the "comic" re-enactment of the story of Exodus, apparently motivated by the implied narrator's desire to give moral tone to grotesque absurdities, ultimately imputes the blame for Tom Sawyer's glaring travesty to the highest level of authority—on which Tom unwittingly relies: the Almighty.

That Clemens is deft where Mark Twain fumbles speaks eloquently of the attitude of The Man in the Iron (comic) Mask, alluded to as "The Iron Mask" by Tom Sawyer (Chapter XXXV), toward his alter ego, Mark Twain. The evasion is a burlesque of Exodus, as it is a burlesque of the flight to freedom itself and of the post–Reconstruction era. Mark Twain plays down the seriousness of Jim's dilemma and returns Huck to a boyish role in ways that grate on serious readers. For Mark Twain all this is merely an unsuccessful attempt to vindicate Tom Sawyer, in whose likeness Clemens caricatures the biblical God. In Clemens' scheme, the concluding section's shortcomings help reveal with emphasis *all* of these aspects of Huck's narrative, and they comprise an indispensable element in this complicated novel's unorthodox design.

VII. Conclusion: Back to the Beginning

At its outset, I suggested that this study is concerned with answering the question posed by the "Notice": How can a reader be prosecuted, banished, or shot by a fiction? As Huck says of Tom Sawyer, explaining to the doctor how Tom came to be wounded, "He had a dream, and it shot him" (Chapter XLI). Huck's lame explanation strikes a humorous note at first, but like so many other experiences he relates, it is not without seriousness, for Tom's wound is the direct result of his dreaming grandiose dreams and scheming the absurd schemes of the evasion.

Tom the conformist will never learn, but Huck has learned that there is no place where he can imagine himself being able to stand "sivilization" any more. He has narrowly escaped prosecution for helping Jim (as Jim has narrowly escaped lynching); he announces his intention to banish himself; and as for being shot, that's only for those who follow Clemens' plot, to which Huck has been oblivious all along.

Metaphorically, to experience the meaning of *Adventures of Huckleberry Finn* from the point of view of the implied author is to empathize with his own experience of ostracism. One is reminded of banished Adam, prosecuted for disobedience to a god Clemens found unworthy of reverence, banished into the wilderness and condemned to mortality. Stanley Brodwin has explored the central position of the Adamic myth in the late writings of Mark Twain. This study focuses on an earlier phase of Clemens' sense of identification with banished Adam.

Through his portrayal of Huck as the prototype of the Adamic Satan/ Christ in whose image Clemens ultimately conceived the character Mark Twain, the author shows his growing consciousness of the chasm widening between himself and his audience. Clemens felt himself banished from the American Eden of his youth. He felt a need to avoid the censure of his public, who held the primary object of his derision, the God of the Bible, sacred. He sensed that life is without inherent meaning and finite—that immortality is a carrot on a stick and hell a goad, both employed to keep the masses on the straight and narrow track of blind conformity. He regarded this path as the truest form of damnation.

To follow Huck and Jim in the company of Clemens is to empathize with his desire to teach people the nature of their evil; to plumb the depths of his irony is to see through the comic mask he chose to wear; to read *Adventures of Huckleberry Finn* as religious satire is to experience both Samuel Clemens' despair and his compassion for "the damned human race." Although the reader risks alienation from the value system of our society, the themes of compassion as the only real redeeming force and of ironic laughter as the only real saving grace transform Samuel Clemens' blasphemy to a blessing on humanity.

CHAPTER SEVEN

Dancing with the Devil

I. The Bigger Picture

Textual evidence and critical interpretations of *Adventures of Huckleberry Finn* presented in the previous chapters establish that the novel could well be what this study says it is: a thoroughgoing satire of Puritan cosmology and religious literalism and fundamentalism. The purpose of the present chapter is more pedestrian. In it are woven together the commentaries of able scholars who have prepared the way for this new assessment of the meaning Clemens had in mind as he composed his acknowledged masterpiece; observations on ways in which some of his other major works of fiction form a context in which *Huck Finn* occupies the place of honor; quotations from Clemens' own statements of his religious views, including excerpts from an untitled essay, not published until 1995 although written in the 1870s, contrasting the God of the Bible to the God revealed by science; and considerations of ways in which students, fans, and decriers of his work should beware of misconstruing Clemens' treatment of mythology in his most "irreverent" works.

If this work should find lay readers who have been generally unaware of the controversies that have swirled around Huck's narrative and other works by Mark Twain over the years, who have heard only the media reports of social turmoil over whether or not it is suitable for inclusion in high school or even college reading lists; to what degree if any it is a racist book; and whether it should be taught in schools at all; this background may shed some much-needed light—not only on Mark Twain and Samuel Clemens, but also on our American obsessions with race, class, social mobility, wealth and its acquisition, the role of religion in shaping our politics and institutions, and matters of tolerance, freedom, and civil and human rights that are prominent in the news today, more than 130 years after Clemens first published *Adventures of Huckleberry Finn* and over a century after his death.

Even for a new generation of literary scholars, who seem to have moved on to other aspects of Clemens' writing career since there has appeared to be "nothing more to write" regarding the controversy that raged over the motive, moral, and plot of *Adventures of Huckleberry Finn* throughout most of the 20th century, this exploration of the arc of Clemens' development as a writer may shed some light on how *Adventures of Huckleberry Finn* fits into the broader context of his writings.

II. Of Critics and Their Work

In the publish-or-perish eco-system of professorships and tenure, the tendency of scholars to focus narrowly on the latest controversy can result in an eclipse of the really valuable work of previous generations:

> We must assume that Mark Twain provided his best book the best ending of which he was capable. Moreover, I propose that the ending of *Huckleberry Finn* recommends itself to us precisely because it *is* bad. First of all, it provides us with one of those critical enigmas upon which academic careers are built: whatever the effect of that ending on Jim's flight from bondage, it has helped countless junior faculty out of slavery into the freedom of tenure.[1]

While the shelf life of articles in scholarly journals is eternal, the attention they command can often be transient. What is needed to assure their more enduring interest, as has been attempted in the previous chapters, is their integration into a comprehensive analysis that presents a unified field theory of Clemens, his masterpiece, and its place in the Mark Twain *oeuvre*—a much bigger subject than can be covered in this chapter, but a few suggestions are in order.

III. *Huck Finn* in the Light of Other Works by Mark Twain

Thus far it has been shown that readers can reconcile many contradictory interpretations of *Adventures of Huckleberry Finn* by attending to the conflicts in point of view among the tale's three tellers: Huck Finn, a clueless persona who is ostensibly relating his adventures and reports only what happened to him and how he felt about it at the time with very little retrospective comment, apart from an occasional aside to the reader; Mark Twain, a character who poses as "THE AUTHOR" and offers a subtext of social satire, pathos, humor, and biblical allusion to Huck's tale that establish his role as a "Mississippi Moses"—a level on which even casual readers can enjoy the book (or not); and Samuel Clemens, who plays off the viewpoints of his twin narrators to have his own say while preserving "plausible deniability" in case anybody should become aware of his puppeteering and "blasphemous" religious satire. *Adventures of Huckleberry Finn* has been both condemned and lauded as a "subversive book,"[2] and for better and worse, it is that—just how subversive—and subversive how—has been the point of this study so far. Now it will set out to explore how this new comprehension of Mark Twain's most popular work contributes to our larger understanding of the author and his major fiction, and how his development in the school of literary burlesque affected his composition of *Huck Finn*.

For one thing, some critics view the contrasts between his genuinely innocent children's books (*The Adventures of Tom Sawyer*, and *The Prince and the Pauper*) and his later, more overtly adult writings (*The Innocents Abroad, Huck Finn, A Connecticut Yankee in King Arthur's Court, Pudd'nhead Wilson, The American Claimant,* and *Personal Recollections of Joan of Arc,* and works of lesser length including *Captain Stormfield's Visit to Heaven* and the unfinished *Letters from the Earth* and *The Mysterious Stranger Manuscripts*) as comprising an arc of increasing anger, cynicism, and despair as the author, allegedly, increasingly identified with "banished Adam" and sank into disillusionment, loneliness, grief, and cynicism. There may be some truth in this broad reading of his major fiction in chronological order, but there is another way of framing his evolution from genial poet to acid-tongued prophet. Mark Twain has been faulted for never writing "another Huckleberry Finn,"[3] but it is nothing short of miraculous that he dared write it at all at the peak of his success and his talent.

IV. Of *The Innocents Abroad*

Although Mark Twain's first book is not usually regarded as fiction, scholars have shown that the anti-religious anger (his disgust with the hypocrisy, stupidity, disrespect for archaeological treasures, cruelty to animals, and vandalism of his fellow-"pilgrims," to name a few of the faults he finds with them in *The Innocents Abroad* [1869]) is evident in his work from early-on.

This best-selling travel book recounting his voyage to Europe and the Holy Land with a band of American Christian "pilgrims" in 1868 bristles with satire, but this is not satire aimed at the sacred beliefs of his readers, but at how those tenets are violated in daily life, both by the pilgrims he accompanies and the European churches that he accuses of hoarding wealth while their congregants eke out a meager and miserable existence in poverty, filth, and disease.

The Innocents Abroad is a sarcastic title, and its subtitle, *The New Pilgrim's Progress,* which aligns the work in the burlesque tradition, underlines Mark Twain's intent and illustrates his life-long struggle with fundamentalist religion. This travel book was one of the most popular of his works during his lifetime. While its tone is often sarcastic on religious matters, it is sarcasm born of righteous indignation, not sacrilegious intent. His American audience ate it up, especially the parts about the shortcomings of *European* mores.

V. *The Adventures of Tom Sawyer* as Literary Burlesque

Clemens wrote his first solo-novel, *The Adventures of Tom Sawyer,* as a book suitable for children that would appeal to his grown-up audience as well, and what religious content he included in it—like Tom's cornering the market in Bible-verse tickets in order to win an award, and everyone in the Sunday school showing off to impress the newly arrived Judge Thatcher, who is showing off, too—is uncontroversial material making gentle fun of human, rather than divine, foibles.

Tom Sawyer is primarily of interest in this discussion because in order to make this story as entertaining to parents as to the children they were meant to read it aloud to, and to give it structure, Clemens resorted to the techniques of literary burlesque that he had been practicing for years, at least since 1862 when he joined the staff of the Virginia City, Nevada, *Territorial Enterprise.*[4] At first he used the technique, which has its roots in parody, mainly for humorous effects in sketches, articles, and the journalistic letters he was commissioned to write for the San Francisco *Alta California* from the then Sandwich Islands, now Hawaii, and on his voyage to Europe and the Holy Land aboard the *Quaker City*, which he later expanded into *The Innocents Abroad.*

Early on in his development as a writer of fiction, Clemens came to rely on literary burlesque as an important part of his creative process, as Franklin Rogers has revealed. In his discussion of *Tom Sawyer,* Rogers, whose insights have been strangely neglected by Mark Twain scholars, explores the burlesque aspects of Mark Twain's first solo novel and finds that a great deal of its humor derives from its burlesque treatment of "the courtship theme" that develops from the puppy love affair between Tom and Becky Thatcher. Rogers observes that "major episodes in the novel are subordinate and contributory to the courtship theme"; he goes on to point out that "Even the knowledge of real murder, the threat of real vengeance, and the hope of real treasure cannot outweigh the courtship in Tom's mind."[5]

Many details of Mark Twain's treatment of this juvenile courtship call to Rogers' mind conventions of the 19th century literary courtship, as seen in *David Copperfield*.[6] The humor of this burlesque would of course be lost on juvenile readers. "Ordinarily," continues Rogers,

> writers using this burlesque device rely upon the incongruity between the actions of the principals and their age and physical size, [...] but Twain has introduced an innovation; retaining the general course of the adult romance, he translates its love-letters, mementos, events, and characters into the notes, gifts, accidents, and people supposedly typical of his own boyhood in Hannibal. [...] The humor of the burlesque depends to a great measure upon the refusal of other characters in the fictive world to recognize and sympathize with the lover's trials.[7]

Thus, when Tom waxes "melancholy" because Becky is ill, his aunt tries to cure him with "patent medicines" (Chapter XII), bringing about the cartoonishly funny incident of "The Cat and the Pain Killer" (*Tom Sawyer*, too, has chapter titles added after the first edition). For young readers, however, the failure of adults in the story to take their growing pains seriously establishes rapport with the author, who does sympathize with the secret sorrows of childhood. The power of burlesque to fill two or more frames of reference simultaneously lent it powerful appeal when Clemens turned his attention to the covert religious satire of *Huck Finn*.

VI. How *The Prince and the Pauper* Burlesques Victor Hugo

The Prince and the Pauper, his second book targeting a younger audience, is a realistic fairy tale written primarily for his own daughters, to whom it is dedicated, and for his wife Livy, who loved it and occasionally referred to it as the type of writing she would like to see more of from him.[8] Nevertheless, Twain's reliance on burlesque techniques in this novel also testifies to their importance in his creative process as he borrows Victor Hugo's plot from *L'Homme Qui Rit* (*The Man Who Laughs* [1869]): "The two parts" of the life of Gwynplaine, the protagonist of Hugo's story, "first as poverty-stricken actor, then as nobleman, suggest the adventures of both Prince Edward and Tom Canty."[9] As Rogers points out, "The source of this structure ... is the [Clemens' own] *Burlesque L'Homme Qui Rit*."[10] Rogers writes that "his purpose in the revision and expansion of his burlesque was ... almost the same as Hugo's," so that "it becomes exceedingly difficult to distinguish between the burlesque and its target":

> Generally, in attitude, tone, and treatment, the two books are almost identical. In *The Prince and the Pauper*, Twain illustrates both in Edward VI and in Tom Canty how poverty fosters mercy and justice. After becoming a victim of his own laws and after seeing the sufferings of others under them, the young king concludes that "the world is made wrong, kings should go to school to their own laws at times, and so learn mercy." Similarly, Hugo's Gwynplaine, after his experiences as an itinerant actor, hopes to reform the laws by informing the lords of what he has suffered.

Many of Edward's experiences, especially, mirror those of Hugo's protagonist. Rogers goes on to point out Clemens' most important departure from Hugo's basic structure: "In *The Prince and the Pauper* Gwynplaine's story is divided between two characters, Prince Edward and Tom Canty. Hugo, himself, however, makes just such a division, splitting Gwynplaine into two personalities, thus furnishing the hint for the actual division."

Noting Clemens' debt, Rogers comments, "It is only fitting that while Prince Edward is with the gang of beggars his chief tormentor is a rogue named Hugo." There are other significant differences that render Mark Twain's novel an original work of art with acknowledged debts to Hugo's work in structure, characterization, plot, and theme, and Clemens was well aware of his borrowing, since his own burlesque of Hugo provided the immediate basis for his romance.[11]

VII. *Huck Finn* Again

Both *Tom Sawyer* and *The Prince and the Pauper* are humorous adventure stories with their roots in the tradition of 19th century literary burlesque. What satire they contain spices and leavens the reading experience, but they are not essentially satires. But the satirist was only sleeping, not comatose, and when Clemens began *Huckleberry Finn* in 1876, it became clear to him that he had found a way to fully express his private anger at the "pernicious influence" he felt the Bible had had on his own mental and emotional development as well as on the mores of his time.[12] It may be that his pigeonholing the manuscript was not, as he later claimed, an act of creative exhaustion, but a case of cold feet as he thought what hell might be unleashed if he were to dare to publish it and critics were to notice its genuine irreverence. It might well have been professional suicide.

Such speculation aside, he did publish the book in 1884 after his wife Livy and William Dean Howells had convinced him that they didn't see anything fundamentally wrong with it, and he probably figured that if they didn't, nobody else would; and even if somebody did, he had left no smoking gun at the scene of the crime, and a little controversy wouldn't hurt sales any. As it turned out, there was more than a little controversy (see Introduction, Section I), although he had concealed his meaning so well that everyone missed the point of his satire for one hundred and thirty years, and controversy did help sales at that. Apparently, he had figured out that America was not that much different from "Arkansaw" in the duke's estimation of rural Southern society in Chapter XXII of *Huck Finn*.

VIII. Reception for *A Connecticut Yankee*

A Connecticut Yankee in King Arthur's Court came next, in 1889, and enjoyed a mixed reception; that is to say, it was well received in the United States and roundly condemned in England due to its ridicule of the Arthurian legends, the Established Church, feudalism, and monarchy with "its several natural props."[13] *Yankee* may never have been well understood on either side of the Atlantic, and a case could be made that this "immediate juxtaposition" of two historical eras separated by 1,300 years, that "emphasizes the salients of both,"[14] as Clemens himself characterized it—for all that Hank Morgan, its protagonist, is contemptuous of the local yokels of sixth century Britain—is neither so flattering to the 19th Century nor so contemptuous of Arthur's age as it has been seen to be in the general run of criticism.

Yankee can be viewed in the grand scheme of his writing as a book-length exploration of "The Dandy Frightening the Squatter," an early sketch in which the armed dandy tries to bully a yokel and winds up with the unarmed squatter punching him in the nose and knocking him into the river. In *Yankee*, however, it is Merlin who delivers the final blow to the protagonist Hank Morgan by casting a spell that sends him back to his own era, contrary to the Yankee's, the implied narrator's, and the reader's disbelief in his magic power. Of course, there is extensive burlesque of Malory's *Morte d'Arthur* that provides the undergirding structure of Clemens' novel.

In both eras, Clemens praises the essential human virtues—kindness, compassion, dignity, and the willingness to sacrifice self-interest for the common good—and he condemns selfishness, brutality, superstition, and vanity in all the guises they wear. The motif of the "moral pilgrimage," which figures large in both *The Prince and the Pauper* as Prince Edward travels with Miles Hendon and learns compassion for his subjects, and in *Huck Finn* as Huck travels with Jim and learns to value Jim's freedom above his own salvation, manifests again in Yankee as King Arthur accompanies Hank Morgan on an incognito tour of his realm. In their travels, both learn important moral and political lessons, or, especially in Morgan's case, fail to learn such lessons.

The wisdom of Samuel Clemens' keeping his criticism of puritanical religion sub-textual in *Adventures of Huckleberry Finn* is amply illustrated by the reception of *Yankee*'s satire on feudalism, as reported by Janet Smith:

> In England, *A Connecticut Yankee in King Arthur's Court* was regarded as the devil's own work. Until 1889, Mark Twain had been adored there, as at home, by the public, although English critics were slower than ours to approve. But in 1889, when *A Connecticut Yankee* appeared, the English sales of Clemens' books shot down by two-thirds and stayed there for six years. This fact is far more remarkable than the furious reviews the book provoked; Mark Twain received such reviews in every country, and for long after his death. But nowhere else did an outraged nation, in effect, boycott his work.
>
> He had been warned. Not even his English publishers dreamed how violent the reaction would be, but they had been perfectly sure that the book would never go down in England.[15]

As Dennis Welland writes, Clemens had not been warned. Yet his response to his English publisher's request for proofs for the preparation of the English edition shows that such a warning was unnecessary:

> Since its publication by Paine in 1917 it has given rise to more misconceptions about their relationship and about the book itself than any other single factor, and the problem is complicated still further by discrepancies between the text of the letter as Paine prints it [cited by J. Smith] and the text received by Chatto [...] which still survives in the Chatto & Windus files.[16]

In what amounts to an unprovoked outburst, Clemens replied to Chatto's courteous request with the following:

> I wanted to say a Yankee mechanic's say against monarchy and its several natural props, and yet make a book which you would be willing to print exactly as it comes to you, without altering a word.
> [...]
> I have taken laborious pains to so trim this book of offence that you'll not lack the nerve to print it just as it stands. I'm going to get the proofs to you just as early as I can. I want you to read it carefully. If you can publish it without altering a single word or omitting one, go ahead. Otherwise, please hand it to J. R. Osgood in time for him to have it published at my expense.[17]

Clearly, the author was not open to advice on the matter of special editing for his English edition, warning or no. Evidently, his letter was pre-emptive, and that is understandable when one considers the rate at which the mails moved in those days and the fact that simultaneous publication in England and America was necessary to protect copyright; and Clemens was pushing for December publication to avail himself of Christmas sales. Continues J. Smith:

But his later regrets about the *Yankee* were not financial. What he bitterly regretted were the things left out. "They burn in me ... but now they can't ever be said."

What he said was enough for the English. But in the United States, the reaction was different. Since feudalism ["monarchy and its several natural props"] did not exist in this country, the American view was that it did not, really, exist anywhere. Therefore the *Yankee* was regarded here mainly as riotous entertainment. "Incidentally," said the *Atlantic Monthly*, "the feudal system gets some hard knocks, but as the feudal system is dead there is no great harm done, and the moral purpose shines."

[...]

Although the English never forgot, they forgave. When Clemens made his last visit to England, three years before his death, to receive a degree from Oxford University, he also received, it was said, "the greatest ovation ever given by the English people to a foreign visitor *not a crowned head*" [italics added].[18]

IX. Of Mark Twain's Waxing Pessimism

Much has been made of the implicit pessimism of Hank's "Tale of the Lost Land," but if one takes in the fullness of its implications as historical—rather than just hysterical—fiction, it is possible to view Hank Morgan as a seed planter who leaves behind in the sixth century a wife and a child who may perpetuate his vision of social, political, and technological progress. Perhaps the most pessimistic feature of *Yankee* is the failure observable in both eras to manifest significant *moral* progress, except, occasionally, in King Arthur himself. Mark Twain interweaves dream vision with realist fiction that affirms his protagonist's positive impact on history even though his project of reforming Arthur's England fails. Suggestive that something like this idea may have been on the author's mind is the fact that the wife Sandy and child Hello Central wind up stranded in France, where 1,200 years later the spirit of democracy bore fruit in the French Revolution, which Clemens regarded as a salutary bloodbath. The author's debts to *Paradise Lost* and perhaps to Dante in this crazy quilt/tapestry make it a generic mix of realist fiction and dream vision, an experiment in literary form as daring in its own way as *Huckleberry Finn*.

Nevertheless, its hostile portrayal of the influence of the Church—a shared characteristic of both eras—on social and moral progress, and its catastrophic ending—although some such catastrophe is necessary in a time-travel story to cover the traveler's historical tracks—are pessimistic features of the story that some critics read as a barometer to measure Mark Twain's emotional and spiritual weather. Most of them have found it to register "Cloudy to Manic-Depressive."

Indeed the English didn't forget the Yankee. In J.R.R. Tolkien's *The*

Return of the King, the final volume of his famed *Lord of the Rings Trilogy*, at the conclusion of the book, in the chapter entitled "The Scouring of the Shire," the hobbit heroes Merry and Pippin return with Frodo to the Shire, their homeland, to find that the rogue wizard Saruman has taken over and wreaked havoc on its lands and people. His title, "The Boss," belongs to Hank Morgan, the scientific sorcerer, in *Yankee*. There are further parallels in Tolkien's chapter, the felling of an ancient, symbolic tree, as in *Joan of Arc*, and the introduction of 19th century industries with their fouled air, soil, and water to Middle Earth, as in *Yankee*. Saruman's ignominious death at the hand of his cowardly servant Worm testifies to Tolkien's distaste for the likes of Hank Morgan, but his "thumbing his nose" at Mark Twain testifies to Clemens' influence.[19]

Another excerpt from J. Smith's commentary that is highly significant follows: "All his life, Mark Twain complained that whenever he wanted to be especially devastating, his irony became so subtle that people missed the point."[20]

This was certainly the case with his early "Petrified Man" hoax-article in the *Territorial Enterprise*, a story that went viral in newspapers about a discovery that, in his description of it, was clearly a joke, a petrified man "thumbing his nose" at the reader. But his readers, one and all, missed the point, as has also been the case with Tolkien's nose thumbing and with *Huck Finn*, for if the reading put forward in this study is correct, readers have been missing the point of its satire for well over a century. Perhaps this is part of the reason *Yankee*'s burlesque of Thomas Malory's *Le Morte D'Arthur*, which is closely related to *Huck Finn*'s biblical burlesque and its send-up of romantic fiction as exemplified by Sir Walter Scott, stand out so boldly.

X. Making Up with *The American Claimant*

The American Claimant (1893) is a romantic comedy that Mark Twain builds around the aristocratic pretensions of poverty-stricken American heirs to English nobility, like his distant cousin from Kentucky who fooled his life away in pursuit of his claim that the present holders of his rightful earldom were usurpers (see Chapter Four, Section I); the character of Col. Sellers, a main character in the story, is a caricature of Clemens' uncle. This tale is a light-hearted novella that like *Tom Sawyer* focuses what satire it contains on human rather than divine foibles and American rather than English traits. It ends, of course, with a marriage that joins the house of the English earl with the family of the American claimant to his titles and lands in a story that deals lightly with its satiric themes and contains plenty of outright farce. The story is thoroughly innocuous, and features Col. Mulberry Sellers, one of Twain's most celebrated characters of his day, to capitalize on that popularity with a farcical treatment of Gilded Age get-rich-quick schemes.

Understanding the damage that he had done to his reputation and sales in England with *Yankee,* the author appears to have written *The American Claimant* as an apology to the English with the message that he held no grudge against them and that he, at least, was willing to live and let live. The six-year "boycott" of his books there did end within two years of *Claimant's* publication, so perhaps it contributed to Mark Twain's peace-making effort.

The novella opens with a dialog between the earl and his son in which they debate the justice of their occupation of Rossmore. Its portrayal of the pragmatic Earl of Rossmore and his idealistic son, who decides to abdicate his title in fairness to the claimant, Col. Sellers, is sympathetic. The son sets out on a pilgrimage to America; there he learns that rank in a capitalist republic is a function of wealth and connections. The English nobility, in the view of the philosophical chair-maker who befriends the destitute young nobleman at the working class boarding house where he settles, are not to blame for the system that perpetuates their privileges. The blame for that Mark Twain puts on the English people, whose continued willingness to support their social and political system constitutes the sole reason for its existence. Thus the heir to Rossmore is not to be held accountable for it, the English people have the right to sustain it if they wish, and Mark Twain makes young Rossmore's idealistic radicalism appear as nonsensical as Americans' pretensions to aristocratic status, exemplified within Col. Sellers' own family.

The story is set in Washington, D.C., after the opening chapter, and satirizes the American system as it recounts the obstacles to the rise of the individual on merit imposed by a corrupt and bureaucratic system of government and labor unions; the generally primitive conditions under which the masses share equality; the hypocrisy of dyed-in-the-wool democrats who would leap at the chance to inherit an earldom; and the aristocratic pretensions that Americans love to affect. At the same time the author shows a high regard for the principles of egalitarianism and democracy, so that he avoids giving offense to his American readership.

XI. The Racial Theme of *Pudd'nhead Wilson*

Having satirized religion, publicly anyway, enough for a while, in *Pudd'nhead Wilson (1893)* Mark Twain focuses his ironic artistry on race: This antebellum story is about the tragic consequences that follow two boys—basically twins with different mothers (one white and one African American, but of indistinguishable complexion)—who are switched in their cradles by the "black" mother, a slave who wants her newborn son to grow up free. The outcome is devastating to all concerned, for though the "black" son, white by appearance, is raised in privilege and freedom, his training makes him arrogant, abusive, and indolent. The "white" son, "black" by training and association, grows up in ignorance, poverty, and servitude. When their having been switched is discovered by David (Pudd'nhead) Wilson by means of fingerprints, and their roles in society are reversed, neither can adapt to his new station, and Roxana, the slave who tried to make her pauper a prince, suffers rejection by the son to whom she tried—and failed—to give freedom and a good life.

A point worth emphasizing about this story is that Mark Twain blames socialization—not race, except in the sense that it provided a pretext for the institution of slavery and for racism itself—for the tragic outcome of the story. In fact, none of the characters is black except in an ethnic sense. He portrays the differences in the twins' characters as being wholly attributable to "training and association," a recurrent theme in *Huck Finn* as it is elsewhere in his writings. As Ron Powers has written, "Thus ... Mark Twain ... speaks through a slave woman to rebuke an America in the lingering throes of its racial dilemma. Roxana, his first fully believable female character, was his last character of enduring significance."

Those still tempted to regard *Huck Finn* as a racist book that indulges "Twain's bias" against African Americans in Huck's language and perception of Jim should consider

> Roxana's rebuke of her actual son, when she finally gathers her outrage and compels the tyrannizing Tom, under threat of damaging disclosure, to kneel before her. "You can't mean it," Tom protests, to which [Roxana,] "the heir of two centuries of unatoned insult and outrage," thunders,
> "I'll let you know mighty quick whether I means it or not! You call me names, en as good as spit on me when I comes here po' en ornery en 'umble, to praise you for bein' growed up so fine en handsome, en tell you how I used to miss you en tend you en watch you when you 'uz sick en had n't no mother but me in de whole worl' ... en you call me names—*names*, dad blame you! Yassir, I gives you jes one chance mo', and dat's *now*, en it las' on'y half a second—you hear?"[21]

XII. Of Clemens' Reverence for Joan of Arc

Next on the list of Clemens' major fictions is *Personal Recollections of Joan of Arc* (1896), another work that may be underappreciated, and one that

Clemens himself thought highly of. It is widely viewed as Clemens' only attempt to write a conventional historical novel, and contemporary reviewers, who at last felt themselves well equipped with critical tools to appraise his success with the genre, found it wanting, as have critics ever since. Many readers find its idealization of Joan dated and unrealistic, her manner more characteristic of the 19th Century than the 15th, and most critics have found it most remarkable as an index of Clemens' declining talent as a novelist, but close attention to the text may someday yield gold where so far mostly lead has been found; William Dean Howells' appreciation of it in *My Mark Twain* (1912) still provides some of the most judicious commentary.[22]

Nevertheless, as in *Yankee*'s satirical take on the Established Church, the focus of the final third of *Joan*'s story is on the process by which she was tried by the Inquisition, sentenced by the Church to death for obeying the voice of the Devil in order to save the Throne of France and its king, and burned at the stake for her "crime" of consorting with demons. Its first book is at least as charming as *The Prince and the Pauper*; in it the narrator does transport the reader into the late medieval worldview of fifteenth century French peasants; its third takes the reader into the depths of human depravity, and it is all the more horrifying because the depravity Joan confronts is the depravity of the Church, "God's representative on Earth." Suffice it to say that its indictment of the ecclesiastical court is damnatory, and Clemens' condemnation is based on the historical record of Joan's trial, which he imports into the novel.

XIII. Of Captain Stormfield's Visit to Heaven

Last in this overview of Clemens' major fictions comes the one that might have headed the list, had he been able to get it into satisfactory form in 1868, when he began it as a burlesque of *The Gates Ajar*, a conventional vision of the afterlife popular in Clemens' day. As it happened, this story proved to be the longest in gestation of all his works: just about forty years[23] (forty years wandering—how's that for irony?). *Captain Stormfield's Visit to Heaven* (1898) tells the tale of a late sea captain of Clemens' acquaintance: his voyage to Heaven, his arrival there, and his discovery of a hereafter that is tailored to the needs of the human soul for interest, change, learning, growth, and appropriate companionship. The harps-wings-haloes-hymns-and-clouds phase proves mercifully brief, and along the way Clemens interlards abundant satire on the conventional view of an eternally static heaven. Captain Stormfield moves on into a heaven that bears pretty close resemblance to the here-and-now, except that there is no degeneration of the body and no need for death, for the institution of which Clemens once acknowledged Adam as "the great benefactor of the human race."[24]

XIV. Of Late Satires and "Fulminations"

These works of fiction published during the author's lifetime, of course, do not comprise an arc of creative degeneration into despair and cynicism as the 19th century ended. Sure, as the 20th century dawned Mark Twain wrote some pretty dark stuff for "posthumous publication," like parts of his *Autobiography*, some short fiction like *The Mysterious Stranger* manuscripts, which tell a series of rather charming tales about a nephew of Satan who visits Earth and performs miracles that have no moral. Sometimes they create, and sometimes they destroy. Phillip Traum, Young Satan, or "44" as he is variously named in these fragments, is guiltless in his own mind, not being burdened with a conscience. And then there are Mark Twain's late politico-religious satires, which he published at the risk of damaging his reputation (which they did), provoked by his outrage at Western imperialism and "The Blessings of Civilization Trust,"[25] with its toxic compound of self-righteousness and rapacious greed, rearing in China, The Belgian Congo, Cuba, and the Philippines; at violations of human rights around the world, including "The United States of Lyncherdom"; and at the abuses of democratic and basic moral principles by Western governments and churches.[26]

These satires are dark, but not as dark as the crimes against humanity they catalog and deplore. And as the elaborate religious satire of *Huckleberry Finn* on the source of the corruption Clemens saw proliferating around the world at the end of his era makes clear, he held the "pernicious influence" of the superstitions known as religion—especially Bible based religion—largely responsible for the evils he observed around him.

In *Huckleberry Finn*, the Bible plays a paradigmatic role; its stories and teachings provide the skeleton that shapes much of the plot. The incidents of the plot are frequently re-dramatizations of these stories without an overlay of reverence toward a god who performs atrocities in every one of them—crimes that no sane human being could condone. His point is not puerile iconoclasm, but to challenge the reader to see that the characters of the novel unconsciously re-dramatize these story patterns in their lives because that is what, underneath all their individual posturing and pretense, gives resonance and meaning to their lives. Whether we are aware of it or not, as human beings we constantly engage in such re-dramatization of the psychological archetypes of our lives, and we constantly recreate situations that validate our personal and societal mythologies.

In "The War Prayer" Mark Twain himself accounts for the origin of the widely held belief that he became a curmudgeon unbalanced by personal misfortunes in his last years. In that literary sermon, he points out that a congregation that gathers to pray for victory in a popular war at its outset is actually praying for the destruction of not just the army of its enemy, but also the community—innocent families of men, women, and children who deserve to live their lives in peace. We don't have to look far for modern examples of this "collateral damage." The silent congregation listens to the "emissary from the Throne" who elaborates to them this dark side of their prayer, and the people conclude, afterwards, among themselves, "he was a lunatic."

In their rejection of the opinions and attitudes he expressed in his diatribes against American and European imperialism and the hypocrisy of our contemporary foreign and domestic policy in both the religious and political spheres, intellectuals who have dismissed these writings as the "fulminations" of a bitterly disappointed man manifest the same deficient logic as the congregation at the end of "The War Prayer."[27]

It was this blindness and stubborn resistance to the possibility of moral progress—the commitment of the whole human race to constantly reliving the past instead of manifesting a more enlightened future—that roused Mark Twain's ire at and pity for "the damned human race," an epithet he often repeated in the last years of his life. It is important to realize that in his anger at and his sorrow for humanity, he intended this epithet as a cry of despair meant not to condemn, but to teach people the nature of their evil so that they could free themselves to "dream other dreams, and better," as Young Satan says in his farewell at the close of *The Mysterious Stranger*.[28] The following extract from his autobiographical dictation of June 25, 1906, sums up his thinking on these matters:

> As to the human race. [...]
> Man is not to blame for what he is. He didn't make himself. He has no control over himself. All the control is vested in his temperament—which he did not create—and in the circumstances which hedge him round, from the cradle to the grave, and which he did not devise and cannot change by any act of his will, for the reason that he has no will. He is as purely a piece of automatic mechanism as is a watch. He is a subject for pity, not blame—and not contempt. He is flung head over heels into this world without ever a chance to decline, and straightway he conceives and accepts the notion that he is in some mysterious way under obligation to the unknown Power that inflicted this outrage upon him—and thenceforth he considers himself responsible to that Power for every act of his life, and punishable for such of his acts as do not meet with the approval of that Power—yet that same man would argue quite differently if a human

tyrant should capture him and put chains upon him and make him a slave. He would say that the tyrant had no right to do that, that the tyrant had no right to compel him to commit murder and then put the responsibility for the murder upon him. Man constantly makes a most strange distinction between man and his Maker, in the matter of morals. He requires of his fellow man obedience to a very creditable code of morals, but he observes without shame or disapproval his God's utter destitution of morals.[29]

We will never know at what point in composing *Huck Finn* it occurred to Clemens that he was liberated not fettered by his reputation as a humorist; perhaps, as this study's reading of Chapter I, paragraph one suggests (see Chapter One, Section III), he knew that before he started. For, be it recalled, that is where he suggests to the reader that Huck Finn's narrative is Mark Twain's book and that Samuel Clemens does not figure in this scheme. At the same time, however, if we allow that the Mark Twain who reports Huck's story is also a character in the fiction, then who is left to make the book but the creator of both?

This question brings us back to what may ultimately be an unanswerable one: Did Samuel Clemens know what he was doing as he penned the religious satire of *Huckleberry Finn*?—to which I must answer with another question: How could he not?—and a reiteration of Janet Smith's observation that "All his life, Mark Twain complained that whenever he wanted to be especially devastating, his irony became so subtle that people missed the point."[30] However, whether and to what extent he knew it, the fact is that the novel lends itself entirely to the reading proposed in this study, and no other explication has ever accounted for so much of Huck's narrative as this one does.

Mark Twain did despair of the human race's potential for social and moral progress to match the dramatic technological progress of the 19th Century, and even though he was tempted to regard life as a persistent nightmare and wrote "The Great Dark," a story that dramatized that dark philosophical idea, he never lost his moral compass and he always came down on the side of any issue where his whole-hearted commitment to the betterment of humanity landed him. If you find that dark, then let there be night.

XV. Sam Clemens' Conception of God

As Lionel Trilling proposed so many years ago, if one is looking for a god in *Adventures of Huckleberry Finn*, a god worthy of reverence, then the river itself provides one very much like "the God of the present day" characterized in Clemens' untitled essay, first published in 1995, well over a century after he wrote it, contrasting the "God of the Bible" with "the God of the present day," a few excerpts from which follow:

> One might represent the Biblical God by a grain of sand on the shore and then draw the proportions of the modern Deity upon the boundless expanse of the waters. [...] One cannot put the modern heavens on a map [...]; but the Bible God and the Bible heavens can be set down on a slate and yet not be discommoded .
> [...]
> Yes, the God of the Bible is justly meted to the scale of the Bible's universe. He found his most consonant employment in superintending the minute domestic affairs of a small coterie of vicious and turbulent fantastics, and his chief joy in inhaling the odors of burnt meat ascending from this toy globe.
> [...]
> A man could contrive the Bible's universe—and manifestly did; but only God could imagine the real universe. The one had neither variety nor grandeur in it—the other bewilders with its variety and appalls with its sublimity.
> To trust the God of the Bible is to trust an irascible, vindictive, fierce, and ever fickle and changeful master; to trust the true God is to trust a Being who has uttered no promises, but whose beneficent, exact, and changeless ordering of the machinery of his colossal universe is proof that he is at least steadfast to his purposes; whose unwritten laws, so far as they affect man, being equal and impartial show that he is just and fair; these things, taken together, suggest that if he shall ordain us to live hereafter, he will still be steadfast, just and fair toward us. We shall not need to require anything more.[31]

Lionel Trilling's 1948 essay introducing *Huckleberry Finn* proposes that Huck "is the servant of the river-god," an entity bearing a close resemblance to the true God Clemens characterizes above:

> *Huckleberry Finn* is a great book because it is about a god—about, that is, a power which, [...] to men of moral imagination, appears to embody a great moral idea.
> [... Huck] comes very close to being aware of the divine nature of the being he serves, and his very intense moral life may [...] derive from his love of the river.
> [...]
> The river itself is only divine; it is not ethical and good. But its nature seems to foster the goodness of those who love it and try to fit themselves to its ways. And we must observe that we cannot make—that Mark Twain does not make—an absolute opposition between the river and human society. To Huck much of the charm of the river life is human: it is the raft and the wigwam and Jim. He has not run away from Miss Watson and the Widow Douglas and his brutal father to a completely individualistic liberty, for in Jim he finds his true father [...]. The boy and the Negro slave form a family, a primitive community—and it is a community of saints.

Trilling's essay, as mentioned earlier (see Introduction, Section I), is one of the foundational opinions in the debate that has gone on for many decades over whether Huck's narrative is great art, a literary hoax, or something in between. His meditation on the novel rings true because it is true to the spirit of Huck and Jim and Mark Twain/Samuel Clemens, whose God was the god of nature and whose reverence was for morality in action rather than in theory. Trilling puts his finger on the pulse of this living work of literature and finds it flowing as strong and deep as the current of the wild river about which Clemens wrote from deep experience.[32]

For this and other reasons, this re-evaluation of Clemens' thought and beliefs is needed to bring interested lay readers up to speed and to educate scholars of American literature who have never been stricken with "delirium Clemens" about the context of biographical, historical, philosophical, and artistic development in which Clemens wrote *Adventures of Huckleberry Finn* over the course of seven or eight years from 1876 to 1884, when it was first published in London.

XVI. Chapter Summary: Who the Hell Was Sam Clemens?

As a cub pilot on the River Comedy, Sam Clemens learned to navigate the crossings from jokes and travesty to wit and parody and from there to humor and literary burlesque, as Franklin Rogers has charted Mark Twain's course. Literary burlesque, as Rogers explains, began as a parodic sub-genre of the English novel, and it reached its full flowering in the nineteenth century, with notable practitioners including William Thackeray, Henry Fielding, and Jane Austin. They all later went on from their apprenticeships in this subgenre to become respected "serious" novelists of the era.[33] Clemens never completed this progression; instead, he pulled literary burlesque up by the roots from the shore of parody and wit, transported it across the Atlantic, and planted it in the soil of American tragic humor, which is a very different place to write from.

As Mark Twain commented in *Pudd'nhead Wilson's New Calendar*, "The secret source of Humor itself is not joy but sorrow. There is no humor in heaven."[34] The humorous narrator—be he Simon Wheeler or his victim, the frame narrator in "The Jumping Frog," Huck Finn, Hank Morgan, Adam, or Eve—is blind to the comic aspects of his/her misadventures, which one might liken to flowers "watered with tears." These characters are at their humorous best only when they are speaking seriously; one hint of double-entendre in their narration would spoil the illusion of innocence and/or ignorance their author has been at pains to create. Never arch, their blindness to their own folly makes them deeply human, and at their best these humorous narrators become tragicomic figures of mythic proportions, as do Huck and Jim.

Arguably, Clemens' most successful burlesque is also his broadest and most multitudinous in the range of its allusions and parody, as far as readers have been able to detect so far. In Huck Finn's *Adventures*, Clemens brought literary burlesque to full bloom as a high art form. Leslie Fiedler was right:

Huckleberry Finn is not a great novel in the same sense that elitist critics find *The Wings of the Dove* great[35]; yet not only did it break upon the scene of American fiction—and world literature—with "the force of nature and revelation," as Justin Kaplan has written,[36] but it also transformed the genre of the novel itself, paving the way for new generations of writers freed from the shopworn conventions of literary form and style: not only the Hemingways and Andersons of twentieth-century American fiction,[37] but also the stream-of-consciousness avant-garde of William Faulkner and James Joyce, who also used everyday people and the occasional idiot to access the archetypal realities of our culture's collective unconscious.

Fiedler was in part right, and so was Seelye, who found *Huck Finn* "abominable," a literary monstrosity of behemoth proportions in which, as Bernard DeVoto, put it, Mark Twain indulges his worst instincts to "cut across lots into burlesque"[38]—even of his own best work—in an ill-timed play for the belly-laugh. But DeVoto is not the only critic to have been confused about what burlesque is; Rogers explores that confusion and its distorting effects on the meaning of Clemens' work, although he himself misses the point of the book's biblical burlesque along with everyone else. Yes, *Huck Finn is* a "bad novel" (Krutch) because even though it has been interpreted as a "serious" novel for generations, it is really just a long, humorous, symbolic narrative that turns aside from the tradition of the English novel to create something new, different, and wonderful.

And in the process Sam Clemens does what the greats like Dante and Cervantes and Chaucer and Shakespeare did before him: Clemens re-invented literary language, laid the foundation of "American" English, and re-envisioned the world in terms that not only the ivory tower elites could contemplate, but also the common man, like Dante's Italians, Cervantes' Spaniards, Chaucer's English, and Shakespeare's Elizabethans.

Huck Finn is a Leviathan of a book, but not a monstrosity. In form it is symmetrical, in Realism convincing, although its "congeries of claptrap" plot detracts,[39] artfully, from that otherwise carefully projected illusion. Clemens develops and sustains its themes of religious satire and the growth of Huck's character and the maturation of his personality and the deep humanity of Jim with admirable subtlety, grace, and humor. The meaning of his story is as clear as its denouement is a historically honest and comprehensive settling of its protagonist's experiences to the satisfaction of "THE AUTHOR"—who "would *like* it, if anybody else does or not"[40]—if not to the satisfaction of readers insensitive to Clemens' allusive burlesque technique. Sam Clemens, it turns out, was Mark Twain's best critic: "Read him right and he explains himself."[41] Who knew?

Allusion is the soul and body of literary burlesque, and almost everywhere in Clemens' works the traces of those who went before him, like pap's tracks in the snow, are there to be seen if one gets out of one's "old sugar hogshead" of assumptions about Mark Twain and assurances from authorities who *ought* to know all about his books, but don't. Clemens' satire was aimed at the very forces of uncritical orthodoxy and conformity and selfishness in our society that too often wave the banners of fundamentalism and conservatism. That was where he perceived the rub that held back the progress of the human race, and the unrelenting storm of resistance to his message shows that his satire was right on target, even though it has never been fully understood. Ultimately, he was not attacking religion, but rather the self-righteous fervor of individuals and groups overwhelmed with *delirium religions* who extend religious sanction to violations of human and civil rights.

Mark Twain championed the rights and dignity of people everywhere. Slavery, in his vision, was a metaphor for all forms of oppression. Arguably, he was the first citizen of Planet Earth. He traveled the world, observed and reported from America, Europe, the Middle East, Asia, Australia, New Zealand, and Africa. He lived a third of his adult life abroad. Almost everywhere he went, he applied the same standards of justice and fairness and of human dignity and equality to his observations of the world around him. That's why *Huck Finn* resonates so strongly around the world to this day. It's not against God or religion; it's *for* the dignity of humanity—even those outsiders who sometimes get excluded from the definition of what it means to be fully human.

AFTERWORD

Sam Clemens Arrives at the Pearly Gates
A Dialog between the Author and the Doorman

"Welcome, Mr. Clemens, you are here at last; we have been looking forward to this day!"

"I wish I could say the same, padre."

"Why, do you have doubts about the outcome of this interview?"

"Oh, no, I wouldn't say that I have doubts; it's just that I seem to have forgotten my asbestos pajamas."

"So you think you might be needing them?"

"I'm not sure. I tried my best to live a high and pure and blameless life, but I didn't always succeed."

"Tell me about that, my son."

"Well, padre, there were certain books and essays I wrote that were not flattering to the Authorities..."

"Flattery is a sin, my son; we do not think that your failure to commit such a grievous offense should bar your way into the Presence."

"Well that's mighty white of you, padre. But He and his Deputies were the ones who were the object of some of the most unflattering things I wrote."

"Hmmmm, that puts the matter in a different light."

"I thought you might see it that way."

"What did you intend to accomplish by these writings?"

"I was trying to do good, padre; all around me I saw people committing the insanest crimes: lying to others and to themselves; coveting their neighbors' possessions and spouses; killing their fellow men and women for motives of blind passion or self-enrichment; taking the name of God in vain even in the places of worship where He was called The Author of a book that was chock-full of even worse crimes and offenses than I saw the people committing—"

"What book was that?"

"They call it The Good Book, padre, and they say it is the Word of God."

"I do not know of such a book, my son. What does it say?"

"It says that God is petty, narrow-minded, jealous to the point of viciousness, vengeful, moody, unkind, forgetful of His promises, a hypocrite who cannot stick to one set of beliefs for more than a century or two; ignorant of astronomy, biology, natural history and most of the other sciences—"

"Peace!—Does it contain anything that is true?"

"Well, that may be the case. That's why I'm wishing I'd been wearing those asbestos pajamas I had my tailor make for me when the end was near. It does turn around and claim that this … this deity is loving, kind, patient, merciful, the Source of all blessings, the enemy of all that is evil (except when He's in a bad mood, or angered by some affront to His vanity, or offended by scientific discoveries that contradict 'His Word'")—

"Enough of this. I get your point, and it sounds like this is another of that class of literary humbug we hear about, rarely, from a few of the many billions of souls who come here every day from all across the universe. I know its genre, if not its details; what was the term for it, now...?

"It's call—"

"No, wait, my son, let me think a moment more …" muttering to himself and rubbing his jaw, "ribald? … hi-balls? … uh-uh; libels? no; … tribal? … closer; idols? … not quite; … Ah! That's it—*bibles!* Yes, we have heard of this category of literature, here. They are a dangerous invention of a few of the young, unruly races who have great difficulty governing their passions."

"I'm relieved to hear you say so, padre. I thought I might get into hot water, or something like that, when I got here because that's what I said most of those unflattering things about, not Him, really. I like God. In fact, some of my best friends are gods."

"Which ones, my son; perhaps we have some mutual acquaintances?"

"Well, there's Jesus, who tried to teach people to love one another, but didn't get too far; and Satan—I hear he used to be called Lucifer around these parts, before he retired to a warmer climate—Some might say I owe it to him that I'm here; then there's Allah, and Krishna—and there's one named Buddha who said he wasn't, but I never met him personally, to tell the truth."

"Hmmm, can't say as I know any of those gods. But then the multitudinous races that have emerged from the Presence and will eventually be absorbed back into It have so many names for the One that there only seem to be many. It is just a trick of the illusory nature of language, which your race has not yet transcended, that causes this fracturing of the Truth into a myriad of illusions. Do not let it trouble you, my son, but be at rest, and enter into the joys of eternal life."

"Why, thank you very kindly, padre! I do appreciate the invitation, but I'm afraid I'll have to decline for the time being. I must ask to be excused because of a previous engagement—some old friends and associates I promised to look up who got here before me, you know. Say, you wouldn't know where I could get a pair of fire-proof pajamas around here, would you?"

From the distance a spectral voice interrupts their conversation: "Train number 666 departing on the hour with stops at Limbo and Sheol.... All aboard that's comin' aboard!"

"Well padre, it's been very nice talkin' with you, and thanks for the outfit. My tailor didn't do half so good a job, and he charged me fancy rates for it too!"

"The pleasure has been mine, my son. Go in peace, and I hope to see you again."

Appendix A

The First Person *Huckleberry Finn* Chapter Titles

For the convenience of readers, here are the chapter titles that Clemens apparently added after the publication of the first edition. Since the recent publication of numerous authoritative texts, these titles, formerly a common feature of *Huck Finn* editions, have come to be omitted in favor of Clemens' original version of the Table of Contents. While I do not know in what edition they first appeared, no less an authority than Bernard DeVoto, first curator of the Mark Twain Papers, includes them in his Easton Press Collector's Edition (1942), from which I have borrowed them.

I append them here for two reasons. First, they provide a remarkably sure guide to the themes the foregoing study discovers in the novel, often directing the reader's attention to aspects of the text that deserve closer consideration, especially matters of religious and social satire. Second, in contrast to the third person objective style of the table of contents of the first edition text, several of these titles, like that of the first chapter, "I Discover Moses and the Bulrushers," are written in the first person, enhancing the illusion that Huck is indeed the author of his story even as they nudge our attention toward "THE AUTHOR's" level of reliable narration:

I. I Discover Moses and the Bulrushers
II. Our Gang's Dark Oath
III. We Ambuscade the A-rabs
IV. The Hair-Ball Oracle
V. Pap Starts In on a New Life
VI. Pap Struggles with the Death Angel
VII. I Fool Pap and Get Away
VIII. I Spare Miss Watson's Jim
IX. The House of Death Floats By
X. What Comes of Handlin' Snake-Skin
XI. "They're After Us!"
XII. "Better Let Blame' Well Alone"
XIII. Honest Loot From the "Walter Scott"
XIV. Was Solomon Wise?
XV. Fooling Poor Old Jim
XVI. The Rattlesnake-Skin Does Its Work
XVII. The Grangerfords Take Me In
XVIII. Why Harney Rode Away for His Hat
XIX. The Duke and the Dauphin Come Aboard
XX. What Royalty Did to Pokeville

XXI. An Arkansaw Difficulty
XXII. Why the Lynching Bee Failed
XXIII. The Orneriness of Kings
XXIV. The King Turns Parson
XXV. All Full of Tears and Flapdoodle
XXVI. I Steal the King's Plunder
XXVII. Dead Peter Has His Gold
XXVIII. Overreaching Don't Pay
XXIX. I Light Out in the Storm
XXX. The Gold Saves the Thieves
XXXI. You Can't Pray a Lie
XXXII. I Have a New Name
XXXIII. The Pitiful Ending of Royalty

XXXIV. We Cheer Up Jim
XXXV. Dark, Deep-laid Plans
XXXVI. Trying to Help Jim
XXXVII. Jim Gets His Witch-Pie
XXXVIII. "Here a Captive Heart Busted"
XXXIX. Tom Writes Nonnamous Letters
XL. A Mixed-Up and Splendid Rescue
XLI. "Must 'A' Been Sperits"
XLII. Why They Didn't Hang Jim
Chapter the Last. Nothing More to Write[1]

Appendix B

Pap Confronts Huck in Chapter V and Genesis 3: 9–24

In Genesis 3 God seeks out Adam in the Garden and Adam hides in fear because he is naked. When God calls him out, Adam and Eve face the wrath of God and He curses them for their sins. In *Huck Finn*, leading up to the parallel confrontation between pap and Huck, Huck has seen pap's footprints near the widow's garden, and he has reacted in fear by hiding not himself, like Adam (v. 10), but the money pap has come for. At the beginning of Chapter V, pap confronts Huck in the boy's room. Pap's abduction of Huck in Chapter VI and Huck's setting a decoy fire at the head of Jackson's Island in Chapter XI complete the "expulsion from the garden" parallel. The following is a parallel transcription of these two texts with verse numbers interpolated into Clemens' text (see Chapter Three, Section III):

9 And the Lord God called unto Adam and said unto him, Where *art* thou?	9–10 I reckoned I was scared of him […] but right away after, I see I warn't scared of him worth bothring about. […]
10 And he said, I heard thy voice in the garden, and I was afraid, because I was naked; and I hid myself.	He kept a-looking me all over. By and by he says:
11 And he said, Who told thee that thou *wast* naked? Hast thou eaten of the tree, whereof I commanded that thou shouldst not eat?	11 "Starchy clothes—very. You think you're a good deal of a big-bug, *don't* you?" "Maybe I am, maybe I ain't," I says. "Don't you give me none o' your lip,"
12 The woman thou gavest *to be* with me, she gave me of the tree, and I did eat.	says he. 17 "You've put on considerable many frills since I been away. I'll take you down a peg before I get done with you. 11
13 And the Lord God said unto the woman, What is this that thou hast done? And the woman said, The serpent beguiled me, and I did eat.	You're educated, too, they say—can read and write. You think you're better'n your father, now, don't you, because he can't? 17 *I'll* take that out of you. 11 Who told you you might meddle with such hifalut'n foolishness, hey?—who told you you could?"
The curse	
[…]	12 "The widow. She told me."
16 Unto the woman he said,	13 "The widow, hey?—and who told

261

I will greatly multiply thy sorrow and thy conception;
In sorrow thou shalt bring forth children;
And thy desire shall be to thy husband, and he shall rule over thee.

17 And unto Adam he said, Because thou hast hearkened unto the voice of thy wife, and hast eaten of the tree, whereof I commanded thee, saying, thou shalt not eat of it: cursed is the ground for thy sake; in sorrow shalt thou eat of it all the days of thy life;

18 Thorns also and thistles shall it bring forth to thee; and thou shalt eat the herb of the field:

19 In the sweat of thy face shalt thou eat bread, till thou return unto the ground; for out of it

wast thou taken: for dust thou art and unto dust shalt thou return.

[...]

Expulsion from the Garden

22 And the LORD God said, Behold, the man is become as one of us, to know good and evil: and now, lest he put forth his hand and take also of the tree of life, and eat, and live for ever:

23 Therefore the LORD God sent him forth from the garden of Eden, to till the ground from whence he was taken.[1]

the widow she could put in her shovel about a thing that ain't none of her business?"

"Nobody never told her."

16 "Well, I'll learn her how to meddle. And looky here—you drop that school, you hear? 17a I'll learn people to bring up a boy to put on airs over his own father and let on to be better'n what *he* is. You lemme catch you fooling around that school again, you hear? Your mother couldn't read, and she couldn't write, nuther, before she died; none of the family couldn't before *they* died. *I* can't; 17b and here you're a-swelling yourself up like this. I ain't the man to stand it—you hear? [...]

Now looky here; you stop that putting on frills. I won't have it. 23 I'll lay for you, my smarty, and if I catch you about that school I'll tan you good. First you know you'll get religion, too. I never see such a son."

APPENDIX C

Samuel Clemens' Burlesque of Milton's Hell

(see Chapter Three, Section V-A)

Part I

From *Paradise Lost,* Book X:
So having said, awhile he [Satan] stood, expecting
Thir universal shout and high applause
To fill his ear, when contrary he hears,
On all sides, from innumerable tongues
A dismal universal hiss, the sound
Of public scorn; he wondered, but not long
Had leisure, wond'ring at himself now more;
His Visage drawn he felt to sharp and spare,
His Arms clung to his Ribs, his Legs entwining
Each other, till supplanted down he fell
A monstrous Serpent on his Belly prone,
Reluctant, but in vain: a greater power
Now rul'd him, punisht in the shape he sinn'd.
According to his doom: he would have spoke,
But hiss for hiss return'd with forked tongue
To forked tongue, for now were all transform'd
Alike to Serpents all as accessories
To his bold Riot: dreadful was the din
Of hissing through the Hall, thick swarming now
With complicated monsters.[1]

From *Huck Finn,* Chapter VI:
I don't know how long I was asleep, but all of a sudden there was an awful scream and I was up. There was pap, looking wild and yelling about snakes. He said they was crawling up his legs; and then he would give a jump and scream, and say one had bit him on the cheek—but I couldn't see no snakes. He started and run round and round the cabin, hollering "take him off! he's biting me on the neck!" I never see a man look so wild in the eyes. Pretty soon he was all fagged out, and fell down panting, then he rolled over and over wonderful fast, kicking things every which way and striking and grabbing at the air with his hands and screaming and saying there was devils ahold of him. He wore out by and by and laid still awhile, moaning.
[...]
"Oh, let a poor devil alone!"

Clemen's Burlesque of Milton's Hell. (See Chapter Three, Section V-B.)

Part II

Satan to the Angel of Death:

Whence and what are thou, execrable shape,
That dar'st, though grim and terrible, advance
Thy miscreated Front athwart my way
To yonder Gates? through them I mean to pass,
That be assured, without leave askt of thee:
Retire, or taste thy folly, and learn by proof,
Hell-born, not to contend with Spirits of Heav'n.
[…]
Each at the head
Level'd his deadly aim; thir fatal hands
No second stroke intend.[2]
[…]
So frown'd the mighty Combatants, that Hell
Grew darker at thir frown; so matcht they stood;
For never but once more was either like to
To meet so great a foe.[3]
[…]
      and now great deeds
Had been achiev'd, whereof all Hell had rung,
Had not the Snaky Sorceress that sat
By Hell-Gate, and kept the fatal Key,
Ris'n, and with hideous outcry rush'd between,
    O Father, what intends thy hand, she cri'd,
Against thy only son? What fury, O Son,
Possesses thee to bend that mortal Dart
Against thy Father's head?[4]
[, ,]
But thou O Father, I forewarn thee, shun
His deadly arrow; neither vainly hope
To be invulnerable in those bright Arms,
Though temper'd heav'nly, for that mortal dint,
Save he who reigns above, none can resist.[5]

Pap's Assault on Huck:

By and by he rolled out and jumped up on his feet looking wild, and he see me and went for me. He chased me round and round the place with a clasp-knife, calling me the Angel of Death, and saying he would kill me, and then I couldn't come for him no more. I begged, and told him I was only Huck; but he laughed *such* a screechy laugh, and roared and cussed, and kept on chasing me up. Once when I turned short and dodged under his arm he made a grab and got me by the jacket between my shoulders, and I thought I was gone; but I slid out of the jacket quick as lightning and saved myself. Pretty soon he was all tired out, and dropped down with his back against the door, and said he would rest a minute and then kill me. He put his knife under him, and said he would sleep and get strong, and then he would see who was who.

So he dozed off pretty soon. By and by I got the split-bottom chair and clumb up easy as I could, not to make any noise, and got down the gun. I slipped the ramrod down to make sure it was loaded, and then I laid it across the turnip-barrel, pointing towards pap, and set down behind it to wait for him to stir. And how slow and still the time did drag along.

(end Chapter VI)

APPENDIX D

Awakening in Paradise

At the beginning of Chapter VIII of *Huckleberry Finn,* Huck wakes up on Jackson's Island after escaping from pap. His narration of this passage bears close comparison to Adam's narration of his own first awakening in Eden as Milton gives it in Book VIII of *Paradise Lost* (see Chapter Three, Section IX):

As new wak't from soundest sleep Soft on the flow'ry herb I found me laid In Balmy Sweat, which with his Beams the Sun Soon dried, and on the reeking moisture fed. Straight toward Heav'n my wond'ring Eyes I turn'd, And gaz'd a while the ample Sky, till rais'd By quick instinctive motion up I sprung, As thitherward endeavoring, and upright Stood on my feet; about me round I saw Creatures that liv'd, and mov'd, and walked, or flew, Birds on the branches warbling: all things smil'd, With fragrance and with joy my heart o'erflowed.[1]	The sun was up so high when I waked, that I judged it was after eight o'clock. I laid there in the grass and the cool shade, thinking about things and feeling rested and ruther comfortable and satisfied. I could see the sun out at one or two holes, but mostly it was big trees all about, and gloomy in there amongst them. There was freckled places on the ground where the light sifted down through the leaves, and the freckled places swapped about a little, showing there was a little breeze up there. A couple of squirrels set on a limb and jabbered at me very friendly.

APPENDIX E

The Duke and the King Introduce Themselves

The Manuscript Text vs. the First Edition Text (italicized): Comparison of Clemens' revised responses for the first edition reveals that he elaborated on the duke's response while downplaying the religious import of the king's (see Chapter Four, Section VII):

The duke: "O, I do lots of things—most anything that comes handy, so it ain't work. What's your lay?" (MS. 166)[1]

"Jour printer; by trade; do a little in patent medicines; theatre-actor—tragedy, you know; take a turn at mesmerism and phrenology when there's a chance; teach singing-geography school for a change; sling a lecture sometimes—oh, I do lots of things—most anything that comes handy, so it ain't work. What's your lay?"[2]

The king: "Gospil-work, mainly—most any kind of gospil work: boosting revivals along, or getting 'em up; working camp meetings; 'occupying' for a preacher that wants to take a week's rest; and missionarying. Thar's more money in missionarying than the others; folks will plank out cash for the heathen mighty free, if you only locate your heathen fur enough off. I've took in as much as seventeen dollars at one grist for the pore benighted Goojoos—invented 'em myself—located 'em away up just back of the north pole. Seeing that that worked so good, I kind of strained myself, next time, and located some in a comet, expecting to jest simply bust the community—but it warn't a go. They wouldn't ante a red—and I come mighty near getting ducked, too."[3]

"I've done considerable in the doctoring way in my time. Layin' on o' hands is my best holt—for cancer and paralysis, and sich things; and I k'n tell a fortune pretty good, when I've got somebody along to find out the facts for me. Preachin's my line, too; and workin' camp-meetin's; and missionaryin' around."[4]

APPENDIX F

Huck's "Great Debate" and Satan's

Passages from *Huckleberry Finn*, Chapter XXXI, and *Paradise Lost* IV, 9–113 are printed here in parallel with subheads emphasizing some of the most salient of the substantive and thematic parallels between these two texts. It is important to note that not only the ideas but also the general outline of Satan's and Huck's thought processes mirror each other. The main difference, on the other hand, is merely in details each author selects to achieve verisimilitude, and the rhetorical styles they choose.

These passages illustrate the burlesque technique described by Franklin Rogers and characterized by him as being "of necessity conscious." Here, Clemens borrows only the ideas and "the result is nothing like the originals when Twain has completed the transplantation, for they become in his hands mere foundations upon which he rears a structure of episode, character-axis, and theme all his own."[1] To recognize the source from which Clemens borrows, however, can vastly enrich a reader's understanding of the meaning of his work, if one is careful not to confuse the theme of the source with that of Clemens' transmutation of it. For a more thorough discussion of the ways Clemens' text burlesques Milton's (see Chapter Four, Section XVIII).

"Nor with Cause to Boast / Begins His Dire Attempt"

Satan, now first inflamed with rage, came down, The Tempter ere th' Accuser of man-kind, To wreck on innocent frail man his loss Of that first Battle, and his flight to Hell: Yet not rejoicing in his speed, though bold, Far off and fearless, nor with cause to boast, Begins his dire attempt, which nigh the birth Now rolling, boils in his tumultuous breast, And like a devilish Engine back recoils Upon himself; horror and doubt distract	After all this long journey, and after all we'd done for them scoundrels, here was it all come to nothing, all busted up and ruined, because they could have the heart to serve Jim such a trick as that, and make him a slave again, all his life, and amongst strangers, too, for forty dirty dollars. [...] And then think of *me*! It would get all around, that Huck Finn helped a nigger to get his freedom; and if I was ever to see anybody from that town again, I'd be ready to get down and lick his boots for shame. That's just the way; a person

267

His troubl'd thoughts, and from the bottom stir
The Hell within him, for within him Hell
He brings, and round about him, nor from Hell
One step no more than from himself can fly²

does a low-down thing, and then he don't want to take the consequences of it. Thinks as long as he can hide it, it ain't no disgrace. That was my fix exactly.

"Now Conscience Wakes Despair"

Now conscience wakes despair,
That slumber'd, wakes the bitter memory
Of what he was, what is, and what must be,
Worse; of worse deeds worse sufferings must ensue.³

The more I studied about this, the more my conscience went to grinding me, and the more wicked and low down and ornery I got to feeling.

"The Plain Hand of Providence"

Sometimes towards *Eden* which now in his view
Lay pleasant, his griev'd look he fixes sad,
Sometimes towards Heav'n and the full-blazing Sun[: ...]
To thee I call
O Sun, to tell thee how I hate thy beams
That bring to my remembrance from what state
I fell, how glorious once above thy Sphere;
Till Pride and worse Ambition threw me down
Warring in Heav'n against Heav'n's matchless King.⁴

And at last, when it hit me all of a sudden that here was the plain hand of Providence slapping me in the face and letting me know my wickedness was being watched all the time from up there in heaven

"He Deserved No Such Return from Me"

Ah wherefore! He deserv'd no such return
From me, whom he created what I was
In that bright eminence, and with his good
Upbraided none; nor was his service hard.
What could be less than to afford him praise,
The easiest recompense, and pay him thanks,
How due!

whilst I was stealing a poor old woman's nigger that hadn't ever done me no harm,

"Miserable Doings"

yet all his good prov'd ill in me
And wrought but malice; lifted up so high
I sdein'd subjection, and thought one step higher

and now was showing me there's One that's always on the lookout, and ain't a-going to allow no such miserable doings to go only just so

Would set me highest, and in a moment quit
The debt immense of endless gratitude,
So burdensome, still paying, still to owe;
Forgetful what from him I still receiv'd.[5]

fur and no further, I most dropped in my tracks I was so scared.

"Destiny"

O had his powerful Destiny ordain'd
Me some inferior Angel, I had stood
Then happy; no unbounded hope had rais'd
Ambition. Yet why not?

Well, I tried the best I could to kinder soften it up somehow for myself, by saying I was brung up wicked, and I warn't so much to blame; but something inside of me kept saying,

"Free Will"

some other Power
As great might have aspir'd, and me though mean
Drawn to his part; but other Powers as great
Fell not, but stand unshak'n, from within
Or from without, to all temptations arm'd.
Hadst thou the same free Will and Power to stand?
Thou hadst: whom hast thou then or what to accuse,
But Heav'n's free Love dealt equally to all?
[...]
       which way shall I
Fly infinite wrath and infinite despair?
Which way I fly is Hell; myself am Hell;
And in the lowest deep a lower deep
Still threat'ning to devour me opens wide,
To which the Hell I suffer seems a Heav'n.[6]

"There was the Sunday-school, you could a gone to it; and if you'd a done it they'd a learnt you, there, that people that acts as I'd been acting about that nigger goes to everlasting fire."

"Only Supreme in Misery"

O then at last relent: is there no place
Left for Repentance, none for Pardon left?
None left but by submission; and that word
Disdain forbids me, and my dread of shame
Among the Spirits beneath, whom I seduced
With other promises and other vaunts
Than to submit, boasting I could subdue

It made me shiver. And I about made up my mind to pray; and see if I couldn't quit being the kind of a boy I was, and be better. So I kneeled down. But the words wouldn't come. Why wouldn't they? It warn't no use to try and hide it from Him. Nor from *me*, neither. I knowed very well why they wouldn't come. It was because my heart warn't right; it was because I warn't square; it was

Th' Omnipotent. Ay me, they little know
How dearly I abide that boast so vain,
Under what torments inwardly I groan:
While they adore me on the Throne of Hell,
With Diadem and Sceptre high advanc'd
The lower still I fall, only Supreme
In misery; such joy Ambition finds.[7]

"Short Intermission Bought with Double Smart"

But say I could repent and could obtain
By Act of Grace my former state; how soon
Would highth recall high thoughts, how soon unsay
What feigned submission swore: ease would recant
Vows made in pain as violent and void,
For never can true reconcilement grow
Where wounds of deadly hate
  have pierc'd so deep:
Which would but lead me to a worse relapse,
And heavier fall; so should I purchase dear
Short intermission bought with double smart.
This knows my Punisher[8];

because I was playing double. I was letting *on* to give up sin, but away inside of me I was holding on to the biggest one of all. I was trying to make my mouth *say* I would do the right thing and the clean thing, but deep down in me I knowed it was a lie—and He knowed it. You can't pray a lie—I found that out.

So I was full of trouble, full as I could be; and didn't know what to do.

At last I had an idea; and I says, I'll go and write the letter—and *then* see if I can pray. Why, it was astonishing, the way I felt as light as a feather, right straight off, and my troubles all gone. So I got a piece of paper and a pencil, all glad and excited, and set down and wrote:

> Miss Watson your runaway nigger Jim is down here two mile below Pikesville and Mr. Phelps has got him up for the reward if you send.
> Huck Finn

I felt good and all washed clean of sin for the first time I had ever felt so in my life, and I knowed I could pray now. But I didn't do it straight off, but laid the paper down and set there thinking—thinking how good it was all this happened so, and how near I come to being lost and going to hell. And went on thinking. And got to thinking over our trip down the river; and I see Jim before me, all the time, in the day, and in the night-time, sometimes moonlight, sometimes storms, and we a floating along, talking, and singing, and laughing [...] and at last I struck the time I saved him by telling the men we had small-pox aboard, and he was so grateful, and said I was the best friend old Jim ever had in the world, and the *only* one he's got now; and then I happened to look around, and see that paper.

It was a close place. I took it up, and held it I my hand. I was trembling

"To Decide, Forever, Betwixt Two Things"

therefore as far
From granting hee, as I from begging peace:
All hope excluded thus, behold instead
Of us out-cast, exil'd, his new delight,
Mankind created, and for him this world.
So farewell Hope and with Hope farewell Fear,
Farewell Remorse: all Good to me is lost;
Evil be thou my Good[9];

because I'd got to decide, forever, betwixt two things and I knowed it. I studied a minute, sort of holding my breath, and then says to myself:

"All right, then, I'll *go* to hell"—and tore it up.

It was awful thoughts, and awful words, but they was said. And I let them stay said; and never thought no more about reforming. I shoved the whole thing out of my head; and said I would take up wickedness again, which was more in my line, being brung up to it, and the other warn't.

Going "The Whole Hog"

by thee at least
Divided Empire with Heav'n's King I hold
By thee, and more than half perhaps will reign
As Man ere long, and this new world shall know.[10]

And for a starter, I would go to work and steal Jim out of slavery again; and if I could think up anything worse, I would do that, too; because as long was in, and in for good, I might as well go the whole hog.

Chapter Notes

Preface

1. Mark Twain, *Following the Equator*, vol. II, in *The Writings of Mark Twain*, Author's National Edition, 25 vols. (New York: Harper and Brothers, 1899–1906: vol. VI, 179. Subsequent citations of this edition are identified as *Writings*.

2. Stanley Brodwin, "The Theology of Mark Twain: Banished Adam and the Bible," *Mississippi Quarterly* 29 (1976): 167–89; 183.

3. Mark Twain, letter to W. D. Howells, in *Selected Mark Twain—Howells Letters*, edited by Frederick Anderson, William M. Gibson, and Henry Nash Smith (New York: Atheneum, 1968), 213.

4. Henry Nash Smith, "Introduction," in *Adventures of Huckleberry Finn*, by Mark Twain (Boston: Houghton, 1958), v–xxix, xviii.

5. Mark Twain, untitled entry, in *Mark Twain's Notebooks and Journals*, edited by Frederick Anderson, et al., 2 vols. (Berkeley, Los Angeles, and London: University of California Press, 1975), vol. II, 493–95.

6. Michael Patrick Hearn, "Introduction," in *The Annotated Huckleberry Finn* (New York: Norton, 2001), xiii-clxv: cxxxix.

7. Janet Smith, editorial commentary in *Mark Twain on the Damned Human Race* (New York: Hill and Wang, 1962), 204.

8. Mark Twain, *Autobiography of Mark Twain*, vol. I, edited by Harriet Elinor Smith (University of California Press: Berkeley, Los Angeles, London, 2010), 212.

9. Mark Twain, "Jane Lampton Clemens," in *Huck Finn and Tom Sawyer Among the Indians and Other Unfinished Stories* (Berkeley, Los Angeles, London: University of California Press, 1989): 82–92: 89.

10. Mark Twain quoted by Victor A. Doyno, in *Writing Huck Finn* (Philadelphia: University of Pennsylvania Press, 1991), 221. The source is not identified.

Introduction

1. *Selected Mark Twain—Howells Letters*, 213.

2. Arnold Bennett, quoted by Hearn, "Introduction," clviii.

3. Harold H. Kolb, Jr., "Mark Twain, Huck Finn, and Jacob Blivens: Gilt-Edged, Tree-Calf Morality in *The Adventures of Huckleberry Finn*," *Virginia Quarterly Review* 55 (1979): 653–69; 669.

4. Henry Nash Smith, *Mark Twain: The Development of a Writer* (Cambridge: Belknap, 1962), 114.

5. H. N. Smith, "Introduction," *Adventures*, vi.

6. Leslie A. Fiedler, *No! In Thunder* (Boston: Beacon, 1960), 264.

7. Leo Marx, "Mr. Eliot, Mr. Trilling, and Huckleberry Finn," *American Scholar* 22 (1953): 423–40; 425.

8. William R. Manierre, "Huck Finn: Empiricist Member of Society," *Modern Fiction Studies* 14 (1968): 57–67: 67

9. H. N. Smith, "Introduction," *Adventures*, xxii.

10. Franklin R. Rogers, *Mark Twain's Burlesque Patterns, as Seen in the Novels and Narratives, 1855–1885* (Dallas: Southern Methodist University Press, 1960), 148.

11. James M. Cox, "Remarks on the Sad Initiation of Huckleberry Finn," *Sewanee Review* 62 (1954): 389–405; 404–05.

12. Kolb, "Mark Twain, Huck Finn, and Jacob Blivens," 653.

13. James M. Cox, *Mark Twain: The Fate of Humor* (Princeton: Princeton University Press, 1962), 180.

14. Burg, "Another View," 307.

15. Carrington, *Dramatic Unity*, 143.

16. Ibid., 147–48.

17. Mark Twain, quoted by H. N. Smith, "Introduction," *Adventures*, f.n. 1, xvi.

18. Kolb, "Mark Twain, Huck Finn, and Jacob Blivens," 658.
19. *Ibid.*, 653.
20. Bruce Michelson, "Huck and the Games of the World," American *Literary Realism* 13 (Spring 1980): 108-21; 119.
21. Leo Marx, "Mr. Eliot, Mr. Trilling," 440.
22. John Seelye, "The Craft of Laughter: Abominable Showmanship and Huckleberry Finn," *Thalia* 4 (Spring-Summer 1981): 19-25; 24.
23. Catherine H. Zuckert, "Law and Nature in *Adventures of Huckleberry Finn,*" *Proteus* 1 (1984): 27-35; 27.
24. Burg, "Another View," 301, 303.
25. John Earl Bassett, "*Huckleberry Finn:* The End Lies in the Beginning," *American Literary Realism* 17 (1984): 89-98; 94.
26. Mark Twain, "Jane Lampton Clemens," 88.
27. Daniel Barnes, "Twain's T*he Adventures of Huckleberry Finn,* Chapter I, *The Explicator* XXIII 8 (April 1965): item 62.
28. Leslie A. Fiedler, *"Huckleberry Finn:* The Book We Love to Hate,*" Proteus* 1 (1984): 1-8; 8.
29. Hearn, "Introduction," cxlviii.
30. Jane Smiley, quoted by Hearn, "Introduction," cxlix; excerpted from "Say It Ain't So, Huck: Second Thoughts on Mark Twain's 'Masterpiece'" (*Harper's Magazine*, January 1996): 61-7; 67.
31. Joseph Wood Krutch, "[*Huckleberry Finn*: A Bad Novel]" from "Speaking of Books" in *The New York Times Book Review*, May 23, 1954; reprinted in Clemens, *Adventures*, 362-3; 363.
32. Hearn, "Introduction," cxlix.
33. Mark Twain, quoted by J. Smith in *Mark Twain on the Damned Human Race* (New York: Hill and Wang, 1962), 203.
34. Mark Twain, quoted by Hearn, "Introduction," cxl.
35. Ron Powers, *Mark Twain: A Life* (New York: Free, 2005): 476.
36. *Ibid.*, 496.
37. Doyno, *Writing Huck Finn*, 228.
38. *Ibid.*
39. *Ibid.*, 239.
40. Victor A. Doyno, "Textual Addendum," in *Adventures of Huckleberry Finn: The Only Comprehensive Edition,* by Mark Twain (New York: Random House, 1996): 365-418, 365.
41. Doyno, *Writing Huck Finn*, 123.
42. *Ibid.*, 122-23.
43. Andrew Levy, "Introduction," in *Huck Finn's America* (New York: Simon and Schuster, 2015),XVII.
44. *Ibid.*, XXII.
45. *Ibid.*
46. *Ibid.*, XXIII-XXXIV.
47. Marx, "Mr. Eliot, Mr. Trilling," 440.
48. H. N. Smith, "Introduction," *Adventures*, xxii.
49. Andrew Hoffman, *Inventing Mark Twain: The Lives of Samuel Langhorne Clemens* (New York: William Morrow, 1997), 317.
50. Rogers, *Mark Twain's Burlesque Patterns*, 155.
51. Mark Twain, letter quoted from A. B. Paine's *Mark Twain's Letters, Ibid.*
52. Cf. W. R. Moses, "The Pattern of Evil in *Adventures of Huckleberry Finn,*" *Georgia Review* 13 (1959): 161-66, reprinted in Clemens, *Adventures*, 387-92.
53. S. L. Clemens, letter to Asa Don Dickenson, in *Mark Twain, A Biography,* by Albert Bigelow Paine, vol. III, 1280-81.
54. Brodwin, "*Theology,*" 188-89.
55. Doyno, *Writing Huck Finn*, 164.
56. Cf. Billy G. Collins, "Huckleberry Finn: A Mississippi Moses," *The Journal of Narrative Technique* 5 (1976): 86-104.
57. Allison Rank Ensor, *Mark Twain and the Bible* (Lexington: University of Kentucky Press, 1969), 75.
58. *Ibid.*, 95-6.
59. Marx, "Mr. Eliot, Mr. Trilling," 440.

Chapter One

1. John Lindberg, *"The Adventures of Huckleberry Finn* as Moral Monologue," *Proteus: A Journal of Ideas* I (Fall 1984): 41-9; 42.
2. Carrington, *Dramatic Unity,* 112.
3. Wayne C. Booth, *The Rhetoric of Fiction* (Chicago and London: University of Chicago Press, 1961), 74.
4. Doyno, "Textual Addendum," 381-2.
5. *Ibid.*, 389.
6. H. N. Smith, "Introduction," *Adventures*, xviii.
7. Lindberg, "Moral Monologue," 42-3.
8. *Ibid.*, 43.
9. Carrington, *Dramatic Unity,* 113.
10. Kolb, "Mark Twain, Huck Finn and Jacob Blivens," 658.
11. Booth, *Rhetoric of Fiction*, 156.
12. *Ibid.*, 73-4, italics added.
13. *Ibid.*, 86.
14. H. N. Smith, "Introduction," *Adventures*, xviii.

15. Manierre, "Huck Finn: Empiricist," 58–64.
16. John Seelye explores the idea that the novel is a literary practical joke in "Abominable Showmanship."
17. Booth, *Rhetoric of Fiction*, 307.
18. Mark Twain, *Autobiography*, 217.
19. Manierre, "Huck Finn: Empiricist," 64.
20. *Ibid.*, 64–5, italics added.
21. Doyno, "Textual Addendum," 365–66.
22. Mark Twain, "Is Shakespeare Dead?" quoted by Hearn in "Notes," f.n. 34, 45.
23. *Ibid.*
24. Kolb, "Mark Twain, Huck Finn, and Jacob Blivens," 658.
25. Anne T. Trensky, quoted in Kolb, "Mark Twain, Huck Finn, and Jacob Blivens," 661.
26. Booth, *Rhetoric of Fiction*, 321.
27. Janet Holmgren McKay, "Going to Hell: Style in Huck Finn's Great Debate," *Interpretations* 13 (1981): 24–30; 29.
28. McKay provides a lucid discussion of Mark Twain's adaptation of Huck's colloquial voice to literary purposes in "'An Art So High': Style in *Adventures of Huckleberry Finn*," in *New Essays on Adventures of Huckleberry Finn*, edited by Louis J. Budd (Cambridge: Cambridge University Press, 1985): 61–81.
29. Mark Twain, *Pudd'nhead Wilson*, in *Writings*, XIV, 230.
30. Mark Twain, quoted by M. P. Hearn, "Notes," in *The Annotated Huckleberry Finn*, 75, f.n. 25
31. H. N. Smith, "Foreword," in Alan Gribben, *Mark Twain's Library*, vol. I, i–xii; i.
32. Alan Gribben, *Mark Twain's Library: A Reconstruction*, 2 vols. (Boston: Hall, 1980), vol. I, 63.
33. Cox, "Remarks," 397.
34. Kolb, "Mark Twain, Huck Finn, and Jacob Blivens," 653.
35. Cox, *Fate of Humor*, 182.
36. Kolb, "Mark Twain, Huck Finn, and Jacob Blivens," 669.
37. *Ibid.*, 661.
38. Cox, *Fate of Humor*, 180.
39. Kolb, "Mark Twain, Huck Finn, and Jacob Blivens," 663.
40. *Ibid.*
41. Norris W. Yates, "The 'Counter-Conversion' of Huckleberry Finn, *American Literature* 32 (1960): 1–10; 8–9.
42. See Cox, *Fate of Humor*, 176–79.
43. Kolb, "Mark Twain, Huck Finn, and Jacob Blivens," 661.
44. Cox, *Fate of Humor*, 23.
45. Brander Matthews, "Biographical Criticism," in *The Innocents Abroad*, vol. I in *Writings*, xxiv.
46. Daniel R. Barnes, "Twain's *The Adventures of Huckleberry Finn*, Chapter 1," *The Explicator* 13 (1965): Item 62..
47. Collins, "A Mississippi Moses," 87.
48. John Milton, *Paradise Lost* in *John Milton: Complete Poems and Major Prose*, edited by Merritt Y. Hughes (New York: Odyssey, 1957): 173–469: I: l. 26.

Chapter Two

1. Barnes, "Chapter 1," n.p.
2. *Ibid.*
3. Kenneth Lynn, *Mark Twain and Southwestern Humor* (Boston: Little, 1960). Excerpts from Chapter 10, "You Can't Go Home Again," sections iii, vii, and viii, reprinted in Clemens, *Adventures of Huckleberry Finn: A Norton Critical Edition*, edited by Sculley Bradley, et al. (New York: Norton, 1962): 421–36: 425.
4. *Ibid.*, 421.
5. C. T. Harnesberger, *Mark Twain's Views of Religion* (Evanston, IL: Schori, 1961), 2.
6. Paine, *Mark Twain*, vol. II, 631.
7. Yates, "'Counter-Conversion,'" 1.
8. H. N. Smith, *Development of a Writer*, 118.
9. Mark Twain, *Following the Equator*, vol. II, in *Writings* VI, 179.
10. Manierre, "Huck Finn: Empiricist," 62.
11. Hearn, "Notes," f. n. 10, 141–42.
12. Mark Twain, "Jane Lampton Clemens," 88.
13. Manierre, "Huck Finn: Empiricist," 64.
14. F. Kaplan, *The Singular Mark Twain* (New York: Doubleday, 2003), 393.
15. Daniel Barnes, "*Adventures...* Chapter I."
16. F. Kaplan, *The Singular Mark Twain*, 3 93.
17. Cf. W. R. Moses, "The Pattern of Evil in *Adventures of Huckleberry Finn*," *Georgia Review* 13 (1959): 161–66, reprinted in Clemens, *Adventures*, 387–92.
18. Hearn, f.n. 34 and 36, 70.
19. *Ibid.*, f.n. 39, 70.
20. Doyno, *Writing Huck Finn*, 139.
21. Hearn, f.n. 9, 140.
22. *Ibid.*, f.n. 17, 189.
23. *Ibid.*, f.n. 36, 198.
24. Yates, "'Counter-Conversion,'" 6–7.
25. Randy K. Cross, "*Huck Finn*: The Sacred and the Profane," *Mark Twain Journal* 21 (1983): 27–8: 27–8.
26. Collins, "Mississippi Moses," 95.

27. Cf. Nielson, "The Savage Prophet."
28. Hearn, "Notes," f.n. 1, 205.
29. Cf. Doyno, *Comprehensive Ed.*, 178–181; Hearn, "Notes," 43–58, 234–37.
30. Joseph B. McCullough, "The Uses of the Bible in *Huck Finn*," *Mark Twain Journal* 19 (1978–79): 2–3; 3.
31. Brodwin, "Theology," 183.
32. Alfred Bigelow Paine, *Mark Twain: A Biography: The Personal and Literary Life of Samuel Langhorne Clemens*, 3 vols. (New York: Harper & Bros., 1912), vol. 3, 1280–81.
33. Brodwin, "Theology," 184–85.
34. McCullough, "Uses of the Bible," 2.
35. Cross, "The Sacred and the Profane," 27.
36. Collins, "Mississippi Moses," 100.
37. Lynn, "You Can't Go Home," in Clemens, *Adventures of Huckleberry Finn*, 431–2.
38. Cf. Genesis 9.
39. The quoted phrases are allusions to Genesis 9: 27.
40. Tom Quirk, "The Legend of Noah and the Voyage of Huckleberry Finn," *Mark Twain Journal* 21 (1982): 21–3: 22.
41. *Ibid.*
42. Hearn, "Notes," f.n. 7, 394.
43. Booth, *Rhetoric of Fiction*, 307.
44. Cross, "The Sacred and the Profane," 28.

Chapter Three

1. Hearn, "Notes," f.n. 24, 35.
2. *Ibid.*, f.n. 23 and 24, 35.
3. H. N. Smith, *Development of a Writer*, 127.
4. Cox, "Remarks," 398.
5. Lynn, "You Can't Go Home," in Clemens, *Adventures of Huckleberry Finn*, 432.
6. *Ibid.*, 422–3
7. Exod. 11: 2
8. Cox, "Remarks," 397.
9. Gary Scharnhorst, "Paradise Revisited: Twain's 'The Man That Corrupted Hadleyburg,'" *Studies in Short Fiction* 18 (Winter 1981): 59–64; 60.
10. Milton, *Paradise Lost* IV: l. 180.
11. *Ibid.*, ll. 173–92.
12. *Ibid.*, ll. 205–820.
13. *Ibid.*, l. 800.
14. *Ibid.*, ll. 839–40.
15. *Ibid.*, ll. 935–39.
16. Mark Twain, "Jane Lampton Clemens," 88.
17. William van O'Connor, "Why *Huckleberry Finn* Is Not the Great American Novel," *College English* 17 (1955): 6–10; reprinted in Clemens, *Adventures*, 371–78; 372.
18. H. N. Smith, *Development of a Writer*, 129.
19. *Ibid.*, 127.
20. *Paradise Lost* V: ll. 775–8.
21. *Ibid.*, ll. 794–802.
22. Samuel Clemens, letter to Orion Clemens, 23 March 1878, http://www.marktwainproject.org/xtf/search?category=letters;rmode=landing_letters;style=mtp
23. F. Kaplan, *The Singular Mark Twain*, New York: Doubleday, 2003, 393.
24. Mark Twain, letter to Orion, op. cit.
25. Milton, *Paradise Lost*, X: ll. 441–584.
26. *Ibid.*, ll. 505–24.
27. *Ibid.*, ll. 629–814.
28. *Ibid.*, ll. 682–688.
29. *Ibid.*, ll. 711–13.
30. *Ibid.*, ll. 719–22.
31. *Ibid.*, ll. 722–30.
32. *Ibid.*, ll. 746–89.
33. *Ibid.*, ll. 811–15.
34. Genesis 22: 10–13.
35. Powers, *Mark Twain*, 320.
36. Briden, "Huck's Great Escape," 17–18.
37. Exodus 2: 11–15.
38. Exodus 11: 2 and 12: 36.
39. Briden, "Huck's Great Escape, 17–18.
40. Exodus 11: 1–2.
41. Exodus 12: 12 and 29–30.
42. Lynn, "You Can't Go Home," in Clemens, *Adventures of Huckleberry Finn*, 422–3.
43. Cf. St. Matthew 2: 13–19.
44. Milton, *Paradise Lost*, II, ll. 892–97.
45. *Ibid.*, ll. 933–39.
46. *Ibid.*, l. 911.
47. Cox "Remarks," 282.
48. Milton, *Paradise Lost* VIII: ll. 253–66.
49. *Huck Finn* Chapter VIII; Gen. 2: 20; *Paradise Lost* VIII: ll. 379–98.
50. Gen. 2: 21–2.
51. Gen. 3: 15.
52. H. N. Smith, "Foreword," in Gribben, *Mark Twain's Library*, i.
53. Quirk, "The Legend of Noah," 23.
54. Brodwin, "Theology," 188.
55. Gen. 3: 24.
56. Stanley Brodwin, "Mark Twain's Masks of Satan: The Final Phase," *American Literature* 45 (1973): 206–27; 227.
57. Mark Twain's manuscript, 179, excerpts in Doyno, "Textual Addendum," 404.
58. Doyno, *Comprehensive Ed.* 372.
59. Cf. Leslie Fiedler, "Come Back to the Raft Ag'in, Huck Honey," in *An End to Innocence* (Boston: Beacon, 1955): 142–51.

60. Doyno, "Textual Addendum," 372.
61. Lynn, "You Can't Go Home," in Clemens, *Adventures of Huckleberry Finn*, 425.
62. Walter Blair, *Mark Twain*: 348-9.
63. Hearn, "Notes," f.n. 6: 140.
64. *Ibid.*, f.n. 10, 141
65. *Ibid.*, f.n. 9, 140.
66. *Ibid.*, f. n. 13, 152.
67. William M. Gibson, *The Art of Mark Twain* (New York: Oxford University Press, 1976), 113.
68. I Kings 3: 7-12.
69. *Ibid.*, 383.
70. *Ibid.*, 377.
71. J. Kaplan, "Introduction," in Doyno, *Comprehensive Ed.*, xi.
72. Vaneta Neilson, "The Savage Prophet, or, Who's Afraid of Samuel Twain?," *Publications of the Utah Academy of Sciences, Arts, and Letters* 43 (1967): 1-7; 5.
73. I Samuel 15: 9.
74. I Samuel, 14: 52-15: 15.
75. Nielson, "Savage Prophet," 4.
76. Cf. Mark Twain's "To the Person Sitting in Darkness," "King Leopold's Soliloquy," and "The War Prayer."
77. Brodwin, "Theology," 183.
78. Nielson, "Savage Prophet," 7.
79. Alfred Bigelow Paine, *Mark Twain: A Biography*, 3 vols. (New York: Harper, 1912): vol. III: 1280-81.
80. Mark Twain quoted by Ensor, *Mark Twain and the Bible*, 95.
81. Hearn, "Notes," f.n. 17, 189-90.
82. Nielson, "Savage Prophet," 5.
83. Cf. Joseph Campbell, *Occidental Mythology*, 105 ff.
84. Genesis 4: 15.
85. Cf. Moses, "The Pattern of Evil."
86. Collins, "Mississippi Moses," f.n. 12, 103-4.
87. *Ibid.*, 94.
88. *Ibid.*, 95.
89. *Ibid.*
90. Exodus 14: 29-30.
91. Collins, "Mississippi Moses," 86.
92. *Ibid.*, 87.
93. *Ibid.*, 89.
94. Hearn, "Notes," f.n. 5, 19.
95. Collins, "Mississippi Moses," 89.
96. Burg, "Another View," 302.
97. Collins, "Mississippi Moses," 89.
98. *Ibid.*, 86-7.
99. *Ibid.*, 88
100. *Mysterious Stranger*, 247.
101. Exodus 2: 11-15
102. Collins, "Mississippi Moses," 86.
103. F. Kaplan, *The Singular Mark Twain*, 393.

Chapter Four

1. F. Kaplan, *The Singular Mark Twain*, 340-49.
2. Mark Twain, *The Autobiography of Mark Twain*, edited by Charles Neider (New York: Harper & Bros., 1959), 29.
3. Kolb, "Mark Twain, Huck Finn, and Jacob Blivens," 658.
4. *Ibid.*, 665.
5. H. N. Smith, *Development*, 123.
6. Mark Twain, quoted by Coley B. Taylor, *Mark Twain's Margins on Thackeray's "Swift,"* (New York: Gotham House, 1935), 55.
7. Cox, *Fate of Humor*, 176-7.
8. Mark Twain, quoted by Blair, *Mark Twain*, 168.
9. Rogers, *Mark Twain's Burlesque Patterns*, 155.
10. Harold Bloom, *The Anxiety of Influence* (New York: Oxford University Press, 1973), 19-45.
11. Alfred Bendixen, "Huck Finn and Pilgrim's Progress," *Mark Twain Journal* 18 (1976-77), 21.
12. Mark Twain, Captain Stormfield's Visit to Heaven," in *The Bible According to Mark Twain*, edited by Howard G. Baetzhold and Joseph B. McCullough (New York: Touchstone, 1996), 129-188, Chapter 3, 147-62.
13. Mark Twain, letter to W. D. Howells, *Selected Mark Twain-Howells Letters*, 250.
14. Vaneta Nielson, "The Savage Prophet, or, Who's Afraid of Samuel Twain?" *Publications of the Utah Academy of Sciences, Arts, and Letters* 43 (1967): 1-7; 2.
15. *Ibid.*, 389.
16. Moses, "The Pattern of Evil," 388-91.
17. *Ibid.*, 387.
18. Gribben, *Mark Twain's Library*, vol. I, 173.
19. W. G. Marshall, "Twain's 'A Curious Dream' and the *Inferno*," *Mark Twain Journal* 21 (1983): 41-3.
20. Thomas Werge, "The Sin of Hypocrisy in 'The Man That Corrupted Hadleyburg' and *Inferno* XXIII," *Mark Twain Journal* 18 (1976): 17-18.
21. Cox, "Remarks," 397.
22. Dante Alighieri, *The Divine Comedy* (Garden City, NY: Doubleday, 1947): Hell [*The Inferno*], Canto XXV, ll. 48-9.
23. *Ibid*, ll. 93-4.

24. Hearn, "Notes," f.n. 1, 264–67.
25. Dante Alighieri, *The Divine Comedy* (Garden City, NY: Doubleday, 1947): *Hell* [*The Inferno*], Canto XVII, ll. 1–26, 86.
26. *Ibid.*, Canto XXI, ll. 40–41.
27. *Ibid.*, anonymous textual notations, 437.
28. *Ibid.*, Canto I, ll. 109–123, 6.
29. F. Kaplan, *The Singular Mark Twain*, 393.
30. E.g., cf. Seelye, "Abominable Showmanship."
31. Hearn, "Notes," f.n. 37, 37.
32. Doyno, "Textual Addendum," 379.
33. Mark Twain, *Adventures of Huckleberry Finn*, edited by Hearn, 206.
34. Mark Twain, MS text, in Doyno, *Comprehensive Edition*, 167.
35. Doyno, op. cit., 177–81.
36. Doyno, "Textual Addendum," 379.
37. Rogers, *Mark Twain's Burlesque Patterns*, 155.
38. Mark Twain, *Adventures of Huckleberry Finn*, MS text, in Doyno, *Comprehensive Edition*, 178.
39. Mark Twain, *Adventures of Huckleberry Finn*, edited by M. P. Hearn, 229.
40. Mark Twain, *Adventures of Huckleberry Finn*, MS text, in Doyno, *Comprehensive Edition*, 178.
41. Mark Twain, *Adventures of Huckleberry Finn*, edited by Hearn, 229–30.
42. Doyno, "Textual Addendum," 380.
43. This invitation occurs only in the final version.
44. Doyno, "Textual Addendum," 380.
45. Mark Twain, *Adventures of Huckleberry Finn*, MS text, in Doyno, *Comprehensive Ed.*, 178–79.
46. Mark Twain, op. cit., edited by Hearn, 229–30.
47. Milton, *Paradise Lost* IV: ll. 76–7.
48. Mark Twain, *Letters from the Earth*, 229–30.
49. *Ibid.*, 381.
50. Doyno, "Addendum," 381.
51. Mark Twain, *Autobiography*, 158.
52. Brodwin, "Theology," f.n. 29, 181.
53. *Ibid.*, 183.
54. *Ibid.*, 183–84.
55. Doyno, "Foreword," xv.
56. Hearn, "Notes," f.n. 17, 272.
57. Hearn, "Notes, f.n. 5 and 7, 274–75.
58. *Ibid.*, f.n. 5, 275.
59. *Ibid.*
60. Bible, editorial introduction to *The Third Book of Moses Called Leviticus*.
61. Ferguson, "Huck Finn Aborning," *The Colophon* (Spring 1938): 171–80, 180; quoted by Hearn, "Notes," f.n. 4, 282.
62. Hearn, "Notes," f.n. 6, 283.
63. *Ibid.*, f.n. 7, 283.
64. Doyno, *Writing Huck Finn*, 71.
65. Mark Twain, MS text, in Hearn, "Notes," f.n. 9, 284.
66. Janet Holmgren McKay, "Tears and Flapdoodle: Point of View and Style in *Adventures of Huckleberry Finn*," *Style* 10 (1976): 41–50; 48–9.
67. Ferguson, op. cit., 175; quoted by Hearn, "Notes," f.n. 9, 284.
68. Hearn, "Notes," f.n. 9, 284.
69. Hearn, "Notes," f.n. 19, 286.
70. Mark Twain, "Bible Teaching and Religious Practice" in *Europe and Elsewhere*, edited by Alfred Bigelow Paine (New York and London: Harper & Bros., 1923), 287; quoted by Hearn, f.n. 22, 287.
71. Mark Twain, manuscript, quoted by Hearn, "Notes," f.n. 30, 289.
72. Ferguson, op. cit., 176; quoted by Hearn, f.n. 1, 291.
73. Hearn, f.n. 1, 291.
74. Doyno, *Writing Huck Finn*, 89.
75. *Ibid.*, 90.
76. *Ibid.*, 89.
77. *Ibid.*, 5–6.
78. *Ibid.*, 90.
79. *Ibid.*, 90.
80. *Ibid.*, 91.
81. Dante Alighieri, *Inferno*, Canto XXXIV, 143.
82. Milton, *Paradise Lost* I: l. 26.
83. Mark Twain, *Letters from the Earth*, in *The Bible According to Mark Twain*: 213–60; 229–30.
84. Kolb, "Mark Twain, Huck Finn and Jacob Blivens," 669.
85. Cox, "Sad Initiation."
86. Manierre, "Huck Finn: Empiricist Member of Society."
87. Romans 6: 23.
88. St. John 15: 13.
89. Yates, "'Counter-Conversion,'" 8.
90. *Ibid.*, 2.
91. *Ibid.*, 10.
92. Milton, *Paradise Lost* IV: l. 15.
93. *Ibid.*: ll. 18–23 and 48–9.
94. *Ibid.*: ll. 58–67.
95. *Ibid.*: ll. 71–8.
96. *Ibid.*: ll. 79–80.
97. *Ibid.*: ll. 81–3.
98. *Ibid.*: ll. 86–97.
99. *Ibid.*: ll. 98–100a.
100. *Ibid.*: l. 102.
101. *Ibid.*: ll. 103–4.

102. *Ibid.*: ll. 108-10.
103. *Ibid.*: l. 111.
104. McKay, "Going to Hell," 24-5.
105. *Ibid.*
106. Carrington, *Dramatic Unity*, 147.
107. I Corinthians 13: 11.
108. Hearn, "Notes," f.n. 14, 345.
109. Cf. Lynn, "You Can't Go Home," in Clemens, *Adventures of Huckleberry Finn*, 428-9; and Lionel Trilling, "[An Introduction to Huckleberry Finn]," in *Huck Finn and his Critics*, edited by Richard Lettis, et al. (New York: Macmillan, 1964): 326-36; 313.
110. Seelye, "Abominable Showmanship," 23.
111. Mark Twain, *Life on the Mississippi*, in *Writings*, vol. IX, 31.
112. F. Kaplan, *The Singular Mark Twain*, 393.
113. Doyno, *Writing*, 120-23; cf. Introduction in this study, IV.

Chapter Five

1. Mark Twain, "Jane Lampton Clemens," 88.
2. Bernard DeVoto, "Introduction," in *Adventures of Huckleberry Finn [Tom Sawyer's Companion]*, edited by Bernard DeVoto (Norwalk: Easton, 1942); ix-lxx; lviii.
3. Cox, *Fate of Humor*, 182.
4. *Paradise Lost* IV: 113.
5. Hearn, "Notes, " f.n. 16, 345.
6. Doyno, *Writing Huck Finn*, 30.
7. *Paradise Lost* IV: 113.
8. *Ibid.*, 159.
9. Frank Baldanza, "The Structure of Huckleberry Finn," *American Literature* 27 (November 1955): 347-55; reprint in *Huck Finn and his Critics*: 371-78; 378.
10. Cross l, "Sacred and Profane," 28.
11. Carrington, *Dramatic Unity*, 112-13.
12. *Ibid.*, 120.
13. *Ibid.*
14. Cf. Doyno, *Writing*, 207-17.
15. Mark Twain, letter to W. D. Howells in *Selected Letters*, 213.
16. Exodus: 3: 10.
17. *Ibid.*, 4: 12.
18. *Ibid.*, 4: 4-16.
19. Collins, "Mississippi Moses," 97-100.
20. Exod. 14.
21. Exod. 13: 21.
22. Stanley Brodwin, "Mark Twain and the Fall of Man," *Dissertation Abstracts* 28 (1968): 5008-9A.
23. *Ibid.*

24. Ferguson, op. cit., 179; quoted by Hearn, "Notes," f.n. 3, 368.
25. Hearn, "Notes," f.n. 3, 368.
26. *Ibid.*, f.n. 2, 375.
27. *Ibid.*, f.n. 4, 368.
28. Mark Twain quoted by Hearn from *Adventures of Huckleberry Finn*, edited by Walter Blair and Victor Fischer (Berkeley and Los Angeles: University of California Press, 1988), 756; Hearn, "Notes," f.n. 4, 387.
29. Hearn, "Notes," f.n. 5, 393.
30. *Ibid.*, f.n. 1, 254.
31. Mark Twain, "Chapters of My Autobiography," *North American Review* (January 18, 1907), 119; quoted by Hearn, "Notes," f.n. 1, 254.
32. Hearn, "Notes," f.n. 6, 140.
33. *American Heritage Dictionary*, "hussy."
34. Hearn, "Notes, f.n. 4, 387.
35. Doyno, "Textual Addendum," 383.
36. Doyno, *Writing*, 164.
37. Doyno, "Textual Addendum," 383.
38. Bernard DeVoto, "Introduction," lviii.
39. Rogers, *Burlesque Patterns*, 148.
40. Doyno, *Writing*, 207.
41. *Ibid.*, 239 ff.
42. Levy, *Huck Finn's America*, 137-38.
43. Doyno, *Writing*, 164.
44. Mark Twain quoted by Victor A. Doyno, in *Writing*, 221.
45. This statement relies on Jungian psychology and study of the writings of Joseph Campbell. Cf. *The Masks of God*.
46. Levy, "Introduction," in Levy, *Huck Finn's America*, XIII-XXXIV.
47. Doyno, *Writing*, 164.
48. Cf. Doyno's discussion of this matter in *Writing Huck Finn*, 211.
49. H. N. Smith, "Introduction," *Adventures*, xxi.
50. Gibson, *Art of Mark Twain*, 113.
51. Chadwick-Joshua, *The Jim Dilemma*, xix.
52. *Ibid.*, 116.
53. Doyno, *Writing*, 237.
54. Ernest Hemingway, *The Green Hills of Africa* (New York: Scribner, 1935): 22.
55. Levy, *Huck Finn's America*, 183-4.

Chapter Six

1. Lindberg, "Moral Monologue," 48.
2. Mark Twain quoted by Victor A. Doyno, in *Writing*, 221. The source is not identified.
3. Mark Twain, "A Little Note to M. Paul Bourget," *Literary Essays* in *Writings*, vol. XXII, 165-81; 171.
4. Rogers, *Mark Twain's Burlesque Patterns*, 155.

5. Brodwin, "Theology," 183.
6. Milton, *Paradise Lost*, VIII, ll. 322-30.
7. Mark Twain, *Letters from the Earth*, 229.
8. Mark Twain, *Pudd'nhead Wilson* in *Writings*, vol. XIV, 19.
9. Milton, *Paradise Lost* I: l. 29.
10. *Ibid.*, VII: ll. 317, 360.
11. Mark Twain, "The Mysterious Stranger," in *The Mysterious Stranger and Other Stories* (New York: New American Library, 1962): 161-253; 252-53.
12. Doyno, "Textual Addendum," 381-2.
13. F. Kaplan, *The Singular Mark Twain*, 393.
14. Hearn, "Notes," f.n. 2, 1.
15. Doyno, "Textual Addendum," 382.
16. H. N. Smith, "Introduction," *Adventures*, xxviii-xxix.
17. Chadwick-Joshua, *The Jim Dilemma*, xii.
18. Bassett, "The End Lies in the Beginning," 94.
19. Trilling, "The Greatness," in *Huck Finn and his Critics*, 312-13; Lynn, "You Can't Go Home," in Clemens, *Adventures of Huckleberry Finn*, 425; Chadwick-Joshua, *The Jim Dilemma*, 121-22.
20. Chadwick-Joshua, *The Jim Dilemma*, 119-22.
21. Lindberg, "Moral Monologue," 42.
22. Doyno, "Textual Addendum," 379-80.
23. Chadwick-Joshua, *The Jim Dilemma*, 129.
24. *Ibid.*, 134.
25. Paine, *Biography*, vol. II, 794.
26. Doyno, "Textual Addendum," 367.
27. Genesis 3: 15.
28. Booth, *Rhetoric of Fiction*, 307.
29. H. N. Smith, "Introduction," *Adventures*, vi.
30. Paine, *Biography*, II, 573-74.
31. Powers, *Mark Twain*, 376.
32. Seelye, "Abominable Showmanship," 24.
33. Paine, *Biography*, II, 745.
34. Lynn, "You Can't Go Home," in Clemens, *Adventures of Huckleberry Finn*, 431.
35. Levy, *Huck Finn's America*, 137-38.
36. Doyno, *Writing*, 167-68.

Chapter Seven

1. Seelye, "Abominable Showmanship," 19.
2. Trilling, "[The Greatness...]," 316.
3. Kolb, "Mark Twain, Huck Finn, and Jacob Blivens," 658.
4. Rogers, *Mark Twain's Burlesque Patterns*, 14 ff.
5. *Ibid.*, 107.
6. *Ibid.*, 103-04.
7. *Ibid.*, 105-06.
8. Hoffman, *Inventing Mark Twain*, 442.
9. Rogers, *Mark Twain's Burlesque Patterns*, 116-17.
10. *Ibid.*, 114.
11. *Ibid.*, 118-121.
12. Cf. Brodwin, "Theology."
13. Clemens, letter to Chatto and Windus, in Welland ["Clemens, Chatto, and the English Edition"], in Clemens, *A Connecticut Yankee*, 313-18; excerpted from *Mark Twain in England* (London: Chatto & Windus, 1978), 313-14.
14. Clemens, quoted in "From *The New York Sun* and *The World Herald*": "[The 1886 Reading at Governor's Island]," in Backgrounds and Sources section of Clemens, *A Connecticut Yankee in King Arthur's Court*,293-96; 296
15. J. Smith, *Mark Twain on the Damned Human Race*, 202.
16. Welland, ["Clemens, Chatto, and the English Edition"], 313.
17. Clemens, letter to Chatto, quoted, *Ibid.*, 314.
18. J. Smith, *Mark Twain on the Damned Human Race*, 202-03.
19. Tolkien, J. R. R., *The Return of the King*, 2d ed. (Boston: Houghton Mifflin, 1993).
20. J. Smith, *Mark Twain on the Damned Human Race*, 204.
21. Mark Twain, *Pudd'nhead Wilson*, quoted by Powers, *Mark Twain*, 550.
22. William Dean Howells, *My Mark Twain* (New York and London: Harper & Bros., 1910): 150-56.
23. *The Bible According to Mark Twain*, 138.
24. Mark Twain, *Pudd'nhead Wilson*, in *Writings*, vol. XIV, 30.
25. Mark Twain, "To the Person Sitting in Darkness," in J. Smith, *Mark Twain on the Damned Human Race*: 3-21; 10.
26. Cf. "King Leopold's Soliloquy," "The War Prayer," "The United States of Lyncherdom," and "To the Person Sitting in Darkness," by Mark Twain.
27. Cf. "The War Prayer," in *Mark Twain on the Damned Human Race*, 64-7.
28. "Mark Twain, *The Mysterious Stranger*, 252.
29. *The Bible According to Mark Twain*, 329-30.
30. J. Smith, op. cit., 204.
31. Cf. *The Bible According to Mark Twain*, Appendix 7: "The God of the Bible vs. the God of the Present Day," 314-17.
32. Trilling, "[The Greatness of *Huckleberry Finn*]," in Clemens, *Adventures*, 312-13.

33. Cf. Rogers, "Burlesque, a Route to the Craft of Fiction," in *Burlesque Patterns*, 3–13.
34. Mark Twain, *Following the Equator*, in *Writings*, vol. V, 119.
35. Fiedler, "*Huckleberry Finn*: The Book We Love to Hate," *Proteus* 1 (1984): 1–8; 8.
36. J. Kaplan, "Introduction," x.
37. H. N. Smith, "Introduction," xxvii ff.
38. DeVoto, "Introduction" in *Adventures*, edited by Bernard DeVoto: ix-lxx; lviii.
39. Seelye, "Abominable Showmanship," 23.
40. Mark Twain, letter to W. D. Howells in *Selected Letters*, 213.
41. Mark Twain, quoted by Hearn, "Introduction" cxxxix.

Appendix A

1. Mark Twain, "Contents" in *Adventures of Huckleberry Finn: [Tom Sawyer's Companion]*, by Mark Twain, edited and with an Introduction by Bernard DeVoto (Norwalk, CT: Easton, 1942).

Appendix B

1. Genesis 3: 9–23.

Appendix C

1. *Paradise Lost*, X, ll. 505–24.
2. *Ibid.*, II, ll. 711–13.
3. *Ibid.*, ll. 719–22.
4. *Ibid.*, ll. 722–30.
5. *Ibid.*, ll. 810–14.

Appendix D

1. *Paradise Lost*, X, ll. 253–66.

Appendix E

1. Mark Twain, *Adventures of Huckleberry Finn*, MS text in Doyno, *Comprehensive Ed.*, 166.
2. *Ibid.*, 1st ed. text in Hearn, 206.
3. *Ibid.*, MS text in Doyno, *Comprehensive Ed.*, 167.
4. *Ibid.*, 1st ed. text in Hearn, 206.

Appendix F

1. Rogers, *Mark Twain's Burlesque Patterns*, 155.
2. Milton, *Paradise Lost*, IV, ll. 9–22.
3. *Ibid.*, ll. 23b–26.
4. *Ibid.*, ll. 27–41.
5. *Ibid.*, ll. 58–61a.
6. *Ibid.*, ll. 61b-78
7. *Ibid.*, ll. 79–92.
8. *Ibid.*, ll. 93–103a.
9. *Ibid.*, ll. 103b–110a.
10. *Ibid.*, ll. 110b–113.

Bibliography

Alighieri, Dante. "Hell" (*The Inferno*) in *The Divine Comedy*. Garden City, NY: Doubleday, 1948: 3-145.

American Heritage Dictionary, 2d college ed., Boston: Houghton Mifflin, 1985.

Baetzhold, Harold G. *Mark Twain and John Bull: The British Connection*, Bloomington: Indiana University Press, 1970.

Baetzhold, Howard G., and Joseph B. McCullough, eds. *The Bible According to Mark Twain*. New York: Touchstone, 1995. Source for *Captain Stormfield's Visit to Heaven* and "God of the Bible vs. God of the Present Day," by Mark Twain.

Baldanza, Frank. "The Structure of *Huckleberry Finn*." *American Literature* 27 (1955): 347-55; reprint in *Huck Finn and his Critics*: 371-78.

Barnes, Daniel R. "Twain's *The Adventures of Huckleberry Finn*. Chapter 1." *The Explicator* 13 (1965): Item 62.

Bassett, John Earl. "*Huckleberry Finn*: The End Lies in the Beginning." *American Literary Realism* 17 (1984): 89-98.

Bellamy, Gladys Carmen. *Mark Twain as a Literary Artist*. Norman: University of Oklahoma Press, 1950.

Bendixen, Alfred. "*Huck Finn* and *Pilgrim's Progress*." *Mark Twain Journal* 18 (1976-77): 21.

Bible. King James Version. Grand Rapids, MI: Zondervan, 1964.

Blair, Walter. *Mark Twain and Huck Finn*. Berkeley and Los Angeles: University of California Press, 1960.

Bloom, Harold. *The Anxiety of Influence*. New York: Oxford University Press, 1973.

Booth, Wayne C. *The Rhetoric of Fiction*. Chicago and London: University of Chicago Press, 1961.

Briden, Earl F. "Huck's Great Escape: Ritual and Magic." *Mark Twain Journal* 21 (1983): 17-18.

Brodwin, Stanley. "Mark Twain and the Fall of Man." *Dissertation Abstracts* 28 (1968): 5008-9A, Columbia University.

———. "Mark Twain's Masks of Satan: The Final Phase." *American Literature* 45 (1973): 206-27.

———. "The Theology of Mark Twain: Banished Adam and the Bible." *Mississippi Quarterly* 29 (1976): 167-89.

Bunyan, John. *The Pilgrim's Progress*. Springdale, PA: Whitaker House, 1973.

Burg, David. "Another View of *Huckleberry Finn*." *Nineteenth Century American Literature* 29 (1974): 299-319.

Campbell, Joseph. *The Masks of God: Occidental Mythology*, 4 vols. New York: Penguin, 1976.

Carrington, George. *The Dramatic Unity of Huckleberry Finn*. Columbus: Ohio State University Press, 1976.

Chadwick-Joshua, Jocelyn. *The Jim Dilemma: Reading Race in Huckleberry Finn*. Jackson: University Press of Mississippi, 1998.

Clemens, Samuel Langhorne [See also Twain, Mark]. *Adventures of Huckleberry Finn: A Norton Critical Edition*. Edited by Sculley Bradley, Richmond Croom Beatty, and E. Hudson Long. New York: Norton, 1962.

———. *A Connecticut Yankee in King Arthur's Court: A Norton Critical Edition*. Edited by Allison R. Ensor. New York: Norton, 1982.

———. Letter to Orion Clemens, 23 March 1878, http://www.marktwainproject.org/xtf/search?category=letters;rmode=landing_letters;style=mtp.

Collins, Billy G. "Huckleberry Finn: A Mississippi Moses." *The Journal of Narrative Technique* 5 (1976): 86-104.

Cox, James M. *Mark Twain: The Fate of Humor*. Princeton: Princeton University Press, 1962.

———. "Remarks on the Sad Initiation of Huckleberry Finn." *Sewanee Review* 62 (1954): 389-405.

Cross, Randy K. "*Huckleberry Finn*: The Sacred

and the Profane." *Mark Twain Journal* 21 (1983): 27–8.

DeVoto, Bernard. "Introduction" in *Adventures of Huckleberry Finn [Tom Sawyer's Companion]*. By Mark Twain, edited by Bernard DeVoto. Norwalk: Easton, 1942, ix-lxx.

Doyno, Victor A., ed. *Adventures of Huckleberry Finn: The Only Comprehensive Edition*. By Mark Twain, with "Foreword to the Text" (xiii-xvii) and "Textual Addendum" (365–418) by Doyno. New York: Random House, 1996.

_____. *Writing Huck Finn*. Philadelphia: University of Pennsylvania Press, 1991.

Eliot, T. S. "[An Introduction to *Huckleberry Finn*]" in *Adventures of Huckleberry Finn*. By Mark Twain, London: Cresset, 1950. Published in the U. S. by Chanticleer: New York, 1950, vii-xvi. Reprint in Clemens. *Adventures*, 320–27.

Ensor, Allison Rank. "Mark Twain and the Bible." *Dissertation Abstracts* 26 (1966): 6696–7A.

_____. *Mark Twain and the Bible*. Lexington: University of Kentucky Press, 1969.

Ferguson, De Lancey. "Huck Finn Aborning." *The Colophon* (Spring 1938): 171–80.

Fiedler, Leslie A. "Come Back to the Raft Ag'in, Huck Honey." In *An End to Innocence*. Boston: Beacon, 1955, 142–51.

_____. "*Huckleberry Finn*: The Book We Love to Hate." *Proteus* 1 (1984): 1–8.

_____. *No! In Thunder*. Boston: Beacon, 1960.

Gibson, William M. *The Art of Mark Twain*. New York: Oxford University Press, 1976.

Gribben, Alan. *Mark Twain's Library: A Reconstruction*, 2 vols. Boston: Hall, 1980.

_____. "Removing Mark Twain's Mask: A Decade of Criticism and Scholarship." *ESQ* 26 (1980): 100–08.

Harnesberger, C. T. *Mark Twain's Views of Religion*. Evanston, IL: Schori, 1961.

Hearn, Michael Patrick. "Introduction" and "Notes" in *The Annotated Huckleberry Finn*. By Mark Twain, edited by Michael Patrick Hearn. New York: Norton, 2001. "Introduction," xiii-clxv.

Hemingway, Ernest. *The Green Hills of Africa*. New York: Scribner, 1935.

Hoffman, Andrew. *Inventing Mark Twain: The Lives of Samuel Langhorne Clemens*. New York: William Morrow, 1997.

Howells, William Dean. *My Mark Twain*. New York and London: Harper & Bros., 1910.

Kaplan, Fred. *The Singular Mark Twain*. New York: Doubleday, 2003.

Kaplan, Justin. "Introduction." In *Adventures of Huckleberry Finn: The Only Comprehensive Edition*. By Mark Twain, edited by Victor A. Doyno. New York: Random House, 1996, i-xi.

_____. *Mr. Clemens and Mark Twain*. New York: Simon, 1966.

Kolb, Harold H., Jr. "Mark Twain, Huck Finn, and Jacob Blivens: Gilt-Edged, Tree-Calf Morality in The Adventures of Huckleberry Finn." *Virginia Quarterly Review* 55 (1979): 653–69.

Krutch, Joseph Wood. "[*Huckleberry Finn*: A Bad Novel]" from "Speaking of Books" in *The New York Times Book Review*, May 23, 1954, reprinted in Clemens. *Adventures*, 362–3.

Lettis, Richard, Robert F. McDonnell, and William E. Morris, eds. *Huck Finn and his Critics*. New York: Macmillan, 1962.

Levy, Andrew. *Huck Finn's America*. New York: Simon & Schuster, 2015.

Lindberg, John. "The Adventures of Huckleberry Finn as Moral Monologue." *Proteus: A Journal of Ideas* I (Fall 1984): 41–9.

Lynn, Kenneth. *Mark Twain and Southwestern Humor*. Boston: Little, 1960. Excerpts from Chapter 10. "You Can't Go Home Again," sections iii, vii, and viii, reprinted in Clemens. *Adventures*, 421–36.

Manierre, William R. "Huck Finn: Empiricist Member of Society." *Modern Fiction Studies* 14 (1968): 57–67.

Mark Twain's Notebooks and Journals, 2 vols. Edited by Frederick Anderson, Lin Salamo, and Bernard L. Stein. Untitled entry. Berkeley, Los Angeles, and London: University of California Press, 1975, vol. II, 493–95. Source of dialog quotations in Preface.

Marshall, W. G. "Twain's 'A Curious Dream' and *The Inferno*." *Mark Twain Journal* 21 (1983): 41–3.

Marx, Leo. "Mr. Eliot, Mr. Trilling, and *Huckleberry Finn*." *American Scholar* 22 (1953): 423–40.

Matthews, Brander. "Biographical Criticism." In *The Writings of Mark Twain: Author's National Edition*, 25 vols. New York: Harper and Brothers, 1899, vol. I, v-xxxiii.

McCullough, Joseph B. "The Uses of the Bible in *Huckleberry Finn*." *Mark Twain Journal* 19 (1978–79): 2–3.

McKay, Janet Holmgren. "An Art So High: Style in *Huckleberry Finn*." In *New Essays on Adventures of Huckleberry Finn*, edited by Louis J. Budd. Cambridge: Cambridge University Press, 1985, 61–81.

_____. "Going to Hell: Style in Huck Finn's Great Debate." *Interpretations* 13 (1981): 24–30.

_____. "Tears and Flapdoodle: Point of View and Style in *Adventures of Huckleberry Finn*." *Style* 10 (1976): 41–50.

Michelson, Bruce. "Huck and the Games of the World." *American Literary Realism* 13 (Spring 1980): 108–21.

Milton, John. *Paradise Lost*. In *John Milton: Complete Poems and Major Prose*, edited by Merritt Y. Hughes. New York: Odyssey, 1957, 173–469.

Moses, W. R. "The Pattern of Evil in *Adventures of Huckleberry Finn*." *Georgia Review* 13 (1959): 161–66, reprinted in Clemens. *Adventures*, 387–92.

Nielson, Vaneta. "The Savage Prophet, or, Who's Afraid of Samuel Twain?" *Publications of the Utah Academy of Sciences, Arts, and Letters* 43 (1967): 1–7.

Paine, Alfred Bigelow. *Mark Twain: A Biography*, 3 vols. New York and London: Harper & Brothers, 1912.

_____, ed. *Mark Twain's Letters: Arranged with Comment*, 2 vols. New York: Harper, 1924.

Powers, Ron. *Mark Twain: A Life*. New York: Free Press, 2005.

Quirk, Tom. "The Legend of Noah and the Voyage of Huckleberry Finn." *Mark Twain Journal* 21 (1982): 21–3.

Rogers, Franklin R. *Mark Twain's Burlesque Patterns as Seen in the Novels and Narratives, 1855–1885*. Dallas: Southern Methodist University Press, 1960.

Scharnhorst, Gary. "Paradise Revisited: Twain's 'The Man That Corrupted Hadleyburg.'" *Studies in Short Fiction* 18 (Winter 1981): 59–64.

Seelye, John. "The Craft of Laughter: Abominable Showmanship and Huckleberry Finn." *Thalia* 4 (Spring-Summer 1981): 19–25.

Selected Mark Twain–Howells Letters. Edited by Frederick Anderson, William M. Gibson, and Henry Nash Smith. New York: Atheneum, 1968.

Smiley, Jane. "Say It Ain't So, Huck: Second Thoughts on Mark Twain's 'Masterpiece.'" *Harper's Magazine* (January 1996): 61–7.

Smith, Henry Nash. "Foreword." In *Mark Twain's Library: A Reconstruction*. By Alan Gribben, i-xii.

_____. "Introduction." In *Adventures of Huckleberry Finn*. By Mark Twain. Boston: Houghton, 1958, v-xxix.

_____. *Mark Twain: The Development of a Writer*. Cambridge: Belknap, 1962.

Smith, Janet. Editorial commentaries in *Mark Twain on the Damned Human Race*. By Mark Twain, edited by Janet Smith. New York: Hill and Wang, 1962.

Taylor, Coley B. *Mark Twain's Margins on Thackeray's "Swift."* New York: Gotham House, 1935.

Tolkien, J. R. R. *The Return of the King*, 2d ed. Boston: Houghton Mifflin, 1993.

Trilling, Lionel. "Introduction." In *Adventures of Huckleberry Finn*. By Mark Twain. New York: Rinehart Editions, 1948; reprinted as "[An Introduction to *Huckleberry Finn*]" in *Huck Finn and his Critics*. New York: Macmillan, 1964, 326–36.

Twain, Mark [dee also Clemens, Samuel Langhorne.] *Adventures of Huckleberry Finn*. In *Adventures of Huckleberry Finn: The Only Comprehensive Edition*, edited with "Foreword" and "Textual Addendum" by Victor A. Doyno and "Introduction" by Justin Kaplan, New York: Random House, 1996.

_____. *Adventures of Huckleberry Finn: [Tom Sawyer's Companion]*. Edited with "Introduction" by Bernard DeVoto. Norwalk: Easton, 1980; source of first person chapter titles in Appendix A.

_____. *Adventures of Huckleberry Finn (Tom Sawyer's Comrade)*. In *The Annotated Huckleberry Finn*. Edited with Introduction and Notes by Michael Patrick Hearn. New York: Norton, 2001; citations of the first edition text and some MS citations are from this edition.

_____. *The Adventures of Tom Sawyer*. In *The Writings of Mark Twain*. Author's National Edition, 25 vols. New York: Harper and Brothers, 1899–1906, vol. XII.

_____. *The American Claimant*. In *The Writings of Mark Twain*. Author's National Edition, 25 vols. New York: Harper and Brothers, 1899–1906, vol. XXI.

_____. *Autobiography of Mark Twain*, Vol. I. Edited by Harriet Elinor Smith, et al. Berkeley, Los Angeles, and London: University of California Press, 2010.

_____. *The Autobiography of Mark Twain: Including Chapters Now Published For the First Time*. Arranged and edited, with an Introduction and Notes, by Charles Neider. New York: Harper & Bros., 1959.

_____. "Bible Teaching and Religious Practice." In *Europe and Elsewhere*. Edited by Alfred Bigelow Paine. New York and London: Harper & Bros., 1923.

_____. "Captain Stormfield's Visit to Heaven." In *The Bible According to Mark Twain*. Edited by Howard G. Baetzhold and Joseph B. McCullough. New York: Touchstone, 1996, 129–188.

_____. *Following the Equator*. Vol. II in *The Writings of Mark Twain*. Author's National Edition, 25 vols. New York: Harper and Brothers, 1899–1906, vol. VI.

———. ["God of the Bible vs. God of the Present Day (1870s),"] untitled essay in *The Bible According to Mark Twain*. Appendix 7, 314–17.

———. "Jane Lampton Clemens." In *Huck Finn and Tom Sawyer Among the Indians and Other Unfinished Stories*. Berkeley, Los Angeles, London: University of California Press, 1989, 82–92.

———. *King Leopold's Soliloquy*. New York: International, 1970.

———. Letter to Orion Clemens, 23 March 1878, by Samuel Clemens, http://www.Marktwainproject.org/xtf/search?category=letters;rmode=landing_letters;style=mtp.

———. *Letters from the Earth*. Edited by Bernard DeVoto. New York and Evanston: Harper & Row, 1962, 1–55; rpt. in *The Bible According to Mark Twain*, 213–60.

———. *Life on the Mississippi*. In *The Writings of Mark Twain*. Author's National Edition, 25 vols. New York: Harper and Brothers, 1899–1906, vol. IX.

———. "A Little Note to M. Paul Bourget." In *The Writings of Mark Twain*. Author's National Edition, 25 vols. New York: Harper and Brothers, 1899–1906, vol. XXII, 165–81.

———. *Mark Twain on the Damned Human Race*. Writings edited with commentary by Janet Smith. New York: Hill and Wang, 1962.

———. *Mark Twain's Notebooks and Journals*, 2 vols. Untitled entry, mid-June 1882. Edited by Frederick Anderson, Lin Salamo, and Bernard L. Stein. Berkeley, Los Angeles, and London: University of California Press, 1975, vol. II, 435.

———. "The Mysterious Stranger." In *The Mysterious Stranger and Other Stories*. New York: New American Library, 1962, 161–253.

———. *Personal Recollections of Joan of Arc*. In *The Writings of Mark Twain*. Author's National Edition, 25 vols., New York: Harper and Brothers, 1899–1906, vols. XVII and XVIII.

———. *The Prince and the Pauper*. In *The Writings of Mark Twain*. Author's National Edition, 25 vols. New York: Harper and Brothers, 1899–1906, vol. XV.

———. *Pudd'nhead Wilson*. In *The Writings of Mark Twain*. Author's National Edition, 25 vols. New York: Harper and Brothers, 1899–1906, vol. XIV.

———. "To the Person Sitting in Darkness." In *Mark Twain on the Damned Human Race*. Edited with an Introduction by Janet Smith. New York: Hill and Wang, 1962: 6–21.

———. *The War Prayer*. New York: Harper Colophon, 1970.

———. *The Writings of Mark Twain*. Author's National Edition, 25 vols., New York: Harper and Brothers, 1899–1906. [Citations of this edition are identified in the notes as *Writings*.]

Van O'Connor, William. "Why *Huckleberry Finn* Is Not the Great American Novel." *College English* 17 (1955): 6–10; reprinted in Clemens. *Adventures*, 371–78.

Wagenknecht, Edward. *Mark Twain: The Man and His Work*. New Haven: Yale University Press, 1935.

Wecter, Dixon. *Sam Clemens of Hannibal*. New York: Houghton, 1952, excerpts 106–9, 147–51, 187–89 reprinted in Clemens. *Adventures*, 257–65.

Welland, Dennis. *Mark Twain in England*. London: Chatto and Windus, 1978; excerpt ["Clemens, Chatto, and the English Edition"] in Clemens. *A Connecticut Yankee*, 313–18.

Werge, Thomas. "The Sin of Hypocrisy in 'The Man That Corrupted Hadleyburg' and *Inferno* XXIII." *Mark Twain Journal* 18 (1976): 17–18.

Yates, Norris W. "The 'Counter-Conversion' of Huckleberry Finn." *American Literature* 32 (1960): 1–10.

Zuckert, Catherine H. "Law and Nature in *Adventures of Huckleberry Finn*." *Proteus* 1 (1984): 27–35.

Index

Aaron (brother of Moses) 27, 70, 91, 92, 169, 172, 173, 177, 179, 182, 200, 201, 231; *see also* Levite; Leviticus; Tom Sawyer
Abel (brother of Cain) 26, 63, 64, 74, 109–11, 199, 229; *see also* Cain; feud
abolitionism 119, 219; *see also* racism; slavery
Abraham (biblical patriarch) 26, 74, 84, 88–90, 168, 182, 228–29; *see also* Genesis; Isaac; "only begotten son"; pap Finn, as Abraham
acts (compared to faith) 15, 70–1, 89, 98, 108, 130, 156, 185, 222, 227, 249; *see also* faith
Acts 17 (biblical) 6, 70, 183, 186; *see also* Aunt Sally; Uncle Silas
Adam (biblical) 26, 63, 74–8, 84–9, 92, 95–8, 104, 116, 152, 191, 206–7, 210, 217, 225, 228, 248, 261–62; *see also* American Adam
Adventures of Captain Simon Suggs 132, 149; *see also* camp meeting; "The Captain Attends a Camp Meeting"
The Adventures of Tom Sawyer 42, 193, 237; as literary burlesque 238–39; *see also* Tom Sawyer
African Americans 6, 17, 21, 22, 60, 87, 101, 112, 127, 135, 184, 198–9, 211–14, 217, 225, 246; enslavement 101, 112, 127, 184; humanity 6, 135, 184, 198–9, 211–14, 217, 225; *see also* bigotry; Jim; n-word; racism; slavery
Agag (biblical) 107–8; *see also* the feud as parable; Samuel (biblical)
Alighieri, Dante *see* *The Inferno*
allusion 5–6, 14, 18–21, 27, 29–30, 38, 41, 44, 48, 53, 55–6, 66–71, 73–4, 77, 89–91, 93, 100–1, 111, 113–14, 116, 120, 123–24, 126, 132, 142, 151–52, 160, 168, 170, 186–87, 190–91, 205, 210, 224, 228–29, 232, 236, 252, 254; ironic 120–21, 229; *see also* burlesque; conflation; echo; inversion; misprision; negation; parallel; parody; resonance
Alta California 238
Amalekites (biblical) 107–8; *see also* the feud; genocide; Samuel (biblical); Saul
American Adam 47, 95–7, 100, 116, 152, 217, 225
American Eden 26, 114, 152, 228, 230, 233
American Egypt 27, 114–15

American society 3, 5, 10, 14–18, 20, 22–3, 26, 28, 47, 52, 55, 59, 71, 77, 97, 108, 110, 113, 117–18, 120, 128–29, 155, 160, 192, 194–95, 199, 201, 207, 209, 217, 225–6, 235, 237, 241, 242–46, 249, 252–54
anarchy *see* Chaos
the Angel of Death 63, 65, 81, 83–94, 116, 152, 160–61, 259, 264; as "only begotten son" 87, 89, 174, 228; *see also* death; Passover; Satan
angle of view *see* point of view
animal 68, 88–90, 92, 115, 182, 237; *see also* Abel (biblical); beast; bestiality; hog motif
animal sacrifice 76, 88–90, 110, 187
anti-imperialism 57, 248–49; *see also* "The Blessings of Civilization Trust"; Twain, Mark, works by: "To the Person Sitting in Darkness," *The War Prayer*
anti-intellectualism 43, 49, 101, 113, 222, 249; Mark Twain as fomenter of 43, 209; *see also* primitivism
apostle 70, 71, 173, 183, 186, 201; *see also* Acts 17; Paul (biblical); Silas (biblical); Silas Phelps; Thomas (biblical); Tom Sawyer, as Thomas (biblical)
archetype 14, 21, 23, 25, 30, 36, 45, 48, 53–4, 57, 67, 78, 83, 85, 88, 96, 104, 109, 113, 120, 132, 138, 152, 155, 168, 195, 227, 229, 249; Judeo-Christian 78, 109, 113, 138, 152, 158, 168, 227, 229; literary 14, 21, 25, 36, 45, 48, 53, 57, 67, 85, 96, 120, 132, 155, 195; *see also* allusion; displacement, mythic; misprision; narrative structure (of *Huck Finn*); resonance
aristocracy 19, 20, 21, 64, 111, 112, 117, 118–19, 138, 140, 144, 231, 244, 245; *see also* democracy; rights; royalty; slavery
Ark of Noah 69–70, 74, 112, 141; *see also* "The House of Death"
art (literary) 2, 4, 7, 9–10, 13, 14–8, 20–1, 23–4, 30, 34, 36–8, 41, 43, 46–8, 50, 54–5, 74, 83, 108, 116, 120, 132, 145, 162, 168, 171, 175, 195, 207, 209, 226, 231, 240, 251–3; *see also* burlesque
atonement 58, 89; *see also* God of the Bible
atrocity 5, 91–2, 248; *see also* cruelty, of God

287

of the Bible; genocide; God of the Bible; punishment; sin, killing
Aunt Polly 42, 95
Aunt Sally 167, 183, 191, 194, 196, 198, 201; as jealous wife 184–5; *see also* Uncle Silas
THE AUTHOR 2, 9, 21, 25, 34, 35, 39, 41, 42–45, 48, 53–5, 88, 102, 108, 115–16, 132, 170, 175–80, 204–9, 227, 236, 253, 259; *see also* author, implied; "Explanatory"; "Notice"
author, implied 2–3, 25, 27, 30, 33, 36–42, 45–8, 50–2, 54–5, 58–9, 65, 76, 80, 88, 92, 94, 102–3, 115, 128, 146, 158–59, 174, 176, 178, 180–81, 185, 189, 196–97, 199, 201, 203–4, 227, 229–33; argument of 20, 55, 102, 119–20, 197, 229; *see also* THE AUTHOR; Mark Twain; narrator, implied, naïve; point of view
"Author of This Universe" (God of the Bible in Milton) 14, 27–8, 36, 48, 55, 59–60, 64, 66, 68, 92, 102, 112–13, 119–21, 139, 144, 147, 170–71, 178–81, 187–88, 190, 200, 202, 208, 227, 229, 232, 255; *see also* authority; god; God of the Bible; hog motif; "Notice"; universe
authority: literary 16, 17–8, 20, 24, 28, 30–1, 34, 37–9, 52, 54, 74, 119–21, 175–76, 187, 194, 200, 202, 205–8, 253–4, 259; moral 55, 63, 74, 113, 119–21, 137, 147, 178–81, 187, 190, 193, 227, 229; social 80, 102, 172, 181, 187, 193, 200, 202, 232; *see also* THE AUTHOR
autonomy: moral 30, 50, 128–29, 153, 161, 167, 170, 174, 208, as goal of Huck Finn's flight 30, 50, 128, 153, 161, 170, 174, 208; social 6–7, 17, 22, 112, 115, 118–19, 127, 153, 197–99; *see also* Doctrine of Total Depravity; Original Sin

beast 91–2, 124, 136, 144, 148, 153, 182, 183, 214; transformation of humans to 144, 148, 182–3; *see also* bestiality; hog motif; serpent motif
bestiality 125–26, 133, 136, 138, 149–51, 183, 190; *see also* beast, transformation of humans to; the brazen serpent
Bible 1, 3, 5–7, 14, 17, 21, 23, 25–31, 36, 38, 48–9, 53–8, 63–77, 89–93, 96–7, 100–4, 107–17, 120–21, 127, 134, 138–39, 141–42, 144, 149, 152, 155, 160, 168–69, 171–75, 178–80, 183, 186–88, 190, 192–93, 195, 197, 199–202, 205–11, 215, 217, 223, 227–33, 235–36, 238, 240, 248, 250–51, 253; Clemens' knowledge of 48; *see also* Bible-olatry; brazen serpent; the feud as parable; idolatry
Bible-olatry 114–15, 121, 142, 230; *see also* Bible; blasphemy; Boggs; the brazen serpent; camp meeting; God of the Bible; heresy; hog motif; idolatry
bigot 44, 53, 59, 69, 81, 101–2, 104–5, 184, 227; Huck as 44, 59, 101–2, 104–5, 227; *see also* aristocracy; mark of Cain; racism; slavery
blasphemy 4–5, 40, 115, 143, 149, 169, 181, 234; *see also* heresy
"The Blessings of Civilization Trust" 108; *see also* anti-imperialism; Twain, Mark, works by, "To the Person Sitting in Darkness," *The War Prayer*
blood 16, 27, 34, 64, 70, 74, 77, 90, 92, 107, 110–11, 119, 137–39, 186, 191, 199, 207, 232, 243; *see also* atrocity; death; the feud; killing; plague of death; war
Boggs 66, 71, 114–15, 137–38, 169, 215, 230; *see also* Bible; Bible-olatry; the brazen serpent; Bricksville; Sherburn
borrowing *see* stealing; sin, theft
the brazen serpent 66, 103, 114, 125, 132–4, 137–38, 152, 169, 188–90, 215, 229–30; *see also* Bible; Bible-olatry; idolatry; serpent motif
Bricksville 66–7, 71, 76, 115, 122, 131, 136, 138, 151, 161, 230; *see also* Bible-olatry; Boggs; lynch mob; Sherburn
Buck Grangerford 65, 106–7, 112, 122, 146; death of 107, 112, 122, 146; *see also* atrocities; Jonathan (biblical); murder
"bulrushers" 54, 71, 259
Bunyan, John *see Pilgrim's Progress*
burlesque 10, 18–9, 21, 25, 29–30, 32, 53–5, 57, 62–3, 65, 68–70, 74–5, 81, 84, 132, 139, 152, 155, 160, 168–69, 172, 174, 178, 180, 182, 188, 190–91, 193, 195, 199–202, 204–5, 209–10, 229–32, 237–241, 244, 247, 252–53, 264, 267; *see also* motif
burlesque Resurrection 69, 71, 172–74, 172, 200–1

Cain (biblical) 63, 74, 109–111, 199, 229; *see also* Abel (biblical); farmer; the feud; fugitive; Jim as bearer of mark of Cain
camp meeting 66–7, 95–6, 127, 131, 133, 135, 137, 151, 215, 230, 266; *see also Adventures of Captain Simon Suggs*; "The Captain Attends a Camp Meeting"; characterization of Huck Finn; hog motif; serpent motif
canoe 93–4, 96, 106, 128, 166, 224, 231
"The Captain Attends a Camp Meeting" 132
caricature 27, 74, 78, 88–9, 168, 229, 233, 244; of Abraham (biblical) 75, 84, 88–89, 168, 182, 228, 229; of God of the Bible 54, 65, 68, 74–9, 83–4, 88–9, 92, 116–17, 120–21, 136, 138, 143–44, 152, 155, 158, 168, 170–72, 178–79, 183, 201, 206–9, 227–28, 230–33, 235, 248, 250–51, 261–62; of Moses 26–7, 43, 53–4, 56–7, 59, 66, 68, 90–1, 111–16, 168, 172–73, 175–77, 179, 182, 190–91, 200–1, 226–29, 231–32, 259; of Noah 69–70, 74, 100, 142–43, 168–69, 228–29; *see also* comedy; Satan
Chaos 53, 81, 85, 92–4, 104, 116, 125, 127–28, 152, 154–55, 160–61, 166, 170–71, 174, 185, 194, 228, 231; as moral womb 91, 94, 98–9, 116, 123, 154, 161, 166, 170, 174, 194, 231; *see also* serpent motif
chapter titles 31, 34, 45, 54, 56–7, 61, 96, 104, 162, 187, 211, 216, 219, 239, 259–60; *see also* point of view

Index

characterization 10, 14, 19, 27, 30, 35–8, 43, 46, 48, 50, 54, 56, 71, 76, 78, 93, 99, 106, 116, 125, 128, 131, 137–38, 150, 151–52, 170, 193, 209–10, 212, 218, 240; of Clemens 36–8, 237; of the duke 131, 143, 161–62, 164; of Huck 10–12, 14, 26, 34–5, 42, 44, 46, 49, 52, 54, 61, 66, 70, 93, 109, 113, 116, 119, 128, 137, 141, 143–44, 150, 158–62, 165–67, 170, 172, 186, 190, 198, 202, 210–12, 216–18, 222, 225, 227, 251–52; of Jim 19–21, 30, 99–100, 105, 126, 161, 198, 210–12, 214, 216, 218, 221–22, 225, 227, 252; of the king 115, 125, 131, 141, 143–44, 149, 151, 161–62, 169–70; of Mark Twain 14, 24–5, 35, 37, 39, 43, 46–8, 53–4, 93, 236, 250; of pap Finn 54, 62, 69, 78, 80–1, 88, 116, 138, 161; of Tom Sawyer 47, 161, 172, 176, 192–93, 239; *see also* point of view

child 11, 13, 19, 22, 33–5, 43–6, 53, 55, 64, 67, 73, 89–92, 98, 100–1, 103, 109, 111–12, 114, 116, 130, 138, 160, 164, 174, 177, 184, 197, 203, 207, 210, 217, 220–21, 228, 231–32, 237–39, 243, 249, 262; David (biblical) as 26, 107, 116; God of the Bible and 43, 64, 67, 89–91, 98, 100–1, 103, 109, 111–12, 114, 116, 174, 177, 207, 220–1, 228, 231, 262; Isaac (biblical) as 26, 74, 84, 88–9, 92; Jesus as 84, 92, 116, 182, 228–29; Moses as 43, 57, 61, 74, 92, 112, 228; Solomon as 59, 101–3; *see also* Buck Grangerford; "only begotten son"; Passover; "plague of death" (biblical)

"children of Israel" *see* Israelites

Christ figure 48, 71, 81, 88–9, 116, 119, 139, 151–52, 160–61, 166, 170, 172–74, 180, 194, 197, 199–201, 210, 222, 225–26, 228–31, 233; *see also* Huck Finn, as Christ figure; Jim, as Christ figure

Christ motif *see* Abraham (biblical); atonement; burlesque Resurrection; Christ figure; Christianity; church; conversion; counter-conversion; Doctrine of Total Depravity; Established Church; Gethsemane; God of the Bible; hell (concept); Hell (place); Isaac (biblical); Huck Finn, as Christ figure; Jim, as Christ figure; salvation; serpent motif; Sunday school; the Temptation

Christian (protagonist of *Pilgrim's Progress*) 36, 53, 120–21, 155, 169; *see also* Huck Finn, compared to; *Pilgrim's Progress*

Christianity 3, 17, 23, 25, 28–9, 36, 38–40, 43, 48, 50, 52–5, 58–9, 63, 65, 67, 71, 73–4, 78, 81, 88–9, 92, 98, 102–3, 108, 111–12, 116–17, 119–21, 127, 131, 139, 149, 151–52, 154–55, 158, 160–61, 166, 169–170, 172–74, 180, 194, 197, 199–201, 204, 210, 222, 225–26, 228–31, 233, 237; *see also* church; cosmology; Doctrine of Total Depravity; Established Church; motif; religion; Sunday school; superstition

Church *see* Established Church

church 5, 36, 56, 61, 64–5, 71, 76, 100, 118, 136, 185, 229, 237, 241, 243, 247–8; *see also* camp-meeting, Christianity; Established Church; sty; worship service

Civil War 17, 51, 56–8, 115, 117, 119, 152, 199, 207, 217, 226, 249; *see also* blood; the feud; war

climax (of *Huck Finn*) 11–13, 26, 29, 35, 50, 54, 58, 71, 88, 123, 131, 134, 154–61, 174, 180, 189, 173, 200, 222, 231; *see also* Christ figure; "deformed conscience"; Huck Finn, "Great Debate" of; parody; "sound heart"

Columbus, Christopher 188; *see also* Tom Sawyer

comedy 12, 105, 123, 132, 199, 201, 209, 212, 244, 252; *see also* burlesque; caricature; humor; parody; satire; tragicomedy; wit

con artist 142, 161; *see also* the duke; Huckleberry Finn; Jim; the king; manipulation motif; Tom Sawyer; the Widow Douglas

conflation 30, 45, 47, 65, 78, 88–9, 108, 138, 150, 152, 158, 169, 181, 190; as cloak masking satire 30, 65, 78, 88–9, 138, 152, 158, 169, 190; *see also* allusion, ironic; misprision; negation

confrontations 26, 73, 75, 78–9, 84, 94, 104, 114, 122, 141, 150, 153, 161, 163, 165, 228, 231, 238, 247, 261

conscience 6, 10–11, 13, 15, 20, 26, 28–30, 36, 44, 48, 50–3, 58, 74, 77, 98, 101, 103, 106, 117, 119–20, 123, 128–31, 152–56, 158–60, 162, 167, 169, 175, 180, 195, 200–2, 214, 219, 229, 231–32, 248, 268; *see also* "deformed conscience"

conversion 11, 52, 54, 58, 62, 64, 81, 122, 130–31, 137, 154–57, 161, 165, 200, 231; *see also* climax; counter-conversion; fraud

cosmology 28, 38, 54–5, 59, 74, 79, 88, 92, 94, 175, 205, 225, 235; *see also* the Bible; god; God of the Bible

counter-conversion 52, 54, 58, 64, 155, 157, 165, 200, 231; *see also* climax

courting 238–39

creation (Clemens' process of) 2, 4, 7, 16, 18, 20–21, 28–9, 32, 34–38, 51, 66–7, 69, 84, 116, 120–21, 139, 141, 152, 168, 171, 178, 198–99, 208, 217, 223, 226, 238–40, 248, 250, 252–5; by God of the Bible 63, 71, 76, 79, 90, 92, 95–9, 104, 116, 186, 206–7, 228, 249, 268, 271; *see also* cosmology; "Notice"

creator 2, 34, 36–8, 67, 69, 76, 97, 104, 186, 198, 206–7, 250; *see also* THE AUTHOR; author, implied; god; God of the Bible; point of view

"cretur" (creature) 197; *see also* bestiality; n-word

crime 20, 66, 73, 76, 92, 108, 116, 124, 130, 189, 207, 224, 241, 248, 255; *see also* con artist; the duke; fraud; God of the Bible; the king; manipulation motif; pap Finn; sin; Tom Sawyer

criticism: archetypal 5, 14, 21, 23, 24, 25, 26, 27, 30, 36, 45, 48, 53, 54, 57, 62, 63, 67, 72, 76, 77, 78, 82, 83, 85, 88, 92, 94, 96, 104, 109,

113, 120, 132, 138, 151, 152, 153, 155, 158, 161, 168, 170, 172, 174, 180, 183, 189, 190, 195, 210, 215, 225, 227, 228, 229, 249, 253; biographical 5, 22, 24, 33, 39, 45–47, 138, 205, 214, 249; formalist 11, 13–15, 24, 107, 123, 226; genetic 16, 20, 24, 39, 45, 194; historical 2, 11, 15–16, 22, 24, 25, 38, 45, 47, 109, 121, 199, 213, 226, 232, 241, 243, 247, 252, 253; moralist 6, 9, 11–15, 17, 20–5, 27–30, 35–7, 41–3, 48–55, 57–8, 60, 62–3, 65–71, 74, 226; reader response 2, 16, 23, 33–4, 43, 80, 133, 145, 178, 198, 205; structural 5, 9, 10, 12, 14, 15, 17–8, 25–6, 28–30, 33, 38, 45–8, 53–6, 68, 74, 93, 106, 110, 112–13, 121, 124, 128, 132, 152, 154, 169–70, 178, 180, 188, 190, 205, 208–10, 213, 226, 231, 238–41, 261–5, 267–71; stylistic 9, 12, 20, 24, 32, 45–7, 52, 120, 130, 145–47, 158–60, 197, 203, 209, 253, 259, 267
criticism, schools of *see* criticism
the Cross (of Christ) 5, 62, 73, 78, 81, 133; *see also* Christ figure; Christianity; God of the Bible
cruelty 53, 58, 97, 104, 108–9, 206, 230, 237; of God of the Bible 97, 104, 108–9, 206
custody dispute 49, 59, 62, 102; resolved by Solomon (biblical) 49, 59, 102, 104–5

damnation 30–1, 43, 54–5, 64, 69, 121, 126, 130, 136, 152, 154, 156, 167, 205, 228, 233–34, 247, 249; *see also* death; hell (concept); Hell (place); sin, wages of
"the damned human race" 55, 152, 167, 234, 249; *see also* damnation
Dante Alighieri *see The Inferno*
"darkey" 10, 99, 215, 217, 220, 227; *see also* n-word
David (biblical) 26, 74, 101, 106–9, 115–16, 168, 200, 229; *see also* kings (biblical)
David Copperfield as source in *Tom Sawyer* 239; *see also* burlesque
death 11–12, 26, 34, 58, 63, 65, 69–70, 77, 81, 83–4, 86–92, 95, 97, 100, 105, 107–8, 112, 115–16, 126, 129–30, 138, 142, 152, 154, 160–1, 167, 173–74, 190, 206, 218–19, 228, 231, 235, 242–44, 247–48, 259, 264; *see also* damnation; deicide; filicide; genocide; homicide; infanticide; killing; murder; patricide; sin; suicide
Death (personified) *see* Angel of Death
defamiliarization (aka *Entfremdung*) 36, 41
"deformed conscience" 10, 20, 51, 101, 103, 230; *see also* conscience; heart vs. conscience; "sound heart"
deicide 26, 76–7, 92, 98, 116, 136, 174; *see also* death
deity 14, 27, 48, 60, 68–9, 74–7, 89, 112, 117, 119, 142, 192, 230–31, 251, 256; *see also* god; God of the Bible
delirium 1, 63, 75, 89, 107, 135–37, 145, 252, 254
the Deluge 26, 69, 70, 228; *see also* flood

democracy 5, 18, 20–1, 28, 63, 70, 117–18, 243, 245, 248; *see also* aristocracy
depravity 16, 59, 62, 76–7, 96–8, 106, 108, 122, 128, 131, 138, 153, 161, 163, 168, 189, 207–8, 227–28, 230, 247; *see also* atonement; Doctrine of Total Depravity
depravity doctrine *see* Doctrine of Total Depravity
devil 78–80, 85–6, 135, 141–42, 149, 162, 164, 166, 230, 235, 242, 247, 263, 267; *see also* Lucifer; Satan
displacement, mythic 24, 62, 70, 77, 92, 95, 104, 115, 155, 160, 166, 174, 194–95, 202, 225, 232, 252; *see also* Abel (biblical); American Adam; American Eden; American Egypt; Cain (biblical); Christ figure; God of the Bible; motif; ritual; Satan
divine right 127, 143, 230; *see also* aristocracy; rights; royalty; slavery
doctrine 45, 54, 119, 144, 186, 207, 214; *see also* bigotry; church; Doctrine of Total Depravity; racism; slavery
Doctrine of Total Depravity 96–8, 106, 138, 153, 168, 189, 207, 228; *see also* doctrine; God of the Bible; rattlesnake-skin; serpent motif
dog 98–9, 148, 151–52, 163, 191–92, 216; *see also* beast; bestiality; hog motif
drunkenness 34, 49, 62–3, 69–70, 81, 85, 90, 100, 122, 197, 211; *see also* pap Finn as exemplar of incontinence
the duke 18–9, 56, 65, 76, 114–15, 119, 122, 126, 128, 130, 132, 136, 138, 143–44, 148, 151, 161–65, 172, 177, 201, 211, 213, 219, 223–24, 230, 259, 266

earl 118, 244–5; *see also* aristocracy; democracy
echo 22, 27, 32, 108; as artistic repetition 32, 90, 92, 97–8, 106, 110, 129, 136, 149, 158, 164–66, 171–72, 179, 181–83, 188–89, 191–92, 195, 198, 201, 214, 232; *see also* allusion; history; repetition with variation; resonance
Eden 26, 30, 65, 76–9, 84–5, 95–9, 104, 114, 116–7, 136, 138, 152, 165, 189, 205–6, 210, 224, 228–29, 233, 262, 268; *see also* American Adam; American Eden/Egypt; Eve; "Notice"
Eden motif *see* Adam; American Adam; American Eden; cruelty of God of the Bible; Doctrine of Total Depravity; Eden; Eve; expulsion from Eden; God of the Bible; Huck Finn, as Adam, as Christ figure, as Eve, as Satan, as serpent; Jim, as Adam; as Eve; pap Finn, as caricature of God of the Bible; as caricature of Satan; rattlesnake-skin (curse); St. Petersburg as American Eden/Egypt; Satan; serpent motif; snake; the Temptation
Egypt 14, 27, 65, 77, 90–2, 112–4, 126, 153, 172, 179–80, 199–200, 205, 210, 226, 230
emancipation *see* manumission
Emancipation Proclamation 17, 103, 119, 192, 198, 231–32; *see also* 13th Amendment

escape (from pap Finn) 10, 18, 49, 64, 70, 76, 85, 90, 92–3, 98, 112, 114, 116, 128, 139, 141, 147–48, 153–54, 161–62, 166–67, 170, 179–80, 182, 184, 188–93, 195, 198–200, 204, 206, 218–19, 224, 226, 228, 232–33; *see also* Chaos

Established Church 118, 241, 247

ethnic cleansing *see* atrocities; genocide

the evasion 10–12, 18, 21, 26–7, 30, 32, 50, 52, 54–5, 71, 77, 119, 153, 170, 183, 188, 194, 201, 204, 216, 225, 231–33; as parody of Huck's flight 19, 28, 32, 182, 188–93, 200–201, 205; as religious satire 18, 26–28, 54–5, 77, 119, 153, 170–92, 196, 199–201, 232–33; as social satire 11, 18, 26, 192, 197–200, 231–33; *see also* serpent motif

Eve (biblical) 76, 84–5, 95–9, 116, 191, 206, 228, 261; *see also* Huck Finn, as Eve; Jim, as Eve

evil 6, 51, 99, 101, 103, 122, 127, 143–44, 153, 158, 169, 188, 212, 247, 249, 256, 271; racism as 6, 99, 212; *see also* sin

Exodus (biblical book) 14, 26–7, 30, 48, 55–7, 64, 66, 68, 70–1, 77, 90, 92, 111–13, 121, 160, 168, 172, 177, 179, 182, 187–88, 201, 229, 232; evasion as burlesque of 177–80

"Explanatory" 2, 9, 25, 34, 39, 41, 45, 227; *see also* THE AUTHOR; "Notice"; point of view

expulsion from Eden 76, 84, 261–62

faith 1, 13, 23, 31, 52, 64–5, 67–8, 71, 96, 108–9, 127, 139, 142, 144, 147, 169, 173, 205, 210, 227, 229; *see also* acts; religion

the Fall (biblical) 26, 74, 76, 78, 84, 97–8, 104, 189, 206–7, 228; *see also* Doctrine of Total Depravity; "Notice"; serpent motif

farmer 64, 110–11, 165, 184–86; *see also* Abel; Cain; the feud; Grangerford; range wars; Shepherdsons

father-son motif *see* God of the Bible, Adam, Christ; Jim, Huck; the king—the duke; Noah—Ham, Japheth, Shem; pap Finn—Huck Finn; pap Finn—the king—Tom Sawyer; Satan—the Angel of Death; Saul (biblical)—Jonathan and older brothers (biblical); Saul Grangerford—Buck Grangerford and older brothers

the feud 64–5, 71, 106–11, 115, 122, 127–28, 131, 169, 189, 199, 223, 229; biblical analogs of 107, 109–13; and Civil War 119, 199–200; as exemplar of violence in *Inferno* motif 115, 122, 131, 223; as parable 107; *see also* murder; sin; war

feudalism 241–43

filicide 89; *see also* death

"firewall of irony" 7, 43, 49, 59, 140, 143, 145, 170; *see also* point of view

first born (cruelty of God of the Bible toward) 89–91, 92, 112, 161, 170; *see also* "only begotten son"

flight to Egypt (of child Jesus) *see* Moses

flight to freedom 10–11, 32, 99, 106, 128, 178, 208, 219–20, 232; *see also* autonomy (moral) as goal of Huck's flight; Jim, as fugitive slave; narrative

the floating house *see* "The House of Death"

the Flood *see* The Deluge

flood (on Jackson's Island) 69, 100, 217; and the Deluge 69, 100, 228

foreordination 229; *see also* predestination; preforeordestination

forty (number motif) 81, 134, 148, 151, 162–63, 192, 225–26, 267

fraud 7, 26, 34, 62, 65–6, 68–9, 73, 115, 119, 122–26, 130–31, 137–38, 141–44, 148–51, 154, 161–63, 165, 169, 172, 182, 189, 204, 225, 230; *see also* con artist; the duke; Fraud; the king; sin; Tom Sawyer

Fraud (Geryon in *Inferno*) 26, 122, 125–26, 131, 151, 230

freedom 6, 10–11, 13–14, 32, 57, 64–5, 82, 90, 95, 99, 106, 114, 128–9, 148, 153–54, 157, 167, 175, 178, 187, 195, 199, 208, 211–14, 218–21, 232, 235–36, 241, 246, 267; artistic 2, 175; *see also* autonomy

friendship 2, 6, 9, 16, 26, 51, 57, 74, 95, 106–8, 122, 129, 130, 143, 153–54, 157, 172, 176, 180, 189, 202, 210, 212–14, 220, 222–23, 245, 256–57, 265, 270; *see also* Huck Finn, as racist

fugitive 10, 65, 97–8, 104, 106, 121, 129, 153, 155, 164, 200, 208, 213, 219, 223–24, 226; slave 6, 19, 69, 104, 110, 127–29, 153, 165, 200, 208, 210, 212–13, 216, 219, 222–24, 226; *see also* Huck Finn, as fugitive; *Pilgrim's Progress*

fundamentalism 5, 23, 228, 235, 238, 254; *see also* delirium

funeral (of Peter Wilks) 144, 147; *see also* mourning

garter snakes 189, 191; *see also* serpent motif

Genesis (biblical book) 48, 63, 69, 74–6, 78, 84, 88, 92, 98, 104, 110, 115, 168, 206–8, 261; *see also* Abel; Abraham; Bible; Cain; Exodus (biblical book); God of the Bible; Isaac (biblical); Leviticus (biblical book); New Testament; Old Testament; pap Finn, as caricature of God of the Bible; serpent motif

genocide 65, 108; *see also* atrocities; crime; death; sin, killing, murder

Geryon *see* Fraud

Gethsemane 154; *see also* climax

the Gilded Age 22, 77, 114, 178, 183, 245; idolatry in 114, 126, 148, 170, 230; *see also* Tom Sawyer, as God of the Gilded Age

Gilgal (biblical place name) 107–8; *see also* atrocities; crime; *delirium*; genocide; murder

giraffe ("giraffft") 149; *see also* beast; bestiality; the king, as bestial

god 31, 126, 149, 164, 183, 230–31, 233, 250–51, 256; THE AUTHOR as 208; Clemens' conception of 6, 31, 77, 84, 98, 250–51, 254–56; "De Lord God Amighty" 140, 150, 170; of the Gilded Age 178, 183, 196; "of the Present Day" 195, 235, 250–51; The Unknown (Acts 17) 183, 186; *see also* atrocities; crime; death; genocide; God of the Bible

God of the Bible 1, 6–7, 26, 30–1, 50, 54–5, 57, 59, 64–5, 67–8, 70, 75–9, 82–5, 88–93, 96, 98, 193, 107–8, 110, 112, 116–17, 120–21, 123, 127, 136–38, 142–44, 149, 152, 154–56, 158, 161, 168, 170–73, 175, 178–80, 186, 201, 206–7, 209, 217, 227–28, 230–31, 233, 235, 247–48, 250–51, 256, 261–62; as Author 92, 207; characterization of God of the Bible 27, 48, 54, 57, 76, 78, 108, 127, 250; *see also* hell (concept); Hell (place); hog, as symbol of God of the Bible; pap Finn, as caricature of; Tom Sawyer; the Trinity

gold 77, 82, 90, 114, 148, 162, 164, 179, 207, 247, 260; as idol 114, 126, 148, 170, 230

Grangerford clan 61, 64–65, 76, 106–7, 109–12, 115–16, 119, 122, 136, 146, 161, 169, 195, 199, 223–24, 229, 259; significance of name 64, 111; *see also* the feud; Rachel (biblical); Saul (biblical); Shepherdson clan

greed 34, 58, 83, 148–49, 207, 248; *see also* sin

grief *see* mourning

Hamlet 20, 169; as source for Huck's dilemma 20, 232; *see also* King Lear; Macbeth; Romeo and Juliet

Hank Morgan (protagonist of *A Connecticut Yankee*) 241–44, 252; *see also* Twain, Mark, works by: *A Connecticut Yankee in King Arthur's Court*

harem 101, 184; *see also* polygamy; rape; slaveholders; slavery; Solomon; Uncle Silas; Young, Brigham

heart vs. conscience 119–20, 180; *see also* criticism, schools of; "deformed conscience"; criticism, moralist; "sound heart"

Hebrews (Israelites) 14, 26–7, 77, 90–1, 107, 111–12, 113, 115, 142, 153, 142, 149, 172–73, 177, 179–83, 192, 199–200, 210, 226; *see also* Israelites; Moses

heifer 144, 146; *see also* bestiality; blasphemy; heresy; revisions

hell 6, 12, 46, 50, 52, 58, 74, 79, 83–6, 109, 113, 115, 120–23, 130, 132, 135–36, 154–61, 171, 174, 176, 180, 189, 194, 207, 214, 222, 230, 232–33, 240, 252, 270–71; *see also* damnation; death; Hell (place); sin

Hell (place name in Dante and Milton) 26, 54, 62–63, 65, 79, 84–5, 87–8, 93–4; Huck's tour of 111, 115, 121–27, 131–32, 136, 154–58, 161, 171, 174, 189, 194, 223, 225, 227, 228–31, 263–64, 267–70; *see also* hell (concept); serpent motif

Hemingway, Ernest 199, 209, 215, 253; *see also* anti-intellectualism; primitivism

herders *see* shepherds

heresy 40, 54; *see also* blasphemy; revisions by Clemens to manuscript

hero 10–11, 15, 19–21, 25, 30, 35, 51, 53, 80, 88, 92, 101, 120, 147, 158, 175, 196, 198, 202, 210, 214, 217–18, 244; *see also* Huck Finn, as hero; Jim, as hero

history 23–4, 47, 71, 74, 119, 138, 140, 193, 197–99, 202, 207, 232, 243, 256; cyclical nature of 23, 188, 195, 199, 202, 232; *see also* echo; criticism, historical; progress

hog 5, 58, 64–5, 68, 76–7, 82, 89, 92, 136, 138, 142, 144, 149–51, 164, 191, 200, 202, 227, 230, 254, 271; as symbol of God of the Bible 76–7, 82, 92; *see also* beast, transformation of humans to; bestiality; hog motif

hog motif 136; *see also* beast, transformation of humans to; bestiality; hog, as symbol of God of the Bible; Huck Finn, ritual deicide/patricide/suicide of; the king, as bestial; pap Finn, as hog, as serpent

hog-god/devil 149; pap Finn as 149; *see also* the king, as bestial

"holy ordinance of servitude" 7, 60, 112; *see also* servitude; slavery

Holy Writ *see* Bible

homicide 89, 114; *see also* death

L'Homme Qui Rit (*The Man Who Laughs*) 239; *see also* Twain, Mark, works by: *The Prince and the Pauper*

homosexuality 99

honor 5, 19, 27, 63, 74, 77, 92, 111, 179, 201, 207, 210, 235

Hooper, Johnson Jones *see Adventures of Captain Simon Suggs*; camp meeting; "The Captain Attends a Camp Meeting"

"House of Death" (floating house) 48, 69, 80, 100, 176, 259

Howells, William Dean 2, 9, 26, 78, 84, 178, 240, 247

Huck Finn: archetypal and real identity shifts of—as Adam 26, 30, 74–6, 78, 84–5, 88, 92, 95–6, 96–100, 104, 116, 123, 139, 152, 155, 161, 166, 172, 174, 180–81, 191, 197, 226, 228, 230–31, 233, 261–62, 265; as adult 14, 88, 153, 158, 167, 197, 210–11, 231; as Angel of Death 63, 81, 83–4, 86–92, 94, 116, 152, 160–61, 174, 228, 259, 264; as anti-pilgrim 25, 28–9, 36, 38, 59, 116, 120–21, 128, 152, 231, 241; as brother to Jim 69–70, 97, 100, 153, 228; as child 11, 13, 22, 33–5, 43–4, 46, 52–3, 55, 73, 89, 92, 98, 100, 105, 109, 114, 116, 130, 138, 160, 164, 174, 197, 203, 228, 231–32; as Christ figure 63, 71, 74, 88–9, 116, 119, 138, 152, 154, 160–61, 166, 170, 172–74, 180, 197, 200–1, 226, 228, 231, 233; as Dante 26, 48, 54, 62, 74, 84, 115, 121–28, 131, 151–52, 169, 209, 223, 225, 229–31; as David (biblical) 26, 74, 106–9, 115–16, 168, 200, 229; as Eve 76, 85, 96–9, 104, 116, 191, 228; gender shifts of 162, 191; as Hamlet 20, 169, 232; as hero 10–11, 15, 20, 30, 35, 51, 88, 101, 120, 147, 158, 196, 202, 218;

Index

as idiot 33, 35, 35–6, 43, 253; as Isaac (biblical) 26, 74, 84, 88–90, 92, 116, 174, 182, 228, 229; as Japheth (biblical) 69–70, 116, 228; as Moses 14, 26–7, 43, 53–4, 56–9, 61, 63, 65, 68, 70, 74, 90, 92, 111–16, 172–74, 177, 179, 182, 190, 197, 200–1, 226–28, 231–32, 236, 259; as naïve narrator 3, 6, 29, 36, 37–8, 40–3, 45–6, 54, 110, 114, 137, 144, 146–47, 158–59, 175–76, 180, 192, 201, 204, 212, 217, 236–37, 252; as object of custody dispute 49, 59, 62, 102, 104, 219; as racist 6–7, 21, 45, 59–60, 104–5, 189, 197–98, 211–14, 217, 220, 228; as realist 2, 30, 34–5, 49, 50–1, 60–1, 63, 92–3, 38, 45–6, 105, 119, 140–41, 143, 152, 166–67, 180, 191–92, 197, 200, 202, 212, 214, 232; as Satan 26, 30, 54, 103, 123, 132, 139, 152–61, 165–66, 170–72, 174–75, 180–81, 194, 197, 231, 233, 267–71; as serpent 189, 223; as Solomon (biblical) 26, 59, 63, 100–1, 103, 106, 109, 116, 339, 239; as son of Jim 20–1, 30, 57, 102, 105, 127, 153, 164, 194, 210–11, 223, 251; *see also* characterization of Huck Finn

Hugo (character in *The Prince and the Pauper*) 240

Hugo, Victor *see L'Homme Qui Rit*

human being 1, 5–7, 12–15, 19–20, 31, 34, 55–6, 59, 65–6, 68–70, 77, 79, 92, 97–8, 101–2, 108, 112, 118–19, 122, 135, 139–40, 144, 148, 150, 152–53, 162, 167, 174, 180, 184–87, 190, 198, 199, 201, 203, 206, 211–14, 216–17, 219, 222, 225, 227, 234, 235, 238, 241, 244, 247–54

humanity (of African Americans) 6, 12, 15, 19, 56, 66, 69–70, 97, 102, 112, 118, 135, 153, 184–87, 198, 201, 203, 211–14, 216–17, 219, 222, 225, 251, 253, 254; *see also* n-word

humor 3, 12, 34–5, 37, 43–5, 53–4, 57, 60–2, 65, 81, 96, 101–2, 132, 137, 140–42, 145, 169, 176, 185, 200, 203, 205, 207–9, 233, 236, 238–40, 250, 252–53; Mark Twain on 252; *see also* comedy; narrator, naïve

"hussy" 184–85; *see also* n-word

hypocrisy 34, 53, 55, 58–9, 64, 113, 122, 140, 144, 147, 150, 184, 187, 200–1, 227, 231, 237, 245, 249; *see also* sin, Uncle Silas

idealism 52, 117
ideology 20, 42, 120, 226
idolatry 114, 126, 148, 170, 250; *see also* Bible-olatry
imperialism *see* anti-imperialism
incontinence (category of sin in Dante) 26, 84, 122, 124, 131; *see also* sin
infanticide 89; *see also* death; sin
The Inferno 26, 28–9, 38, 62, 74, 111, 117, 121–27, 130, 151–52, 166, 170, 209–10, 223, 230–31; as source for *Huckleberry Finn* 121–27
Inferno motif *see* camp meeting; climax; counter-conversion; damnation; devil(s); drunkenness; the duke; as exemplar of violence; the feud, the God of the Bible; Huck Finn, as Dante, as Satan/Lucifer; idolatry; Jim, as Virgil; the king, as demon Geryon (Fraud), as bestial, as devil, as exemplar of Fraud, as heir to pap Finn, as Judas figure, as Noah, as "old Leviticus," punishment of the Inquisition 247; *see also* Established Church

intention, authorial 1, 7, 9, 18, 20, 24, 28, 30, 70, 97, 109, 113, 116, 120, 123, 127, 145, 151, 161, 176, 179, 193–94, 197, 203–9, 231, 232–33; *see also* THE AUTHOR; author, implied

intrusion, authorial 24, 33–5, 38, 41–3, 46, 143–44, 158–60, 208; *see also* author, implied; narrator; point of view; criticism, stylistic

inversion 20, 54, 69, 120, 154, 185, 205, 230; *see also* allusion, ironic; conflation; negation

irony *see* firewall of irony

Isaac (biblical) 26, 74, 84, 88–9, 92, 116, 174, 182, 228–29; precursor of Christ's crucifixion 84, 89, 116, 182, 228–29; *see also* animal sacrifice; hog motif; Huck Finn, as Isaac figure; ram

Israelites 14, 26, 77, 90–1, 107, 112, 115, 142, 153, 172–73, 177, 179–80, 182, 192, 199, 210; *see also* Hebrews

Jackson's Island 25, 56, 94–9, 104, 116, 166, 189, 191, 215–16, 225, 228–29, 261, 265; as Eden 95–9, 104; as setting of Deluge 69–70

Jesus 67, 71, 84, 173–74, 200, 225, 256; as child 92; *see also* Christ; Savior

Jim: as Adam 96 7, 99, 104, 116, 191, 199, 210, 217, 225–6, 230; as bearer of mark of Cain 110; as brother to Huck 69–70, 97, 100, 153, 225, 228; as Christ figure 187, 199, 210–11, 222, 225–26; as "darkey" 10, 99, 215, 217, 220, 227 as developing character 19, 21, 30, 99, 105, 106, 126–29, 170, 198–99, 210–27; as Eve 95–6, 99; as exemplar of nobility 19–21, 30, 210; as father figure, as friend to Huck 129, 153–54, 157, 210, 213, 215, 221–22; as hero 210, 217; as King Lear 19; as prisoner representative of freed slaves after Reconstruction 11, 17, 26–7, 53, 59, 102, 197–9; as representative of Hebrews captive in Egypt 14, 26, 153, 192, 199, 210; as Shem, son of Noah 69–70, 210, 228; as slave 17, 27, 64, 70, 79, 96, 99, 100–6, 112, 115, 118–19, 127, 129, 153–54, 181, 184, 186–87, 192, 197–99, 208, 212–18, 221–24, 227; as Virgil (Dante's guide) 122, 125–27; *see also* Miss Watson; serpent motif

Jonathan (biblical) 26, 74, 106–8, 200, 229; *see also* Buck Grangerford

Joshua (biblical) 183; *see also* ram

Judas (biblical) 151–52, 225; the king as, figure

Judith Loftus 80, 144, 162

juvenile courtship 238–39; *see also* courting

killing 3, 7, 63, 76, 80, 86–92, 94, 96, 99, 107, 110, 114, 124, 129, 137–38, 162, 198–99, 219, 228, 239, 255, 264; *see also* death; sin
the king 19–20, 44, 56, 62, 65, 68, 76, 113–15, 119, 122–28, 130–32, 137–38, 141–51, 161–66, 169–73, 179, 182–83, 189, 201, 211, 224–25, 230, 260, 266; as bestial 20, 76, 114, 124–26, 130, 141, 149, 151, 169, 189, 230; as demon Geryon (Fraud) 124–26; as devil 230; as exemplar of Fraud 26, 65–6, 68, 119, 122–23, 125–26, 131, 142; as heir to pap Finn 62, 65–6, 68, 76, 113, 114–15, 119, 122–27, 131–32, 137–38, 141–49, 151–52, 161–62, 165–66, 169–70, 172, 179, 182–83, 224–25, 230; as Judas figure 151–52, 225; as monarch 144, 230; as Noah 141–42; as "old Leviticus" 141–43, 182; as pap Finn's priest 230; punishment of 126; *see also* aristocracy; bestiality; con artist; devil; the duke; fraud; Fraud (demon Geryon); hog motif; Levite; Lucifer; manipulation motif; The Royal Nonesuch; serpent motif; sin, punishment of
King Lear 18–20, 169; *see also Hamlet*; Jim, as King Lear; *Macbeth*; *Romeo and Juliet*
kings (biblical) *see* David; Saul; Solomon
The King's Camelopard *see* The Royal Nonesuch
"the king's speech" 145–48, 170; *see also* characterization, of Huck Finn

Levite (priest of Israel) 142, 182; the king as 143, 169, 172; Tom Sawyer as 172, 182; *see also* Aaron (biblical); "old Leviticus"
Leviticus (biblical book) 141–2; *see also* the king, as "old Leviticus"; Tom Sawyer, as Aaron (biblical)
"light out" 12, 27, 52, 58, 115, 153, 195, 197, 200, 231, 260; as allusion to Lucifer/Satan 52, 115, 153, 195, 197, 199, 231
literary archetype (source text) *see* criticism, archetypal
log cabin 49, 81–2, 85, 90, 141, 162, 186, 189–91, 196, 212
loyalty 20, 123, 129, 150, 153, 168, 210–12, 222–23; *see also* friendship
Lucifer 151, 197, 225, 231, 256; *see also* Satan, Huck as
luck 94, 96–8, 106, 127, 189, 229; as analog of Doctrine of Total Depravity 96–8, 106, 189; *see also* serpent motif
lying 3, 11, 42, 57, 61, 82, 122, 150, 157, 163–64, 177, 194, 198, 213–14, 216, 231, 255; *see also* sin
lynch mob 46, 138–39; *see also* Sherburn

Macbeth 169; *see also Hamlet*; *King Lear*; *Romeo and Juliet*
Malory, Sir Thomas *see Le Mort D'Arthur*
manipulation motif 148, 161–66, 221; *see also* motif
manumission 129–30, 161, 169, 190; of Jim 129–30, 161, 169, 190; *see also* holy ordinance of servitude
manuscript of *Huckleberry Finn* 16–17, 21, 29–31, 34, 62, 66, 83–4, 99–100, 104–6, 115, 130–37, 140–41, 143–45, 147–51, 160, 167, 169, 171, 181, 187–89, 194, 198, 208, 213, 240, 266; characterization of Huck in 30, 137, 141, 143–44, 158–60, 170
mark of Cain 110, 210; *see also* Abel; Cain; the feud; Jim as bearer of; murder
Mark Twain as fictional character 2, 10, 24–5, 28, 30, 34–5, 36–44, 47–48, 50, 53–4, 58, 60, 65, 88, 102–3, 155, 160, 174–75, 177, 178, 181, 193–94, 201, 215, 227, 232–33, 235; *see also* narrator, implied; point of view; Twain, Mark, works by
Mars 183; Tom Sawyer as, 183, 212, 226; *see also* Acts 17; Mars' Hill; Tom Sawyer, as God of the Gilded Age
Mars' Hill (setting of Acts 17) 183
Mary Jane Wilks 143, 150–51, 162–63, 170, 213; as Beatrice (in Dante) 170
Master (Tom Sawyer) *see* Mars
Matthews, Brander 5, 53; *see also* criticism, biographical
meritocracy 118
Milton, John *see Paradise Lost*
ministry *see* Levite
minstrel show 10, 101, 211; *see also* Jim, as "darkey"; n-word
misprision 74, 120, 152; *see also* allusion, ironic; conflation; negation
Miss Watson 36, 39–41, 43, 60–1, 63, 71, 96, 102–3, 128–130, 157, 169, 177, 190, 215–16, 218, 223, 251, 259; *see also* conscience; manumission; Providence
"Mississippi Moses" 53, 68, 111, 236; *see also* author, implied, argument of; narrator, implied, argument of
Mississippi River 3, 25, 40, 65, 70, 77, 79–81, 94–8, 100, 104, 112, 116, 122, 126–28, 130, 134, 152, 161, 165–66, 169, 171, 177, 180, 196, 215, 220, 228, 230; as Chaos 81, 92–4, 98–9, 116, 123, 127–28, 152, 154–55, 160–61, 166, 170–71, 174, 194, 228, 231; as deity 251–2; *see also* Chaos
monarch 82, 104, 144, 230, 241–43; *see also* aristocracy; as exemplar of aristocracy; the king, as exemplar of fraud, as monarch; kings; the Throne (of biblical Monarch); right, divine
money *see* gold
"moral" (of *Huckleberry Finn*) 2, 6, 9, 11–15, 17, 20–25, 27–30, 38, 41, 48–55, 70, 77, 88, 98, 128, 132, 138, 144, 152–55, 158, 160–61, 168, 171, 174, 180–81, 193–95, 198, 200–2, 203–9, 212, 225–27, 232, 241; *see also* motif; "motive"; "Notice"; "plot"
moral authority *see* authority
moral autonomy *see* autonomy
moral pilgrimage 241; *see also Pilgrim's*

Index

Progress; Twain, Mark, works by: *A Connecticut Yankee in King Arthur's Court*; *The Prince and the Pauper*

Le Morte D'Arthur 241, 244; *see also* Twain, Mark, works by: *A Connecticut Yankee in King Arthur's Court*

Moses (biblical) 14, 26-7, 43, 53-4, 56-70, 74, 77, 90-2, 103, 106, 111-16, 168, 172-83, 190, 197, 201, 226-32, 236, 259; as adult 197; as child 43, 74, 112, 228; as fugitive 114

Moses motif *see* Aaron; American Egypt; Angel of Death; the brazen serpent; "bulrushers"; cruelty, of God of the Bible; Egypt; Exodus; the feud; first born; forty (number motif); Grangerford clan; Hebrews; "holy ordinance of servitude"; Huck Finn, as Moses; Israelites; Jim, as representative of Hebrews captive in Egypt; the king, as Levite, as "old Leviticus," as pap Finn's priest; Levite; Moses; Passover; pharaoh; Promised Land; slavery; Tom Sawyer, as Aaron (biblical), as God of the Gilded Age, as heir to pap Finn, as "his Grandfather's ram," as Levite; "torchlight procession"; the Widow Douglas, as pharaoh's daughter; "wonders"

motif *see* Christ; Eden; father-son; forty (number motif); hog; *Inferno*; manipulation; Moses; Noah; *Paradise Lost*; rebirth; serpen; three (number motif); twins

"motive" (of *Huckleberry Finn*) 18, 21, 25, 41, 50, 158, 194, 204-6; *see also* "moral"; "Notice"; "plot"

Mount Nephates 30, 155; *see also* climax; Lucifer; Satan

mourning 19, 107, 111, 146, 234

murder 34, 63-4, 71, 73, 80, 88-91, 95, 109, 115, 122-24, 129, 138-39, 161-62, 173, 188, 190, 192, 215, 218, 228, 239, 250; *see also* Abel (biblical); Boggs; Buck Grangerford; Cain (biblical); death; God of the Bible; Grangerford clan; Jim, as Huck's murderer; killing; Miss Watson, conscience of, guilt of; pap Finn, as victim; Shepherdson clan

myth 14, 24, 26, 29, 37-8, 47, 54-5, 59, 62, 70-1, 74, 77, 80, 84, 91-4, 95-9, 109-10, 115-19, 129, 136, 152, 155, 160, 166, 172-74, 177, 180, 183, 195, 197-99, 202, 206, 225-235, 249, 252; *see also* allusion, ironic; American Adam; American Eden; American Egypt; criticism, archetypal; archetype; Bible; displacement, mythic; Promised Land; ritual

narrative (of slave's flight to freedom) 208, 212, 232; *see also* flight to freedom

narrative structure 43, 53-7, 60, 62, 67-8, 77, 89, 93, 100-2, 123, 127, 132, 152, 155, 158, 169-70, 172, 175-76, 180, 201, 205-9, 227, 231-33, 250, 251, 253; *see also* allusion, ironic; burlesque; echo; misprision; negation; resonance

narrator: implied—25, 29, 36-8, 40-3, 45-55, 57-9, 63, 65, 80, 93, 102, 113, 115, 154, 158, 159, 174, 176-78, 180-81, 190, 194, 201, 204, 227, 231-32, 241, argument of 52, 102, 113, 175, 201; naïve 3, 34, 38, 45, 99, 145, 227; reliability of 3, 37, 42-5, 99, 227, 259; *see also see also* author, implied; Huck Finn, as naïve narrator; narrator, implied; Mark Twain; point of view view

negation 12, 19, 30, 60, 88, 120, 120, 138, 160; *see also* allusion, ironic; misprision

New Testament 48, 70, 89, 111, 138, 154, 186-87, 201-2; *see also* acts; Acts of the Apostles; Acts 17; Bible; Christian (protagonist of *Pilgrim's Progress*); Christianity; church; Established Church; Huck Finn, as Christ figure; Jim, as Christ figure; John (gospel); Matthew (gospel); Old Testament; prayer; salvation; Savior; Sunday school; Tom Sawyer, as God of the Gilded Age

"nigger" 3, 6, 60, 79, 82-3, 98, 101-2, 105, 123, 134-35, 156-57, 163-65, 177, 181, 196, 198-99, 213-16, 220-21, 223, 225, 267-70; *see also* Huck Finn ... as racist; n-word; racism; slavery

Noah (biblical patriarch) 48, 56, 66, 69-70, 74, 97, 100, 141-43, 168, 210, 228-29; the king as 141-43, 169, 210, 228; pap Finn as 69-70, 100, 116, 141; *see also* Huck Finn, as Japheth; Jim, as Ham, as Shem; the king, as Noah; pap Finn, as Noah

Noah motif *see* Ark of Noah; the Deluge; flood (on Jackson's Island); Genesis; "House of Death"; Huck Finn, as Japheth; Jim, as Ham, as Shem; the king, as Noah; Mississippi River; Noah; pap Finn, as Noah; the raft, as Ark; slavery; voyage (of raft)

Noah's Ark *see* Ark of Noah

nobility *see* aristocracy; ideology; Jim, as King Lear; the king, as monarch; patrician; rights, divine; royalty

"Notice" 2, 4, 9-10, 25, 30, 34, 39, 41, 45, 54, 72, 115-16, 120, 203-9, 218, 227, 233; *see also* punishment; serpent motif; sin; three (number motif) Trinity

"nub" 204-5; *see also* "moral"; "motive"; "plot"

n-word 6, 213-14; *see also* African American; "cretur" "darkey"; "hussy"; "nigger"; "wench"

"old Leviticus" 141-43, 182; *see also* the king, as Levite; Levite

Old Testament 26, 48, 54-7, 75-7, 92, 106, 110, 139, 141-2, 168, 172, 175, 199; *see also* Bible; Exodus; Genesis; God of the Bible; Leviticus; New Testament; serpent motif

"only begotten son": of Abraham (biblical) 88-9; of Clemens, Samuel L. 89; of God of the Bible 89, 228; of pap Finn 75, 87-8; of Satan 87, 264

Original Sin 75, 96, 189; *see also* Doctrine of Total Depravity; God of the Bible; "Notice"; serpent motif; sin; the Temptation

ostrich 151, 164; *see also* beast, transformation of humans to; bestiality; the king, as bestial; "soldier plumes"

pap Finn 11–12, 34, 49, 54, 61–3, 69–70, 74–91, 136, 138, 141–4, 146, 149, 160–62, 164–69, 171–72, 174, 177, 183, 188–91, 194, 196, 201, 211, 215, 218–19, 222, 227–28, 230, 254, 259, 261, 263–65; as caricature of Abraham (biblical) 84, 88–9, 92, 22–29; as abusive father 12, 34, 48–9, 88, 218; as caricature of God of the Bible 54, 63, 74–80, 84, 88–92, 138, 144, 149, 152, 164, 174, 201, 215, 218, 227–28, 230, 261; as caricature of Noah 69–70, 142–3; as caricature of Satan 54, 74, 78–9, 91–2, 138, 152, 160, 164–65, 168, 171–72, 174, 215, 218, 227–28, 230; as corpse 80, 100, 168, 176, 218, 228; death of 11–12, 91, 168, 190–91, 219; as Egyptian 90, 191; as exemplar of incontinence (drunken, profligate, wrathful) 49, 62, 84; as father figure to Tom Sawyer 177, 183, 188; as head of "unholy trinity" 80, 168; as hog 91–2, 136, 149; as murder victim 1, 168; as personification of the Moral Sense 48; as racist 69, 71, 222; as secessionist 82–3; as serpent 85–6, 188–89, 263; as type of the king 169, 230; as victim of Huck's ritual patricide/deicide 91; *see also* hog-god/devil, hog motif; the king, as pap Finn's priest; pap Finn as; serpent motif; Tom Sawyer, as heir to pap Finn

parable 22, 107–9, 138, 140, 199, 231; *see also* allusion, ironic; the feud as

Paradise Lost 21, 25–6, 28–9, 38, 55, 73, 75, 78, 83–5, 87, 99, 116, 117, 136, 152, 155, 160, 165, 168, 189, 194, 206–9, 218, 227, 231, 243, 263, 265, 267; Clemens' knowledge of 78, 84; *see also* motif

Paradise Lost motif *see* Adam; allusion, ironic; beast, the brazen serpent; burlesque; Chaos; confrontations, Adam and Eve with God, Huck with conscience, pap with the Angel of Death, pap with Huck, Satan with the Angel of Death, Satan with conscience; cosmology; Death (the Angel of); Eden; Eve; hell (concept); Hell (place); Huck Finn, as Adam, as Angel of Death, as Christ figure, as Satan; inversion; Lucifer; negation; "only begotten son"; pap Finn, as caricature of God of the Bible, as caricature of Satan, as serpent; parody; rattlesnake-skin (curse of); Satan; serpent motif; Sin (Satan's daughter); theology

parody 10, 19, 21, 27–9, 121, 132, 168–9, 173, 180, 182, 188, 190–3, 200–1, 205, 219, 229, 232, 238, 252; evasion as self-parody 188, 190–3, 200–1, 205, 219, 229, 232; *see also* allusion, ironic; comedy

Passover 65, 90–1, 111, 114, 191; rites of 90; *see also* animal sacrifice; the evasion; the feud; Huck Finn, escape from pap; ritual

patrician 61, 112; *see also* aristocracy; divine right

patricide 82, 98, 116, 136, 174; *see also* death; myth; ritual

Paul (apostle) 70, 183, 186; *see also* Acts 17; burlesque Resurrection; Thomas (apostle)

the peculiar institution 14, 60, 64, 68–70, 101, 142, 185, 213; *see also* racism; slavery, biblical props of

perspective 2, 6, 9, 24, 29, 33, 36, 41, 43, 47, 52, 54, 58, 62, 65, 80, 132, 142, 145, 152, 159, 176, 194, 203–4, 220, 227, 231, 232; *see also* angle of view; point of view

persona *see* narrator, naïve; point of view

Peter Wilks 126, 144, 162, 260; *see also* death; funeral; mourning; six thousand dollar fortune

pharaoh 26, 61, 74, 90–2, 112–14, 177, 179, 200, 228–29

Phelps *see* Aunt Sally; Uncle Silas

Pilgrim's Progress 25, 28–9, 36, 38, 59, 73, 116–17, 120–21, 152, 231, 238; *see also* allusion, ironic; Christian (protagonist of); conversion; counter-conversion

plague 65, 90, 113, 179, 182; biblical plagues 65, 90, 113, 179, 182; Tom Sawyer's advent as arrival of 182

"plague of death" *see* Passover; plague

"plot" (of *Huckleberry Finn*) 9–10, 17–18, 20–1, 25–6, 30, 41, 44, 61–2, 71, 80–1, 84, 89, 104, 110, 120–2, 124, 126–27, 149, 161, 166, 180, 188, 190–94, 201, 204–6, 209–11, 215–16, 220, 222–23, 233, 236, 239–40, 248, 253; *see also* "moral"; "motive"; "Notice"

point of view 2–6, 9, 15, 21, 24–5, 29, 33–43, 45–50, 52–4, 58, 60, 63, 65, 80–1, 93, 96, 100, 105, 116, 132, 142, 145, 147, 152, 155, 158–163, 174–7, 181, 186, 194, 198, 201–204, 212, 216–17, 219–21, 224, 226–27, 231–33, 236–37; threefold ~ 2, 25, 29, 36–9, 41–3, 45–54, 58, 63, 65–8, 93, 96; *see also* author, implied; intention (authorial); intrusion (authorial); narrative; narrator; "Notice"; perspective; viewpoint

polygamy 220; *see also* harem; rape; Solomon; Young, Brigham

prayer 40–3, 45, 54, 58–61, 175, 227, 249; *see also* Christianity; church; hypocrisy; Providence; religion; Sunday school; superstition

predestination 168, 229; *see also* foreordination; preforeordestination

preforeordestination 168, 229; *see also* foreordination; predestination

priest 113, 115, 142, 172, 182; the king as 142, 230; *see also* as caricature of God of the Bible; the king, Levite; as Levite; pap Finn, Tom Sawyer, as Aaron (biblical)

primitivism 33–4, 98, 209, 245, 251; *see also* anti-intellectualism
progress 5, 23, 117–18, 127–28, 197–98, 212, 243, 249–52, 254; moral 117–18, 128, 212, 243, 249–50, 254; technological 23, 243, 250; *see also* echo; history
Promised Land 74, 112, 115, 152, 226, 228
Providence 39–40, 59, 141, 148–49, 162, 165–66, 179, 268
punishment 65, 67, 84–5, 124, 126, 151, 189; *see also* hell (concept); Hell (place)

"the quality" (gentry) 65; *see also* aristocracy; white trash

Rachel (biblical) 111; *see also* Agag (biblical); Amalekites (biblical); Exodus; the feud; God of the Bible; Passover; Samuel (biblical); Saul (biblical); Saul Grangerford
Rachel Grangerford 111, 116, 169; *see also* the feud; Grangerford clan; Rachel (biblical); Saul (biblical); Saul Grangerford
racism 6–7, 15–17, 21–2, 27, 34, 45, 58, 70–1, 99, 119, 184, 189, 193, 198–99, 212, 214, 216–17, 225, 228, 246; as Original Sin of American Adam 99, 189, 212, 217; *see also* hypocrisy; slavery
raft 1, 18, 26, 44, 65, 70, 96, 98, 100, 104, 106, 111, 113, 122, 124, 127–31, 142, 154, 157, 163–70, 175–76, 189, 191, 196, 216, 219–24, 227, 230–31, 251; as Ark of Noah *see* Noah
Raftmen's Passage 106; *see also* characterization
ram 89, 182–83; *see also* Aaron (biblical); Abraham (biblical); animal sacrifice; beast; bestiality; Huck Finn, as Isaac (biblical); Isaac (biblical); ram; Tom Sawyer, as Aaron (biblical), as Levite, as Mars/Ares, as ram
rape 101, 184–85, 201; *see also* atrocity; harem; rights, human; Solomon; Uncle Silas; wench
rattlesnake-skin (curse) 96–8, 104, 106, 116, 128, 152–54, 189, 191, 219, 223, 259; *see also* Doctrine of Total Depravity; luck; serpent motif
reader response criticism 2, 16, 23, 33–4, 43, 80, 133, 145, 178, 198, 205; *see also* criticism, schools of
reading strategy 53, 83, 140, 145, 159, 169, 178, 203, 226; *see also* firewall of irony; point of view
realism 2, 6, 11, 13, 17, 22, 30, 34–5, 38, 45–6, 49–51, 63, 92–3, 105, 148, 152, 161, 166, 178, 180, 194–95, 197, 199, 212, 214, 224, 239, 243, 253; *see also* Huck Finn, as realist
rebirth motif *see* conversion; gender shifts of; Huck Finn, archetypal and real identity shifts of, burlesque Resurrection of, counter-conversion of, death/escape from pap of; rebirths of
Reconstruction 17, 59, 178, 193, 197, 199, 201, 217, 226, 232; *see also* burlesque; evasion, as self-parody; social satire
religion 1, 3, 5, 18, 20, 27, 28, 40–1, 50, 57–9, 64, 73–4, 76, 89, 102–3, 107–8, 113–14, 116, 119, 121, 127, 135–37, 139–40, 142, 144–45, 149, 152, 158, 169, 171, 183, 185–86, 227, 229, 231–32, 235, 238, 242, 245, 248, 254, 262; *see also* acts; Christianity; church; conversion; counter-conversion; God of the Bible; hell (concept); Hell (place); serpent motif; Sunday school; superstition
repetition with variation 18–9, 32, 44, 142, 172, 177, 189, 200; *see also* allusion, ironic; burlesque; echo; resonance
resonance 32, 64, 89, 94, 100, 110, 114, 141–42, 174, 182, 248; *see also* allusion; echo; repetition with variation
revisions (by Clemens of manuscript) 19, 21, 30, 66, 104–5, 111, 132–7, 141, 143–7, 150, 160, 170, 181, 187, 192, 194, 207, 209, 219, 239; *see also* characterization
rights 22, 73, 81–3, 103, 112, 118, 127, 143–44, 184–85, 187, 197, 201, 222, 230, 235, 244, 245, 248, 250, 254; civil 22, 103, 112, 127, 185, 187, 197, 201, 235, 248, 254; human 22, 112, 185, 187, 201, 235, 248, 254; *see also* aristocracy; democracy; divine right; slavery
ritual 26, 49–50, 65, 76–7, 88–90, 93, 114, 116, 136, 154, 157, 161, 166, 174, 195, 228, 231; *see also* criticism, archetypal; myth; ritual; sacrifice
Roman Catholic Church *see* Established Church; Inquisition
Romeo and Juliet 169; *see also Hamlet; King Lear; Macbeth*
The Royal Nonesuch 124, 138, 161, 189, 230; as burlesque of *Inferno* 124–126, 230
royalty 66, 119, 122, 126, 141, 150–51, 154, 161, 162–63, 165, 225, 230, 259–60; *see also* aristocrat; rights, civil, human; slavery

sacrifice 13, 15, 26, 74, 76, 84, 88–90, 116, 172, 174, 182, 187, 198, 209, 211, 225, 228, 241; animal 76, 88, 89, 90, 110; human 13, 15, 26, 74, 84, 88, 89, 116, 182, 187, 211, 225, 228, 241; self- 13, 187; *see also* Abraham (biblical); Cain (biblical); death; deicide; hog; hog motif; Huck Finn, "Great Escape" of; pap Finn, as victim of Huck's ritual patricide/deicide; ram; ritual; suicide; *see also* hog motif
St. Petersburg 11, 12, 25, 61, 73, 76, 78–80, 94, 97, 99, 114, 116, 121, 157, 195, 218, 230; as American Eden/Egypt 76, 78–80, 114, 121, 230; *see also* American Eden; American Egypt
Sally Phelps *see* Aunt Sally
salvation 15, 63, 98, 129, 134, 136, 138, 154, 174, 187, 222, 241
Samuel (biblical) 65, 74, 107–11, 168, 200, 229; *see also* Agag (biblical); Amalekites (biblical);

atrocity; the feud; genocide; God of the Bible; Saul (biblical); Saul Grangerford

Satan (*Paradise Lost*) 26, 30, 50, 54, 74, 77–89, 92–4, 103, 116–7, 117, 120, 123–24, 132, 136, 138–39, 152–61, 165–66, 168–72, 174–75, 180–81, 188–89, 194, 197, 206–7, 227–28, 230–31, 233, 248–49, 256, 263–64, 267–71; Huck as 26, 29–30, 50, 54, 88, 92–4, 103, 116, 123, 131–32, 139, 152–61, 165–68, 170–72, 174–75, 180–81, 194, 197, 231, 233, 267–271; as secessionist 83; *see also* Lucifer; pap Finn, as caricature of Satan; serpent motif

Saul 26, 65, 74, 106–8, 111–12, 116, 168–69, 200, 229; *see also* kings (biblical); Saul (biblical); Saul Grangerford

Saul (biblical) 26, 65, 74, 106–8, 111, 168, 200, 229; *see also* the feud; God of the Bible; kings; Passover; Rachel (biblical); Samuel (biblical)

Saul Grangerford 111–12, 116, 169; *see also* the feud; Rachel (biblical); Rachel Grangerford; Saul (biblical)

Savior 84, 154; *see also* Christ; damnation; Jesus; salvation

Scripture *see* Bible

secessionism 82–3; *see also* pap Finn, as secessionist; Satan, as secessionist

self-sacrifice 13, 172, 187; *see also* Huck Finn, as Christ figure; Jim, as Christ figure; sacrifice

serpent *see* beast, transformation of humans to; bestiality; the brazen serpent; hog motif; serpent motif; snake

serpent motif 188–90; *see also* beast, transformation of humans to; the brazen serpent; Doctrine of Total Depravity; hog motif

servitude *see* "holy ordinance of"; Jim, as bearer of mark of Cain, as brother to Huck, as fugitive slave, as Ham, son of Noah, as prisoner representative of freed slaves after Reconstruction; mark of Cain; racism; slavery

Shakespeare, William 18–20, 169, 210, 253; Clemens' knowledge of 169; *see also Hamlet*; *King Lear*; *Macbeth*; *Romeo and Juliet*

shepherd 64, 109–11; *see also* Abel; the feud; Hebrews; range wars; Shepherdson clan

Shepherdson clan 64, 76, 109–11, 115, 122–23, 136, 199, 223, 229; *see also* the feud, Grangerford clan, Rachel Grangerford; Saul Grangerford; shepherd

Sherburn 46, 114–15, 119, 138–40, 230; *see also* intrusion, authorial; point of view

Silas 70–1, 113, 119, 165, 167, 183–87, 196, 200–1, 225; companion of Paul (biblical) 186; *see also* Acts 17 (New Testament); Uncle Silas

sin 6, 67, 75, 79, 85, 89, 96–7, 102, 110–11, 135–36, 154, 156–57, 172, 189, 228, 231, 255, 261, 263, 270; mother of Death (Sin personified) 87; punishment of 65, 67, 84–5, 124, 126, 151, 189; *see also* Angel of Death; bigot; death; evil; fraud; greed; hypocrisy; incontinence; killing; lust; lying; murder; Original Sin; punishment of sin; racism; rape; theft; treachery; violence

Sin (Satan's daughter in Milton) 87, 264

six thousand dollar fortune: Huck's 11, 62, 82, 114, 148, 161, 230; Wilks girls' 123, 148, 219, 230; *see also* idolatry, of gold; Wilks inheritance; yaller boys

skepticism 27, 53, 65, 102, 146, 220; *see also* the Bible, Clemens' attitude toward

slaveholders 65, 100

slavery 5–7, 11, 14–7, 19, 27, 34, 45, 51, 55–60, 64–5, 68–71, 79, 90, 96, 99–106, 111–15, 118–19, 123, 127–29, 135–36, 139, 142, 147–48, 150, 153–54, 158, 161–63, 165, 176–77, 181, 184–89, 191–94, 197–201, 207–8, 212–20, 222–24, 226, 229–31, 236, 246, 250–51, 254, 267, 271; biblical props of 7, 27, 53, 55–7, 60, 64, 69–70, 100, 112, 115, 127; *see also* Acts 17; aristocracy; "holy ordinance of servitude; Jim, as bearer of mark of Cain, as fugitive slave; Uncle Silas

snake 85–6, 96–9, 104, 106, 116, 124, 128, 138, 152–54, 162, 179, 189, 191, 217, 219, 223, 229, 259, 263; *see also* beast, transformation of humans to; bestiality; serpent motif

snakeskin *see* Doctrine of Total Depravity; Original Sin; rattlesnake-skin, (curse); serpent motif; sin; Sin (Satan's daughter); snake

soliloquy (Satan's) 30, 155–60; *see also Hamlet*

Solomon (biblical) 26, 49, 59–61, 63, 74, 89, 100–4, 106, 109, 116, 140, 168, 184, 211, 219–20, 229, 259; as child 103; *see also* kings (biblical)

sons of Noah *see* Huck Finn, as Japheth; Jim, as Ham, son of Shem

"sound heart" 6, 10, 13–4, 20, 46, 51, 101, 103, 153, 154, 159; *see also* "deformed conscience"; heart vs. conscience

stealing 77, 90, 179, 191, 229; *see also* sin, theft

structure of *Huck Finn*: as religious satire 5, 9, 25–6, 28–30, 38, 48, 53–6, 67–8, 74, 93, 106, 112, 121, 124, 128, 132, 152, 154, 169–70, 178, 180, 188, 205, 208–10, 213, 226, 231, 261–5, 267–71; *see also* motif

sty 65, 76, 136; church as moral; *see also* hog motif

suicide (Huck's ritual escape) 26, 92, 98, 116, 136, 166, 174, 240; *see also* death; ritual; self-sacrifice

Sunday school 36, 44, 58–9, 61, 156, 181, 238; *see also* Christianity; church; God of the Bible; religion

superstition 1, 31, 39, 41, 59, 67, 96–7, 99–100, 104, 134, 137, 167, 178, 187, 205, 215, 229–30, 241, 248; religion as 31, 59, 67, 99–100, 104, 134, 137, 167, 178–9, 187, 205, 215, 229, 230,

248; religion vs. 39, 41, 96, 215; *see also* religion

the Temptation 67, 96, 116, 138, 189–90, 206–9, 229, 267; *see also* "Notice"; religion; serpent motif; superstition
Territorial Enterprise 238, 244
three (number motif) 9, 11, 18, 33, 36, 38, 41–2, 49, 69–70, 88, 93, 104, 107, 110, 114, 119, 128, 130, 138, 143, 147–148, 160–61, 163, 167, 173–74, 176, 181, 191, 196, 199, 203, 206–8, 224, 231; *see also* the Trinity
13th Amendment 11, 119, 198, 201; *see also* Emancipation Proclamation; manumission; Reconstruction
Thomas (biblical) 70–1, 173, 200; *see also* burlesque Resurrection; Tom Sawyer, as Thomas (biblical)
the Throne (seat of biblical God or monarch) 18, 83, 91, 143–44, 157, 247, 249, 270; *see also* God of the Bible; the king, as monarch, as pap Finn's priest; monarch; pap Finn, as God of the Bible
Tom Sawyer: as Aaron (biblical) 27, 70, 172–73, 177, 179, 182, 200–1, 231; as authoritarian 17–18, 28, 30, 71, 119, 170, 17–72, 187, 193, 195, 200, 202, 232; as Christopher Columbus 188, 201; as con artist 11, 16, 24–5, 28, 77, 142–43, 161, 163, 172, 176–77, 180, 182–83, 187, 190–93, 195, 200–1; as conformist 72, 126, 233; as envious of Huck 192, 200; as God of the Gilded Age 172, 179–80; 187, 192–93, 201–2; as heir to pap Finn 177, 179–80, 183, 188, 192, 201; as "his Grandfather's ram" 182–83; as Levite 172–73, 179, 182; as Mars/Ares 183; as perpetrator of fraud 183, 187, 190–91; as Thomas (biblical) 173, 201; *see also* beast, transformation of humans to; bestiality; "cretur" (creature); evasion, as parody of Huck's flight; manipulation motif; Mars (Ares); racism; ram; serpent motif
"torchlight procession" 179, 196
tour of Hell: Dante's 122–27; Huck's 54, 83–4, 86, 111, 115, 122–27, 132, 152, 154, 161, 171, 176, 180, 223, 225, 229, 231
tragedy 11, 19, 52, 65, 74, 89, 151, 169, 175, 217, 246, 252; *see also* comedy; tragicomedy
tragicomedy 12, 114, 119, 175, 252; *see also* burlesque; comedy
transformation 1, 12, 14, 16, 19, 25, 54–5, 74, 81, 85, 90, 105–16, 124, 132, 136, 144, 148, 151, 155, 160, 174, 179, 183, 193, 209–11, 220, 229, 231, 234, 253, 263; *see also* beast, the brazen serpent; conversion; counter-conversion; hog motif; of humans to; idolatry; serpent motif
travesty 7, 15–6, 20, 28, 71, 190, 193–95, 200, 202, 204, 232, 252
the Trinity 5, 80, 88, 91, 161, 168, 174, 208; *see also* God of the Bible; "Notice"; pap Finn, as head of "unholy trinity"; skepticism; three (number motif)
Twain, Mark: letters—to Asa Don Dickenson 109, to Olivia Langdon (1868) 78, to Orion Clemens (1858) 78, (1878) 83–4; works by— *The Adventures of Tom Sawyer* 10, 11, 35, 42, 45, 57, 73, 109, 193, 216, 237–240, 244, *The American Claimant* 118, 237, 244–45, *The Autobiography of Mark Twain* 41, 138, 248, "Bible Teaching and Religious Practice" 149, *Captain Stormfield's Visit to Heaven* 121, 237, 247–48, *A Connecticut Yankee in King Arthur's Court* 241–45, 247, *Following the Equator* 1, *L'Homme Qui Rit* (*The Man Who Laughs*) 239, ["God of the Bible vs. God of the Present Day"] (untitled essay) 31, 250–51, "The Great Dark" 250, "How to Tell a Story" 33, 35, *The Innocents Abroad: The New Pilgrim's Progress* 237–38, "Jane Lampton Clemens" 60, *Life on the Mississippi* 106, 167, 169 "A Little Note to M. Paul Bourget" 205, *Mark Twain's Notebooks and Journals* 3, *The Mysterious Stranger* 249–50, *Personal Recollections of Joan of Arc* 237, 244, 246–47, "The Petrified Man" 244, *The Prince and the Pauper* 237, 239–41, 247, "To the Person Sitting in Darkness" 100, *The Tragedy of Pudd'nhead Wilson* 237, 245–46, untitled notebook dialog between deckhands 3, *The War Prayer* 249, to William Dean Howells (1879) 78

Uncle Silas 70, 167, 183–87, 196, 201; *see also* Acts 17; Aunt Sally; rape; slavery; sin, hypocrisy, racism
Uncle Tom's Cabin 15–16
universe 48, 51, 98, 207, 251, 256; *see also* god

viewpoint *see* point of view
violence 5, 26, 34, 44, 46, 55, 73, 115, 122, 124, 131, 158; *see also* the feud; sin; war
voyage (of raft) 26, 44, 70, 111, 113, 124, 127, 128–29, 142, 154, 159, 166–67, 169, 189, 191, 216, 219, 222, 224, 227

wages of sin 154; *see also* sin
The Walter Scott (steamboat) 21, 146, 162, 188, 219, 244, 259
war 17, 51, 56–7, 59, 64, 83, 102, 107–8, 110, 112, 115, 117, 131, 139, 152, 183, 192, 199, 207–8, 226, 231, 249; *see also* anti-imperialism; Civil War; the feud
water-moccasins 189; *see also* serpent motif
"wench" 134–35, 184–85; *see also* Aunt Sally; camp meeting; "hussy"; n-word; racism; slavery
white trash 104–5, 211, 214, 220–22
Widow Douglas 11, 36, 39–42, 49, 51, 59–63, 75–8, 84–5, 90, 101–2, 112, 114–15, 118, 130, 140, 154, 161, 164–66, 170–71, 215, 219, 228, 251, 261–62; as pharaoh's daughter 61, 112,

228; views on divine Providence 39, 40; *see also* manipulation motif
Wilks inheritance *see* six thousand dollar fortune
wit 9, 34, 41, 151, 204, 252; *see also* comedy
"wonders" (God of the Bible's) 91

"yaller-boys" (gold pieces) 114, 148, 195; *see also* six thousand dollar fortune
Young, Brigham 220; *see also* polygamy; Solomon

www.ingramcontent.com/pod-product-compliance
Lightning Source LLC
Chambersburg PA
CBHW051209300426
44116CB00006B/497